CATCHING *our* FLAG

ALSO BY JAMES E. ROGAN

"Dear President Truman"
(*American Heritage*, 1994; *Readers Digest*, 1995)

My Brush with History
(Contributor, 2001)

Rough Edges
My Unlikely Road from Welfare to Washington
(2004)

Catching Our Flag
Behind the Scenes of a Presidential Impeachment
(2011)

And *Then* I Met...
Stories of Growing Up, Meeting Famous People, and
Annoying the Hell Out of Them
(2014)

"On to Chicago"
Rediscovering Robert F. Kennedy and the Lost Campaign of 1968
(2018)

Shaking Hands with History:
My Encounters with the Famous, the Infamous, and the
Once-Famous but Now-Forgotten
(2020)

CATCHING *our* FLAG

BEHIND THE SCENES *of a* PRESIDENTIAL IMPEACHMENT

JAMES ROGAN

SHENANDOAH PRESS

CATCHING OUR FLAG

Copyright © 2011, 2021 by James Rogan

Library of Congress Control Number: 2021936657

Hardcover ISBN: 978-1-7351317-7-1
Paperback ISBN: 978-1-7351317-6-4
ebook ISBN: 978-1-7351317-9-5

Printed in the United States of America

For the Patriots Who Caught Our Falling Flag
1998–1999

CONTENTS

The question before the House is not a question of sex. Sexual misconduct and adultery are private acts and are none of Congress' business. It's not even a question of lying about sex. The matter before the House is a question of lying under oath. This is a public act, not a private act. This is called perjury. The matter before the House is a question of the willful, premeditated, deliberate corruption of the nation's system of justice. Perjury and obstruction of justice cannot be reconciled with the office of the president of the United States.

The president is our flag-bearer. He stands out in front of our people, and the flag is falling. Catch the falling flag as we keep our appointment with history.

—HENRY J. HYDE
HOUSE JUDICIARY COMMITTEE CHAIRMAN
CLINTON IMPEACHMENT CLOSING ARGUMENT, 1998

FOREWORD

Within hours after my approving the appointment of Congressman Jim Rogan to the House Judiciary Committee in January 1998, the Monica Lewinsky scandal became public. Thus, we began a 13-month ordeal that shocked America and crippled the administration of President Bill Clinton.

Jim Rogan was a key player in the Clinton impeachment saga. One of President Clinton's lawyers said later that the White House referred to Jim, a former Los Angeles County gang murder prosecutor and state court judge, as "The Domino." The Clinton team felt if they could persuade Jim to vote against impeachment, enough members who respected his judgment might follow his lead and end the Administration's bleeding.

After Jim's decision to vote for Clinton's impeachment, his colleagues called upon him to help lead the debate in the House of Representatives. Following the adoption of two articles of impeachment, the House selected Jim as one of the Managers to prosecute Clinton in the United States Senate. A riveted nation watched the first ever impeachment trial of a popularly elected American president. During the trial, Jim won acclaim from both sides for his fair, dignified, and effective presentation of the evidence.

Because of Jim's role, President Clinton and the national Democrats named Jim as their number-one target for retribution in the next congressional election cycle. Jim battled back in what became (and remains to date) the toughest and most expensive House race ever. He paid the price of political defeat for insisting that elected officials uphold the rule of law. In losing his race for reelection, Jim earned the respect of millions of Americans for his courage.

From his first day on the House Judiciary Committee, Jim (a lifelong student of history and government) foresaw this historic event before it unfolded. He knew that if the scandal ever led to impeachment proceedings, future accounts would suffer from faulty memories or faulty motives. To combat this threat of factual error, Jim kept copious notes and diaries during every significant meeting relating to impeachment. It was his purpose to record the comments, strategies, arguments, and biases of insiders as they uttered them. He did this so there would be a complete and accurate chronicle, leaving for historians the best evidence of what really happened behind the scenes in Congress during the unfolding drama. This historically important archive is unmatched in its thoroughness and integrity.

After all these years, Jim has opened his private diaries for history by penning the ultimate insider's story on what led a very reluctant House of Representatives to impeach a then-very-popular American president. He wrote it with his eye on truth, not spin. This first-hand narrative provides a fascinating inside tale of politics, power, expediency, and intimidation. Other books on this subject invariably rely on fading recollections (or wholesale fantasies). Congressman James Rogan was more than a witness; he was a leading figure in the most important trial in our country's political and legal history.

It is a story only he can tell.

NEWT GINGRICH
FORMER SPEAKER, U.S. HOUSE OF REPRESENTATIVES

The Usual Rules

Democrats weren't the only ones for whom Bill Clinton's impeachment created a dilemma.

When Republican Governor George W. Bush ran for president in 2000, his campaign played Clinton's impeachment as its background music. While his opponent, Vice President Al Gore, tried desperately to distance himself from his scandal-tainted leader, Bush hung the disgrace around Gore's neck like an ethical millstone. Bush's impeachment dagger sliced subtly; I don't think he ever uttered the unhappy "I" word. Instead, in almost all of his stump speeches, Bush held up his hand dramatically and declared, "When I raise my hand on the Capitol steps next January, I will be doing more than taking an oath to protect the Constitution. I will be vowing to restore honor and integrity to the presidency." The message couldn't have been any clearer.

George W. Bush liked impeachment and used it successfully in his White House race. He just didn't want to get any of it on him.

I experienced his aversion in my own doomed congressional reelection race that same year. As one of the first House members to endorse Governor Bush's presidential candidacy, I met with him in Washington one week after the Clinton impeachment trial ended. Putting his arm around my shoulder, he filled me with praise: "You did a great job in the impeachment trial, Jimmy, and I'm really proud of you. I'm going to do all I can to help you win in 2000 and help you keep your seat." Impressively, Bush even knew that the makeup of my anti-impeachment Democrat district (home to many Hollywood movie studios and their employees) promised to make my reelection the toughest and most expensive House race in congressional history. To cement our connection, Bush pulled me in closely and whispered in my ear, "You avenged my father," a reference to candidate Clinton defeating President George H.W. Bush in 1992.

When we met again a few months later, Bush repeated the same theme with the same arm thrown around my shoulder. "I'll be there to help you," he pledged to me. "We'll campaign a lot together in your district."

During the 2000 general election campaign, Bush (by now the GOP presidential nominee) brought his campaign to my district twice. Both times, my reelection team organized the rallies and turned out thousands of volunteers. Both times his campaign called at the last minute and asked me not to come. I honored each request and assumed it came from staff rather than from the grateful candidate who pledged to help me for doing the right, but unpopular, thing. Still, it stung later to learn that at each of those rallies, Bush looked out upon a sea of hundreds of "Rogan for Congress" signs and never once mentioned my name or asked anyone to help me. As one of my volunteers told me later, "It was like he came into the district of a congressman under indictment."

After my defeat, I told House Majority Whip Tom DeLay I hoped the incoming Bush administration would find a temporary spot for me until the school year ended the following June, when we planned to return home with our young children to California. Tom said he would call Karl Rove, Bush's chief advisor, and have him take care of this "no-brainer" request. A couple of days later, Tom called back. He sounded embarrassed and angry. According to Tom, Rove told him, "We love Jim Rogan. He's a hero. Nobody served in Congress with greater distinction. But Tom, you're not asking us to nominate him for something, are you? With Senate confirmation required and that whole impeachment issue? Don't get me wrong. If it hadn't been for impeachment, we probably wouldn't be here. We just don't want to bring up that subject now."

When longtime Democrat lobbyist Jack Valenti (an old friend who supported me for an administration position) heard about this, he complained to Senator Patrick Leahy (D-VT), ranking Democrat on the Senate Judiciary Committee. Leahy told Valenti that I served honorably during impeachment and did what I thought was right. Pat Leahy—the Prince of Darkness in many Republican fundraising letters (including a few of my own)—said that he would call Rove personally and offer to handle any nomination bumps I might encounter. It was only after receiving this assurance that President Bush nominated me for a slot. Later, when I came before a Democrat-controlled U.S. Senate, they confirmed me unanimously.

What a bizarre dynamic: Democrats angry with me over impeachment; a Republican president grateful to me because of it. Yet only when angry Democrats interceded did the grateful Republican president throw me a life preserver.

How do we explain this illogical scenario? I suspect it is because whenever America goes through a political cataclysm—in this case, the impeachment of a president with a 73 percent job approval rating—the usual rules no longer apply.

From the time President Clinton assumed office, he suffered an almost unbroken string of scandals. Through it all, the country endured repeated examples of the usual rules not applying:

- In the mainstream media, Clinton (the sexual harassment defendant) became the victim, and the victim (Paula Jones) was dubbed "trailer trash";

- Judge Kenneth Starr, the respected former federal judge charged by President Clinton's own attorney general to investigate these scandals, was branded as the villainous out-of-control prosecutor prying into the personal lives of others;

- Monica Lewinsky, the young intern exposed and humiliated in a sex scandal with Clinton, defended him even after Clinton executed plans to have his close associates smear her in the press as a crazed stalker-whore;

- When other women came forward with credible claims of Clinton's sexual misconduct, the well-known national "women's groups" fell silent. Later, when pressed on the subject, these same groups defended the accused man and ignored the violated women—even after he admitted lying about his behavior;

- The more Clinton sullied the dignity of his office, the higher his job approval poll numbers climbed;

- America demanded to know the truth, and then they grew outraged at those who told it;

- In a true abandonment of the usual rules, a handful of politicians cherishing reelection as a top priority volunteered to defend an unpopular principle of law in the face of over 70 percent of the voters demanding they not enforce it and threatening ballot box retribution if they did.

During Bill Clinton's impeachment, the typical conventions of political engagement turned upside down. The usual rules did not apply, and because of it, history changed.

This is an inside account of what happened behind the scenes in Congress during that fractious battle when right looked wrong, wrong looked right, and indifference looked preferable to either.

PART ONE:
The House

1

My Confession

(And Many of You Won't Like It)

At a GOP members-only congressional meeting with Dick Morris (Clinton's longtime political adviser), one congressman mentioned that Clinton was likeable and charming personally. Morris stated without emotion, "No, he isn't. Clinton is like a solar battery. He draws energy from those around him and emits an energy that comes off as care and empathy. But when the people aren't around him from which he can draw that energy, he is like a cold lump of steel. He really is not a very likeable guy."
—ROGAN DIARY, MAY 14, 1998

Since this book is about the truth, I am compelled to begin with a confession: I have a soft spot for Bill Clinton.

"You have a what?" I hear conservatives stammering. "Is this the same Jim Rogan

- who insisted on holding accountable the disgraced president in the House Judiciary Committee for abusing his power, committing perjury and obstructing justice;

- who helped lead the fight in the U.S. House of Representatives to adopt formal articles of impeachment against Clinton;

- who prosecuted Clinton in the United States Senate impeachment trial, and;

- upon whom the forces of Clinton-directed surrogates trained their cannons to destroy him politically?"

Oh, I see you remember me.

Judging from experience, I expect this confession makes me (in the minds of many fellow conservatives) something of a traitor. One typical response happened in 2008, when a *Washington Post* gossip columnist mentioned that Clinton and I exchanged a few post-impeachment notes since we both left Washington. Our infrequent correspondence was nothing earth shattering; just a handful of mutual pleasantries between ex-combatants.

This news blip appeared while the Democrat-controlled U.S. Senate considered my pending nomination to the federal bench. Despite earning the highest "well qualified" rating from the American Bar Association (hardly a bastion of conservatism), the Democrat leadership had not held a hearing on my nomination. The *Wall Street Journal* blasted the Senate for this neglect, laying blame directly at the feet of Senator Hillary Clinton (D-NY) as retribution for her husband's impeachment. In an effort to gin up pressure on the committee, my former political director Jason Roe called a respected columnist for a national conservative magazine who befriended me during my time in Congress. To Jason's and my surprise, the columnist rebuffed him.

"Rogan's not a true conservative," he alleged. "I saw that *Post* story about him and Clinton being pen pals." By comparison, the columnist referenced another Republican congressman who once declined a Clinton White House party invitation because he apparently didn't want to breathe any Clinton-exhaled air. The columnist suggested the other congressman showed the sort of anti-Clinton fervor that any true conservative would exhibit.

Jason exploded: "Are you kidding? Rogan impeached Clinton! Rogan fought against him harder than anybody you know, and he paid a political price higher than anyone you know. How can you compare that to some guy who refused to go to a party?" My writer friend remained unimpressed.

If exchanging a few innocuous notes with Clinton triggered the gag reflex of a political pro, then the opening lines of this chapter probably presage my expulsion from the conservative fraternity. Still, I hope these purity custodians will permit the condemned this brief allocution. When the Clinton armies turned their firepower on me, I battled their forces in the most costly and hard-hitting congressional campaign in history. After I'd spent 30 years working toward the goal of serving in Congress, my constituents tossed me out soon after arriving because of Bill Clinton's expressed desire to rid Washington of me. I probably have as much reason to dislike him as anyone (with the exception of people like Juanita Broaddrick, who accused Clinton of raping her many decades ago). Despite our post-warfare cordial correspondence, when they called the roll for volunteers willing to engage Bill Clinton in hand-to-hand combat, I stepped forward.

Still, that soft spot lingers even after our blistering collision.

No, I wasn't snookered by his now-famous lower lip biting or his endless claims of victimization. Also, I remained immune to his superficial glad-handing charm we politicians recognize (and mimic). I have no idea how many of the scandals that swirled around his presidency were true, half true, untrue, or (worse) undiscovered. I do know he was caught dead-bang on some of it. As for the rest, there certainly was enough heat and flame to stoke my suspicions.

Nor did I think him a great president, or even a good one (although he signed some great legislation when our Republican congressional majority forced his hand). I felt he weakened national security, limited freedom with higher taxes and federal power grabs, embarrassed his office—and that was after giving him the benefit of the doubt on the most serious allegations against him. I prosecuted him because he abused his power, obstructed justice, and committed felony perjury. Despite the folklore, Clinton didn't fight impeachment out of nobility to defend the Constitution. He did it to save his own hide. I knew that in voting to impeach him, I was voting to end two political careers: his and mine.

Given all of this, how can I possibly have that bothersome blind spot?

First, I can't help but look at a part of Clinton's life and see an eerily familiar shadow of my own. Young Bill Clinton came from a poor family, never knew his biological father growing up, lived amid an alcohol-hazed dysfunctional family, yet still persevered through life while dreaming he could be president one day. I came from a poor family; I never knew my biological father growing up, I lived amid an alcohol-hazed dysfunctional family, and I persevered through life while dreaming I could be a congressman one day. (Okay, since I promised to tell the truth in this book, I'll admit it—I dreamed I could be president, too. I settled for congressman.)

Second, my reverence for the presidential office created by our Founders is such that I can't help projecting some degree of respect and decency on any occupant even though (for some) this presumption is both unearned and unwarranted.

Third, I never forgot the kindness then-Arkansas Attorney General Bill Clinton showed me when I was a young college student 20 years before our impeachment clash (more about that later). In addition, no matter how often I stomped on President Clinton's foot in Washington—and despite my throwing the kitchen sink at him—he showed repeated graciousness to my family during my Washington service.

All these excuses pale next to the real reason: As one who enjoys the Lord's pardon for my own unending trail of temptation and sin,

I don't think it wise for me to begrudge God's forgiveness to anyone else. Besides, how much moral snootiness would you take seriously from an author who bartended his way through law school on Hollywood's Sunset Strip in places like female mud-wrestling bars—all while dividing my time between half-hearted studying in lecture halls and full-hearted dating the cocktail waitresses at my shift's end?

Anyway, in reflecting on Bill Clinton's personal failings, I try avoiding my instinctive drift into judgmental hypocrisy by recalling two Scripture verses: "There is none righteous, no, not one," (Romans 3:10), and "Don't worry about the sliver in another man's eye; worry about the log in your own eye," (Matthew 7:3). To those purists who see unpardonable sin both in Bill Clinton's soul and in my entertaining some possible measure of decency lurking inside him, please return my missing log.

• • •

Finally, before I pull back the veil and begin my impeachment story, I need to mention an unrelated scandal so that you will understand the template from which this book is written. It has to do with former U.S. Senator Bob Packwood (R-OR), whose experience, in my opinion, has been bad for history.

The longtime senator meant for his private diaries to be his post-mortem monument to the role he played in Washington. Faithful to this intended legacy, he dutifully spent half an hour recording his thoughts and observations each day for 25 years. In one of the more unfortunate Capitol "oops" moments in memory, he often allowed his pen to drift into indiscretion by describing his sexual fantasies, libidinous observations, and pick-up attempts aimed at female Hill staffers and lobbyists during that same quarter century.

All this information normally would have remained buried somewhere in Packwood's attic. However, when allegations of unwelcome sexual advances from over 30 women leaked against him, the existence of his diaries became known and the Senate Ethics

Committee subpoenaed them. Before long, the steamy passages of his chronicles became grist for tabloid journalists and late-night television comics. In a tearful speech, he resigned from Congress before the Senate voted to expel him.

Although he was gone from Congress by the time I arrived in January 1997, Packwood's legacy remained. I encountered it the first time I started jotting down notes in an early impeachment strategy meeting. A curious congressman sitting next to me watched as I recorded the discussion on a yellow legal pad.

"Are you keeping a diary?" he asked incredulously.

I told him yes. I thought it important to keep an accurate behind the scenes record for future historians.

"You're breaking *The Packwood Rule*," he whispered.

When I said I didn't know what that meant, he stated, "It means they can't subpoena what doesn't exist. Look around. Do you see anyone else keeping a diary in here?"

I scanned the two dozen or more congressmen seated around the large conference table. Other than some scratch pads bearing random and infrequent notations, statistics, or doodles, nobody else kept notes. It was a scene replicated in almost every future meeting throughout my congressional service.

"Hmmm, it looks like you're right," I told my colleague as I resumed writing. The flustered congressman turned away from me.

"Dumb ass," he muttered.

• • •

I never anticipated the likelihood of President Clinton's impeachment until just hours before it happened. However, from the moment the Monica Lewinsky story broke in January 1998 I knew that if the unthinkable occurred, revisionist histories would continue long after death stilled the tongues of the witnesses. I kept writing out of a conscious determination to keep an accurate journal. Whenever I attended a private meeting, conference call, or strategy session of any apparent significance, I tried to write down the words as their authors spoke them or at least get their substance. Also, I conducted no interviews of other participants when writing this account. My goal was to get it right, not to get it sanitized. As you read this book, all of my diary entries (as opposed to the story narrative) are printed in **bold typeface.**

• • •

This book is not a history of the Clinton White House scandals. Neither is it a global overview of his impeachment and trial. It certainly is not an apology. Rather it is an account of what I saw and experienced behind the scenes. The account is not always pretty—it is sometimes bloody, embarrassing, and profane.

It is also true.

Soon after the impeachment trial ended in 1999, publishers waving contracts wanted me to write this book. I turned them all down because it was too close to the event. I thought it prudent to let overheated passions cool, including any that I harbored. Also, I didn't want to be tempted to color facts to pacify a very angry electorate back home in my district.

Almost a quarter-century has passed since the media force-fed America a steady diet of Monica Lewinsky's blue dress, a wagging presidential finger, and the parsing of phrases like "it depends on what the meaning of the word 'is' is." Many of the participants are now gone from Washington; some are gone from Earth. It is time to tell what I witnessed and experienced behind the scenes.

I offer this account for posterity.

2

Sonny's Timing

But for a twist of fate, I would have missed what Henry Hyde called "our appointment with history."

A week after my election to Congress in November 1996, the House leadership invited all newly elected members to Washington for a biennial rite of passage: Freshman Congressman Orientation Week. This tradition is something of a Bataan Death March of manufactured photo ops, policy briefings, press availabilities, new staff interviews, lobbyist meet and greets, and jockeying—lots of jockeying.

Key committee assignments, freshman class officer positions, interview requests by the crème of the Washington press corps, and other indicia signaling one's arrival are best not left to chance. The Darwinian competition among new members, though often masked by nonchalance, is significant. Future colleagues and D.C. powerbrokers look for the "smoke signals" from the freshly minted class as to who will likely be the future players in town.

I ran for Congress as a conservative Republican in overwhelmingly liberal Los Angeles County (my district encompassed much of the Hollywood entertainment community). I won that year with a bare 50.1 percent of the vote when President Clinton won my county by 20 points. As my staff reminded me, we needed to start worrying about my 1998 reelection campaign the day after I won in 1996.

Like it or not, reelection depended on raising a massive campaign war chest, a job always made easier for congressmen on key "juice" committees. Thanks to the lobbying efforts of my predecessor, outgoing Congressman Carlos Moorhead (R-CA), and the insistence of Speaker Newt Gingrich that his most vulnerable members get the best assignments, I came to Washington with a good chance of winning a coveted slot on the House Commerce Committee.

The oldest committee in Congress, Commerce also is one of the "juiciest." A lobbyist told me that its former chairman, Congressman John Dingell (D-MI), used to enjoy demonstrating his committee's powerful reach by inviting new members into his private office and then pointing to a map on the wall.

"What's that?" Dingell would ask.

"A map of the world," came the standard reply.

"Wrong," the chairman corrected. "It's the jurisdiction of my committee."

Near the end of orientation week, I learned that Speaker Gingrich appeared personally at the private meeting of the House Steering Committee (where committee assignments are made) and demanded they give me the desirable Commerce slot. That same day, the venerated chairman of the House Judiciary Committee, Henry Hyde (R-IL), sent word that he wanted to speak to me.

With over two decades of congressional service, the 73-year old chairman cast perhaps the most commanding shadow on Capitol Hill. Tall, hulking, and with thick snow-white hair, Chairman Hyde exuded elegant Chesterfieldian manners. A hearty laugh and lilting voice animated his raconteur's gift of possessing an unending fund of stories. When he turned those talents to policy debates, nobody in Congress spoke extemporaneously and made it sound more like literature. Despite being a passionate champion of conservative causes—from banning abortions and flag burning to balancing the federal budget and arming anti-communist rebels worldwide—he held the bipartisan respect of his Democrat colleagues.

I returned Hyde's call. After offering congratulations on my election, he got to the point:

"Jim, I know all about you. You were named as one of California's most effective gang murder prosecutors. You were the youngest sitting state court judge when you were appointed by your governor. As majority leader of your state legislature, your colleagues ranked you as number one in both integrity and effectiveness. You're pro-life and pro-Second Amendment. You're just the kind of man I want on the House Judiciary Committee."

To this day I am hard-pressed to recall a greater professional compliment. And, if there was a better assignment for an ex-prosecutor and judge, I couldn't imagine it. The Judiciary Committee was my heart's true desire. However, anticipating what Chairman Hyde might say, I sought advice from a senior future colleague before I returned his call.

Congressman Bill Paxon (R-NY), chairman of our National Republican Congressional Committee (in charge of overseeing House GOP reelection efforts) argued against my accepting a Judiciary Committee assignment if offered: "First, all Judiciary will do is put you up on a bunch of bad votes back home. I know you'll vote pro-life and pro-gun, but your district is pro-abortion and anti-NRA. You'll keep voting your conscience and you'll keep getting the shit kicked out of you every week by the *Los Angeles Times* and your local newspapers. Second, you need to raise money for 1998. Every business in the world has an interest before the Commerce Committee, so you'll have contributors lining up at your doorstep. This is an easy decision: tell Henry no if he asks."

With this advice in mind, I thanked Hyde profusely when he tried recruiting me to Judiciary. He made a few failed attempts to overcome my reasons for declining before telling me that he understood. "I'll give up lobbying you for now," he told me, "but only temporarily. Let's talk about this again next year after you get settled."

• • •

Commerce Committee Chairman Tom Bliley (R-VA) ran a tight ship, and he showed little interest in the uninformed contributions of his junior members. His committee staff usually didn't distribute to newer members copies of the complex bills under consideration until the morning of the hearing, which left no time for meaningful preparation. During committee hearings, after the chairman and senior members made their introductory remarks, Bliley made it known he preferred that his junior members submit their comments in writing. He also didn't value independent spirits from his GOP ranks when it came to Virginia's parochial interests. Before he signed off on my joining Commerce, he called me during orientation week.

"Newt wants my blessing on you," he said in his southern drawl. However, before he consented to my joining the committee, Bliley said he needed my assurance on a vital question. Was I going to give him any trouble over "The Golden Weed"?

The Golden Weed?

"Well, Mr. Chairman," I began, "as a former prosecutor, I'm afraid I have a problem with legalizing marijuana. It leads to—"

"I'm not talkin' about marijuana!" he snorted. "I want to make sure you won't give me any troubles with *tobacco*. I don't need another pain in the ass Californian on my committee like Henry Waxman." I surmised Congressman Waxman's (D-CA) anti-tobacco crusade so irked Bliley that he assumed everyone west of Atlanta wanted to treat tobacco as if it were crack cocaine. I assured him that I had libertarian values on The Golden Weed. The deal was done.

• • •

From the time Speaker Gingrich swore me in as a member of the 105th Congress in January 1997, I found my participation on the Commerce Committee frustrating because I could rarely get staff there to provide me with advance information on the pending matters. Chairman Hyde sensed my committee blues. He made multiple friendly overtures regarding my joining Judiciary, and he peppered each one with the flattery of his needing me. In October 1997, he ratcheted up the lobbying. Inviting me to his office for a cup of coffee, he zeroed in on my policymaking "Achilles heel" and aimed his dart with precision.

"Jim," he noted, "your area in Los Angeles has most of the movie, TV, and music industries in it. I would think that intellectual property [copyrights, patents and trademarks] is the lifeblood of your local economy. All those issues filter through the IP Subcommittee of the Judiciary Committee. I'll bet that if you were on that subcommittee, the entire employment base of your district would be very pleased. Wouldn't that be good for you in your reelection as well as interesting for you?"

He was right on both counts. Despite Congressman Paxon's earlier warning, I folded.

Hyde noted two minor problems. First, the Commerce Committee is one of the few "exclusive" committees, meaning that its members cannot serve on any other committee without two-thirds of the entire House membership voting to allow it. If I wanted to remain on Commerce (despite its tedium, I did—to raise campaign money), I needed to get a rule waiver. Second (and more practically), he told me that there were no vacancies on the IP Subcommittee, and he didn't expect any until after the 1998 elections.

"So, here is what we will do," he concluded. "You just stay on Commerce for the rest of this term, but when we get our vacancy in 1999, you are my boy for that spot."

Another deal was done.

• • •

The legendary Sonny Bono had the Midas touch. He wasn't terribly articulate, but long before he became a politician, he was a chart-topping pop singer and a successful songwriter. He really couldn't sing well, yet he had ten gold records and some 80 million sales worldwide. He couldn't act, but his television show was a top-rated network hit for five years. When his entertainment career peaked, he transitioned into thriving businessman and restaurateur. Following this record of success (and despite a reputation for ditziness), he added "politician" to his resume: Palm Springs voters elected him mayor in 1988; six years later, they sent him to Congress.

As a young kid in the 1960s listening to Sonny and Cher singing their string of hits on the radio or watching their prime-time comedy show in the early 1970s, I never dreamed that one day I'd serve in Congress with this goofy guy on TV wearing those bell-bottom pants, Eskimo boots, cheetah fur vest, and droopy mustache. Yet, of all my 534 colleagues, he became my favorite.

Our friendship started shortly after I arrived in D.C. when we both were scheduled to address a group of disadvantaged students. Sonny arrived late to the event and stood in the back of the room listening as I discussed my early life far from Washington's powerful center of gravity. I spoke of being the illegitimate son of a bartender and cocktail waitress; of growing up in San Francisco's hardscrabble Mission District and never knowing my father while my mother (a convicted felon) raised four kids on welfare and food stamps. Later, after running with a rough crowd, I got expelled from high school and never went back. With no diploma, I fell into a variety of jobs ranging from the crummy to the seamy— everything from cleaning toilets to selling door-to-door vacuum cleaners. Later I "graduated" to Hollywood bartending gigs in places as varied as a Hells Angels biker bar, a strip joint, a female mud and hot oil wrestling club, a rowdy cowboy bar, and at the late mobster Bugsy Siegel's old haunt on the Sunset Strip. I did this while scrapping through night school and community college, and then U.C. Berkeley and UCLA Law School on my way to becoming a prosecutor, judge, state legislator, and congressman.

Sonny liked what he heard. Later he came over to me on the

House floor. "You're a no-bullshit guy who doesn't put on airs," he said. "Some of these other guys around here really have their heads up their ass." We became friends. On late night votes, Sonny often plopped himself next to me in the House chamber and talked about everything—from Hollywood, his three ex-wives, his current family, the private sex lives of almost every colleague in sight (I couldn't believe how much he knew), and the old days of Sonny and Cher.

Sonny remained humbled by the privilege of serving in Congress. I felt the same way, but he harped on it too much during one particularly long day. This floor session had begun about 10:00 a.m.; by 2:00 a.m. the next morning an unending string of procedural votes kept us trapped on the House floor with no end in sight. While Sonny and I sat in the back of the chamber together, he jabbered endlessly about what a thrill it was to be a congressman. "Damn, Jimmy," he chimed out like an excited kid. "Look at this place! Here we are: members of the United States House of Representatives!"

"Yeah," I replied disinterestedly. "Here we are."

He became more emphatic: "Abraham Lincoln served here!"

"Yeah, Lincoln."

"And Webster!"

"Right. Webster."

"And all those presidents! Kennedy, Johnson, Nixon, Ford—all of them!"

"Yeah. All of them."

He grew irked that I wasn't in the proper spirit. He smacked me with his rolled-up papers and grew serious: "Here you are—a guy who used to bartend on the Sunset Strip. Here I am—a guy who used to drive a meat truck on the Sunset Strip. Don't you ever look around this chamber and wonder how in the hell we ever got here?"

I put my hand on Sonny's shoulder and said mischievously, "Sonny, I sit here all the time, look around this chamber, and wonder how in the hell *you* ever got here! I know how *I* got here, you jackass—I went to law school!"

Sonny laughed so hard that the speaker called for order in the chamber.

• • •

Although he sometimes lacked political polish, nobody could diffuse a hostile situation like Sonny. Halfway through my first year in Congress, Newt Gingrich's speakership almost collapsed when a rump group of disgruntled conservatives tried to depose him in a coup. As leaked news stories of the secret rebellion stunned Capitol Hill, Newt summoned his 228 troops to a confrontational private meeting in the Capitol basement. Angry charges of treachery and lying flew among the rebels, Newt's leadership team, and outraged members. I watched helplessly as the wheels appeared to be falling off the historic Republican Revolution.

Late into the tense evening, Sonny rose to speak. A few chuckles broke out. Whenever he talked, everyone expected it to end up being funny (intentionally or otherwise). As usual, he couldn't resist slipping into a nostalgic look at his Tinseltown years while trying to tie in a lesson.

"I remember being on top of the entertainment world," he began. "I had a hit show, a great wife, and a beautiful little girl. I had everything. Then, in a single day, it was gone." He spoke about the demise of both his marriage and his Hollywood career.

Oblivious to the eye-rolling glances of some colleagues, he continued: "I ended up being one of those celebrities spending all of his time trying to regain his fame. I knew I had hit rock-bottom when I became a regular on a TV show that was the elephant graveyard for washed-up celebrities: *Fantasy Island*."[1]

The titters grew as he told of sitting in his trailer getting drunk while waiting to shoot a scene: "The script called for me to walk

---

1   *Fantasy Island* was a dramatic television series that ran on ABC from 1977 to 1984. See https://en.wikipedia.org/wiki/Fantasy_Island (accessed August 6, 2020).

up to Herve Villechaize [the little person actor who played Tattoo, the island host's diminutive assistant], and say, 'Isn't it a beautiful day, Tattoo?' Instead, I said, 'Isn't it a lovely day, Harpoon?' I don't know where the hell 'Harpoon' came from. The director yelled, 'Cut!' Herve started yelling at me and calling me a stupid asshole. So, I'm just standing there looking at him and thinking to myself, 'I've lost my money, my family, and my fame. I've lost it all. I've written ten gold records, and now all I have to show for it is I have to stand here and get screamed at by a goddamned midget.'"

The room broke into howls. It no longer mattered if the story had any relevance. Sonny had returned calm to the fractured caucus.

"Let's retire for the evening to reflect on the lesson of the gentleman from California," Newt proclaimed. "Meeting adjourned." The next morning, the Republicans started working together again.

Later that night, Sonny told me, "Washington is just like Hollywood entertainment—execs love you when you're on top, but when you're down and out, they wouldn't piss on you if you were on fire. So, in both of these towns, you run a big risk of falling hard if you ever start believing your own bullshit or your own press agent. People need to keep a sense of perspective."

Sonny's message—at least that one tumultuous night—was heard.

• • •

I expected a hectic first year in Congress, but I didn't anticipate how draining the countless late-night votes, twice weekly or more cross-country flights, unending district appearances, and incessant fundraising would be. Trying to accomplish this while maintaining balance as a husband and father of preschool twins left me exhausted by the end of the year. I couldn't wait to get home to California for the extended holiday recess.

On the last night of the 1997 congressional session, a cheerful Sonny walked up to me. "Hey, Jimmy, what're you and Christine doing for Thanksgiving? Mary and I wanted to invite you guys over for dinner if you're going to be in town. It'll be the best spaghetti you ever had!"

I blew off the invitation without much thought. "Sorry, buddy," I said, "but I'm out of here. We'll be in California for the holidays. Thanks anyway."

"Well, give me a call if you change your mind," he said as he stuck out his hand and wished me a Happy Thanksgiving.

As Sonny turned to leave the chamber, the significance of his invitation hit me suddenly. I trotted over to the exit where he stood. Putting my arm around him, I said, "It just sank in that you and Mary invited us over for Thanksgiving dinner. Thank you. That means an awful lot. Thanksgiving is for family."

"Yeah, I know," he said with a big smile and a back slap, and then he headed down the House steps and into the night.

I never saw him again.

• • •

Home for the 1997 Holidays in California recharged my batteries. Just before returning to Washington for the start of the 1998 congressional session, I received the tragic news on January 5, 1998: while skiing in South Lake Tahoe, Sonny had struck a tree and died instantly. Grief and shock overcame me as I remembered our last conversation—Sonny's Thanksgiving invitation that I declined. I couldn't believe he was gone.

A few minutes later my chief of staff, Greg Mitchell, called to offer condolences. Then he said hesitantly, "I hate to mention it, but Sonny was on the Judiciary Committee and the IP subcommittee. Someone's going to have to take his place."

A few days later, I attended Sonny's funeral in Palm Springs. Thousands of people crowded St. Theresa's Catholic Church. A military honor guard escorted former President Ford, Cher, members of Congress and other dignitaries into the small chapel used as a VIP holding area. Chairman Henry Hyde arrived and sat next to me. Wiping away tears with his handkerchief, he said, "We can discuss this later, but remember, Jim: you're my number one boy to fill Sonny's slot on the committee."

I suggested that perhaps this wasn't the place for us to discuss the subject. Henry nodded in silent agreement and continued blotting his eyes. Just then I leaned over and whispered to him, "But I'll take it." He said he would go to work on Speaker Gingrich to get the necessary rule waiver as soon as we returned to D.C.

On January 14, Henry sent the speaker a two-page letter outlining why he needed me on his committee and why he wanted the rule waiver granted: "Jim is impressive; he is smart, capable and hard working. Also, as a former state court judge, Jim will bring an important expertise to the judicial issues the committee must address. Granting the rule waiver is in the best interest of the Congress."

On the night of January 20, word reached me from Chairman Hyde that Speaker Gingrich approved the rule waiver. I would be Sonny's replacement on the House Judiciary Committee.

Less than 12 hours later, all hell broke loose in the press around a former White House intern who preserved in her closet a DNA-stained blue dress.

3

Mouse Maze

On January 21, 1998, I first learned of President Clinton's Monica Lewinsky scandal while sipping a hurried cup of coffee and reading the early edition of the *Washington Post*. I shrugged off yet another tale about Clinton's private life: tacky and embarrassing, but of no congressional concern. Because I caught a predawn cross-country flight, I missed the media firestorm that broke out in those early hours.

To show how flawed my instincts were about this story's significance, the Lewinsky story was my last, brief diary entry for that date. After all, it wasn't the first time Clinton had yanked us down this road with him. During his first presidential campaign, the Clinton "war room" kept busy staving off or knocking down threatened "bimbo eruptions" (their phrase, not mine). That's why I initially ignored this new Lewinsky revelation. If America didn't care before they elected Clinton president, why care now? Besides, this sounded minor in comparison with his other scandals. It seemed at times the sun never set on the Clinton White House without some new outrage du jour. Some claims were serious, others tenuous; many created infernos, others discharged lots of black smoke. However, no First Couple had ever exposed the presidency to the sheer magnitude of disturbing allegations as did Bill and Hillary Clinton.

During their White House residency, the Clintons added a completely new lexicon to our political vocabulary: Chinagate, Travelgate, Filegate, Troopergate, Pardongate, and so forth. Their White House had more "gates" than a lab researcher's mouse maze. Consider the following sampler of pre-and post-Lewinsky allegations:

- Military Technology to China: China obtained top-secret U.S. missile technology through both theft and over-the-table technology transfers granted by the Clinton Administration. These transfers and thefts enabled China to develop, test, and deploy nuclear weapons on par with America's arsenal. As a result of Clinton's technology transfers, the House of Representatives passed a resolution in 1998 on a nearly unanimous vote condemning Clinton for failing to act in the national interest by allowing Chinese-launched satellites to carry highly sensitive U.S. missile technology. In another near-unanimous show of outrage over Clinton's recklessness with our military secrets, the House voted to block Clinton from approving any further missile technology exports. MSNBC News reported later that the chairman of the aerospace company involved in these Clinton-approved technology transfers donated hundreds of thousands of dollars to the Democrat National Committee and to Democrat Party coffers.

- Donorgate: A huge web connecting illegal campaign fundraising, money laundering, and direct access to President Clinton. The drumbeat of news accounts seemed endless:

  » The Clintons turned the White House Lincoln Bedroom into a bed and breakfast for their major donors. A 1997 CNN report claimed Clinton's Lincoln Bedroom slumber parties netted at least $5.4 million to the Democrat National Committee during 1995 and 1996 alone.

  » Piling sacrilege upon sacrilege, President Clinton personally ordered a burial waiver at Arlington National

Cemetery for a major campaign donor who fabricated a military record. When authorities discovered the lie, his family disinterred his remains and reburied him elsewhere.

» Large campaign donations that netted direct access to President Clinton at the White House. According to the *New York Times*, Democrat fundraisers said they explicitly sold invitations to White House coffees for $50,000 to $100,000. White House and campaign records later released showed the Clinton campaign projected one hastily scheduled presidential meeting could bring $500,000 in donations.

» Clinton Commerce Secretary Ron Brown, a former Democrat National Committee chairman and close friend of the president, allegedly used Commerce Department trade missions for political fundraising. One of Brown's trusted business associates said under oath that Brown told her that both Bill and Hillary Clinton approved the sale of seats on official government trade missions to those donating at least $50,000 to the Democrat National Committee. Brown died in a mysterious plane crash before he could testify in a criminal investigation about the allegations.

» Johnny Chung donated $366,000 to the Democrat National Committee (a portion of which he later admitted came from China's military intelligence). He delivered a $50,000 campaign check inside the White House to a senior Clinton aide while seeking favors. Granted access to the White House for 49 separate visits, he later said he viewed the Clinton White House like a subway: "You have to put in coins to open the gates."

» Charlie Trie made an illegal contribution of $460,000 to President Clinton's legal defense fund, along with an additional donation of $220,000 to the Democrat National Committee. According to *Time* magazine, Trie visited the White House 23 times before his name surfaced in news reports, including a controversial White House coffee to which Trie brought a Chinese arms dealer as his guest.

» John Huang raised at least $3.4 million for the Democrat Party. Later convicted of campaign money laundering violations, according to the *New York Times* he made at least 65 White House visits in 1996 alone—the year of Clinton's reelection race.

» Buddhist nuns coordinated an illegal temple fundraiser attended by Clinton's vice president, Al Gore. The destitute monks with whom Gore dined later "donated" $140,000 to Democrat Party coffers. It turned out the temple was used as a front to launder illegal foreign money to the Democrat National Committee. A jury later convicted Gore's longtime fundraiser, Maria Hsia, for her participation in the scheme.

• Pardongate I (Friends and Donors): Pardons and commutations signed by President Clinton for friends, family, and major political donors—including 140 separate pardons and commutations signed on his last day in office. Even Congressman Barney Frank (D-MA), one of Clinton's fiercest defenders on the House Judiciary Committee, called the pardons "contemptuous" and "a betrayal." In what smelled like an exchange of executive clemency for money and favors, the list included:

» Fugitive Marc Rich, the veritable poster boy of the pardon scandal. Before Clinton signed Rich's pardon, Rich's ex-wife reportedly paid to furnish Bill and Hillary Clinton's presidential retirement home; she also donated almost $500,000 to the Clinton Library, more than $1,000,000 to the Democrat Party, and steered $100,000 to Mrs. Clinton's 2000 U.S. Senate campaign. After the surprise pardon, Clinton's own Justice Department U.S. Attorney prosecuting Rich said, "It is inconceivable that President Clinton chose to pardon the biggest tax cheat in the history of the United States."

» Sixteen members of FALN, a Puerto Rican terrorist group responsible for over 100 U.S. bombings that left many dead and injured. These terrorists faced federal prison sentences ranging from 35 to 105 years for conspiracy and sedition. As former Clinton political adviser Dick Morris noted, "These terrorists never even asked for a pardon, but because Hillary wanted to ingratiate herself with the Hispanic population in New York during her first Senate race, [the FALN terrorists] were suddenly granted a commutation of their sentences." Congress condemned the commutations by huge bipartisan margins and started an investigation; Clinton invoked executive privilege and refused to turn over key documents.

» Four Hasidic Jewish felons convicted of stealing $40 million from taxpayers. Clinton granted this pardon at the request of New York's Orthodox Hasidic leaders, who afterward delivered their community's votes for Hillary Clinton in her Senate race by the lopsided result of 1,400 to 12.

- Pardongate II (A Family Affair):

  » Clinton pardoned his brother Roger for an earlier federal narcotics conviction. With his own pardon pending, several drug kingpins hired Roger Clinton to lobby for their pardons as well. The *New York Times* reported that one convicted drug felon told prosecutors he paid Roger Clinton $225,000. In another case, Roger Clinton received a huge fee and a Rolex watch for seeking a pardon for a member of the Gambino crime family.

  » Narcotics peddler Carlos Vignali, who served only six years of a 15-year federal sentence before Clinton freed him. Convicted for trafficking 500 pounds of cocaine, Vignali paid Hillary Clinton's brother, Hugh Rodham, more than $400,000 to lobby for clemency. Vignali's father also contributed more than $150,000 to the Democrat Party.

  » Edgar and Vonna Jo Gregory, pardoned for bank fraud. The Gregorys contributed over $100,000 to Democrat races, including Hillary Clinton's Senate race. The Clintons also entertained them at their Camp David presidential retreat. The press later reported that the Gregorys forgave a $107,000 loan to Hillary Clinton's younger brother, Tony Rodham.

  » Almon Braswell, pardoned for mail fraud and perjury. Unbelievably, Clinton pardoned Braswell while the U.S. Department of Justice and FBI conducted an ongoing federal investigation into new charges of money laundering and tax evasion. Braswell paid about $200,000 to Hillary Clinton's brother, Hugh Rodham, to lobby

Clinton for the pardon.

» Incidentally, while Hillary Clinton's two brothers raked in some $700,000 in fees for pardon-lobbying their presidential in-law, both brothers lived in the White House. When confronted with these revelations, both Bill and Hillary Clinton expressed shock.

- Chinagate: According to news accounts, the Clintons left the White House at the end of their term with nearly $200,000 in china, gifts, and 44 pieces of White House furniture as well as art, clothing, and historical artifacts worth another $400,000. Half of these gifts never received an independent appraisal beyond the Clintons' own stated valuation. After a congressional committee referred the matter to the U.S. Justice Department for possible criminal investigation, the Clintons returned much of the loot. Of the removal, the usually supportive *Washington Post* editorialized: "[This] demonstrates again the Clintons' defining characteristic. They have no capacity for embarrassment."

- Associate U.S. Attorney General Webster Hubbell: President Clinton appointed one of Hillary Clinton's former Arkansas law partners, Webster Hubbell, to a key Justice Department position. Soon after taking office, Hubbell pleaded guilty and went to federal prison for mail fraud, tax evasion, and bilking former clients. Following his felony conviction for stealing over $400,000, and while awaiting his prison surrender, Hubbell collected over $700,000 in "consulting fees" from Clinton friends. Meanwhile, the White House gave Mrs. Hubbell a high-paying job while her husband sat in federal prison. The evidence pointed to this being "hush money" paid to buy Hubbell's silence. In a secretly recorded telephone call from jail between prisoner Hubbell and his wife, he told her that he'd have to "roll over one more time" for her to keep her White House job; Mrs. Hubbell said the "squeeze play" they were feeling was just "part of the game."

- Whitewater: Governor and Mrs. Clinton invested money with Jim and Susan McDougal in an Arkansas vacation home development known as Whitewater. When this (and some of their other investments) failed, the McDougals tried to cover their losses with funds from the savings and loan institution they operated. A jury convicted both McDougals of fraud and conspiracy and they received federal prison sentences. Later, Clinton-appointed Attorney General Janet Reno and a three-judge panel appointed former federal judge and U.S. Solicitor General Kenneth Starr to investigate the Clintons' Whitewater involvement. Former Arkansas banker and state court judge David Hale testified that then-Governor Clinton pressured him to make an illegal $300,000 loan to Susan McDougal. Judge Starr subpoenaed the McDougals to testify before the grand jury. Jim McDougal agreed to cooperate; however, he died in prison unexpectedly before telling his story. Susan McDougal refused to testify about Clinton's involvement, preferring to receive an additional 18-month prison sentence for contempt. Mrs. McDougal later claimed she refused to testify because investigators pressured her to lie. On President Clinton's last day in office, he issued Mrs. McDougal a full and unconditional pardon.

- Travelgate: The Clinton White House ordered the FBI to conduct what proved to be a bogus investigation of longtime White House Travel Office employees, then used that investigation as a reason to fire the employees so that Clinton's cousin could take over the operation. Under intense media scrutiny, the Clintons rehired the original employees and sent their Arkansas relative and her friends packing. The FBI and U.S. Department of Justice investigated this outrage. Independent Counsel Robert Ray later issued a report stating that Mrs. Clinton made false statements to investigators, but given the high burden of proof in criminal court there was insufficient evidence to obtain a perjury conviction against the First Lady.

- Filegate: The Clinton White House hired Democrat Party operative Craig Livingstone to head the White House Office of Personnel Security. Livingstone (whose only prior "security" experience came from working as a bouncer at a D.C. nightclub) improperly obtained and rifled through up to 900 national security background files on high level Republican government officials. Claims arose that senior White House figures, including Hillary Clinton, read the files looking for political dirt. A later investigation revealed insufficient evidence to file criminal charges.

- Vincent Foster Suicide: President Clinton appointed another of Hillary Clinton's former law partners, Vincent Foster, as Deputy White House Counsel. Foster handled many of the scandals and indignities miring down the newly installed Clinton Administration. Upon receiving news of Foster's suicide, senior White House aides searched Foster's office and removed files and documents before the FBI arrived to investigate. A later U.S. Senate report criticized a "pattern of stonewalling" from the Clinton White House.

- Missing Billing Records: As noted above, the Clintons' Whitewater investment partners Jim and Susan McDougal operated an Arkansas savings and loan. The McDougals later hired Mrs. Clinton as their attorney to represent their S&L before the Arkansas agency overseeing S&L operations—whose members were appointed by then-Governor Clinton. Later, during the federal Whitewater investigation, Justice Department investigators subpoenaed Mrs. Clinton's billing records. She claimed they were lost. Two years later, and after the firestorm ebbed, her files appeared inexplicably on a table in the First Family's private White House reading room.

- The Draft: Clinton undertook extraordinary efforts to avoid military service. Retired Colonel Eugene Holmes (a decorated World War II hero and Clinton's former Army ROTC commander at the University of Arkansas) stated that while in college, Clinton "purposefully deceived me, using the possibility of joining ROTC as a ploy to work with the draft board to delay his induction and get a new draft reclassification." Meanwhile, enraged veterans heard reports that Clinton allegedly said during his conscription-sidestepping days that he avoided service because he "loathed" the military. Colonel Holmes made this public observation during Clinton's 1992 race: "There is the imminent danger to our country of a draft dodger becoming Commander in Chief of the Armed Forces of the United States."

- *Wag the Dog*: This was the name of a 1997 movie where a scandal-plagued U.S. president started a phony war with Albania to divert domestic attention from his problems. The film became a precursor of life imitating art. While enmeshed in the thick of the Lewinsky scandal, President Clinton placed American armed forces in harm's way by ordering sudden and unexpected overseas military assaults, the timing of which proved too coincidental to all but Clinton's most hardy defenders. These operations included:

» A three-day bombing campaign in Iraq that began without any provocation *the night before* the U.S. House of Representatives debated Clinton's impeachment;

» Clinton ordering sudden missile strikes against supposed "terrorist" targets *a few hours* after he admitted in a nationally televised speech that he had an affair with Lewinsky. Further, the White House timed the missile strike announcement to occur just moments before Monica Lewinsky completed her much-anticipated grand jury testimony. Clinton's main target turned out to be a harmless Sudanese pharmaceutical factory. By destroying this important civilian source of needed medical supplies, Germany's ambassador to Sudan later told an interviewer that untold numbers of Sudanese children died from lack of medicine.

This walk down memory lane doesn't include all the ladies crossing the stage with allegations against Clinton ranging from extramarital affairs to harassment and sexual assault. Paula Jones, Dolly Kyle Browning, Elizabeth Gracen, Juanita Broaddrick, Kathleen Willey, and Sally Perdue were some of the names joining Gennifer Flowers and Monica Lewinsky in the Clinton-generated tabloids.

Given this mind-numbing history of scandal and alleged wrongdoing, it's no wonder I didn't think (at least initially) that the Lewinsky story rated particular notice. Yet, as the layers peeled back slowly from this newest humiliation, it did rate higher and it changed more than Clinton's presidency. It changed our culture.

• • •

Within hours of the Lewinsky story unfolding, First Lady Hillary Clinton branded the allegation a lie. She blamed it on a "vast right-wing conspiracy that has been conspiring against my husband since the day he announced for president."

If House Republican chieftains (presumably the ringleaders of Mrs. Clinton's web of conspirators) wanted to use this new revelation as an excuse to depose Clinton from office, they did a great job of hiding their intentions from me. Both before and after Lewinsky made headlines, Speaker Gingrich privately urged the House Republicans to ignore the swamp of Clinton scandals and keep focused on policy. I heard him take this position upon my arrival to Washington more than a year before anyone ever heard of Monica Lewinsky. At a members-only meeting with newly elected freshmen Republicans, Newt gave us his template for dealing with Clinton and his troubles:

Diary, Freshman House Republicans Meeting, November 15, 1996

Speaker Newt Gingrich shared his view of President Clinton: "Clinton is a customer I'll always deal with as long as the check clears before I give him the product. But we'll never give him the product on consignment." He cautioned us to focus on our policy agenda and forget about Clinton's unending scandals: "We [Republicans] will do everything we can to make him successful," Newt affirmed, "but 'successful' on our terms. We don't need to beat up Bill Clinton. As Woodrow Wilson said, 'Never murder a man in the process of committing suicide.' We will make Bill Clinton uncomfortable when we send him good policy. Our goal will be to force him to sign it. Our center of gravity is the American people, not Bill Clinton."

After the Lewinsky revelation, I heard this sentiment echoed repeatedly in the House GOP leadership ranks. Commerce Chairman Bliley told me he didn't want to see Bill Clinton impeached, "although I wouldn't mind seeing him bleed for three more years." On February 18, at a private dinner I attended with Judiciary Chairman Henry Hyde and conservative members of Hollywood's entertainment community (we gathered in a very small room), Henry told those assembled that if the latest scandal was just about sexual relations with an intern, he didn't think it would be an impeachable offense.

My own diary notes written the night the Lewinsky scandal became public repeated the same political reality: for Republicans, Bill Clinton wounded was better than a new and invigorated replacement president.

Diary, January 21, 1998

It is alleged that Clinton told Lewinsky to lie about the relationship under oath in a deposition. Clinton has issued a vehement denial.

The interesting political equation for the GOP: if he is guilty, does the GOP really want him impeached halfway through his second term? As much as Republicans dislike Bill Clinton and would like to remove him, it is not in our political interest to have Vice President Al Gore as an incumbent president moving into the 2000 presidential election.

Most people now forget that two months before the Lewinsky story broke, Congressman Bob Barr (R-GA) introduced a resolution authorizing an impeachment inquiry against Clinton for his foreign campaign money laundering connections. If Mrs. Clinton's "vast right-wing conspiracy" supported this, its membership must have missed Bob Barr's invitation to the dance. Only a handful of Bob's 228 GOP colleagues cosponsored his resolution; not one of them served in the Republican leadership.

The reason Bob Barr had no meaningful support is that the overwhelming majority of Republican House members thought impeaching Clinton was a bad idea. Only days after the Lewinsky news became public, 1996 GOP vice presidential nominee Jack Kemp headlined a fundraiser for me in San Diego. In our private discussion, Jack expressed dismay at Bob's television interviews trying to bootstrap his resolution onto these new revelations. "Why is Bob doing this?" Jack asked. "It makes us look silly. Newt [Gingrich] handled himself beautifully in interviews when he urged caution and not jumping to conclusions until we get all the facts."

Not long afterward, I ran into former Vice President Dan Quayle (whom Clinton defeated for reelection in 1992) at a Capitol Hill Club reception. As we discussed Bob's proposal (now getting plenty of media attention since the Lewinsky scandal aired), Dan felt that it was better politically for the Republican Party to see Clinton survive the tsunami.

Another person unhappy with Bob's impeachment proposal was the man who controlled the committee of jurisdiction for impeachments: Chairman Henry Hyde. Shortly after Bob introduced his resolution, and two months before the Lewinsky saga, I asked Henry if he thought enough evidence would ever merit an impeachment inquiry against Clinton. He shrugged: "There's no smoking gun yet on the president," he said, "but we all know he is dirty." When I asked him why he thought Bob Barr introduced an impeachment resolution before our committee received the anticipated referral from Independent Counsel Kenneth Starr (who was concluding a four-year investigation into earlier Clinton scandals), Henry scowled: "Publicity," he grumbled, "pure and simple."

Later that afternoon I ran into Bob, who seemed disinterested in what anyone else thought about his effort. I asked if he felt there was enough evidence to impeach Clinton right now.

"No," he conceded. "There's a lot of smoke, though. Nailing Bill Clinton is like trying to nail a fart to the wall. There's a lot of smell and you know it's there. You just aren't sure where to nail."

4

Poker Hand

The question "Did he or didn't he?" quickly switched to "Would he or wouldn't he?"

The Lewinsky bomb detonated six days before Clinton's annual State of the Union message. Considering the awkward timing, pundits expressed unending speculation as to whether he would appear before a joint session of Congress. Cloakroom rumors swirled: Clinton will resign; Clinton canceled the speech; Republicans are boycotting; the leadership revoked his speech invitation, and so forth. There was one certainty: if Clinton appeared, it would be the most controversial State of the Union speech ever.

The White House had good reason to worry over one of those rumors: Clinton's congressional allies might not rally to his defense. How deeply or for how long this panicked the administration I do not know. However, in the days immediately following the Lewinsky story's unfolding, I do know that the greatest backstage anger and frustration I witnessed came from Clinton's own Democrats.

A couple of days after Lewinsky became public, I attended a private luncheon at Walt Disney Studios in Burbank with CEO Michael Eisner and Jack Valenti, the longtime head of the Motion Picture Association of America. Both men were major Democrat fundraisers and friends of Clinton. Now they spoke of their fury at him over the startling revelation. Eisner agreed when Valenti said, "Clinton's sexual appetite is so great that he has led himself, foolishly and recklessly, to disgrace and probable ruin. He may survive the scandal, but his presidency's effectiveness will not."

Echoing that same theme, my old friend Michael Dukakis (former Massachusetts governor and 1988 Democrat presidential nominee) expressed great disappointment in how the scandal threatened to undo all the Democrats tried to accomplish. Over lunch in Mike's small UCLA office a few weeks after the Lewinsky revelation, he defended Clinton as a talented and competent president. But when we discussed the political fallout, he looked dejected: "Just when we got the country believing after five years that he was a good president, this new scandal breaks." His voice then trailed off.

Around the same time, I ran into Congressman Howard Berman (D-CA), a respected senior Democrat on the House Judiciary Committee and fellow Southern Californian. Howard vented when I asked what he thought about the scandal: "Clinton is self-destructing," he said angrily. "He's destroyed our agenda and all we've tried to do. I feel betrayed by him. He's killed us!"

It didn't take long for the White House to try cauterizing the bleeding with a full-blown credibility assault. Along with Mrs. Clinton's almost daily television appearances blasting this "lie" as a right-wing fabrication, Clinton now played the victim publicly. He called a cabinet meeting to assure each member of his administration personally that the Lewinsky allegations were untrue. Simultaneously, and within hours of the scandal breaking, he underwent a succession of back-to-back interviews where he pounded away on the same theme:

Clinton Interview with Jim Lehrer, PBS, January 21, 1998

Q: The news of this day is that Kenneth Starr, independent counsel, is investigating allegations that you suborned perjury by encouraging a 24-year-old woman—a former White House intern—to lie under oath in a civil deposition about her having an affair with you. Mr. President, is that true?

A: That is not true. That is not true. I did not ask anyone to tell anything other than the truth. There is no improper relationship. And I intend to cooperate with this inquiry. But that is not true.

Q: "No improper relationship"—define what you mean by that.

A: Well, I think you know what it means. It means that there is not a sexual relationship, an improper sexual relationship, or any other kind of improper relationship.

Q: You had no sexual relationship with this young woman?

A: There is not a sexual relationship—that is accurate.

Q: Just for the record, to make sure I understand what your answer means, there's no ambiguity about it?

A: There is not.

Clinton Interview with National Public Radio, January 21, 1998

Q: Many Americans woke up to the news today that the White-water independent counsel is investigating an allegation that you, or you and Vernon Jordan, encouraged a young woman to lie to lawyers in the Paula Jones civil suit. Is there any truth to that allegation?

A: No, sir, there's not. It's just not true.

Q: Is there any truth to the allegation of an affair between you and the young woman?

A: No, that's not true, either. The charges are not true, and I haven't asked anybody to lie.

Q: Mr. President, where do you think this comes from? Did you have any kind of relationship with her that could have been misconstrued?

A: I'm going to do my best to cooperate with the investigation. I want to know what they want to know from me. I think it's more important for me to tell the American people that there wasn't any improper relation. I didn't ask anybody to lie, and I intend to cooperate. And I think that's all I should say right now, so I can get back to the work of the country.

Clinton White House Press Availability, January 22, 1998

Q: Could you clarify for us, sir, exactly what your relationship was with Ms. Lewinsky, and whether the two of you talked by phone, including any messages you may have left?

A: The allegations are false. I would never ask anybody to do anything other than tell the truth. [T]he American people have a right to get answers. We are working very hard to comply and get all the requests for information up here, and we will give you as many answers as we can, as soon as we can, at the appropriate time, consistent with our obligation to also cooperate with the investigations. And that's not a dodge, that's really why I've talked with our people. I want to do that. I'd like for you to have more rather than less, sooner rather than later.

Then, in one of the most unforgettable moments of his presidency, a steely-eyed Bill Clinton wagged his pointed finger at a White House audience while America watched, listened, and (according to the polls) believed:

White House News Conference on Education, January 26, 1998

"I want to say one thing to the American people. I want you to listen to me. I'm going to say this again. I did not have sexual relations with that woman, Miss Lewinsky. I never told anybody to lie, not a single time—never. These allegations are false. And I need to go back to work for the American people."

All of Clinton's denials came a few days after he testified in Paula Jones' federal sexual harassment lawsuit against him. Since Clinton's defense in that suit boiled down to calling Jones a liar, her lawyers needed to show Clinton's pattern of conduct. Jones' legal team understood that if President Clinton now used the prestige of his office to obtain sexual favors from female subordinate federal employees, then this corroborated Jones' claim that Governor Clinton did the same thing with subordinate Arkansas state employees. Once Jones' lawyers learned about Monica Lewinsky, they found the substantiation they needed.

Nobody had to explain any of this to Bill Clinton. Along with facing grave political jeopardy, he knew that losing the Jones lawsuit exposed him to paying her vast sums in damages and legal fees out of his own pocket. Given the lay of the land, beating Paula Jones became doubly important. However, he faced a critical risk: any generic finger-wagging Lewinsky denial (if later proven a lie) might cost him political capital and prove personally humiliating, but he had to make any Paula Jones deposition denial under oath. If Clinton lied there, losing political capital was his least worry. He faced impeachment, felony criminal perjury charges, and possibly imprisonment. The table stakes for Bill Clinton could not get any higher.

The president arrived for his Paula Jones deposition on January 17, 1998. After being sworn in, Clinton (a Yale-trained lawyer, constitutional law professor, former state attorney general and governor, and the only federal official charged in the U.S. Constitution, in Art.

II §3, to "take Care that the Laws be faithfully executed") pushed in all of his poker chips and called the dealer's hand:

Q: Did you have an extramarital sexual affair with Monica Lewinsky?

A: No.

Q: If she told someone that she had a sexual affair with you beginning in November of 1995, would that be a lie?

A: It's certainly not the truth. It would not be the truth.

Q: I think I used the term "sexual affair." And so, the record is completely clear, have you ever had sexual relations with Monica Lewinsky?

A: I have never had sexual relations with Monica Lewinsky. I've never had an affair with her....

Q: At any time were you and Monica Lewinsky alone together in the Oval Office?

A: I don't recall. It seems to me she brought things to me once or twice on the weekends. In that case, whatever time she would be there, [she'd] drop it off, exchange a few words and go.

Q: So, your testimony is that it was possible that you were alone with her, but you have no specific recollection of that ever happening?

A: Yes, that is correct. It's possible that while she was working there, she brought something to me and that at the time she was the only person there. That's possible....

Q: Have you ever met with Monica Lewinsky in the White House between the hours of midnight and six a.m.?

A: I certainly don't think so. Now, let me just say, when she was working there, there may have been a time when we were all working late. On any given night, when the Congress is in session, there are always several people around until late in the night, but I don't have any memory of that. I just can't say that there could have been a time when that occurred. I don't remember it.

Q: Certainly, if it happened, nothing remarkable would have occurred?

A: No, nothing remarkable. I don't remember it.

The Bill and Hillary Clinton press assault worked: America believed him. His poll numbers first held steady, and then increased to a whopping 67 percent approval rating. Democrats in Congress heaved a sigh of relief. Clinton returned to their embrace.

After the president played this defensive hand successfully (and congressional Democrats exhaled after seeing his post-denials polling data), the gossip over canceling his speech ended. Speaker Gingrich said that the invitation stood, and the White House announced Clinton would proceed as scheduled.

On the evening of January 27, 1998, the 105th Congress reconvened for the president's State of the Union message. Entering the House chamber, I saw Chairman Hyde surrounded by Republican colleagues praising him for yet another round of successful appearances on the Sunday morning interview shows discussing the Lewinsky scandal. Henry had handled himself judiciously and insisted that there be no rush to judgment.

When the crowd thinned, I sat with Henry and then added my congratulations. "Thank you," he said. "I sure fielded a lot of questions about the Clinton scandals."

"Oh, I'm not congratulating you on your answers, Henry," I said in mock solemnity. "I'm congratulating you on your ability to answer all those questions about Clinton possibly getting impeached and not bursting into a big shit-eating grin."

He returned my grave countenance and replied, "Well, now that you mention it, my jaw was quivering just a little bit!"

After laughing at his own joke, he grew serious and said he expected Special Counsel Kenneth Starr to deliver his investigative report later this year: "I think Ken Starr will give us the goods on Clinton," Henry whispered to me. "When that happens, I predict the Democrats will want Clinton out. He's imploding."

A couple of hours before Clinton's scheduled speech, Speaker Gingrich summoned the House GOP conference to a private meeting in the Capitol. Newt focused his remarks on Clinton's upcoming address and how he wanted Republicans responding to him: "We need to avoid being negative," Newt admonished us. "Be positive. The *Contract with America* [1] was a positive message. 'No comment' is better than a dumb comment." As for rumors that many Republicans intended to turn their backs on Clinton or walk out of the chamber, Newt showed great intensity addressing this threat:

---

[1]   During the 1994 congressional midterm elections, House Republican candidates published their *Contract with America,* a set of legislative promises to voters. It helped secure the first House GOP majority in 40 years and brought Newt Gingrich to the speakership.

Diary, House Republican Conference Meeting, January 27, 1998

Newt said, "Americans are angry and confused with Clinton. They're ashamed of him, but they want to be patriots. If Clinton is going to be brutalized in the end, and I suspect he is, we can't be part of the mob. We have a system in place to deal with it. Henry Hyde's committee will act accordingly. You salute the uniform, not the person. This speech tonight is a state function. I expect every member to stand when the person of the president of the United States walks in and walks out.

This country wants to know there is a Party providing stability. Let's hold off commenting on Bill Clinton's problems. If we don't comment, the media will be forced to go to the Democrats to get their comments. Let them be the ones to answer how they can stomach him. I've learned my lesson from 2-1/2 years of getting the crap beaten out of me."

Suggesting a comparison between a positive message and political popularity, Newt argued that his own recent approval ratings in the polls reflected a payoff for his change of tone. "*USA Today* has me at my highest approval rate ever!" Newt said excitedly. At that, Congressman Wally Herger (R-CA) leaned over and whispered with a smirk, "Yeah, now he's at 12 percent."

Before the conference adjourned and members proceeded to the chamber for the president's speech, Conference Chairman John Boehner (R-OH) added his own cautionary words: "Any little nuance will be picked up by the cameras. Please don't make any faces."

Despite the uncertainty leading to the president's speech, no unruly demonstrations or disruptions occurred. Congressmen interrupted his 72-minute speech over 100 times with applause. Clinton covered the bases of his expansive spending agenda: education, federally run childcare, crime, and trade. He mentioned everything but Lewinsky.

At the end of the address, most members rushed from the chamber and headed for the scores of television cameras crowded into Statuary Hall. This post-speech stampede is another congressional tradition: satellites beam the interviews to the members' various local television media markets. As I looked over my notes while making my way out of the chamber, I heard one Republican congressman walking behind me say to another:

"I hope Clinton enjoyed giving that speech. It's the last one of those he will ever do."

5

A Closing Window

The circus atmosphere surrounding Clinton's State of the Union appearance died with his departure from the Capitol; the suspicion and unrelenting gossip did not. He and Monica Lewinsky still topped the rumor charts playing in the Capitol cloakrooms and hallways. Despite this massive distraction, everything settled down to business as usual for me. After dodging Henry Hyde's entreaties to join his committee for a year, now I looked forward to adding Judiciary to my portfolio of responsibilities. With my maiden appearance as a member of the committee just days away, I hit an unexpected bump: Speaker Gingrich had second thoughts about ratifying my appointment.

Pulling me aside at a Capitol Hill Club reception and showing symptoms of buyer's remorse, Newt said he was reconsidering his decision. Citing polling data from my district, he felt the mere *possibility* of a future impeachment inquiry might be tough for me to overcome in my first reelection campaign later that year:

Diary, January 29, 1998

Newt grew serious during our discussion: "I've been getting calls and letters from Henry Hyde and all of Hollywood about appointing you. Is that what you really want? Does this hurt your reelection? You need to be reelected. Can you do it?"

I reminded Newt that Hollywood's intellectual property interests remained the primary job creator in my district, so the industry shouldn't complain about the appointment. Besides, as a former prosecutor and judge, I wanted a committee assignment that allowed me to use my expertise. "I'm a natural for this," I insisted. I asked him not to rescind the appointment.

Newt stared at me for a few moments, and then he sighed heavily. "Okay" he said, "then it's done."

A lobbyist watching my discussion with Newt later walked over to me: "I don't know what that was all about with Newt," he said, "but it looks like you're getting your way with him."

He was right; I was getting my way. Whether I would later regret it remained to be seen.

• • •

Following Clinton's State of the Union address, Newt and the House Republican leadership continued trying to steer the GOP conference away from impeachment and scandal. Just as stubbornly, the House Republican rank-and-file refused to move off topic. At our first conference meeting a week after Clinton's speech, Speaker Gingrich gave a lengthy overview of our policy agenda for the coming months. Clinton's woes came last and merited only a cursory comment. Congress' current poll numbers showed a healthy 58 percent approval rating, Newt said, and suggested it was because we remained above the Clinton fray.

Despite Newt's efforts, at the end of the meeting, members peppered him with Clinton questions. Some said their constituents demanded we hold Clinton accountable for perjury. Others reported schoolchildren asking embarrassing sexual questions about Clinton and Lewinsky. Newt tried to brush off these statements, but his desire to move on went ignored. Finally, he tossed a small bone to his Clinton-obsessed colleagues and quoted former Clinton communications advisor David Gergen: "If this scandal is true, then Bill Clinton is a scoundrel and he must resign." Even this failed to quell the perseveration on Clinton:

Diary, House Republican Conference Meeting, February 4, 1998

In frustration, Newt threw up his hands and said, "Look, Clinton denied having an affair with Lewinsky. This means he has set a very low bar for himself. If he lied, we will know by spring. The election isn't until November. Let's just be patient. My guess is that before this is over, Henry Hyde is going to give each of you the chance to be part of a very historic drama."

That brief comment was the first time I ever heard Speaker Gingrich hint at a possible impeachment vote against the president of the United States, and he said it only after the House GOP conference dragged it out of him.

• • •

A week later, the Republican conference met in Williamsburg for our annual members-only retreat. Once again, the scene from the previous week played out. Newt and his leadership team tried to present a policy-laden game plan for 1998, and the Republican members wanted to know what we were going to do about Clinton.

Diary, House Republican Retreat, Williamsburg, February 10, 1998

Referencing Clinton's recent State of the Union message, Newt said, "We must be the contrast to the White House and not the opposition. We must offer a better market product with positive

alternative solutions based on freedom and limited government."

After shooting pool with a few colleagues, I said good-night to the gang about 11:30 p.m. As I left the bar, Newt called me over to his table. He said that from now on, he wanted our team to refer to me as "Judge Rogan, not Congressman Rogan," adding that Special Counsel Ken Starr "made a mistake in dropping his judicial title. Starr would have more credibility today if he used his title of judge. That's why we want the press to call you Judge Rogan."

Newt then grabbed my arm and pulled me aside: "Listen," he said, "Henry Hyde really wanted you on the Judiciary Committee. You should be proud that he has so much faith in you. But you need to prepare yourself. You are going to have the pleasure of sitting on a very historic committee, and you guys are going to make history."

For the second time that day, our don't-talk-about-impeachment speaker dropped a hint that the unmentionable might happen. This time, he made the remark free from duress.

I returned to my hotel room that night thinking Newt knew something was brewing. This suspicion heightened a few days later when I attended a private dinner with Henry Hyde and some IP industry leaders. Mitch Glazier, a senior Republican staff attorney with the Judiciary Committee, confided that Henry expected Judge Starr to deliver his evidentiary report to the committee in May. He and other staff attorneys on the committee believed Judge Starr's investigative team collected substantial evidence against Clinton over the Whitewater fraud and other non-Lewinsky scandals. Mitch and the committee staff were confident there would be an impeachment inquiry. It was just a matter of time.

• • •

I ran into President Clinton a couple of times in the few weeks following his State of the Union message. These were our first face-to-face meetings since I joined the Judiciary Committee and the Lewinsky story became public.

On February 5, I attended the White House arrival ceremony for British Prime Minister Tony Blair's first official trip to Washington. When both leaders appeared, President Clinton looked poised and dignified. His commanding presence might have been accentuated standing next to Blair: the slight, youthful prime minister looked more like a junior White House staffer than the heir to Churchill. Following brief speeches from both leaders, Clinton and Blair retired to the Blue Room to greet guests.

During my brief greeting with Clinton in the receiving line, he looked far more haggard than was apparent from a distance:

**Diary, White House Reception for
Prime Minister Tony Blair, February 5, 1998**

While we chatted briefly in the Blue Room, I noticed Clinton's eyes had dark circles and bags—more pronounced than when he appeared for his recent State of the Union speech. This is probably a result of the stress he has been under as he tries to salvage his presidency from the scandal.

A month later, Newt's office sent me an invitation to attend the speaker's annual St. Patrick's Day luncheon in the Rayburn Room of the Capitol. I had received a similar invitation the previous year and declined; I assumed the event was some corned beef and cabbage smorgasbord reception. This year I also planned to skip it, but as noon approached I found myself both hungry and nearby, so I headed over hoping to grab a quick bite. My miscalculation became apparent upon arrival: a room decorated elegantly, a string ensemble playing, an Irish tenor singing, and Secret Service agents posted everywhere. "Something tells me they aren't passing out sandwiches here," I said to a staffer checking names at the table.

"Oh, no," she said. "This is one of the hottest tickets in town. Only a dozen or so House members are invited, and just a few senators. This is a very exclusive luncheon." The staffer then handed me a card showing my table assignment: Table #2, seated with President Clinton, Speaker Gingrich, Irish Prime Minister Bertie Ahearn, Ireland's 1998 Nobel laureate David Trimble, Senator Edward Kennedy, and a couple other congressional colleagues.

President Clinton arrived looking cheerful and relaxed. He sported a green necktie and a clump of shamrocks protruding from his coat pocket. His high spirits surprised me. Aside from his ongoing Lewinsky problem, another scandal bomb had just dropped on him. In a nationally televised interview only two days earlier, Kathleen Willey (one of his former staffers) accused Clinton of groping her in the Oval Office. If any of these troubles weighed on his mind, he showed no sign of it. He laughed and joked with guests.

During lunch, the table conversation turned to sports. Clinton sang the praises of one highly ranked basketball team, and then added with pride that Arkansas beat them. "Sorry, Mr. President," I told him, "but that's improper. You can't build up one team and then brag that your home state team clobbered them. It's a clear conflict of interest!"

Clinton and Congressman Jack Quinn (R-NY) continued the discussion when, suddenly, the only awkward moment of the otherwise pleasant luncheon occurred:

Diary, Speaker's St. Patrick's Day Luncheon, March 17, 1998

Jack Quinn (R-NY) asked if Clinton ever followed women's basketball. Clinton said he did, and then he became quite animated: "Have you ever seen the physiques on some of those women basketball players?" Clinton asked. "They are

these tall, sculpted women with sinewy muscles." As Clinton described their bodies admiringly, everyone at the table looked around at each other. Clinton appeared oblivious to the sudden discomfort level. With the current claims made against him, perhaps such observations were best left unspoken.

Other than this minor blip, it was a splendid luncheon. Clinton and Newt held their pints aloft in a mutual toast; they exchanged gifts with Prime Minister Ahearn, and all the speeches were laudatory and complimentary. As the afternoon wound down, Clinton made a point to come over and thank me for attending. I mentioned the speech note cards I saw him read, and I told him that it reminded me of how I had talked then-Governor Ronald Reagan into autographing and giving me his speech note cards for my collection when I was a young boy. He asked if I still had the notes. When I said I did, he took his speech note cards, signed and dated them with a flourish and handed them to me. He did me an unexpectedly gracious favor.

Of all the events I attended in Washington during my congressional service, this occasion remains high on my list of fond memories. For this brief event, everyone was Irish, and that meant we were all friends. To this day, in my judicial chambers hangs a photograph on the wall depicting President Clinton and me sharing a laugh on that St. Patrick's Day. When visitors see it, they usually ask if it predates the impeachment because they assume the harmonious moment captured by the photographer did not occur after the storm clouds gathered. Sadly, they are right.

The window for sharing similar moments was about to close.

6

Blood on the Floor

"Speaker Gingrich's spokeswoman issued an emphatic statement this week that the incumbent intends to retain the job until 2003, when he would be required to relinquish the post under House GOP rules. It is widely believed—despite repeated protestations to the contrary by Gingrich—that Gingrich will leave his current post [soon] to mount a presidential bid."

—*CONGRESS DAILY*, MARCH 1998

As if House Republicans didn't have enough distractions with which to contend, the rumor of Newt's sudden presidential ambitions went beyond backroom whispering. Now, Gingrich allies like Ways and Means Chairman Bill Archer, Majority Leader Dick Armey, and Appropriations Chairman Bob Livingston became candidates to succeed Newt. This sudden jockeying for speaker got so bad that a letter signed by 16 GOP committee chairmen went to the entire Republican conference requesting that we not assist in any leadership struggle until after the November 1998 elections.

Diary, March 4, 1998

I think Newt wants to run for president, but after surviving a coup attempt last year, I don't think he wants to telegraph that desire too strongly right now. He probably fears another insurgency to replace him early, claiming our conference needs a "full-time speaker."

As it turned out, Newt didn't run in 2000, but the timing of this presidential rumor coincided with a curious shift in his thinking. After the Lewinsky story first aired in January, he spent the following months cautioning his GOP members to treat the subject like a hot potato: toss it into the lap of the Democrats and Judge Starr but don't touch it yourself. All that changed during the spring of 1998, and he reversed course on impeachment almost to the day that the presidential campaign gossip took flight.

Roll Call reporter Jim VandeHei wrote that Newt accepted the counsel of his House GOP leadership when they urged him to take the fight to Clinton personally. Soon after this story ran, Newt throttled into full public attack mode. He began his blitz with a speech before the Republican grass roots GOPAC group on April 27. "There is something profoundly demeaning and destructive to have the White House systematically undermine [Judge Kenneth Starr], an officer of the Department of Justice," he said. "When I watch these paid hacks on television, to be quite honest, I am sickened by how unpatriotically they undermine the Constitution of the United States on behalf of their client. I have decided to speak out. And I will never again, as long as I am speaker, make a speech without commenting on this topic."

The next day in the House chamber, Newt accused the Clinton administration of obstructing the congressional investigations. He also charged the Democrats with participating in a cover-up: "The American people have the right to expect that the rule of law will prevail," he proclaimed, "and that no one is above the law."

Newt's new approach set the tone for others on his leadership team. Tom DeLay chimed in, calling Clinton a "sexual predator." Dick Armey called Clinton "shameless," and suggested he resign. At a GOP member-only conference meeting on May 20, Rules Committee Chairman Jerry Solomon reported that his committee would take up the president's treason on the China missile issue. Conference Chairman John Boehner cut off Solomon, saying, "I hope nobody here, from a communications standpoint, will repeat that word *treason*."

Solomon replied dryly, "Oh, you do, huh?"

The worst of it occurred when Chairman Dan Burton spoke of Clinton to reporters: "This guy's a scumbag," Burton said, "and that's why I'm after him." House Democrats retaliated by filing ethics charges against Burton for his intemperate comments. They also filed a resolution seeking his removal as chairman of his investigative committee, claiming he could no longer provide Clinton a fair hearing.

Given the timing of this rhetorical switch, one might suspect that Newt's sudden desire to whack Clinton was more than a coincidence. Did Newt hope to grab the presidential nomination by positioning himself as leading an impeachment crusade? I doubt it. All the polls at that time showed impeachment was very unpopular, and he read the polls closer than most. Although I never discussed the timing of these two events with him, I suspect he changed course on impeachment when the Judiciary Committee's radar picked up signals of a damning report against Clinton from Judge Starr. As speaker, I believe he felt obliged to take charge of what the Constitution deemed the sole responsibility of the House of Representatives. Although the Gingrich presidential boomlet proved short-lived, one thing is certain: by spring 1998, Newt went from avoiding the contagious impeachment leper colony to wanting to lead a conga line through it.

• • •

Ever since the attempted coup against him in mid-1997, Newt included me in his small "kitchen cabinet" meetings. In early March, I arrived for one of those meetings to find him in his shirtsleeves at the head of the table in his "Dinosaur" room (named for a large fossilized dinosaur skull on display; Newt told visitors it reminded him daily of another species that viewed itself as big and powerful and ended up extinct). He raised the Clinton issues and offered what sounded like a serious insider tip:

Diary, Office of the Speaker, March 5, 1998

Newt declared authoritatively, "We will get 'the boxes' [Special Counsel Ken Starr's impeachment report] in May. When the boxes finally come, this thing will be huge: Filegate, Travelgate, Whitewater, Lewinsky, and so on. Starr won't seek to indict a sitting president. There is too much uncertainty over whether he can do it legally. Still, he'll have a ton of stuff and he might seek to indict Hillary Clinton. When it comes, we need to be very cautious. We should invite the Democrats to join us in crafting a solution as to how to proceed. We need to appear judicious and fair in all we do when we handle this. It will be very sensitive."

Newt said that Judge Starr now had former Arkansas Governor and Clinton ally Jim Guy Tucker cooperating in his investigation, as well as former Clinton Whitewater partner Jim McDougal. Showing no reticence in his demeanor, he added, "With Tucker and McDougal helping, Starr could give us enough to impeach Clinton."

Two weeks later, on March 18, Newt called a press conference with a publicly supportive (but privately dejected) Chairman Hyde at his side to announce a special task force to review any material Judge Starr forwarded to Congress. Newt's idea was to appoint senior House members (including Hyde) to consider Judge Starr's evidence. Instead of Chairman Hyde waving the impeachment baton, Newt's proposal relegated Henry to the orchestra pit.

. . .

In the world of veteran congressmen, they just didn't come much grumpier than John Conyers.

Republicans disliked the cranky senior Democrat on the Judiciary Committee, and the feelings appeared mutual. First elected to the House in 1964, the 69-year-old Michigan liberal knew that the only thing now standing between him and the chairman's gavel was a switch of six Republican House seats to the Democrat column. John waited a long time for this chairmanship, so it wasn't surprising that he brushed off new Republican members as irritants.

None of that mattered to me. As a teenager, I sat spellbound watching the 1973–1974 televised Judiciary Committee impeachment hearings against President Nixon. Now, 24 years later, John remained the last Watergate member still serving on the committee. As a lifelong political junkie, I longed to hear him share his first-hand account of that historic period. Yet whenever I tried talking to him, he offered me little more than a discontented grunt before walking away. I formulated a plan to crack through his unresponsiveness.

Having collected old political campaign memorabilia since the age of ten, I knew from experience that most politicians never saved their own campaign items and regretted it years later. Determined to find an icebreaker with John, I rummaged through my collection for a relationship building opportunity.

The next time I saw him sitting alone on the House floor, I invited myself to join him. Before he could run me off, I asked if he remembered doing a campaign rally with Senator Edward Kennedy in Michigan almost 30 years earlier. He said he had thought about it just the other day: "This was back when everyone believed Ted Kennedy would be the next president," he said. "It was the biggest rally I ever had in my district." I asked John if he remembered seeing yellow campaign badges there with the legend, "The People's Choice in 1972: Edward Kennedy for President—John Conyers for Vice President."

"I remember those badges!" he said excitedly. "In fact, I wanted my staff to save one for me, but they never did." Before he could ask the obvious question ("How do you know about that badge?"), I reached into my pocket.

"I saved one for you, John." Pressing the badge into his hand, I smiled and walked away.

My childhood passion forged a new friendship.

John's later kindness toward me caused more than a few raised eyebrows at my maiden appearance as a member of the House Judiciary Committee. On March 3, 1998, Lindsey Graham (R-SC), another new committee member, and I attended our first hearing. As the senior Republican, Chairman Hyde drew the duty of making the welcome speech for Lindsey and me. After Henry finished and then called up the first bill, John Conyers interrupted unexpectedly: "Mr. Chairman, will you yield to me?"

Everyone looked around nervously. "Here it comes," remarked a congressman seated behind me. Republicans hunkered down for another partisan tirade. Instead, jaws dropped as he made a lovely speech embracing my membership on Judiciary. As he extolled my virtues, Republican members began eyeing me suspiciously. Even Henry looked baffled. To make things worse, after he finished welcoming me, he gazed icily at Lindsey and remarked, "Mr. Chairman, I yield back the balance of my time."

• • •

Chairman Hyde worked diligently to keep the irascible Conyers mollified, but with little success. After Henry requested from Speaker Gingrich $1.3 million to hire additional staff for Department of Justice oversight, Conyers and committee Democrats accused Henry and the Republicans of using this as an early impeachment war games exercise. At our March 24 committee hearing, Conyers railed so angrily that our otherwise courtly chairman banged his gavel and stomped out of the hearing room. Publicly, Henry maintained his poise. He seethed privately:

Diary, Republican Judiciary Committee Meeting, March 26, 1998

Henry grew angry as he recounted John Conyers' and Barney Frank's claims that he never consulted with them: "You can't trust 'em," he sputtered. "Conyers lied; he told the press a bald-faced lie!" Remembering his earlier admonition about not being sucked into a verbal battle with the Democrats, Henry apologized for his sudden blow-up. "I should have just told Conyers to go fill his prescription," he chuckled.

Then, as if to confirm Conyers' charge, Henry added, "Of course, if we hire the additional staff for this investigation, and we later move to an impeachment inquiry, it is logical that some of these new hires will be used for an impeachment review. But that is a collateral issue."

When Henry first called this particular meeting of Judiciary Republicans, he said he wanted to address the Conyers staffing squabble. As it turned out, he had much bigger news to share: he confided that he had a "correspondent" in Ken Starr's office who told him that Starr's evidence against Clinton "will move people uncommitted toward impeachment. It will be credible, and it will be heavy evidence against Clinton."

"If we have to do an impeachment inquiry," Henry said, and then stopped speaking. After looking around the room at each of us, he continued: "Oh, hell: it's not if—it's when. And when we do get into this, there will be blood all over the floor."

As other members absorbed this revelation, he addressed his initial plans for the Judiciary Committee in the face of this constitutional bombshell:

"When Starr advises us formally that he has evidence against Clinton, we will receive it in executive session. I will control the follow-up hearing closely. There will be no cross examination of Starr. I won't let it become a circus. We will invite the president's lawyers to testify for balance. This hearing, when it happens, will form the basis for a resolution of impeachment against Clinton. We will look petty and partisan unless we can move Clinton off his high poll numbers, and we can't do that unless we show unassailable testimony. Starr needs an opportunity to put his story out and defend himself from the unrelenting abuse he is getting from the White House and their friends in the press. If necessary, I'll rig the goddamned room. I'll install a mute button so I can shut off the Democrats' microphones if they become abusive or get out of hand."

Henry noted that during the 1973 Watergate impeachment inquiry, the Judiciary Democrats' lead investigator John Doar hired 90 new staffers. "We'll need more," he added. Henry also announced he already hired his choice to be our committee's lead investigator: David Schippers of Chicago. "Dave's a former U.S. Attorney," Henry told us. "I've known him for 30 years. He's a Democrat and he voted for Clinton, but he is one tough son of a bitch."

He then turned to Speaker Gingrich's latest idea floated a week earlier: the creation of a select committee to review any report Judge Starr sent to the Capitol. Even though Newt arm-twisted Henry into joining in the speaker's press statement favoring that approach, he privately derided the notion of any congressional review outside the purview of the Judiciary Committee: he called Newt's plan "a disaster" and "a dumb idea" that would be "seen as a partisan witch hunt on Newt's part." He added that creating a select committee hurts Republicans, and he predicted that Democrat Minority Leader Richard Gephardt "will appoint all of his 'bomb throwers'—Barney

Frank, Maxine Waters, Charlie Schumer, and John Conyers—to the select committee." Henry warned that the Democrats will try to make this a partisan fight: "We can't take the bait," he stated.

Henry adjourned the meeting; when I rose to leave, he motioned me into his small private office. He asked if I agreed that Newt's select committee was a bad idea. Flattered that the chairman sought advice from a freshman on his committee only a few weeks, I felt obliged to be candid. I said doing anything outside the normal precedents of the House gave the Democrats ammunition to claim the Republican leadership was trying to rig the system. We'd end up spending our energy defending the creation of the extraordinary committee rather than pressing forward with an impeachment review. I reminded him that Newt often threw out ideas just to see how they echoed around the room, but if Newt entertained this notion seriously, I suggested that Henry force his hand: "If I were you, I'd tell Newt you won't participate in any model that goes outside the jurisdiction of your committee. Newt needs you in this because of the House's bipartisan respect for you. If you threaten to pull out, I think Newt's idea will go away." Henry listened but said nothing.

Henry then asked what I thought about him appointing David Schippers as our committee's lead investigator. I grimaced: "Mr. Chairman, other than the fact he's a Democrat, he's from Cook County, and he voted for Clinton, I have no problem with the guy."

Henry rose from his chair, put his arm around my shoulder, and led me out of the office. "Jim, I've known Dave for a long time," he said. "Trust me on this guy. He'll root it out and get to the truth. Just meet with him and keep an open mind. Will you do it?" As he spoke, he steered me into a nearby office and closed the door from the outside. I found myself alone with our committee's new lead investigator.

Looking back, I'm not sure why I liked Dave Schippers instantly. Maybe it was because the short, bearded, 68-year-old father of ten came with the Henry Hyde seal of approval. Knowing he tackled

Chicago mob bosses like Sam Giancana certainly didn't hurt. Ultimately, it was the gut instinct of one ex-prosecutor sizing up another. Dave and I spoke the same language. Our goals synced: follow the evidence wherever it led. As far as I was concerned, he was our guy.

7

Homework from Newt

(Part One)

Question: Mr. Speaker, the Associated Press reports today that you've recruited Representative James Rogan, a former judge, to review past congressional hearings on wrongdoing by the Clinton administration. Is that true?

Gingrich: Absolutely. Jim Rogan is a first-class former judge, former prosecutor, and very widely respected.

Question: What do you want him to do?

Gingrich: Chairman Henry Hyde of the Judiciary Committee and I agreed that Congressman Rogan would go back and review, from Watergate through Iran-Contra to the present, all the major congressional investigations and offer us advice if—and again, this is if—Judge Starr does issue a report to the Congress. What should we do, and how should we do it? We think that Congressman Rogan is absolutely one of the finest people serving in the U.S. House and a man of impeccable personal reputation.

—*LARRY KING LIVE* WITH SPEAKER NEWT GINGRICH, CNN, APRIL 8, 1998

Huse Republicans used to joke that Speaker Gingrich suffered from Attention Deficit Disorder (truthfully, when they said it, not everyone was joking). The synapses of his brain fired at too high a rate, making it hard for him to focus on any single topic for too long, and harder for his troops to follow him into multi-front battles. By the time we absorbed his newest powerful idea, Newt was off on ten new topics, all brilliant and all worthy of immediate focus. The practical problem was that nobody could keep up with the most peripatetic mind in Washington.

My first exposure to this phenomenon caught me unaware. A few months after I joined Congress, Newt announced our newest Republican assault: eliminate the IRS and simplify the entire federal tax code. He decided to get America's input on two alternatives: the flat tax or the national sales tax. As the next long congressional recess approached, he urged our GOP members to carpet bomb our constituents with the news, and then report back to him when we returned to D.C. so we could choose the better option for which to fight.

Newt's tax reform crusade fired me up. I mailed thousands of surveys and articles on the two alternatives and I blitzed my district with dozens of town hall meetings, speeches, and television and radio interviews. As Newt suggested, I told constituents it wasn't a question of whether to rid America of the oppressive federal tax code, it was just a question of which system we would use to replace it.

Back in Washington after the recess, Newt called our first House Republican conference to order. Over the course of an hour, he never mentioned the flat tax or national sales tax. Baffled by this oversight, I approached the speaker after we adjourned. I briefed him on all I did to promote his tax reform revolution and I asked when we would jump-start our modern-day Boston Tea Party.

"Clinton never would sign that bill," Newt said blandly, and then he turned to address another member's concern. I stood there, mouth slightly agape, holding all my constituent replies under my arms. A veteran congressman listening to my enthusiastic report apparently had been down this path before. He patted me on the shoulder and said, "You're new here, aren't you?"

By now, I was sensitized to Newt's sudden bursts of inspiration. When I heard through the grapevine that Newt had some major assignment for me, I ignored the rumor. Had I shown some haste in speaking to him, perhaps I might have learned about the new project before America did.

Diary, March 19, 1998

Judiciary Committee Chief Counsel Tom Mooney [Chairman Hyde's closest aide] called and told me he heard that Newt Gingrich wants me to study the potential pitfalls of a congressional proceeding against President Clinton, including a possible impeachment review. Tom said, "This isn't our committee's drill. Henry doesn't want this. We just want $1.5 million from the speaker to beef up our committee staffing, but Newt wants us to do this, so we'll need to do this. And the speaker wants you to do it because of your training and experience as a prosecutor and judge."

Later in the evening, while walking through Statuary Hall, I ran into Newt's press secretary, Christina Martin. "I hear the speaker has some sort of homework for me," I said.

"He didn't talk to you first, did he?" she asked. When I said he hadn't, she rolled her eyes. "Well, you can read all about it in tomorrow's morning edition of *USA Today*." She walked away mumbling, "This is so Newt."

The next morning, I read the article in which Newt said that any referral from Judge Starr would go directly to him and not to any committee. He said his first step would be to consult with the Republican leadership and Chairman Hyde and then call a bipartisan leadership meeting. Newt also announced my appointment to "review all the lessons learned procedurally" during previous House investigations of the Clinton Administration. This *USA Today* piece proved illuminating on two scores: aside from confirming my new responsibility, Newt's interview signaled that he saw himself, and not the Judiciary Committee, as the gravitational center of the impeachment galaxy.

With the story out, reporters descended on my office that morning. Few believed me when I told them I never consulted with the speaker and only learned of my new duties while reading the morning paper. "Isn't it true you've been put on Judiciary to beef up the committee for a future impeachment?" one asked me.

"No," I replied, "I only stumbled onto Judiciary in the wake of Sonny Bono's premature death."

"Then why did you come on the committee?"

"I came to work on copyrights, patents, and trademarks," I said, unable to contain the grin that I knew would make the implausible answer sound even less sincere. Audible groans filled their ranks. Later I pulled one aside and showed her a copy of Henry's letter to Newt requesting my appointment to Judiciary, dated almost two weeks before the Lewinsky story aired.

"Okay," the reporter told me, "I believe you. But you just ruined a damned good lead for me."

The following day I received a bit more clarity on Newt's assignment, albeit indirectly (again):

Diary, March 20, 1998

Tom Mooney called to say he met last night with Speaker Gingrich and Chairman Hyde. Tom said Newt wants me to interview people who have conducted earlier Clinton scandal hearings and met with minimal success, like Senator Fred Thompson and Congressman Dan Burton. He also needs me to identify the "problems" of running an investigative hearing against Clinton based on their experience.

Despite these messages, I still did nothing to begin any investigation—my bulging "flat tax vs. national sales tax" data notebooks were reminders of what happened when one jumped at the speaker's signals prematurely. Reporters expressed continuing frustration at my candid answer to their now daily questions: I had not conferred with the speaker and wasn't investigating anything until I did.

A full ten days went by before Newt called me:

Diary, March 28, 1998

Newt said he wants me to report to him on previous investigations of the Executive Branch. He told me to find out what had worked in the past, and why it would or would not work with the Clinton White House. Newt said he wanted me to prepare two separate reports: a "bulleted report" for his personal review, and a separate sanitized report "suitable and designed for reproduction on the front page of the *Washington Post*."

"Republicans are just learning how to do investigations," Newt said. "We now need to learn how to do them in the current atmosphere, with Clinton aggressively smearing everyone who tries to investigate him."

• • •

Henry Hyde assigned two of the Judiciary Committee's best lawyers, Jon Dudas and Joseph Gibson, to work with me. We assembled a bipartisan list of 11 senior congressional leaders (past and present), most of whom led or played key roles in the investigation of potential White House misconduct over the last 25 years. We decided to use the same template for the interviews: ask each person to assume Judge Starr's office just delivered an impeachment referral and then pose these questions:

- What are the first things the speaker should do to protect the integrity of the referral and the integrity of the House as an institution?

- How should we handle the information? Should it go to the House Judiciary Committee? A specially created select committee? A joint House-Senate committee?

- During your investigative experience, what helped maintain bipartisan cooperation that you can now recommend for any future review?

- Did you make any mistakes that hurt bipartisan cooperation? How can we avoid those mistakes in a future review?

On March 30, Jon, Joseph, and I began the first interview.[1] Six weeks later, with the interrogations complete, we compared notes and found two distinct themes: one offered by all the Democrats, and a very different theme by the Republicans. The Democrats' common advice on its face involved no surprises or outlandish requests. They urged the House Republican majority to do everything possible to make the hearings bipartisan: seek common ground with the Democrat minority whenever possible, involve them in all decisions regarding process, avoid any surprises, and clear everything in advance through their ranking member.

Beyond these egalitarian demands, for the most part we were unable to mine the Democrats for any detailed or meaningful help. They entered each interview with a deep suspicion over our motives (or of Newt's motives). When we arrived at Lee Hamilton's office, his

---

1   We interviewed Senator Fred Thompson (R-TN); former Senator Howard Baker (R-TN); Speaker Gingrich; Congressmen John Dingell (D-MI), Dan Burton (R-IN), Peter Hoekstra (R-MI), and Don Young (R-AK); former Congressmen Peter Rodino (D-NJ), Lee Hamilton (D-IN), Tom Railsback (R-IL), and William Clinger (R-PA).

greeting typified the attitude of our Democrat subjects: "You're trying to impeach the president," Lee said. "What help do you expect to get from me?" Yet, despite the Democrats' reluctance to offer detailed answers, their "equality" approach sounded perfectly reasonable.

The only Democrat exception to this otherwise "name, rank, and serial number" approach was former House Judiciary Committee Chairman Peter Rodino, who led the impeachment hearings against President Richard Nixon. Ironically, Rodino started as the most uncooperative and suspicious interviewee of all. As I will explain later, cracking that code came about through dumb luck and a quarter-century old coincidence.

• • •

Not surprisingly, the Republican interviewees with Clinton investigative experience also offered uniform suggestions. What did shock me was the nature of their shared advice: when investigating the Clinton White House, invoking the Marquess of Queensberry Rules with the Democrats guaranteed only frustration, ineffectiveness, and failure.

At the conclusion of these interviews, Jon and Joseph drafted a confidential memorandum to me setting forth the astonishing shared experiences of Republican congressional leaders who challenged the Clintons:

Dudas and Gibson Confidential Memorandum: Common Themes Expressed by Republicans Interviewees, March-May 1998

- *The White House will relentlessly attack anyone who is conducting an investigation. All Republicans investigating Clinton scandals felt that private investigators went to their districts to dig up information.*

- *In each case of investigating Clinton, Congressional Democrats worked closely with the White House and did everything possible to delay and derail the investigation.*

- *In responding to subpoenas, the White House will use every possible device to delay. They will announce publicly that they want to cooperate, and then they will insist on endless meetings. They will not produce incriminating documents until forced to do so by a contempt citation.*

- *The White House tactic is to dump a mass of harmful documents on a Friday evening and leak one small tidbit to reporters. By doing so, they get the reporters to focus on that one thing. The stories then miss the context and many other bad things that may be contained in the documents. They will also blame you for leaking the documents.*

- *Because of these tactics, the chairman should have as much power as possible to issue subpoenas, release documents, and take other procedural steps on his own without taking a committee vote.*

- *Do not give in to the Democrats' procedural demands. Do what you think is fair and do not worry about their complaining. You will get mainstream press stories saying you are unfair no matter what you do, so do not let Democrats dictate procedure.*

- *The Chairman and his top staff must be perceived as fair-minded. They are the faces by which the public will remember the institution of the House.*

When we began the interviews, I focused more on developing the protocol for the receipt of Judge Starr's report; I paid less attention to Republican interviewee complaints that sounded more like whining than warning.

Looking back, I see the tactics that Jon's and Joseph's memorandum identified became prologue for what lay ahead.

8

Homework from Newt

(Part Two)

Senator Fred Thompson, our first interviewee, chaired the Senate committee investigating Clinton's connection to illegal Chinese campaign contributions. In our interview, he expressed grave doubt that any protocol we adopted would bring bipartisanship. His experience investigating the Clinton White House left him believing the congressional Democrats would be obstructionist, even if evidence from Judge Starr merited their cooperation:

**Diary, Meeting with Senator Fred Thompson,
The U.S. Capitol, March 30, 1998**

Thompson said any witnesses affiliated with the Clinton White House will not tell the truth, so we will have to expose the facts as gathered by others. He also warned us not to agree to any deadlines: it will give the Democrats an incentive to run out the clock on the investigation.

Thompson cautioned that the mainstream press would be unhelpful, whether through laziness or political enmity: He said the press wants a story that is new, simple, and explosive. Reporters get no reward for connecting the dots and they will not do it on their own. If the story is not simple, it is easy for them to fall back on the "partisan breakdown" story line. The Democrats can always provoke that story. Thus, it is essential to plan in every hearing what the simple factual story will be. Focus on broader public opinion and not the Washington Beltway opinion. These two often are quite different, and it is the larger public that must be convinced.

Thompson spoke angrily about Senator John Glenn (D-OH), who served as the ranking Democrat on Thompson's committee. As one of the original seven NASA Mercury astronauts, Glenn became the first American to orbit the earth in 1962. On the opening day of their hearings, Glenn denounced the Republicans and suggested that they offered daily legislative quid pro quos for special interest money in Washington. As the *New York Times* reported the next morning, Glenn's nasty and unprovoked assault left Thompson clearly "taken aback." Thompson suspected the Clinton White House blackmailed Glenn into adopting his slash-and-burn approach by holding hostage Glenn's scheduled return to space (at age 77) aboard the Space Shuttle Discovery later that year. Saying this made him mad enough to "cut the balls off" Bill Clinton, Thompson added in sadness:

"These guys in the Clinton White House will do anything, whatever it takes, to win. When they can get a man like John Glenn to do what he did and behave as badly as he behaved during my hearings, you see just how dirty they can be."

• • •

Fred Thompson's assessment of Team Clinton was almost positive compared to Congressman Dan Burton, who loathed Clinton (and the feelings were mutual). Earlier, Clinton surrogates assaulted Burton in the press as "a loon" and "a kook," and leaked that Burton fathered an illegitimate child. A Clinton-aligned lobbyist accused Burton of trying to squeeze illegal contributions from him, prompting Clinton's attorney general to open a criminal investigation against Burton. The Department of Justice closed their investigation and found no evidence of Burton's wrongdoing but withheld publicizing that finding until Clinton's last days in office. Burton returned fire against the White House. He called Clinton "a scumbag" while opening investigations into multiple Clinton scandals: Filegate, Vince Foster's suicide, and the Chinese money connection to Clinton and the Democrat Party.

Burton offered us no greeting when we arrived at his office. Instead, he charged across the room toward us and pressed a two-page document into my hand. "Here, read this before we start," he stated. The caption atop his discussion points read:

INVESTIGATING THE CLINTON WHITE HOUSE
WHAT YOU ARE UP AGAINST:
THE ABC'S OF THE CLINTON ATTACK MACHINE

A   Attack the investigators and accusers (the House Democrats will assist the White House with this by constant internal attacks, planted news stories, hit pieces, etc.).

B   Bluff and misinform and assume the bluff won't be called and opponents won't take risks.

C   Cover-up.

D   Delay, disinform, deny, distract, and dissemble.

Burton said that Clinton spent 10 percent of his entire presidential budget on lawyers from Washington's biggest firms, and each lawyer coordinated with the White House and the press. Further, he claimed that House Democrats pipelined everything discussed privately to the White House and would use their committee resources and staff to smear Republicans rather than conduct an honest investigation. Finally, he warned that we would be foolish to rely on any good faith negotiations with the White House or with their Democrat enablers in Congress.

• • •

In our next interview, Congressman Peter Hoekstra echoed the same generic themes regarding Democrat obstruction. As an aside, later I met with Newt and a small group of members including Hoekstra, Newt wanted an update on Hoekstra's current investigation of indicted Teamster Union leaders. Hoekstra's chief counsel Joseph diGenova told Newt that committee Democrats threatened to put his law license in jeopardy with the District of Columbia Bar by filing ethics complaints against him. If that happened, diGenova demanded Newt's assurance that the speaker would view this as "nuclear war" on the Democrats. Newt's comments on how to handle the obstreperous minority proved illuminating.

**Diary, Office of the Speaker,
The U.S. Capitol, April 28, 1998**

Newt replied coolly, "I understand how some of these Democrats work. They tried to destroy me personally. They tried to bankrupt me. They tried to end my political career and kick me out of Congress. They are thugs."

Newt said there were many ways to get the Democrats to cooperate with the committee investigation "by continuing up the escalation ladder. It's all laid out in the movie, *The Untouchables*. If they pull out a knife, you pull out a bigger knife. If they pull out a gun, you pull out a bigger gun."

Although Newt's movie quote was off slightly, his point was not lost. By the time I completed these first three Republican interviews, it sounded like we'd need more than a bigger gun. We'd need napalm.

• • •

Of all the interviews we scheduled, the one with former Congressman Peter Rodino (D-NJ) proved the most meaningful. It also proved the hardest to get. The retired Judiciary Committee chairman who presided over the Watergate investigation and President Nixon's impeachment vote 25 years earlier had no interest in cooperating with me.

A decorated World War II veteran and lawyer, Rodino began his 40-year congressional career in 1948. He served a quarter-century in congressional anonymity until 1973, when seniority elevated him to the chair of the House Judiciary Committee. Within weeks, the Nixon White House began unraveling under the weight of the Watergate scandal. Before the untested new chairman loomed a grave constitutional challenge. Ultimately, his Judiciary Committee passed articles of impeachment against President Nixon in July 1974; two weeks later, Nixon resigned. Rodino's calm approach during Watergate made him a national hero. He remained committee chairman until he retired from Congress in 1989. Now almost 90, the former chairman still taught law at Rutgers University in Newark.

On April 4, I called Rodino at his home. He listened politely while I explained my assignment from Speaker Gingrich, but he told me that he opposed Clinton's impeachment and feared a visit from me might be misinterpreted. It took a great deal of prodding to get him to agree to see me, "But 30 minutes is all I will give you," he stated firmly. Having no position from which to bargain (and hoping to change his mind once we got there), I agreed.

Aside from wanting to get Rodino's advice for Newt's project, I looked forward to meeting him to satisfy my insatiable curiosity about Watergate. As a teenager, I watched his televised Judiciary Committee's gavel-to-gavel coverage during that tumultuous period. I never suspected that I might one day discuss his impeachment experiences while I served as a member of the same committee facing the same constitutional issue. It felt surreal.

Dave Schippers, Jon Dudas, and I flew to Newark to see Rodino on May 11. They agreed with my suggestion that they remain in Rodino's outer office when I went in to see him. Given his hesitancy, I feared the presence of our chief investigator and deputy chief counsel might trouble him further.

A secretary ushered me into Rodino's cramped faculty office. After a perfunctory handshake, the short, stocky Rodino introduced me to an unsmiling faculty colleague seated next to him behind the desk. Rodino told me he wanted a witness to our discussion. The professor turned on a small tape recorder. My 30 minutes had begun.

Our brief time involved very few questions from me. Instead, Rodino launched into a half-hour soliloquy detailing how he approached the impeachment inquiry against President Nixon. He viewed it as a constitutional question and not as a partisan one, and he warned that respect for the Constitution must always remain paramount.

Near the end of my allotted time (and his filibuster), Rodino looked at me sternly and said, "Now I have shared my thoughts with you. I need to know where you are on this issue and how you view it." I explained that I sought no partisan gain from any review. In fact, given the Democrat makeup of my district, my own political fortunes improved if the allegations against President Clinton proved unfounded. Like Rodino in the 1970s, I had an unpleasant job before me. Like him, I said I would do my duty.

When the faculty witness signaled our time was over, Rodino stood and thanked me for coming. Anticipating this moment, I deployed my secret weapon: as we shook and said goodbye, I thanked him for keeping his two promises to me.

"Two promises?" he asked.

"Yes, two," I replied. "You met with me today for half an hour; that was promise number one." Then I handed him a piece of paper: "Here is promise number two."

I was a teenager almost 25 years earlier in 1975 when I made my first trip to Washington, D.C. I wrote to Chairman Rodino (then fresh off the Nixon hearings), told him about my law and political aspirations, and I asked if I could meet him during my visit. He replied with an apologetic letter advising me that he would be out of town that week. He promised to give me a rain check on a future date. After winning my seat in Congress, I sent him a copy of this letter along with a note saying I hoped to meet him during my service.

Rodino stared at the letter and then at me. He hadn't made the connection until now that I was the same new congressman who wanted that handshake as a kid so long ago. He kicked out the witness ("And take the tape recorder with you when you leave."), he invited Dave and Jon to join us in his office, and we were still in there talking with him three hours later.

He held back nothing and offered us plenty of advice (and a few warnings):

- If you begin any impeachment inquiry, expect to be investigated yourself.

- If the independent counsel sends evidence to the House, have the Judiciary Committee chairman and ranking member review the evidence together and then bring it to the committee. Otherwise, have the chairman select an impartial group of committee members to make an initial review of the evidence, and let them report their findings to the full committee. If these members find evidence of impeachable offenses, have it reported to the full committee. Republicans and Democrats should look at Starr's materials together.

- Keep Independent Counsel Ken Starr away from your hearings. There are too many questions raised about his bias.

- Work with the independent counsel's office and keep them informed, but the committee should do its own supplemental investigation to fill in any gaps.

- Never set a final date. This will encourage your opposition to stonewall. A target date might be appropriate in some circumstances.

- Hire impartial and nonpartisan staff. Do not let them make any statements or render any opinions until the inquiry is complete. If they do, fire them.

- If you get to the stage of having live witnesses, allow the president's lawyers to ask questions.

- If your review gets too late in the year, do not hesitate to roll it over to the next Congress after the November elections.

- The press needs to know this is an inquiry to see if substantial evidence exists to warrant impeachment. It is not a prosecution.

He warned that starting an impeachment investigation would subject each of us to intensive political (and possible legal) investigations and that we must brace for it: "People in Washington always play rough, and during our Watergate investigation Nixon played for keeps." He said that he later learned that Jeb Magruder, Nixon's imprisoned former special assistant, approached former New Jersey Congressman Cornelius Gallagher while both were inmates in a federal penitentiary. Magruder allegedly promised Gallagher a presidential pardon if he would help produce dirt to "get Rodino." He added that such tactics never intimidated him. "I came up the ranks alongside hardball masters like Lyndon Johnson and Bobby Kennedy. Those were two tough sons of bitches, and I learned from them," he said with a grin.

He remained convinced that bipartisan cooperation was the only way the country would retain any confidence in the process, but he had no solution for how to make that work successfully without cooperation from the minority. He said that during Watergate, he and Congressman Ed Hutchinson (the ranking Judiciary Committee Republican) reviewed jointly the first tapes of Nixon's secretly recorded Oval Office conversations. "When we listened to the first tape," Rodino recalled, "we heard Nixon calling Jews 'kikes' and Italians 'guineas.' I told Ed Hutchinson I'd never report those remarks and I didn't." He also shared his subpoena power with Hutchinson and agreed that no subpoenas would issue without the approval of both sides.

Speaking about his role in history, he said that when he cast his vote to impeach Nixon, "My voice was almost inaudible. When it was over, I left the committee room, went to my private cubbyhole office, and called my wife. I told her, 'I hope I did the right thing.' Then I began to sob like I never sobbed before."

He called it a quirk of fate that one of the young committee lawyers he hired, 26-year-old Hillary Rodham, would bring around to the hearings her boyfriend, Bill Clinton. "She introduced him to me as a future president," he said. "They had it all planned out, even then." He told me that although he did not support any impeachment effort against him, Clinton as president disappointed him personally.

Throughout our three-hour talk, I worried that Rodino's advanced age might cause him to tire. He kept brushing aside my concerns and wanted to continue. In fact, at the end of three hours, he invited Dave, Jon, and me to his home for dinner so that we might continue our conversation. Much to my everlasting regret, Jon reminded me that we had to return to the Capitol for a late meeting. However, I promised that on my next New Jersey visit, I would call him and take a rain check on his gracious dinner invitation—just as he gave me a rain check on our 1975 meeting.

Rodino's most significant advice came as we spoke our goodbyes. He said that before Watergate he had spent 25 years as an unnoticed congressman voting the liberal party line and trying to help his district. Suddenly, in 1972, longtime Judiciary Committee Chairman Emanuel Celler lost his Democrat primary race in a stunning upset. The following November, Democrats held the House and Nixon won reelection in a landslide. Because of seniority, Rodino took Celler's place as chairman. Within weeks, Watergate revelations bombarded the Capitol. When the senior House Democrat leadership realized that one of the biggest political stories in history might land in the lap of their new and untested chairman, they panicked. Congressional Party leaders pleaded with Democrat Speaker Carl Albert to yank responsibility for Watergate from Rodino and give it to a special committee or a select committee (precisely what Speaker Gingrich now wanted to do). Despite incredible pressure, Carl Albert stood firm. He reasoned that being speaker put him in the constitutional line of presidential succession. He did not want the House leadership vulnerable to accusations that they had changed the rules to depose a Republican president and replace him with a Democrat one.

"Once Carl Albert made that decision," Rodino told me, "he announced to everyone that 'Peter's my man.' He never had any hand in selecting committee staff, he never interjected himself in the committee's operation, and he didn't make any statements about impeachment—and certainly not like the ones Newt Gingrich is making now. Anytime a reporter asked Albert about Nixon's impeachment, he told them, 'Go talk to Chairman Rodino.'"

Rodino's voice grew firm: "*That's why, under no condition, should Newt Gingrich be involved in any way.*"

In these few minutes of fortuitous and offhand reminiscing, Rodino gave me the most profound and lasting advice I received during any of my 11 interviews.[1]

• • •

As an aside, the opportunity to return to Newark did not present itself until seven years later when I accepted a speaking invitation at Rutgers Law School. I debated whether to call Rodino. He was almost 96 years old. Would he remember me? If he did, would he be angry that I ended up playing a key role in impeaching a president he didn't want impeached?

Despite my reservations, I kept my promise and called. To my delight, he remembered me, and he expressed joy in hearing from me. I felt humbled when he told me that even though we were on opposite sides of the issue, he thought that I did an outstanding job during the Clinton impeachment. He said I conducted myself with fairness and dignity at all times.

---

1   In 2019, 21 years after my meeting with Peter Rodino, the House of Representatives impeached another president, Donald Trump. Throughout that proceeding, former House Speaker Newt Gingrich appeared on television and radio almost daily and blasted the Democrat-led House procedures used to bring articles of impeachment against Trump. He contrasted the sham rules adopted under House Speaker Nancy Pelosi against "The Rodino Rules" that he adopted based upon my 1998 meeting with Rodino, and the advice Rodino gave me to pass along to Gingrich. During the Trump impeachment, Gingrich wrote, "Everyone interested in better understanding how fair people used judicial standards and basic fairness in 1973 and 1998 should read former GOP Congressman James Rogan's personal account of the process in an important book, *Catching Our Flag: Behind the Scenes of a Presidential Impeachment*. https://www.foxnews.com/opinion/newt-gingrich-pelosis-rigged-game-and-hyde-rodino-rules-for-fairness (accessed August 8, 2020).

I told him of my upcoming Newark trip and suggested completing our elusive dinner plans. He apologized and said that now was not a good time for it. He was home recovering from major surgery, and he wasn't receiving visitors. However, as our call progressed, he sounded more chipper. "Maybe you could pick up dinner and bring it over," he suggested. Still later, near the end of our call, he was naming Italian restaurants where we could go during my visit. The more he talked about my upcoming visit, the more his desire to get out of bed increased.

The only melancholy note during our chat came when we talked about his recuperation. "I served in Congress for 40 years," he told me sadly. "I chaired the Judiciary Committee for 15 of those years. Now I'm recovering from major surgery and *nobody* from Washington calls me. In fact, the one guy who does call is a congressman with whom I never served and is in the wrong Party to boot. When you're gone from Congress, life goes on and people forget you so quickly."

I thought I heard his voice crack with emotion, and so I tried to lighten the mood: "In my Democrat district, everybody was so mad when they voted me out of office that the sooner they forget me the safer I'll be!" He chuckled politely, but he still sounded low.

I took one more stab at cheering up the ailing veteran legislator: "Mr. Chairman, you left Congress more than 15 years ago. Yet, when the House of Representatives faced the grave duty of considering another presidential impeachment, a Republican controlled Judiciary Committee adopted your precedents. You set a standard for fairness that outlasted your service. In fact, Henry Hyde and Newt Gingrich kept saying publicly that we Republicans were relying on *The Rodino Rules*. If you don't mind my saying so, that's a hell of a legacy for a kid who grew up in a Jersey tenement."

He perked up. He told me he looked forward to our dinner, and that he was sure he'd be well enough to take me to his favorite Italian haunt by the time I arrived. We made our date for late May,

I promised to be on time, and he promised to be well enough to leave the house.

Sadly, it was not to be. A few days after my call, he died on May 7, 2005. For the second time, Peter Rodino left me with a much-appreciated rain check.

9

Hardball

In the midst of my interview project, we learned that Judge Starr expanded his investigation into possible "hush-money" payments to now-ousted senior U.S. Justice Department official Webster Hubbell, Hillary Clinton's former law partner. During the brief period between Hubbell's DOJ resignation in disgrace and the start of his 15-month prison sentence for fraud and tax evasion, Clinton friends and donors paid Hubbell $700,000 in cash for "consulting fees." In adding this issue to his own expanding investigative portfolio, Chairman Burton said, "The American people should know if senior White House officials conspired to buy Webb Hubbell's silence." After Burton's committee investigators pored through hundreds of hours of recordings of Hubbell's taped telephone calls from federal prison, Newt called a private House Republican conference to discuss the Hubbell situation:

**Diary, House Republican Conference Meeting,
April 29, 1998**

Chairman Dan Burton believes he may find evidence of a cover-up; he reported that 92 people from the Clinton Administration (or connected closely with it) have either fled the country to avoid testifying or have invoked the Fifth Amendment. He also said that when his committee obtained approval from the U.S. Department of Justice to offer witness

immunity to four people, the Democrats on his committee voted in lockstep to block the immunity grant.

Gingrich noted that when Democrats filed ethics charges against him a year ago, he fulfilled every request for documents. He also waived any attorney-client privilege and he agreed voluntarily to reimburse the House for all costs of the investigation. "There is a big difference between me and the way Clinton is handling his scandals," Newt said. "Fifty-four of his people took the Fifth Amendment; 34 fled the country. We should be appealing to honest Democrats to call their Democrat congressmen to help in a search for the truth." Newt then urged us to read *New York Times* reporter Jeff Gerth's recent article that suggested Clinton transferred nuclear ballistic missile technology to China. Newt said that transfer financially benefited the Loral Corporation, whose chairman is the single largest contributor to Bill Clinton.

After making this point, Newt declared firmly, "My personal belief is that the president of the United States is engaged in a vast criminal conspiracy that has allowed our military secrets to be funneled to the Chinese. The president is engaged in systematic cover-ups and briberies. Can you stomach a president of the United States paying out $700,000 in hush money to Webster Hubbell?"

Chairman Henry Hyde rose and said that calling Clinton a "scumbag" (a reference to Dan Burton's controversial characterization last week) may be "mild," but the Judiciary Committee must appear judicious. "When we get Starr's report, we will run with it even if we get it on Christmas Eve."

Shortly after this meeting, Burton stepped into another public relations sinkhole. His committee staff released edited transcripts of Hubbell's taped prison conversations. Democrats again cried foul, so Burton released the tapes unedited. When doing so, his committee counsel stood on a chair in the hearing room and tossed the tapes into the air toward the outreached hands of grasping and shouting reporters like a vendor tossing bags of peanuts at the baseball park. This televised visual infuriated Newt, embarrassed the Republican leadership, and cost the attorney his job:

Diary, House Republican Conference Meeting, May 6, 1998

"Our job as a group is to take on Clinton this fall and survive," Newt declared angrily. "All of you need to lock this in your head: it is the sworn duty of the White House and the Washington press corps to divert attention from Clinton's embarrassments." As Newt began to discuss the evidence on the Hubbell tapes as an example, he assured us that Chairman Dan Burton felt embarrassed by what occurred in the last few days [the "scumbag" comment and the Hubbell tape dissemination spectacle]. Burton interrupted Newt and shouted from his seat in the audience, "I'm not embarrassed."

Newt swirled in his seat and glowered at Burton: "You're not embarrassed?" Newt snapped. "Well, those of us who have had to defend you on national television are embarrassed. Thanks for interrupting someone who is trying to help you out. If you're not embarrassed, then let me rephrase it. You *should* be embarrassed. Let me rephrase it again for you: I'm embarrassed for you. You had your press secretary throwing out Hubbell tapes as though he was in a circus carnival. Your colleagues are embarrassed for you." Burton stared straight ahead during the dressing down and said nothing.

Regaining his calm, Newt returned to the Hubbell tapes issue. "The curious aspect of the tapes is where Hubbell and his wife complain about a White House 'squeeze play' against him to pressure his silence, and his comment about having to 'roll over again.' I ask the press who complain to me about Dan Burton's comments, 'Have you been to the White House to ask if they are worried about White House pressure on Hubbell to obstruct justice?' These are not scandals we are talking about; these are crimes that were committed. Ask reporters if it concerns them who committed the crimes. I don't know if the president committed any crimes. I don't know if anyone did. It's time to find out. The president is the elected leader of the government. He should be helping us get to the truth."

As the one tasked with developing a bipartisan protocol, this ongoing cacophony made my job of asking the Democrats to be helpful an exercise in silliness. That is why Peter Rodino's advice to get Newt out of the impeachment story came none too soon. As Dick Morris (Clinton's longtime political strategist) told me during this period, "Tell Newt that Clinton is not your enemy. [House Democrat Leader] Dick Gephardt is your enemy. Why take on a guy with a 60 percent approval rating?"

Another voice trying to steer Newt away from impeachment came from former Senator Howard Baker, who 25 years earlier was the ranking Republican on the U.S. Senate's Watergate Committee. After I shared private insights with Henry Hyde about my initial interview with Baker, Henry asked me to set up a second confidential Baker briefing for Newt. He wanted Newt to hear Baker's advice first-hand based on his Watergate experience:

Diary, Office of the Speaker, The U.S. Capitol, May 12, 1998 (Meeting with Newt Gingrich, Howard Baker, and Henry Hyde)

Baker warned us not to rely too heavily on the Watergate model: "We Republicans back then decided simply to get

to the truth," he said. "But unlike the Republicans during Watergate, the Democrats under Clinton have made a decision to 'circle the wagons.' The Democrats will stay with him as long as his poll numbers are strong."

Baker said Gingrich should avoid any action that is different from the "regular order" of the House: "Any deviation from standard operating procedures, even by a degree, will be pounced on by the Democrats as a partisan attempt to rig the proceedings or make it a witch hunt."

He suggested gingerly that it was appropriate for Newt to go on offense with Clinton over his stonewalling. Newt jumped in and said, "You're right. Our base really likes it when I talk about White House crimes." Newt missed the nuance of what Baker and Hyde tried to suggest—that Newt should not be talking about Clinton's "crimes." Newt has been bashing Clinton, which in turn has subjected him to Democrat attacks stating he is unable to lead a fair hearing.

Baker criticized Dan Burton's for calling Clinton a "scumbag" and for saying he was "out to get" Clinton. "Burton can no longer proceed under the guise of fairness because nobody in the country will view him in an impartial light," Baker concluded.

When the briefing ended, Baker said he wanted to sneak out of Newt's office without reporters knowing he had been there. When I asked if he needed my help in leaving unnoticed, he brushed me off: "Rogan, if there's one thing I learned in all my years in Congress, it's how to get out of a building without the press knowing."

● ● ●

With all of these developments blurring the horizon, we still had one last interview to conduct—the one with Speaker Gingrich.

On the appointed day, Newt escorted us to his outdoor Capitol office patio facing the Mall toward the Washington Monument. It was a muggy day with a blinding glare reflecting off the terraces. Newt rejected my suggestion that we might be more comfortable moving inside where it was cool and shaded. "I prefer to sit outside," he told me. "It helps me to think." We got down to business very quickly:

Diary, Gingrich Interview, May 20, 1998

I asked Newt the same preliminary question I had asked the other interviewees: how did he think we should handle a call from Judge Starr saying a report of impeachable offenses was en route to the Capitol?

He smiled: "Very carefully," he said, and then the smile vanished as quickly as it appeared as he answered the question: "Henry Hyde and I would call a press conference. We would announce jointly that Judge Starr had delivered to us a report with the following highlights. We would announce that we will take our time reviewing the materials and not be rushed. The investigation probably would not be completed by the end of this Congress unless the evidence was weighty or the president resigned.

"Henry and I would set up the first phase review, which would be an internal review at the senior member level. We would establish a select committee, with a select subcommittee consisting of senior members. The committee or subcommittee size should be no more than 5-to-3 or 6-to-4 Republican/Democrat ratios, or Henry will be trying to manage a zoo.

"Henry and I would pick a day during the August recess when there was nothing to compete against on television. Ken Starr would come to the Hill with his associate prosecutors. Questioning would be done by members of the select committee we created. We might possibly invite the

president's attorneys to come up and make the case for summary judgment to the select committee. Then the select subcommittee would render an opinion to the full committee. Starr's testimony must be live, and it must be posted on the Internet ASAP."

Although I favored Starr testifying personally, I played devil's advocate and asked him why he thought it wise for the politically unpopular Starr to appear before the committee. He replied sternly, "There is nothing more destructive than to allow six months of vicious White House character assassination against Starr to proceed. I feel strongly that Starr must be given the chance to defend himself."

He declared confidently that we would have a report from Starr by mid-July. "Starr understands it cannot be any later," he said. "If the Republicans lose the Congress in November, then his investigation is over—and he knows it." When I asked if we should delay a hearing until after the elections in the event Starr reported to us too close to November, he brushed off my question dismissively: "That is not a contingency for concern," he said.

Finally, I asked if he saw any unanticipated obstacles to our hearing. Without missing a beat, he replied, "Read Jimmy Breslin's book on Watergate, *How the Good Guys Finally Won*. It shows how the Left responded to destroy Nixon during Watergate. The Left will be far more vicious against us. They will dredge up everything they can to smear Hyde or anyone else."

Other than asking a few open-ended questions, I kept silent during Newt's presentation. Finally, and for the first time since he gave me the assignment, he asked my opinion. Now it was my turn to smile:

"Mr. Speaker, my only problem with your game plan is your constant insertion of the personal pronoun 'I.' Why are you involved in all of this?"

His countenance showed great irritation at my question, which appeared to touch a nerve. Jabbing a finger in my direction, he snapped impatiently, "In case you haven't noticed, I happen to be the speaker of the House. In case you also haven't noticed, I happen to be the titular head of the Republican Party."

My earlier lesson from Peter Rodino prepared me well for my reply: "Respectfully, in case you haven't noticed, you're also the only member of the United States House of Representatives in the constitutional line of presidential succession. That makes you the only member with a constitutional conflict of interest." With that, I shared Rodino's story of how Speaker Carl Albert rejected the calls to create the precise sort of committee Newt now contemplated. I passed along Rodino's concern that Newt ran a grave risk of appearing to be on an opportunistic witch-hunt unless he did the same. Rodino thought Newt should send any referral through regular channels—the Judiciary Committee—and I agreed with him. Based on this model, I recommended that Newt get as far away from Clinton and his scandals as possible. "Mr. Speaker, you need to stand in front of your shaving mirror each morning and practice saying 15 times, 'Go ask Chairman Hyde your question.' If you can't say that to reporters each day and mean it, then don't come to work that morning or you will do harm."

Newt's momentary prickliness vanished, and he grew reflective. "Maybe you're right," he said.

"I don't think there's a 'maybe' on this one, Mr. Speaker."

Being blunt with Newt never concerned me. I knew he wanted and would appreciate meaningful advice, not sycophancy. Still, after Jon and I left Newt's office, Jon turned to me and said, "No disrespect intended, but you're a freshman congressman. Can you talk to the speaker that way?"

"I'll let you know, Jon."

• • •

Peter Rodino's advice changed Newt's perception of his role.

As explained earlier, before I began working on the speaker's project of drafting a protocol for any impeachment referral, I wanted to make sure this wasn't another Gingrich goose chase. Two weeks before I interviewed Rodino, the ghost of that damned "flat tax vs. national sales tax" debate rose from the grave. With my interviews not yet completed, Newt jumped in front of my efforts and announced publicly his decision to take the impeachment inquiry away from the Judiciary Committee. Making matters worse, he designated himself as the lead Roman soldier tasked with spearing Clinton.

On April 23, Jim VandeHei of *Roll Call* reported that Newt told a closed-door meeting of his House Republican leadership team that the Judiciary Committee was not prepared to handle an impeachment investigation: "Gingrich is concerned that Judiciary Republicans lack the staff to go head-to-head with Democrats and their "vicious attack machine." Gingrich is leaning toward a smaller panel of seasoned investigators and GOP women run by Judiciary Chairman Henry Hyde (R-IL). This panel would hold public hearings for Starr to explain his report to Congress and make the final call whether to proceed with the first [presidential] impeachment hearings in Congress since 1974."

A few weeks later, after I shared Rodino's advice with him, Newt took a totally different tack. Inviting VandeHei to join him on the same patio overlooking the Mall where we had met for my interview with him, Newt outlined his plan for any future referral from Judge Starr. The next day, *Roll Call's* headline read, "Gingrich Promises to Focus on Taxes, Not Impeachment—Speaker Reverses His Strategy of Attacking Clinton." In the interview, Newt said he came to several conclusions:

- He had washed his hands of Clinton's tribulations and would play no role in any impeachment review. "Henry [Hyde] and

I have a very clear relationship right now," Newt declared. "If the word begins with 'I' [impeachment], you talk to him. If the word begins with 'T' [taxes], you talk to me."

- He would make no further comment on allegations of Clinton's perjury, suborning perjury, and obstruction of justice. "I will rely on Henry's judgment for additional remarks," he said.

- Newt said that Henry Hyde and the Judiciary Committee would handle any impeachment review. He scuttled all previous suggestions regarding a special or select committee.

VandeHei noted that these comments showed a radical departure from the pledge Newt made never to give another speech as speaker without commenting on Clinton's refusal to cooperate with Judge Starr's investigation. VandeHei wrote this was a far different tack from Gingrich's recent accusation that Clinton bore responsibility for "the most systematic, deliberate obstruction of justice, cover-up, and effort to avoid the truth we have seen in American history."

Later that afternoon, Jon Dudas sent me a copy of the article with a note scribbled across the top reading, "I wonder where he got this idea?" The idea came from Peter Rodino; I was just the messenger.

Newt and I ran into each other a few days later as we both headed for the showers in the House gym. He asked when I might deliver to him my written report. I suggested we dispense with it: Henry Hyde remained concerned about a formalized report leaking to the press. Besides, I said, my conclusions echoed what he expressed in his *Roll Call* interview. Finally, I told him that all the Republicans who investigated Clinton complained of White House operatives' stonewalling and smear tactics (hardly a revelation for Newt). He agreed that he no longer needed anything in writing and then thanked me for my effort. This marked the first time the teacher ever gave me a passing grade for not turning in my homework assignment.

I left the brief encounter with a clear understanding that from here on, Chairman Henry Hyde would determine the details of how to proceed upon receipt of any impeachment referral from Judge Starr.

10

Big Buggy Ride

"There's nothing left to say. There's not any point now in putting the country through an impeachment, since the president isn't making any pretense of innocence now.... Now that the president has admitted wrongdoing, he should resign."

—BILL CLINTON, DEMOCRAT CONGRESSIONAL CANDIDATE, SPEAKING OF PRESIDENT RICHARD NIXON DURING WATERGATE, 1974

Chairman Henry Hyde was back in the driver's seat. Calling a confidential meeting of Judiciary Committee Republicans, Henry made each of us promise we would not share what he was about to say with our families, our staff, and especially the press.

Diary, Judiciary Republicans Meeting, June 25, 1998

After swearing each member to secrecy, Henry told us, "We are going to get a report from Ken Starr, and it will be a mas-

terpiece. It will include an executive summary sanitized for release to the press. Our procedures upon notification from Starr are not yet definite because the speaker keeps changing his mind. However, Gingrich will tell Starr to report directly to the House Judiciary Committee."

Tom Mooney [the committee's chief counsel] said, "We are preparing to receive Starr's report the first week back after the July 4th congressional recess." Dave Schippers [the committee's chief investigator] added that all the materials received from Starr will be in a guarded room and with cameras to keep them from being taken or leaked.

Henry told us, "When we receive the materials, we will go to the House floor with a resolution regarding procedures. The Democrats will scream because the resolution will give me a lot of authority. So, if you won't come to meetings or back me up on procedural votes then tell me now. We can't have the same situation they had on Dan Burton's committee. The Democrats will run us ragged if they can. That is why I need authority to subpoena witnesses, hold them in contempt, etc.

"Once we pass the resolution, we will get the Starr materials, and then the Judiciary Committee will go into executive session. Copies of the executive summary will be distributed to the press after a decent interval. At some point in open session, the clerk will read the summary and the television cameras will have a field day. After the reading, we will pass out the report summary to the press. Then we will go back into executive session.

"Our committee will divide into bipartisan teams, and we will go through all the materials laboriously. This will take a long time, but it must be done. We then will make the decision whether to lay before the public the materials by way of opening an impeachment inquiry. If that happens, we will draft an impeachment resolution for the House floor.

"Also, I don't want to bring in Starr to testify before the committee and subject him to three days of bashing. Instead, we'll call witnesses. If the Democrats have questions or have a quarrel, let them take it up with the witnesses.

"Don't make any plans for summer. You all have been drafted. Pearl Harbor is next month."

Henry fretted that the delivery of the referral and the time involved to examine the materials might push into the November elections and beyond: "If it gets too close to Election Day, we run the risk of people thinking this is politically motivated." He offered no solution to a problem that remained out of our control. However, he noted that we did have control over one aspect of the impending entanglement—our public demeanor:

"Our people who go on myriad talk shows do a terrible job of defending Ken Starr. The issue isn't Ken Starr. The issue is Bill Clinton, and you guys are playing into it.

"We need to avoid the temptation of talking to the press, but when we do, we will be acting more in sorrow than in anger as we march inexorably toward that wonderful day in the Senate where we can wave the Constitution. Some of you will be on that team addressing the Chief Justice in a Senate impeachment trial. So be good, be on time, and read your materials.

"We need to be very circumspect and treat this like, 'We are so sorry that this has happened to the highest officer in the land, but there it is—so out you go, you bastard.'"

Henry concluded with a warning:

"They will go through your trash. They will look for big liquor bills. They will do all they can to get garbage on you.

If it gets too bad, we may look at bringing obstruction of justice charges."

Taking a long puff on his ever-present cigar, Henry said in a quiet voice, "Get ready for a big buggy ride."

• • •

July came and went, and then August, and then September—and still no referral. Newt's and Henry's repeated assurances that Starr *had* to report well in advance of the mid-term elections fell flat. But with November approaching, it became clear our House GOP seers were reading political stars not followed by the Office of Independent Counsel.

• • •

As the edgy summer months dragged along, I ran into President Clinton a couple more times in neutral, friendlier surroundings.

On June 11, I attended the annual summer White House picnic for congressional families with my wife Christine and our five-year-old twin daughters Dana and Claire. The warm, beautiful evening found my girls more interested in catching fireflies than in adult socializing. It took some coaxing to get them to come meet the president. It amazed me to see how many senior members of Congress didn't hesitate to cut in front of all the small children and maneuver themselves to the front of the line. After it happened a few times to my kids, Christine and I picked up the girls to avoid the sharpened elbows of some of my overzealous colleagues.

When Clinton finally reached us, I introduced him to my family. Our overly affectionate daughters (too young to appreciate either protocol or partisan rancor) recognized him from television: assuming he was an old family friend (or maybe one of Dad's congressional staffers), they threw their arms around Clinton's neck and kissed his cheek. His eyes brightened. "Well, my goodness, look at these two!" he exclaimed as he scooped up our giggling girls in his arms. Cameras clicked as he posed for pictures with the girls before they returned to their firefly adventure.

Later in the evening, as the girls and I prepared to return to the lawn party through the Diplomatic Reception Room, an agent asked us to wait briefly: "We need to clear the path for the First Lady," he whispered. "She's retiring to the family quarters." As Mrs. Clinton approached, once again my sociable twins recognized her from their steady C-SPAN diet. Thinking they knew her, too, they walked over with outstretched arms. Mrs. Clinton's fatigued look vanished into one of joy at their spontaneous affection. It was a darling sight to watch them trade hugs and hellos.

"Do they know who I am?" Mrs. Clinton asked me with a broad smile.

"Oh, yes," I replied. "They know you're the president's wife."

Leaning down to Claire, Mrs. Clinton beamed as she asked, "Do you know who I am?"

"Yes," replied little Claire with gusto, "you're Mrs. Dole!"

Even Mrs. Clinton's Secret Service detail had difficulty suppressing their grins over Claire's confusion that she was meeting the spouse of Clinton's recently defeated Republican presidential campaign rival. Mrs. Clinton's smile faded as she looked at me. Fearing that she thought I put my kid up to this, I scratched the back of my head and said, "Gee, I can't imagine where she got that."

A month later, on July 26 (the same day that Judge Starr subpoenaed him to testify before the grand jury), President Clinton and I attended the commissioning ceremony of the carrier U.S.S. Harry S Truman near Norfolk, Virginia.

Diary, Newport News, Virginia, July 26, 1998

The rain gave way to a sweltering, muggy day under a broiling sun. Escorts assembled us in our places on the flight

deck overlooking the bay and the thousands of spectators below. When President Clinton arrived, Secretary of Defense William Cohen introduced him. Clinton read from a prepared speech; I found his pledge to keep the Navy strong an empty one given his recently announced plan to dismantle our 600-ship fleet and reduce it to 200 ships. This so infuriated Republicans that many chose to boycott his speech at this commissioning ceremony.

When we chatted briefly at the end of the ceremony, I thought Clinton looked fatigued. I didn't know it at the time, but Judge Starr had earlier today subpoenaed him to testify before the grand jury. The threat to bring down his presidency continues to grow.

This brief encounter was the last time Clinton and I spoke before the impeachment deluge. It would be a long while before we exchanged any friendly words again.

• • •

While writing this book, I read my impeachment diaries for the first time. I found them replete with references of what others told me about how they felt; I discovered a glaring absence in them of how I felt. When the Lewinsky story first aired, my former supervisor from the Los Angeles County District Attorney's office, now-Superior Court Judge Terry Green, called me and said, "You need to mentally put back on your old judge's robe during all of this. Don't decide anything until all the evidence is in and the matter is submitted." Based on the very few instances where I jotted down a personal opinion on all that agitated around me, I guess I took Terry's advice subconsciously.

Others in Congress didn't operate under the same self-imposed restrictions. The debate intensified on both sides. One diary entry records a common sampling of what I heard almost every day:

Diary, July 27, 1998

While working out in the House gym, I listened to Budget Chairman John Kasich (R-OH) and Congressman Gary Condit (D-CA) discuss the merits of Starr's investigation of Clinton. "Hey, if all Clinton did was get sex with a young bimbo and then lie about it to his wife, who cares?" Kasich said. "It's not impeachable stuff." He thinks Clinton will finish out his term.

Congressman Dana Rohrabacher (R-CA) disagreed, saying he just heard a rumor that former White House intern Monica Lewinsky met with Starr's prosecutors today and gave information to them against Clinton. "Ahh," said Rohrabacher gleefully, "the dam is starting to break!" Kasich replied that he still thinks this is much ado about nothing.

Among my Republican colleagues, Kasich's indifference put him in the distinct minority. Most agreed with Rohrabacher that Lewinsky's immunity agreement with Judge Starr and her bargained-for cooperation signaled a noose tightening.

Around this time, I also noted a greater tendency of some of my Democrat acquaintances to dump on Clinton privately. I wasn't sure if their comments signaled scandal fatigue, moral outrage, or a calculation that replacing Clinton with his vice president would be better for the Democrats in the 2000 presidential election. Whatever the reason, Democrat lips grew looser during these sweltering summer days:

Diary, July 15, 1998

I had lunch today with Ambassador Chuck Manatt, the former chairman of the Democrat National Committee. Manatt said he has known Clinton for 20 years and that

Clinton always had a voracious sexual appetite. He attended many, many events when Clinton was governor of Arkansas and Manatt was DNC chairman. According to Manatt, Clinton would have his state bodyguards scope out beautiful women in the room and then approach the women and ask if they would like to come to the Governor's room later. "Clinton would get one out of every three women to say yes," Manatt said. "That's a hell of a lot of women over the years."

Diary, July 28, 1998

Former Congressmen Rod Chandler (R-WA) and Tom Downey (D-NY) hosted a fundraiser for me at their lobbying firm offices today. Over lunch, Downey (a longtime Clinton and Gore friend and supporter) said Clinton's sexual appetite is "compulsive" and that Clinton had always been that way since Downey first met him. He called Clinton "a weak person who gets himself into trouble because he can't keep his pants zipped."

Despite such ongoing private observations, as long as Clinton's poll numbers held, Democrat loyalists weren't jumping ship. On a flight from Washington back to Los Angeles, my colleague Howard Berman (D-CA) told me the House Democrat Caucus had a basic strategy: continue defending Clinton, keep claiming that Judge Starr's investigation is just about sex, and keep repeating that Congress should spend its time talking about other issues.

One colleague keeping noticeably silent was Speaker Gingrich. I saw Newt on the House floor one night in late July and wanted to pass along to him a rumor I heard about Starr's investigation. Newt smiled as he replied, "When I was younger and irresponsible,

I would have taken to the House floor to announce this to the world. Now I have to behave."

• • •

As the fall of 1998 approached, I felt like a man straddling tandem train tracks while watching two locomotives—one marked *Impeachment* and the other *Reelection*—hurtling toward me. My goal was to keep my mouth shut about the Clinton scandals publicly until I saw the evidence while simultaneously finessing the subject so as not to anger my heavily Democrat constituency. Judge Terry Green's earlier suggestion to remain in mental "judicial mode" remained sound advice both on merit and as realpolitik analysis.

Meanwhile, I pursued reelection in 1998 aggressively. Looking for ways to mollify my liberal constituency, I saw an easy lift when Congressman Joseph Kennedy (D-MA) asked me to co-sponsor his bill to name the U.S. Department of Justice building after his assassinated father, former Attorney General and presidential candidate Robert F. Kennedy. Political opportunism motivated me, but there was a degree of sincerity behind it as well. As a fifth grader, I discovered my love for politics during Kennedy's doomed 1968 campaign. After I had followed his race as a class project, his brutal murder moments after winning my state's presidential primary left a lasting memory with me as a ten-year-old budding political aficionado.

Long after I signed onto the bill, Joe Kennedy told me that despite earlier GOP assurances, his bill lay dead for some unknown reason. I agreed to see if I could discover what happened. Later that day, I ran into Newt's chief of Staff, Arnie Christensen, who told me that Newt was taking significant heat from conservatives opposed to the measure. A few days later, I approached Newt on the House floor and explained the reason for my support. Because his speakership depended on a handful of seats like mine remaining in the Republican column, I presumed asking him to push this window-dressing bill and then letting me take a bow for it wouldn't be a big deal.

Diary, June 17, 1998

Newt told me, "If working to name DOJ after Bobby Kennedy helps you with Democrats in your district, then go for it and take full credit for it. Just don't ever ask me to move the bill. That bill is dead—*dead*. Even DOJ is opposed to it."

When I asked Newt why it was dead, he said many conservatives didn't want anything named for Bobby Kennedy. "Overlook for a minute what kind of guy Bobby Kennedy was personally," he said. "Just go ask [Republican Congressman] Denny Hastert why he won't vote for something as a favor to Joe Kennedy."

Looking back, I should have sought any additional information from Denny Hastert. Out of freshman ignorance, and missing an obvious social cue, I pursued the issue with Newt and asked why others wouldn't vote for the bill as a favor to our colleague Joe. Newt's eyes narrowed at the mention of "our colleague Joe":

Newt snapped at me: "When a guy like Joe Kennedy spends ten years up here shitting on people and then he asks you to name a building after his father, the typical response to someone like that is, 'Screw you.' Go ask Hastert why he won't vote for anything for Joe Kennedy. He'll tell you it's because Joe Kennedy's been an asshole his whole career in Congress."

Oh.

• • •

Although helping to get DOJ named for Bobby Kennedy might have merited me a good press release, and maybe a few appreciative votes from old-time Democrats, it wasn't going to fill my need for (in Jesse

Unruh's famous phrase) the mother's milk of politics: campaign contributions. That came from endless fundraising to ensure a sufficient war chest to defend my seat in 1998. As Election Day drew nearer, I was thrilled to learn that 85-year-old former President Gerald Ford agreed to do a rare campaign event for me. This would draw a lot of attention, a lot of press interest, and most importantly, a lot of money.

After we confirmed the event, we sent out the invitations, cashed the checks, and hired the photographers and caterers. Then I received a telephone call from my pal and former State Assembly colleague, Brooks Firestone, an old Ford family friend (Brooks' father served as Ford's ambassador to Belgium).

Diary, August 15, 1998

Brooks said Gerald Ford just called him and said he noticed I wasn't "on" as a co-sponsor of HR 2409, a bill Ford and his wife are pushing. Ford's pet bill required federal law to treat substance abuse like other illnesses under private health insurance coverage. Ford told Brooks that if I didn't co-sponsor the bill, Ford would not come out for my fundraiser. This is extortion. I can't believe an ex-president, and former Republican House minority leader to boot would pull such a stunt.

Ford backed me into a corner: cancel the event and stand on principle or give in to a blackmailing ex-president and allow the bill's author to list me as a co-sponsor.

I caved.

The day after Gerald Ford's arm-twist got me to cry "uncle," I got a call from former Judiciary Chairman Rodino:

Diary, August 14, 1998

Peter Rodino called and told me, "Jim, I know you are a Republican, but you are one of the individuals upon whom the responsibility [of impeachment] will fall. It will be incumbent upon you to preserve the process. I know you are committed to doing the right thing"

I was glad Chairman Rodino wasn't on the extension phone when I surrendered to Gerald Ford out of political expediency.

• • •

By August, President Clinton had lost his court battles to keep aides off the witness stand under claims of privilege. This forced his friends, advisers, and even his Secret Service agents to testify before Judge Starr's grand jury. Lewinsky testified under a grant of immunity, and reports continued surfacing that she was now cooperating with the investigation. Although polls showed voters in record numbers wanted Clinton to finish out his term, his personal approval ratings on "honesty" and "respect" had plummeted. Meanwhile, Bill and Hillary Clinton continued their daily assault on Republicans. Amid the White House's unending assault on Judge Starr, the independent counsel subpoenaed President Clinton. Starr withdrew the formal subpoena after Clinton agreed to testify voluntarily on August 17 from a video feed at the White House.

Soon after Starr subpoenaed Clinton, information surfaced that decimated the Clintons' eight-month "vast right-wing conspiracy" victimization strategy. Reporters learned that Lewinsky turned over to the FBI a blue dress that she said contained Clinton's semen stain. Judge Starr got a court order to obtain Clinton's DNA sample to compare against Lewinsky's dress. If the evidence matched, it meant that Clinton's January denial under oath during the Paula Jones sexual harassment lawsuit constituted felony perjury, which made impeachment the least of his legal woes. Perjury and obstruction of justice in a federal court case meant possible criminal prosecution and imprisonment.

Suddenly, Clinton faced a Hobson's choice: continue repeating his earlier denial at his forthcoming grand jury appearance or admit he lied under oath in his Paula Jones deposition last January. Making the decision harder, the independent counsel wasn't sharing the results of their DNA test before Clinton testified.

Diary, House Floor, July 30, 1998

During our cloakroom discussion about Clinton, Newt grew serious and asked me, "Do you know why Hillary will never let Clinton admit anything? Because in her mind he must remain president since he is her ticket to a presidential pardon for all of her crimes. If he perjures himself again, he's gone and they both know it. She and her husband are boxed in."

Senate Judiciary Committee Chairman Orrin G. Hatch (R-UT) made the rounds of interview shows offering Clinton an olive branch: if Clinton lied earlier, Hatch didn't believe it required removal from office as long as Clinton now came forward and told the truth. Just before we recessed, Newt discussed with me the movement by Hatch and others to force a public mea culpa from Clinton in exchange for legal constitutional forgiveness.

Diary, August 6, 1998

On the House floor, Newt and I talked about the advice Clinton was getting to "come clean" and admit he lied in the Paula Jones lawsuit. Now, with Monica Lewinsky testifying before the grand jury, he appears (according to published news accounts) ready to confess.

A colleague mentioned that last year Newt paid $300,000 out of his own pocket to reimburse the government for the cost of the ethics investigation directed at him. The colleague said we should now demand Clinton do the same for the millions expended by the independent counsel to investigate his lies. Newt's demeanor turned solemn: "This shows you why Washington is such a horseshit town," he said. "In Virginia, they sentenced someone to six months in jail for lying under oath about an affair. Here, the media and the Left excuse it when it is one of their own who does it. This sends the message to every criminal in America that if you are caught and you just go on television with a quivering lip and say, 'I'm sorry,' everything will be OK. But that's all right, we'll keep our cool, let the facts come out on their own, and then let Clinton get his brains beat out over all this."

• • •

On August 17, President Clinton became the first sitting president to testify under oath before a federal grand jury investigating him. Later that evening, he addressed the nation in a five-minute televised speech in which he said that his Paula Jones deposition answers denying any sexual relationship with Monica Lewinsky were "legally accurate." Clinton then offered a vague admission that he had a relationship with Lewinsky that was "not appropriate," "wrong," and constituted a "lapse in judgment and a personal failure." He denied asking anyone to break the law. Finally, he turned defiant and attacked Judge Starr's investigation. As for his increasingly perjurious-sounding testimony in the Jones deposition, he looked into the camera and told America, "It's nobody's business but ours."

For a politician feted for his shrewd instincts, this Clinton performance laid a public relations egg. *Washington Post* reporter Howard Kurtz's quick opinion compilation demonstrated that television commentators panned the president's performance almost uniformly:

Fox News:

"This really is the 'I didn't inhale' defense." —Fred Barnes

"This was Slick Willie in operation." —Morton Kondracke

ABC News:

"A heavily lawyered speech where he conceded nothing legally."
—Jeffrey Toobin

"He didn't come clean with the country." —Sam Donaldson

CBS News:

"The president has been using the White House, White House staff, and White House lawyers to defend this lie." —Scott Pelley

Clinton "set a new standard" for evasion. —Steve Kroft

NBC News:

"I'm not sure he's come to terms with how much he has soiled his presidency." —Jonathan Alter

As for the print media, even the traditionally liberal and supportive newspapers weren't much kinder:

The New York Times:

"Expressing regret for creating a 'false impression' is not an adequate response when he lied to the American people for seven months. The investigation of subornation of perjury and other obstruction issues must continue, and Mr. Starr ought to move quickly to conclude it. [N]othing now known about the grand jury testimony or revealed in the speech warrants abandonment of that inquiry."

The Washington Post:

"'It is time, in fact it is past time, to move on,' the president said, suggesting that the only issues remaining in the case were private ones having to do with him and his family, 'nobody's business but ours.' But that's not so. The basic questions as to whether he broke the law remain. [F]ailure to examine the facts seriously would be an abdication of Congress' constitutional obligation to weigh the evidence in a case as serious as this. What it cannot do is ignore an allegation, if one is made, of criminal conduct by a sitting president. However unpalatable this matter has become, Congress has no more right to blink it away than does Mr. Clinton."

USA Today:

"No matter how strong the urge is to forgive and forget Clinton's actions, doing so in this context, and after the extreme damage Clinton has brought to those around him and to the nation, would be to define the presidency downward. His claim to a right to be left alone ended once he forced his nation and those closest to him to bear the cost of his denial."

The Los Angeles Times:

"If Starr presents a compelling case against the president on allegations of perjury or obstruction of justice, or both, it would be difficult for the House to brush it aside. Bill Clinton made a similar confession before and suggested it was all in the past. It wasn't. On this issue, he has no credibility."

Members of Clinton's own team felt he botched his presentation. According to Dan Balz of the *Washington Post*, "President Clinton's speech Monday night was increasingly seen by Democrats yesterday as a political failure that has unleashed a torrent of anger among some of the president's most loyal supporters and created problems no one at the White House anticipated."

Although I tried scrupulously not to make any judgments against Clinton prematurely, I wrote privately what I would not say publicly:

Diary, August 17, 1998

President Clinton gave a speech tonight admitting he had an "improper relationship" with former White House intern Monica Lewinsky. His deportment appalled me. There was no contrition in his voice or demeanor, just sheer defiance. He continues to be an embarrassment to the presidency.

Once again forced into damage control mode, Clinton underwent another "Apology Tour," expressing repeatedly the remorse and humility that evaded him the night of his nationally televised address. This time, even the mea culpas uttered through the lip biting failed to work their usual magic. Aside from the blistering press reviews garnered, Democrat Congressmen Paul McHale (D-PA) and Gene Taylor (D-MS) both urged him to resign. The federal judge before whom Clinton testified in the Paula Jones lawsuit now threatened to hold him in contempt for giving false answers. Respected Senator Joseph Lieberman (D-CT) condemned Clinton's conduct as "immoral" and "disgraceful" in a much-watched Senate floor speech. Other esteemed Democrats such as Senators Daniel Patrick Moynihan (D-NY) and Bob Kerrey (D-NE) echoed Lieberman's comments. Senator Dianne Feinstein (D-CA) said Clinton's admission left her faith in his credibility "shattered." At a luncheon with Democrat colleagues, she almost wept as she recounted how Clinton looked her in the eye and lied. Senator Robert Torricelli (D-NJ) laughed in reply, "The president looked me in the eye and told me the same thing on many occasions. And

I'm not upset. Do you know why? Because I never believed him in the first place."

• • •

On September 8, I met *Wall Street Journal* columnist Paul Gigot for lunch near the Capitol. During our chat, he posed a hypothetical question to me: "What if I told you Judge Starr would deliver his referral to Congress tomorrow, and I also told you its entire focus was Monica Lewinsky—how would you feel?"

I laughed off the suggestion and told Paul that I hoped he didn't pay for a tip that stupid. I said that after over four years of investigating everything from Whitewater to laundered Chinese campaign contributions to Webster Hubbell hush money, Judge Starr must have a mountain of evidence against the president. I predicted confidently that if the independent counsel sent Congress an impeachment referral, the late-developing and unexpected Lewinsky story would at best merit a footnote in the saga.

As I lectured Paul about not accepting foolish gossip under the guise of news tips, he just kept nodding his head, taking occasional notes—and smiling.

11

The Shower

"An independent counsel shall advise the House of Representatives of any substantial and credible information which such independent counsel receives . . . that may constitute grounds for an impeachment."
—PUBLIC LAW 103-270 §3(G), 108 STAT. 734

Eight months of unending and bitter Lewinsky warfare induced a battle fatigue that brought both sides together, albeit temporarily. The top brass of both parties grew tired of wondering what Ken Starr was doing and tired of waiting for him to do it. If the House needed to draft legislation to receive and disseminate any referral from the independent counsel, they wanted to know about it—now.

On Wednesday, September 9, in a rare act of bipartisan cooperation, Speaker Newt Gingrich, Minority Leader Richard Gephardt (D-MO), and their leadership teams held a joint press conference. Newt said he and Gephardt agreed to publish any report from Starr because "the public has a right to know." Gephardt suggested that perhaps Congress should let Clinton see the report in advance so the president could fashion a reply before it became public. Newt remained noncommittal on that suggestion, but he nodded in agreement as Gephardt assured the press, "[W]e have made a good start at making this a nonpartisan effort. [N]ext to declaring war, this may be the most important thing that we do, so we have to do it right."

As I watched their joint meeting on television, two things surprised me. First, after months of silence, Newt was back in the center of the action. Henry Hyde had only a brief supporting role at this key press conference. Second, knowing Dick Gephardt to be a severe partisan, I didn't expect to see him breaking political bread with Newt over such a hot topic. Later, when I ran into my friend and "Freshman Ghetto" next-door neighbor, Rod Blagojevich (D-IL), I mentioned that Gephardt impressed me with his new-found moorings. Rod laughed and told me it was all for show. He said that since Gephardt didn't know what might be in the report, he was playing it safe. He added that once the House published the referral, the Democrats would wait a day or two to see which way the polls ran. If Clinton's numbers held, he said they would come after us Republicans mercilessly.

Just prior to their joint appearance, Gingrich and Gephardt ordered senior Judiciary Committee staffers to call Judge Starr's office and demand to know what type of material he would send and when it would arrive. Starr's chief deputy Jackie Bennett told the callers that Judge Starr was out of the office. Bennett called back a few hours later with an unexpected message: Two vans were en route to the Capitol to deliver an impeachment referral, along with 36 sealed cartons of exhibits—where did we want them to drop off the boxes?

After four years of speculation, the waiting ended. Judge Starr believed the president of the United States committed acts meriting his impeachment and removal from office. Now, on a balmy Wednesday afternoon, his staff dumped it in our laps with no warning.

By the time the vans pulled in front of the House steps, chaos reigned on the Capitol plaza. Guards corralled tourists, reporters, photographers, television camera crews and staffers who crowded and jostled to get a close-up glimpse of the historic handover. Uniformed police unloaded the vans and surrendered their contents to House Sergeant at Arms Bill Livingood, who ordered everything sealed and guarded in secured rooms at the Ford House Office Building down the street. Nobody would see any of Starr's material until the House Rules Committee passed, and the full House approved, a resolution directing the manner of release.

Diary, September 9, 1998

I was visiting constituents in my office this afternoon when, at about 3:30 p.m., I learned that Judge Starr delivered his impeachment referral to Congress. Later, in the House chamber, Republicans tried hiding their glee. But there is a sense among many of pending vindication and that this report will expose Clinton as the liar and fraud many believe him to be.

As members rushed to the chamber to be present when the referral was received formally, both caucuses passed out their respective media talking points slapped together for the occasion. Our GOP crib notes suggested we get "on message" with the same basic response: members must reserve judgment until we have a chance to review Judge Starr's report, and we will not make any decisions until we have all the facts.

In the House chamber, the clerk read Judge Starr's cover letter; amid the bedlam, nobody paid attention to these words buried in the body of the document:

"Many of the materials in the referral contain information of a personal nature that I respectfully urge the House to treat as confidential."

• • •

The next morning, Republicans members had to fight their way through a phalanx of reporters to get into our GOP conference meeting. Rules Committee Chairman Jerry Solomon (R-NY) began the meeting by circulating a handout reminding us about the House rules of decorum during floor debate. His lecture on propriety provoked laughter, because he tended to be one of our bigger debate hotheads. "Is this the pot calling the kettle black?" one member yelled from the back of the room.

Chairman Hyde received a standing ovation when he rose to speak. He began with a warning: once this report is unsealed and we begin the process of reviewing it, "The other side will be vicious and partisan."

Diary, House Republican Conference Meeting, September 10, 1998

Henry said, "We were surprised yesterday by Judge Starr's referral. It consists of one three-ring binder with 445 pages, and over 2,000 pages of appendices. We are negotiating a date with the Democrats to look through the appendices. Many of the Democrats also want it publicized so they can plan their fall campaigns. They need to decide whether to cut and run from Clinton or whether to embrace him."

At yesterday's Gingrich-Gephardt joint press conference, both leaders left unanswered whether they would release materials in full or publish a redacted version. Henry now sounded as if leadership decided this issue:

"We will release immediately the 445-page report," Henry said. "It will give folks something to chew on over the weekend." Conference members chuckled over Henry's

unintentional double entendre, prompting him to grin and reply, "I've never seen such an assemblage of dirty minds!

"The guts of this report will be public by the weekend. We probably should redact some personal stuff, but it would be too hard to do it.

"We will need to change our House and committee rules to have an orderly transfer of the materials from the custody of the House Sergeant at Arms to the Judiciary Committee. We will also need to modify the 'Access Rule' [allowing any members to review any committee document]. As much as all of you want to see the materials, the Democrats want to see it more so they can leak it to the press."

Jerry Solomon reported that most members of the Rules Committee wanted the information made available. He said his committee was drafting a rule to make the entire 445-page referral available; the 2,000-page appendices will be available after review by the Judiciary Committee. He suggested Judiciary get the appendices for ten days to sift through it first, and then remove (with bipartisan approval) any irrelevant materials.

Speaker Gingrich then briefed the conference on his immediate goals for the coming days. Like me, Newt presumed the referral to be heavy-laden with non-Lewinsky impeachable offenses:

"First," said Newt, "we will handle the entire investigatory process, including Chinese missile technology transfers, Teamster money laundering, campaign finance irregularities, etc. in a dignified way."

"So much for Paul Gigot," I thought to myself. "I knew Starr would send a referral based on weighty issues and not just Lewinsky. How could Paul be so hoodwinked?"

Meanwhile, Newt continued:

"Second, on the House floor, we need to impose a level of decorum higher than the level the Democrats displayed toward me. This is not *The Jerry Springer Show*.[1] This is the United States House of Representatives. Third, we need to keep moving the legislative process. We need to focus on legislation and let the press focus on scandals." After completing his checklist, Newt said that we had the best man in Congress—Henry Hyde—to handle this referral because "we picked the best person for the job."

Newt then made a comment almost in passing that caught nobody's attention, but it soon had significant consequences on the ultimate impeachment dynamic:

"Once we vote tomorrow to pass the resolution to post the information on the Internet, within minutes the world will have the information available. My guess is that this weekend an astonishing number of people will be learning how to use their computers."

Thus, the Republican and Democrat leaders of the House of Representatives decided jointly to avoid congressional elitism, release the referral immediately on the worldwide web, and let America in on the historic decision as to whether Congress should terminate a presidency over criminal conduct:

"During Watergate," Newt said, "the Peter Rodino-led Judiciary Committee held 24 secret meetings, and then met for six months after eight months of Senate hearings. By contrast, we are releasing the information to the country within 48 hours of receiving it."

---

1   *The Jerry Springer Show* was a tabloid talk show that aired on television from 1991 to 2018.

Newt said the White House requested an advance copy of the report. "Since that same courtesy was not made available by the Democrat majority in their Iran-Contra investigation of President Reagan and President Bush, we are not in a position to establish a precedent for that request."

Although Newt still maintained public neutrality on impeachment (despite his previous comments), others in his leadership circle felt no compulsion to follow suit. Immediately after our conference adjourned, I attended a whip meeting called by Majority Whip Tom DeLay:

**Diary, House Majority Whip Meeting,
The U.S. Capitol, September 10, 1998**

DeLay said he is intent on getting Clinton to resign. As he spoke of Clinton's immorality, he grew visibly irritated. It is clear he views Clinton as a total disgrace to America and to the presidency. He passed out to each of his deputy whips a thick binder filled with Clinton scandal information and historical impeachment data for us to use in making the argument for Clinton's removal.

That afternoon, while I stood in the House chamber talking with a couple of fellow freshmen members, Newt walked over and joined our conversation:

Diary, House Floor, September 10, 1998

Newt asked me, "Are you satisfied with the procedures so far?" This was in reference to the earlier homework assignment he gave me. I told him I thought the tenor of public bipartisanship was helping the House and the Judiciary Committee. Newt nodded in agreement.

Newt then launched into an unexpected tirade against Independent Counsel Ken Starr. He fumed over the way Starr's people delivered his report with no notice to him and in the way he "dumped it"—literally—on the House yesterday. He called Starr's actions "unprofessional and total horseshit."

Dentist-turned-Congressman Charlie Norwood (R-GA) lightened the mood when he came over and said Newt's hair didn't look good at his earlier press conference. Newt cut Charlie off with a wave of his hand and a chuckle: "When I need grooming advice, I get it from a dentist. When I need my teeth fixed, I'll go to a beautician."

My diary from that day also contains a passage reflecting the awe settling in as I contemplated the job ahead:

In these last two days, I gave many interviews. The attention from the national press over my position on the Judiciary Committee is incredible. I'm not excited or thrilled by it; I feel sobered by the whole prospect of sifting through the Starr report and potentially impeaching a president. I'll do my duty fairly.

Late that evening, the House Rules Committee met to consider H. Res. 525, which authorized transferring jurisdiction of the entire referral and attachments to the Judiciary Committee. The resolution directed the immediate public release of the 445-page Starr narrative, with the remaining materials received in executive session and subject to release in two weeks, unless the Judiciary Committee voted for confidentiality. The resolution ordered that only Judiciary Committee members would gain access to the executive session materials until its release.

Although the Democrat committee members protested some of the individual resolution provisions during debate, the Rules Committee passed the resolution to release the Starr report immediately on the Internet by a unanimous vote of all Democrats and Republicans. Under the terms of the resolution, the Judiciary Committee had two additional weeks to decide whether to hold back any of the 2,000-page appendices or other exhibits.

The next morning, the entire House voted to release Starr's report immediately, and to transfer jurisdiction of the entire referral over to the Judiciary Committee, by an overwhelming vote of 363 to 63. Given the later avalanche of lies that Republicans in the House foisted upon America a salacious report, before reviewing and sanitizing it, I restate the previous facts—and highlight them in bold so the reader does not overlook them:

> ***The House Rules Committee passed the resolution to release the Starr report immediately on the Internet by a unanimous vote. It passed on the floor of the House with an overwhelming margin of 363 to 63. House Democrat leader Richard Gephardt, every single member of his entire Democrat leadership team, and 80 percent of every House Democrat voted to post Judge Starr's report immediately on the Internet.***

After the resolution passed, Chairman Hyde called a private meeting of Judiciary Committee Republicans. Henry entered the committee meeting room carrying a large envelope delivered by messenger that contained Bill Clinton's formal "response" to Starr's referral. Reminding everyone of Clinton's complaint that it would be unfair to release the report before he got an advance peek at it. Henry held aloft Clinton's prepared response now delivered before the release of Starr's report and before any of us had yet seen it

"As you can see, they really were hampered by our failure to give Clinton a pre-release copy!" he laughed.

**Diary, Judiciary Committee Republican Meeting,
September 11, 1998, 12:30 p.m.**

"The request of President Clinton to get an advance copy
of the report is rubbish," Henry said. "During Watergate,
there were 134 Democrat Judiciary Committee staffers to
the Republicans' 12 staffers. The Democrats never gave
Nixon a 'head's up.' They let Nixon's lawyer sit in but didn't
allow him to ask questions. We'll do the same for this White
House, but no more.

"Gingrich and Gephardt are involving themselves deeply
in the process," he griped. "Decisions are changing from
minute to minute. It's hard to keep all of you in the loop." He
added that both Gingrich and Gephardt put on "a brave show
of bipartisanship, but I'm not easily fooled. The Democrats
are very bitter and very angry."

Henry said he promised to deliver a copy of the Starr
referral to Clinton by 1:30 p.m. Committee staff would
deliver a hard copy to each congressional office by 4 p.m. He
said that all members of the Judiciary Committee would have
access to the appendices. "But we still need to establish my
subpoena power, contempt power, immunity, and deposition
issues, etc. We can't let the Democrats tie us up."

Anticipating the referral's unfavorable contents, Henry then
set forth his game plan for the coming weeks. Although the House
leadership still expected to adjourn the 105th Congress in early
October so members could return home for the last weeks of the
campaign season, Henry said Congress would not adjourn sine die[2]:

---

2   *Sine die*: to adjourn a meeting or body without any future date to return. At the end of each
     Congress, the body's final adjournment is *sine die*.

"We will remain at the call of the chair," Henry said. "During this period, Dave Schippers [our chief investigator] and his staff will winnow out the appendices and make the case for Clinton's impeachment. Then Dave Schippers and Gephardt's lawyer Abbe Lowell will brief our committee. At the end of all this, we will have a draft of an impeachment resolution to recommend to the House."

Dave Schippers added that he hoped to be ready to brief the committee before the October adjournment. He said the Democrats wanted to put off any briefing until after the November elections.

• • •

Because of a technical glitch, the committee had to fax the referral to congressional offices instead of delivering printed copies. My press secretary, Jeff Solsby, agreed to allow ABC News anchorman Peter Jennings and the network's congressional correspondent Linda Douglass to broadcast a live feed from my office showing the delivery of the report to a Judiciary Committee congressman.

On camera during this live national broadcast, Jeff started handing me batches of pages from the long-anticipated report. With Linda Douglass looking over my shoulder and with Jennings interviewing me through an earpiece, I scanned those first sheets looking for words like "Whitewater," "Hubbell Hush Money", "Travelgate," and "Chinese Missile Technology Transfers." Instead, the live network cameras depicted me suppressing shock as I read to myself phrases like "exposed his genitals," "oral sex," "masturbating into a bathroom sink," "oral-anal contact," and "the president inserted a cigar into Ms. Lewinsky's vagina, then put the cigar in his mouth and said, 'It tastes good.'"

After absorbing this information, I stopped seeing words printed across the pages: instead, I saw the face of The *Wall Street Journal*'s Paul Gigot smiling at me over lunch a couple of days ago when I explained to him the foolishness of his hint that any referral from the independent counsel would be "All Monica."

Paul knew.

For 445 pages, it was Monica Lewinsky and every excruciating detail of her sexual relationship with Bill Clinton, as well as Clinton's Herculean efforts to cover his tracks when the Paula Jones lawyers picked up the perjury and obstruction of justice scent.

If true, what did all of these allegations mean? It meant the president of the United States perjured himself in the Paula Jones deposition. It meant Clinton suborned perjury from others. It meant Clinton obstructed justice. It meant he committed multiple crimes to protect himself from civil liability in a legitimately filed federal civil rights lawsuit. It meant that he tried to deny a lone woman's claim of sexual harassment against him with a web of felonious conduct. It meant he violated his constitutional duty under Article II §3 to "take Care that the Laws be faithfully executed." It meant he violated his oath of office to "preserve, protect, and defend" the rule of law. It meant Congress had a duty to investigate and, if true, call him to account for his actions.

It meant one more thing. As I told a colleague after I finished reading the referral, to prove all of this, "We're going to have to stand under the faucet and get sprayed by a miserable shower of shit."

12

Three Little Words

Mercifully, my need to get to the airport gave me an excuse to end the live Peter Jennings-ABC News interview. While on the plane back to California, I began reading the independent counsel's voluminous referral. It cited 11 areas of potentially impeachable offenses, including allegations that President Clinton:

- lied under oath at a civil deposition while he was a defendant in a sexual harassment lawsuit;

- lied under oath to a federal grand jury;

- attempted to influence the testimony of a potential witness who had direct knowledge of facts that would reveal his deposition testimony lies;

- obstructed justice by helping and encouraging a witness' plan to refuse to comply with a subpoena;

- obstructed justice by encouraging a witness to file an affidavit he knew was false, and then made use of the false affidavit at his own deposition; and

- obstructed justice by lying to potential grand jury witnesses knowing that they would repeat those lies before the grand jury.

- Judge Starr concluded that these acts and others "were part of a pattern that began as an effort to prevent the disclosure of information about the president's relationship with a former White House intern . . . and continued as an effort to prevent the information from being disclosed in an ongoing criminal investigation."

That weekend, while America digested the sordid details, Clinton's lawyers flooded the news shows trying to keep their client from facing both impeachment and criminal indictment. Clinton put his attorneys in the unenviable position of arguing that Clinton didn't commit perjury by denying he had sex with Monica Lewinsky because he gave "legally accurate" answers. How could this be, given Clinton's televised admission last month to an "improper" sexual relationship with her? Clinton now claimed that when he testified under oath that he didn't have sexual relations with Monica Lewinsky, this was technically true because she had sex with him, not the other way around.

Clinton's legalistic "she had sex with me" defense bombed in the court of public opinion. Even congressional Democrats found that claim indefensible. Dan Balz and Peter Baker reported the fallout in Monday morning's *Washington Post*: "Senate Minority Leader Thomas A. Daschle (D-S.D.) and House Minority Leader Richard A. Gephardt (D-Mo.) yesterday criticized the White House legal defense strategy, calling on President Clinton and his advisers to abandon what Daschle called 'hairsplitting' about his testimony denying a sexual relationship with Monica S. Lewinsky. . . . Gephardt and Daschle were reacting to what one Democrat called a 'disastrous' performance by the president's legal advisers over the weekend. [The White House now wants] to shift attention away from Clinton's contention that he was "legally accurate" if misleading in his January 17 deposition in the Paula Jones case [and] back to the president's admissions of wrongdoing."

Balz and Baker also noted correctly that, "Those comments reflected the complicated dilemma Clinton now faces. As long as he is in legal jeopardy, either from Congress or the independent counsel, his lawyers will resist any acknowledgment that he lied under oath. But that very defense may hinder efforts to find a compromise short of impeachment, particularly before the November midterm elections."

On Sunday, the Republican leadership team scheduled a 5:00 a.m. (PT) conference call to discuss communications strategy with all Republicans appearing that morning on the national news shows. Since ABC News scheduled me for an interview on their program *This Week* (appearing via satellite from the West Coast), I dialed in to the call. Leading it were House GOP Conference Chairman John Boehner (R-OH), National Republican Congressional Committee Chairman John Linder (R-GA), House Republican Conference Secretary Jennifer Dunn (R-WA), and Republican National Committee Chairman Jim Nicholson. After complaining that Clinton still enjoyed high job approval ratings despite the unsavory revelations, they suggested we use these sound bites when discussing Starr's report on television:

Diary, GOP Media Strategy Conference Call, September 13, 1998

- **Use the phrase Clinton "lied under oath" instead of "perjury." It is easier for people to understand what he did.**

- **Remind everyone that Clinton held only two cabinet meetings this year: one in January to lie to his cabinet and tell them there was no truth to the Lewinsky** story, the other last month to apologize for lying to them in January.

- Use the word "dishonor" when discussing Clinton's behavior and the way he has handled his presidency.

- The last federal judge impeached and removed from office suffered his indignity at the hands of a Democrat Congress. They removed him for lying under oath—after he won an acquittal in his underlying criminal case.

- If the Democrats complain about the release of these lurid details, remind everyone that every Democrat in leadership voted to release the materials, as well as 80 percent of all House Democrats.

- Clinton's position of power and his age differential with Lewinsky makes his conduct akin to a high school principal "mashing" one of his young students. [Mashing? Urging us to go on national television and use this antiquated phrase for propositioning a young woman should have tipped me off early that our Republican communications strategy was doomed.]

When congressional Democrats hit the airwaves that Sunday morning, they wisely dumped Clinton's initial "she had sex with me" defense. Instead, on *This Week*, Democrat Congressman Vic Fazio preceded my segment and minimized Clinton's behavior by saying the president's lies were "only about sex" (the Democrats' new and improved mantra). In response, I jettisoned the GOP conference call advice and focused on the legal precedent set if we accepted the Democrat defense:

First, it grieves me to hear my friend Vic Fazio say, "It's only about sex." This was about sexual harassment. A federal judge in a sexual harassment lawsuit ordered the president of the United States to give testimony about sexual conduct with subordinate federal employees. The judge said Clinton had to answer these questions because it might show a pattern of sexual harassment [relevant to the Paula Jones case]. This is critical in sexual harassment cases because harassers don't usually commit their conduct under a harsh spotlight. They do it behind closed doors. Paula Jones was trying to find out if there was any other pattern of similar conduct to bolster the credibility of her claim. [Clinton defenders] now come on these shows and say these lies were "only" about sex and ask why we care? That attitude sends a message to any woman victimized by sexual harassment that she might as well not come forward, because if the man testifies in her case and lies about it, and if—in the unlikely event—we find out it is a lie, he can just say it was only about sex. Everybody can shrug their shoulders and say, "Why are we looking at this?" That attitude won't just weaken sexual harassment laws in this country; it will decimate them.

My focus on the implication for sexual harassment laws was (I thought) a more than worthy rebuttal to Clinton's newfound "it's about sex" defense. I was dead wrong. Clinton's defenders hit public relations pay dirt with their alternate theme: it allowed them once again to position the culprit as the victim and then pivot to blame Starr and the Republicans. My argument was sound legally, but it took three paragraphs to explain; Clinton's took three words. It may not have been fair or true, but it was brilliant.

Clinton lawyer David Kendall now argued vociferously that Starr released the specifics of the Clinton-Lewinsky relationship solely "to harm the president." This put Republicans on defense: Senate Judiciary Committee Chairman Orrin Hatch countered that Judge Starr "had to put all the [sexual] details in because of [Clinton's] dissembling on the law." Hatch was correct. However, right now, we weren't fighting in court. We were fighting a political battle, and in politics, the necessary is not always the prudent. The sordid truth, made compulsory by Clinton's verbal contortions, caused a massive public backlash. The more I studied the report, the more I knew that the voters' recoil would extend to anyone defending it.

• • •

Word reached the House cloakrooms that the Clinton team vowed a "scorched earth" policy in retaliation for the House moving forward with the impeachment referral. This meant that their henchmen would investigate the personal lives of congressmen and use the information to smear anyone coming after Clinton. It didn't take long to learn they meant business. When the first domino fell, the victim was an unexpected target.

On September 16, *Salon.com* published details of Henry Hyde's 1960s-vintage extramarital affair. Our humiliated but resolute chairman issued a statement: "The statute of limitations has long since passed on my youthful indiscretions. [The affair] ended and my marriage remained intact. The only purpose for this being dredged up now is an obvious attempt to intimidate me, and it won't work."

This leak created a new undercurrent of Republican fury directed at Team Clinton. Newt Gingrich and Dick Armey wrote to FBI Director Louis J. Freeh demanding an investigation into whether this was part of a White House-orchestrated "campaign of slander and intimidation." At a press conference, Tom DeLay said he had no evidence connecting Clinton to it, but he added, "We have reason to believe that top aides with access to the Oval Office have been orchestrating a conspiracy to intimidate members of Congress by using their past lives."

At our next Republican Judiciary Committee meeting, our members arrived early to express support for Henry and outrage over the revelation. He entered the room late. His head hung low and he didn't look at any of us. He took his seat, mentioned a few unrelated matters, and then adjourned the meeting without saying a word to our group about the affair disclosure—then or ever.

• • •

Under the House Rules, the Judiciary Committee's upcoming tasks involved multi-tiered hurdles, each with ascending levels of difficulty and each with a corresponding increase in the political and emotional stakes:

- First, review the entire Starr referral;

- Second, decide what to withhold or release from the materials, including tangible evidence like the videotapes of President Clinton's Paula Jones deposition from January and his August grand jury testimony;

- Third, report to the House whether sufficient evidence exists to warrant a formal investigation;

- If the House of Representatives approved the inquiry, the Judiciary Committee would begin hearings on whether to recommend the president's impeachment;

- After holding these hearings, if a majority on the committee felt the president committed impeachable offenses, the committee would draft and debate articles of impeachment and recommend any approved articles to the full House;

- If one or more articles passed a vote of the entire House, then the president was impeached;

- In the final step, the Senate would try the president's case and determine whether to remove him from office. The House case would be presented through its designated "Managers"— the Judiciary Committee members selected to prosecute the president.

As we began the first phase of this daunting process, only Judiciary Committee members had access to the Starr materials, which remained guarded by police at the Ford House Office Building until we voted to release them. Like other committee members, I spent hours sifting through the evidence in the off-site location.

Dave Schippers and I watched the video of Clinton's August 17 grand jury testimony. I found nothing remarkable besides his continuing evasiveness and the interrogators' polite and (sometimes irritatingly) deferential attitude toward him. The prosecutors let Clinton begin his testimony by reading a lengthy canned answer to one of their key questions. Later, they allowed him to refer back to this prepared answer and "stand by it" when they pressed him. Dave and I felt the prosecutors missed many chances to pin him down and force him to answer. We wouldn't have played by the same polite rules with a deceptive witness who kept reading his law-firm-drafted canned answer to almost every uncomfortable question.

To me, watching Clinton jump through hairsplitting hoops trying to redefine what it meant to be "alone" in the White House with someone, and what sort of intimate, mutual sexual contact counted as "sex" made him look more silly (and guilty) than victimized. The defining moment came when the off-camera prosecutor noted that Clinton sat next to his attorney at the Paula Jones deposition and made an adoptive admission to his lawyer's statement that "there is absolutely no sex of any kind, in any manner, shape or form" between Clinton and Lewinsky:

Question: That statement was made by your attorney in front of Judge Susan Webber Wright, correct?

Clinton: That's correct.

Question: The statement that, "there is no sex of any kind, in any manner, shape or form with President Clinton" was an utterly false statement. Isn't that correct?

Clinton: It depends upon what the meaning of the word "is" is. If "is" means, "is and never has been," that's one thing. If it means, "there is none" [going on at this moment you are asking me a question], then that was a completely true statement.

The internal Republican debate over whether to publish this videotape was by no means pro forma. Speaker Gingrich called a House Republican conference to discuss the proposed release. Surprisingly, we had a number of dissenters in our ranks; one of them provoked an unfortunate outburst by Newt:

Diary, House Republican Conference, September 16, 1998

Congresswoman Nancy Johnson (R-CT) said she felt it would be unfair to Clinton if we released the videotape of his grand jury testimony. Members booed her for making that comment. Newt looked angry when she again insisted that we hold back the videotape. He shouted at Nancy, "Bill Clinton is a liar. He lied yesterday, he's lying today, and he'll be lying tomorrow. He's a misogynist monster. So, you're saying it's OK [for television news] to show footage of him saying, 'I'm sorry' three times each day, but it's not OK to show him lying?"

As expected, Newt's statement leaked to the press almost before he drew his next breath. The Democrats again accused Newt of secretly driving the impeachment bus while Henry Hyde rode along as his stooge. Henry answered that this persistent claim was yet another lie hatched to undermine the credibility of the Judiciary Committee. As for Newt, he recognized almost immediately that he had missed another opportunity to keep quiet and stay away from Clinton's problems. At our next conference, he assured his GOP colleagues, "I will return to not commenting on Clinton's impeachment and I will refer all such questions to Henry Hyde."

• • •

Over the next two days, Chairman Hyde met privately with Judiciary Republicans to seek consensus for handling the incendiary contents of the Starr referral. Specifically, he wanted to discuss possible limitations on releasing things like reports of past sexual assaults committed by Clinton against women, the graphic sexual descriptions of the Lewinsky saga, and whether to make public Clinton's videotaped testimonies in whole, in part, or (as the Democrats demanded) in transcript form only:

Diary, Judiciary Committee Republican Meeting, September 16, 1998

In arguing for release of Clinton's videotaped grand jury testimony, Henry Hyde said, "The demeanor of the deponent is a part of the truth-seeking process." We then debated whether to release only the transcript as the Democrats wanted, or whether we should release both the video and the transcript. Every committee Republican voted to release the video and the transcript except for two: George Gekas (R-PA) and Asa Hutchinson (R-AR).

Diary, Judiciary Committee Republican Meeting, September 17, 1998

George Gekas again argued that we should postpone the video release of Clinton's testimony to avoid the Democrats charging us with partisanship. Others now agreeing with him were Elton Gallegly (R-CA), Asa Hutchinson (R-AR), and Ed Pease (R-IN). Most members felt we should release it immediately. Charles Canady (R-FL) said we can't flinch in the face of Democrats screaming "partisanship." I argued for the release of the videotaped testimony in whole, and suggested we redact other materials only if they were gratuitously graphic and unrelated to the charges against Clinton.

Just as with our internal debate over whether to release Clinton's videotaped testimony, there was no unanimity on whether to withhold other materials with graphic sexual descriptions found in the referral:

Diary, Judiciary Committee Republican Meeting, September 16, 1998

Committee staff attorney Mitch Glazier briefed us, saying the Starr materials locked away in the Ford Building also contained two FBI interviews with a woman who denied previously any sexual relationship with Clinton, but now she told the independent counsel that Clinton in fact forced himself on her when she refused his advances back in 1978. Henry Hyde interrupted Mitch, saying, "In other words, rape."

Mitch said that (so far) the Republican staff was at 60 percent agreement with the Democrats on what to edit from the remaining materials. He said some suggested deletions are where Lewinsky referred to Mrs. Clinton and their

daughter Chelsea. Henry interjected that we needed to remove such comments, "or else they'll accuse us of hurting Clinton's daughter."

Henry discussed the overall "pornographic" nature of Starr's report: "It consisted of language not fit to be in a locker room no less than the Internet. But the president's semantic evasions made it necessary."

Diary, Judiciary Committee Republicans Meeting, September 17, 1998

Calling Clinton a "Machiavellian jerk," Bob Inglis (R-SC) said he wants all the graphic details of Starr's referral published, "so people can see what kind of a man Clinton really is."

• • •

On September 17, Chairman Hyde called to order our first full Judiciary Committee hearing since the independent counsel's referral arrived at the Capitol less than two weeks earlier. Over the next two days, Republicans and Democrats met in executive (private) session. Already, our committee staffers had sifted through the 18 boxes and 60,000 pages of raw material; now it was time for us to consider what to do with it.

Diary, House Judiciary Committee Meeting, Executive Session, September 17, 1998

After opening statements, Henry made a formal motion to release all the materials as redacted [by previous Republican and Democrat staff agreement]. Maxine Waters (D-CA) objected, complaining that she had not been given enough

time to read all the materials and wouldn't have time to do so in the near future because of her "busy schedule of appointments." Their colloquy continued:

The Chairman: Your staff has read it.

Ms. Waters: My staff hasn't.

The Chairman: Well, your minority committee staff has read it. Don't you trust them?

Ms. Waters: I might trust them if we had more of them.

The Chairman: Maybe you would trust them more if we gave you the same number of staff that you gave us during Watergate, when we Republicans had 12 and you Democrats had 127.

The bells clanged, signaling a pending House floor vote and bringing the confrontation to a convenient end. When the committee resumed in executive session in the late afternoon, Waters reprised her grievance:

Maxine Waters again complained about not having time to review the materials. Steve Buyer (R-IN) told her to go down to the tables below the dais and review it now. An argument broke out between them. Buyer walked over to the tables where the materials lay, pointed to the boxes, and called, "Come down here, Maxine, and do your job."

During a break, Congressman Barney Frank (D-MA) added a little comedic relief. An openly gay man, Barney walked over to where a group of us stood and cracked, "All this talk about heterosexual sex bores the shit out of me."

As the daylong meeting progressed, we reviewed and discussed the jointly proposed edits. These included unnecessary personal information, material still under seal in the Jones v. Clinton lawsuit, national security matters, information relating to innocent third parties with no connection to the case, and materials relevant to Starr's charges but overly lurid or graphic. As to the latter topic, two colleagues proposed amendments that set off another firestorm:

> Bob Inglis filed a formal amendment to change the description of redaction #3, so that the published reason for redaction would read, "Description of oral-anal sexual contact between the president and Monica Lewinsky." The Democrats exploded over the suggested change. Steve Rothman (D-NJ) expressed "concern" that the definition would suggest Clinton performed the act on Lewinsky, instead of vice versa. Inglis countered that he would accept "any perfecting language." When we voted on Inglis' motion, many Republicans voted either "no" or "pass." Inglis looked stunned over so many Republican defections. "So, we lose our [Republican] unanimity on the very first vote," he grumbled.
>
> Bob Barr (R-GA) offered an amendment that would release publicly the information describing Clinton penetrating Lewinsky's vagina with his cigar. Barr argued this information needed to be included in the public materials because it goes to Clinton's evasive definition of the sexual activity that he denied under oath having with Lewinsky.

In the coming weeks, I often reflected during moments like this that if Sonny Bono hadn't met his fate on a Lake Tahoe ski slope, I'd be considering things like satellite deregulation bills in the Commerce Committee instead of pondering creative cigar uses.

• • •

The next morning, our committee (still in executive session) completed our preliminary review of the most controversial Starr referral materials:

**Diary, House Judiciary Committee Meeting,
Executive Session, September 18, 1998**

In arguing against release of the Clinton grand jury video-tape, Steve Rothman (D-NJ) made an emotional and specula-tive argument that maybe Starr's prosecutors were making off-camera "faces" at Clinton to intimidate or anger him to make him look bad on tape. Republicans dismissed this as a silly and weak claim. Hyde's motion to release Clinton's videotaped testimony passed on a Party-line vote.

We fought the escalating propaganda war across the notepads and camera lenses of the press. Elbowing our way to their microphones now became an almost hourly ritual. Republican and Democrat staffers fed packets of talking points into our hands like infantrymen feeding ammo belts into machine guns. GOP message points urged us to accentuate details like these:

- Perjurers Go to Prison: Since Clinton became president, his Department of Justice prosecuted and convicted 489 defendants for perjury, 323 of whom went to prison for their crime. Their average prison sentence was two and a half years.

- The president has made it necessary to release his grand jury testimony. His lawyers insist he testified truthfully in the Paula Jones deposition and before the grand jury. Now Congress and the American people must assess the credibility of the president's answers. This requires close examination of the president's carefully chosen words and his demeanor when using those words.

- In an overwhelmingly bipartisan vote, the entire House decided to release all of the independent counsel's documents (except for highly personal information and references to innocent people). The Democrats now attacking us for releasing the report shows that they are hypocritical frauds.

The Democrats never shared their talking points with me. I didn't need to see a copy. Ours came in packets of stapled pages, while they could write theirs on a popsicle stick:

"It's about sex."

After adjourning our September 18 hearing, Chairman Hyde tried to reflect optimism by telling reporters that our two days of closed-door debates were vigorous yet civil. He said, "I would say the spirit of bipartisanship is alive and flourishing." Barney Frank, one of the senior Democrats on the committee (and one of the most combative), interrupted Henry's answer and called the hearings "a very one-sided, partisan effort to release material to make the president look bad."

When a reporter from National Public Radio asked my opinion about the Judiciary Committee Democrats, I didn't bother putting the same cheery smile on the proceedings that Henry offered: "For them to come out and say that releasing this material is 'partisanship at its worst' is intellectually dishonest when 75 percent of every Democrat in the House, and 100 percent of every Democrat leader in the House voted to release the [Starr referral] material. [They have] continued to litigate this issue with bitter and rancorous characterizations."

It had been a long and exhausting two weeks, and our work had barely begun. Carrying reams of materials under my arms, I trudged out of the committee room that night and headed back to my office. Looking up, I saw Speaker Gingrich approaching from the opposite direction in a Rayburn Office Building hallway. He smiled an impish grin as he passed by me:

"So," he asked, "are you having fun yet?"

13

A Real Piece of Work

"Those who argue that Mr. Starr should never have inquired into Mr. Clinton's truthfulness about his sex life fail to consider his legal mandate. As an officer of the court, operating under Justice Department aegis and the supervision of three federal judges, he would have been derelict if he had walked away from evidence of potential perjury. Mr. Starr, based on the available evidence, has not exceeded his legal authority as a federal prosecutor. He would, on the other hand, have been guilty of a grave offense if he had failed to investigate false swearing by a president or if, once the likelihood of such conduct was established, he had hidden that information from Congress and the public. Mr. Clinton reportedly still believes that he can secure a deal without confessing to his sworn lies, and the Republicans cannot and should not accept that."

    —THE *NEW YORK TIMES*, EDITORIAL, SEPTEMBER 24, 1998

"Plainly, there are offenses so minor as to permit a before-the-fact judgment that, even assuming the worst, they are not impeachable. Perjury and obstruction of justice, however, are not among them. The [Judiciary] Committee needs to find the facts."

    —THE *WASHINGTON POST*, EDITORIAL, OCTOBER 2, 1998

Any expectation that the Judiciary Committee Democrats might approach the Starr referral with an open mind, or reciprocate even a fragment of the public bipartisan cooperation Republicans gave them during the Watergate investigation of Richard Nixon, proved delusional. Before Chairman Hyde ever banged his gavel to begin the committee's first hearing to review the contents of the Starr referral, disruptions and distortions erupted from most committee Democrats whenever a live microphone or camera pointed in their direction.

The Democrats' unending "partisan witch hunt" yelps kept from public view an important detail: the entire Judiciary Committee—Democrats and Republicans—reviewed thousands of pages in the Starr appendices. Dave Schippers later estimated that both sides reached mutual agreement on about 99 percent of the issues with little or no dispute. However, to hear the Democrats tell it, just the opposite was true. With the Republican compass needle pointing to felonious conduct and the Democrats bound by a poll-driven decision to ignore it, a mêlée became inevitable barring some creative intervention.

• • •

Over the days leading to the next installment of this melodrama (a Judiciary Committee hearing to decide whether Starr's evidence warranted recommending a full-blown impeachment investigation), the Democrat and Republican spin machines continued cranking out the talking points for both sides. Ours carried three general themes:

Democrat Doubletalk

- *The Democrats demanded we follow the Watergate model. When we said we would, they then opposed the Watergate model. The Democrats now want to set a deadline, narrow the inquiry scope, and define what is an impeachable offense—all issues that the Democrat majority rejected three times during Watergate in 1974.*

- *During Watergate, John Conyers voted three separate times against setting a time limit on the investigation. Now he and the Democrats demand a 30-day time limit to review and investigate over 60,000 pages of referral materials. The Democrats also claim they need more information from the Office of Independent Counsel and insist we cannot move forward until we get it. Which is it?*

Bipartisanship is a One-Way Street

Chairman Hyde has made extraordinary overtures to the Democrats in the name of fairness and bipartisanship, granting every request committee Democrats made:

- *We agreed to use the Democrats' Watergate model for the investigation;*

- *We agreed to investigative power sharing with the Democrats;*

- *We agreed to send a bipartisan delegation to Starr's office to review materials the Democrats demanded to see; and*

- *We agreed to call a hearing on the issue of what is an impeachable offense in response to Democrat requests.*

Getting to the Truth: Which Side Cares?

- *According to the sign-in logs, Republicans have spent over 114 hours at the Ford Building reviewing the materials sent by Judge Starr. The Democrats have spent just over 21 hours.*

How can they want to narrow the scope of the investigation when they don't even know what is in the referral from Judge Starr?

- *Six committee Democrats never visited the evidence room. David Schippers confirms that the most vocal Democrat attacking Judge Starr for having no evidence—Barney Frank—never showed up to view the evidence.*

- *We have serious documented felony allegations against the president. He apologized, but he denies any crimes. What is the truth? Has the president played by the same rules as the rest of us, or has he committed felonies and undermined the rule of law? A vote against an inquiry is a vote against getting to the truth.*

Diary, House Judiciary Committee Republicans Meeting, September 19 and 22, 1998

According to Henry and our committee staff, Democrat committee members have been AWOL from the Ford Building to review the evidence. "We will use the attendance logs to show their dereliction at the appropriate time," Henry said. According to our staff, Sheila Jackson-Lee (D-TX) walked in and demanded to know where Clinton's "phone sex" tapes were located. When told no such tapes existed, she waved her hand dismissively and proclaimed, "Then you have nothing," and walked out.

Henry said, "There are two Democrat Parties in the House: the Party on the floor and the Party in our committee. These committee Democrats are the unreconstructed hardliners." As an example, he decried Barney Frank's acidic bias and suggested we dismiss him in the press by saying "His sister [White House Communications Director Ann Lewis] works for Clinton. He just wants to save her job."

"I implore all of you to be patient," Henry said. "Once we release the materials, we have plans that will gratify the coldest heart. We will be in control."

Sadly, the Democrat committee members couldn't even show comity when they pre-arranged it with us. When the full committee met to finish its review of the Starr referral, Henry and Ranking Democrat John Conyers agreed in advance to a cordial finale. It failed, but through no fault of Henry's:

Diary, September 25, 1998

Before this morning's closed Judiciary Committee hearing, our Republican counsel Mitch Glazer said that Henry and ranking Democrat John Conyers would introduce a series of ten joint motions today to show bipartisanship.

Later, toward the end of the hearing, and after we adopted all of the Hyde-Conyers motions, Democrats started offering delaying motions while Conyers and Barney Frank slipped away and rushed to the television cameras waiting outside. There they both decried once again the "bitter partisanship" going on inside the closed hearing. It is all hogwash.

This continuing scenario had a familiar ring. In cartoonist Charles Schulz's classic *Peanuts* strip, Charlie Brown was the placekicker and Lucy was his football holder; she always pulled the ball away at the last moment, leaving Charlie flat on his back. We Republicans were Charlie Brown; the Democrats were Lucy offering us unending private promises of bipartisanship. We kept running forward to embrace the promise, and they kept pulling it back, leaving us to topple (as my longshoreman grandfather used to say) ass over teakettle.

Once the committee voted to release Clinton's videotaped grand jury testimony, his White House team started playing the time-honored Washington game of shifting expectations. Before the release, they claimed falsely that the grand jury videotape showed Clinton lashing out at his critics angrily and stomping out of the room. The tactic was an old psychological ploy to get viewers to expect the worst, and then later shrug their shoulders after thinking what they just saw wasn't so bad.

Diary, September 19, 1998

I spent another day at the Ford Building going through the Starr exhibits, and again watching the videotape of Clinton's August 17 grand jury testimony. He looked his usual slick self while using legal gymnastics to explain that a woman having sustained oral sex upon him in the Oval Office doesn't amount to a "sexual relationship." It's absurd, but it probably will push his favorable poll rating higher. Amazingly, the more Clinton covers himself in sludge, the higher his poll numbers climb. Clinton lies, cheats, and destroys people's lives. He gets away with it time after time. I don't understand what is wrong with America.

Despite my privately expressed feelings, my public comments remained muted:

Diary, September 20, 1998

I debated Congresswoman Maxine Waters (D-CA) on the *Fox News Sunday* show with Tony Snow. When asked, I declined the opportunity to call Clinton "a liar." I just don't feel that such public comments are constructive to the process. Despite my personal feelings about Clinton, I want to continue showing respect for the office of the presidency.

On September 21, the committee released Clinton's four-hour videotaped grand jury testimony and unsealed all the pre-approved Starr materials. The television news networks aired Clinton's tape in a continuous loop. As usual, the Democrats decried the release and the "harsh partisanship" behind it. They even made a religious objection, complaining it was sacrilegious to turn over Clinton's screed during Rosh Hashanah.

While all of this percolated, Chairman Hyde faced dual pressures over the Starr report. On his right flank, many Republicans (like me) felt we should expand the committee's inquiry beyond the salacious Lewinsky facts and investigate other potential impeachable offenses (like transferring missile technology to Communist China). From the left, the Democrats demanded (with public opinion polls supporting them) a quick end to the review.

As to expanding our inquiry, Henry discussed the prospect with assembled Republican House members at our next weekly conference:

Diary, House Republican Conference Meeting, September 19, 1998

Mike Castle (R-DE) asked Henry when Starr would send to the House the rest of his materials on other scandals like Whitewater, Filegate, and Travelgate. Henry again teased that Lewinsky's saga was just part of the trail the Judiciary Committee would follow. He didn't know when Starr would deliver additional materials, "but I expect we will have an interesting Thanksgiving. I also don't view our committee charter as being limited to reviewing only what Starr sent us."

A few days later, Henry raised the issue again in a private meeting with committee Republicans:

Diary, Republican Judiciary Committee
Republican Meeting, September 22, 1998

Someone asked if our committee investigation would ever get into the other Clinton scandals that Starr investigated. Hyde replied, "May I suggest that won't happen before the election." Committee counsel Tom Mooney added that after the resolution authorizing an impeachment inquiry passes the House, the committee staff can keep working and investigating these other areas. He suggested we could begin that inquiry right after the November elections."

Another member asked whether we should pursue issues like Juanita Broaddrick's rape allegation against Clinton dating back to 1978, detailed in FBI reports sent to us by Starr but not included in his published referral:

Henry said, "The series of FBI interviews carry very substantial but uncorroborated claims of sexual abuse, including Juanita Broaddrick's rape claim from 1978. My concern is that we end up piling on with irrelevancies unrelated to Starr's allegations. I propose we withhold all this now and keep it in the drawer until a later inquiry."

Dave Schippers added that Starr's investigators still have Kathleen Willey's claim [of Clinton assaulting her sexually] "on the table." He expects Starr to issue an indictment over this.

As to the second pressure of setting a narrow investigation time limit, House Democrat Leader Gephardt now attacked Republicans daily for wanting to "drag out the process to feed their narrow political interests." He demanded the House complete its entire impeachment review against Clinton within a mere 30 days. Chairman Hyde accused the Democrats of talking from both sides of their mouths:

"The president had eight months to tell the truth," Henry said, "but instead he sent his staff out to declare his innocence to the world. Now the Democrats want to shut down an inquiry of his behavior in 30 days…. The House only received the independent counsel's report two weeks ago." Noting that the Democrats' Watergate review took nine months, Henry mocked the minority for saying they wanted an expeditious process finished within 30 days while also claiming they needed more materials from the independent counsel's office to resolve the matter fairly.

• • •

Although most Republicans kept their powder dry publicly, it appeared that the House Judiciary Committee would move toward recommending a formal impeachment inquiry not long after the first boxes of the Starr materials were unsealed. Just a week after the referral arrived, our committee investigator Dave Schippers had already finished his preliminary review of the sequestered materials:

Diary, September 19, 1998

Dave Schippers told me his evidentiary review was complete. "I'm already writing," he said, a reference to his drafting a recommendation for a formal impeachment inquiry based on the Starr referral.

Dave showed me the FBI reports of Clinton's alleged rape of nurse Juanita Broaddrick in 1978, which he believed to be true based on all the evidence and corroboration. Dave, a lifelong Chicago Democrat, now spoke of the man for whom he had twice voted: "This guy's a real piece of work," he growled in disgust.

Later, at our meeting of Republican committee members, Dave expanded on our anticipated direction:

Diary, Judiciary Committee Republican Meeting, September 19, 1998

Dave Schippers said sometime in October he would do a report for the full committee. He also expected Starr to issue perjury indictments. "Clinton entered his August 17 grand jury testimony so cocky," Dave said, "because his team thought they had 'taken care' of Kathleen Willey" by intimidating her into silence. By then they also obtained a false affidavit from Lewinsky in which she denied that she ever had a sexual relationship with Clinton.

At the same meeting, Henry Hyde told us to expect a House floor debate on October 8-9 (just three weeks before Election Day) on whether to authorize the Judiciary Committee to conduct a formal impeachment inquiry:

"Be patient," Henry counseled. "We are working on so many things. As Al Jolson once said, 'You ain't heard nothing yet.'"

In preparation for the debate on whether to recommend an impeachment inquiry to the full House, Henry handed out a list of assigned member and staff responsibilities for preparing the various arguments. The main areas covered were as follows:

- The nature, authority, and significance of the independent counsel referral;

- The importance of the rule of law;

- The law of perjury and the fundamental importance of truth in our legal system;

- Obstruction of justice and witness tampering;

- Sexual harassment implications;

- The analogy to the Military Code of Conduct;

- This is public behavior, not personal behavior;

- This case is not about sex, but about obstruction of justice, witness tampering, and perjury.

Attached to this memorandum was a House Resolution discussion draft conspicuously marked, "SECRET." The opening sentence was unambiguous:

Resolved: That the Committee on the Judiciary . . . is authorized and directed to investigate fully and completely whether sufficient grounds exist for the House of Representatives to exercise its constitutional power to impeach William Jefferson Clinton, president of the United States of America.

• • •

On my first day back in D.C. following a brief district break, Henry Hyde summoned committee Republicans to a private meeting at which he announced that the full committee would convene to debate the inquiry issue on Monday, October 5:

Diary, Judiciary Republicans Meeting, September 29, 1998

Jim Sensenbrenner (R-WI) warned that the Democrats would want to put Ken Starr on trial at our hearing and suggested we need to stop them from doing so. Henry replied, "Is attacking Ken Starr all they want to do? Won't any of the Democrats defend Clinton? I can't stop them from trying to subpoena Starr. We need to bring back the focus of our hearings to what Bill Clinton, and not Ken Starr, has done.

"I will be very liberal on subpoena authority, but it's because I want to impose my subpoena power on some 'interesting people.' I won't say who they are now. You need to trust me on this. I will allow Democrats to issue subpoenas, but they will be subject to the approval of the chairman and appealable to the full committee.

"We have to be fair—not because we want to be but because we need to be. This is the only way we can drive down Clinton's 60 percent-plus approval ratings. So, when we bring that big impeachment question forward, America will be ready for it."

• • •

As we moved closer to the full committee hearing date, I continued working almost round-the-clock studying the Starr referral materials in the secure evidence rooms of the Ford Building:

Diary, September 30, 1998

Mary Bono (R-CA) [who had been elected to fill her husband Sonny's seat after his tragic death] and I watched Bill Clinton's videotaped January 1998 deposition in the Paula Jones case. When I compared this deposition testimony to the answers he gave to the grand jury in August, I saw several examples of dead-bang perjury.

Mary told me Clinton disgusts her: "Now that I'm single again," she said, "he reminds me of why I need to be careful when I start dating. Some men are pigs."

• • •

At a private strategy session of committee Republicans held before the hearing, Henry Hyde caught everyone's attention as he opened the meeting:

Diary, Judiciary Committee Republicans Meeting, October 1, 1998

Henry told us, "We are on the threshold of a very major event. The Democrats have had the momentum for a long time. Next Monday, it is going to shift.

"We will start in executive session on Monday at 9 a.m. and immediately vote to open the hearing to the public. Once we hear opening statements from myself and John Conyers, I will recognize Dave Schippers for one hour, and then Abbe Lowell on behalf of the Democrats for one hour. Then we will have opening statements from all members in seniority order. There will be members' questions of counsel [Schippers and Lowell], but they will be confined to requests for additional information or for clarification."

Henry asked Dave Schippers to outline for us what he would say in his formal committee presentation. Although Henry had just indicated that our committee would not limit its review exclusively to Lewinsky, Dave's case would focus exclusively on the contents of Starr's referral as it related to her:

Dave said he will set forth 15 different impeachable offenses to show that Clinton, Lewinsky, Vernon Jordan, and Betty

Currie were all part of a criminal conspiracy. [Starr alleged that Clinton friend Jordan got Lewinsky a job in New York at Clinton's request to get her out of town. After Paula Jones' attorney subpoenaed Clinton's gifts to Lewinsky, Clinton's personal secretary Currie picked them up from Lewinsky and hid them under her bed.] Dave said for now he will only bring up details relating to the Clinton-Lewinsky scandal since that is all Starr sent our committee in his referral.

In preparing his overview, Dave told his staff to approach their review of Starr's materials as though each investigator represented Clinton. He also made sure his investigators left out no exculpatory material.

Jim Sensenbrenner (R-WI) said he wants Schippers to focus on Clinton's conduct, which was not "to hide his relationship with Lewinsky from his wife and country. It was to defeat the lawsuit of poor little Paula Jones, a clerk in the Arkansas bureaucracy." Steve Buyer (R-IN) said he wants Schippers to focus on Clinton's betrayal of trust.

Toward the end of the meeting, Henry raised a side issue causing discomfort in the ranks. Over a period of months, the press had been reporting that two of our Republican members, Asa Hutchinson (R-AR) and Lindsey Graham (R-SC), had been meeting regularly with Democrat Judiciary Committee members Howard Berman (D-CA) and Bill Delahunt (D-MA). The four told the press the purpose of their meetings was to maintain a bipartisan dialogue. This revelation galled Henry, who told me that he believed that this group was really trying to position itself as impeachment "deal cutters." He grumbled to me frequently and privately about these get-togethers, but he took no action. Then, in late September, the quartet published their letter to Judge Starr asking him to end his investigation and turn over the evidence to the committee. For Henry, this was the final straw. He told the press (through Tom

Mooney) that their "breakfast club" was nothing more than a White House pipeline for pushing a censure resolution as an alternative to impeachment.

Now, at our meeting, a clearly irritated Henry raised the issue of two of our junior Republican members playing public footsie with the Democrats outside of the committee process. It brought a rare rebuke from the chairman and from some of our colleagues:

> **Henry called on the carpet Lindsey and Asa: "Berman and Delahunt are nothing more than conduits for [Democrat House leader] Dick Gephardt," Henry snapped. "They want us to limit the scope of our inquiry to just Lewinsky. We *won't* narrow our scope."**
>
> **Bob Barr (R-GA) demanded that Lindsey and Asa tell us if they "are up to something we need to know about." Asa defended the meetings but said that everything he and Lindsey discussed with the Democrats during them "is kept secret." Ed Bryant (R-TN) raised the same concern as Bob, adding, "By Lindsey and Asa trying to look 'bipartisan' in the press, it makes the rest of us look partisan." Neither Asa nor Lindsey responded to the comment.**

• • •

On Friday, Speaker Newt Gingrich summoned all House Republicans to the Capitol for an emergency meeting:

> **Diary, House Republican Conference Meeting, October 2, 1998**
>
> **Henry Hyde again briefed our conference: "The Democrats' plan is to try and limit the scope of our inquiry. No way. There is plenty out there against Clinton. We'd be nuts to narrow the scope. They also will demand a time limit; our**

answer will be no. Fred Thompson said it was his greatest mistake to agree to a time limit in his Senate investigation of Clinton because the Democrats just ran out the clock.

"We got a strong letter from [House Democrat leader] Gephardt urging us to use the Watergate model. After he sent the letter, he went back and learned the Democrats weren't too generous to the Republicans during Watergate, so now they don't want Watergate to be the model. They are standing on two stools that are separating and I hope they get a hell of a hernia.

"The Democrats on the Judiciary Committee are the most extreme liberals—the hardest of the hard liners. The Democrats don't want this question on the House floor, but it will be on the House floor. The bottom line is this: if the president can't tell the truth and has no credibility at home or abroad, that should decide the issue for you and for me."

House Banking Committee Chairman Jim Leach (R-IA) reported that 14 criminal convictions came out of Starr's investigation of Whitewater, which involved 41 criminal acts, including two frauds against the U.S. Government. He suggested the Judiciary Committee use this information in its review. Majority Whip Tom DeLay added, "The entire picture of Clinton shows a pattern of conduct demonstrating his unfitness to be president."

Speaker Gingrich urged Republicans to avoid a civil war over the next ten days that would divert attention from Clinton's problems. "We need to appear calm and in control as we proceed," he said. "The odds are one-in-three that Clinton will find a way to shut down the government in the next few days. Clinton continues to show his 'contrition-confrontation continuum.' Nobody knows where he'll be next week."

Newt closed the meeting solemnly:

"Your vote next week on whether to have an impeachment inquiry is a vote of conscience. The whip organization will apply no pressure on any member. Democrats should take the same pledge. It is a constitutional question. The key is not the outcome; the key is how our grandchildren will view our effort 50 years from now."

Following this GOP conference, Henry again asked to meet briefly with the Judiciary Republicans. Once we assembled, he suggested we mention in our weekend press interviews that fairness dictates—and we will allow—the president to have the opportunity to mount a defense before the committee. Then he told us all to go home and spend a little time with our families before the fireworks started anew.

As he got up to leave the room, Henry paused by the door, turned, and then looked back at us.

"Come Monday," he said solemnly, "we will all be a part of history."

14

Dress Rehearsal

Sunday, October 4, was the day before the Judiciary Committee began hearings on whether to recommend that the House begin formal impeachment hearings against President Clinton. That morning I awoke to the sound of my home fax machine humming as it cranked out a stack of talking points. I had little time to do more than skim these documents, since ABC News again scheduled me for a morning debate on their *This Week* Sunday news show.

In the pile that morning was a list of "key questions" our staff urged us to ask in every interview and speech over the next few days:

- Would you expect the law to hold one of your constituents accountable for lying to a federal grand jury or to a federal judge?

- Does lying to a federal grand jury or to a federal judge undermine the rule of law?

- Does the president's oath of office require him to uphold and abide by the rule of law?

After arriving at the ABC television studio, I joined Senate Majority Leader Trent Lott (R-MS) and House Democrat Leader Dick Gephardt (D-MO) in the green room. My Judiciary Committee colleague Barney Frank and I were to debate in one segment; he arrived late and not long before airtime.

Diary, October 4, 1998

When Barney Frank joined us in the green room, he said nothing other than grunting an acknowledgment to our cheery "good morning," and then he plopped down in the middle of our group and began working a crossword puzzle. Aside from mumbling occasional side comments (and never looking up from his puzzle while doing so), he remained silent.

Lott asked Gephardt what tomorrow's House Judiciary Committee meeting would be like. Barney chimed in sarcastically, "It will be 37 people all trying to do their very best Barbara Jordan imitation [Jordan, a congresswoman during the committee's Watergate hearings, became a national celebrity with her dignified, stentorian voice].

Gephardt teased Barney for being so antisocial and asked why he worked a crossword puzzle instead of joining our conversation. Barney (still not looking up), said, "I knew there wouldn't be any conversation of substance in this room, so I thought, 'Why bother?'"

Across town, Chairman Hyde appeared on Fox News with Tony Snow. Henry made headlines (and raised his colleagues' eyebrows) when Snow asked how long any formal impeachment deliberations might last: "My New Year's resolution is to end it by the New Year. If [the Democrats are] forthcoming, they could give us a series of stipulations now and not force us to prove things. If they would do that, we could short-circuit this immensely." Although Henry later explained he meant the Democrats could stipulate to Clinton's perjury, obstruction of justice, and the charges that Dave Schippers would lay out tomorrow, the Democrats jumped on his "end it by the New Year" comment as fodder to push their proposal to limit the entire review to 30 days.

• • •

On Monday morning, October 5, shortly before Chairman Hyde convened our committee, he scheduled his usual pre-hearing meeting of Judiciary Republicans:

Diary, Judiciary Republicans Meeting, October 5, 1998

Henry mentioned his Tony Snow interview yesterday where he said his New Year's resolution is to end the inquiry by year's end. "We won't be bound by that date," he assured us. "It invites delay. When these guys [the Democrats] have subpoena power, they will use it and abuse it."

I argued against an artificial deadline: "With no deadline, this committee controls the inquiry. With a deadline, we give control of the process to those from whom we are trying to obtain evidence. We are here to search for the truth, and that should be a search where our committee controls the process."

Moving to another topic, Henry said, "The Democrats are insisting we study the 'standards for impeachment' before we review the evidence. In Watergate, Peter Rodino rejected that as a dumb idea. The Founders gave us a general standard of what defines an impeachable offense. The Democrats just want to use this as an excuse to play semantic games."

I also raised the suggestion that we might want to surprise the Democrats today and accept their alternative motion to hold a hearing on what constitutes an impeachable offense. I felt this wouldn't prejudice our case, it would take some of the political wind out of their sails, and it would push the threat of Clinton's impeachment to the sidelines until after the November elections. Henry dismissed the idea outright, saying, "It's too late for that."

"As for the scope of our inquiry now," Henry said, "we will only be looking at what is contained in the Starr report. There are other things of which we need to be cognizant, like Whitewater, Filegate, and so on. We may need to review these things later."

We took our seats in the crowded Judiciary Committee room. Henry banged his gavel; after he and John Conyers made opening statements, each committee member received five minutes for the same opportunity, with the chairman alternating between Republicans and Democrats in seniority order. Since I was near the bottom of the ladder, I had a couple of hours before he recognized me.

As the morning wore on, Henry passed the gavel so he could take a break and leave the committee room. A few minutes later, chief counsel Tom Mooney asked me to join the chairman in his private office. Closing the door, Henry chomped on his big cigar while letting off steam. He still seethed over our two Republican committee members—Asa Hutchinson (R-AR) and Lindsey Graham (R-SC)—for holding and then publicizing their side meetings with Democrats. Although mad at both, he reserved special grumpiness for Asa:

Diary, House Judiciary Committee Hearing, October 5, 1998

Henry thinks Asa is not a team player and that he is playing into the hands of the Democrats by trying to cut side deals with them through his breakfast club meetings. Henry said if Asa doesn't clean up his act, he won't be on the Judiciary Committee next year.

I told Henry I had gotten to know both Asa and Lindsey well and that he could count on them. Further, I told him several committee Republicans attended one or more of these breakfasts at their joint invitation. I went to one myself and found it to be more of a coffee klatch than anything of particular significance. I offered to speak to them about these ongoing meetings (which is what I think Henry wanted and the reason he raised the issue with me). In any event, whatever irritation Henry harbored about Asa and Lindsey dissipated. When we later moved to full impeachment mode, both ended up as key players who enjoyed the chairman's complete confidence.

Changing subjects, Henry again expressed confidence that Dave Schippers' presentation today would reverse Bill Clinton's sky-high poll approval ratings:

"When Schippers makes his presentation today, people will get their first good look at what this is about." Looking ahead, he told me that when and if this goes to the Senate for trial, he will have a great management team to try the case against Clinton there, "and you will play a big part in it."

By that last comment, I assumed Henry meant I would be there as a junior member helping to support our senior colleagues tasked with the job of prosecuting Clinton. I'm not sure how I would have felt had I interpreted his words differently.

• • •

I returned to my seat in the committee room for my own five-minute opening statement. Knowing this occasion was historic, I labored on my brief speech over the weekend. That's why my seatmate Lindsey Graham surprised me as our turn to address a national audience approached: he sat doodling on a pad with no prepared remarks in front of him. When I suggested he should draft something for this important event, he just shrugged.

"What are you going to say?" I asked.

Lindsey put down his pencil, turned toward me and replied, "Jim, I'm the first Republican elected in my district since Reconstruction. I'm not sure what I'm going to say here today. I only know that when I say it, I'm going to leave myself a big back door."

After committee members concluded their opening remarks, Hyde recognized the Republicans' lead investigator, David Schippers, to present formally his interpretation of the evidence against President Clinton:

Dave Schippers sat at the witness table surrounded by photographers. Beads of sweat moistened his brow as he began reading his 48-page speech setting forth the list of impeachable offenses and the evidence that shows President Clinton committed them. In a slow, clear, and effective presentation aided by charts, he laid out the grounds to impeach Clinton.

When Dave finished, Abbe Lowell for the Democrats reviewed the same evidence and came to a far different conclusion: Clinton only wanted to hide an embarrassing extramarital affair. Like so many Democrat committee members earlier, Lowell went beyond an evidentiary discussion and attacked Judge Starr, saying he tried to "usurp the constitutional role of the House." Lowell concluded that Clinton committed no acts that rose to the constitutional impeachment standard of "high crimes and misdemeanors."

Following these presentations, Chairman Hyde introduced a resolution recommending that the House authorize the Judiciary Committee to begin a formal impeachment inquiry. Rick Boucher (D-VA) introduced an amendment to Henry's resolution to limit the review to 30 days. As my diary notes from this hearing indicate, once Boucher introduced his resolution:

Every Democrat sought recognition on the amendment. Chairman Hyde wanted to move the debate along, but his press secretary insisted that a Republican committee member speak after every Democrat so that the Democrats didn't dominate the debate for the television audience.

Boucher's amendment went down to defeat on a straight Party-line vote, as did another amendment by Howard Berman (D-CA) to limit the scope of the review. Other Democrats had additional amendments, but as the evening wore on, John Conyers called a caucus of his members. When they returned to the committee room, the Democrats withdrew their stack of additional amendments. According to our staff, Conyers feared that the continued presentation of dilatory amendments would make the Democrats "look bad on after-dinner television."

• • •

Late that evening, the committee approved Chairman Hyde's resolution to recommend the House authorize an inquiry into whether President Clinton deserved impeachment. With passage of the resolution, the measure now moved to the House floor for debate. Adopting the resolution in committee by a straight Party-line vote fed the Democrats repeated charge of partisanship. A White House spokesman chimed in, claiming the refusal of any committee Democrat to back the resolution proved its passage was "unfair and unwarranted." I felt the only truly "unfair" result of our committee's action was the willingness of many in the mainstream press to give Democrats the story they sought.

As their opening statements showed, most Republicans remained temperate and desirous of keeping an open mind. Several stated specifically they would not support impeachment unless the evidence warranted such drastic action. By contrast, not a single Democrat made the reverse pledge: to keep an open mind and vote to impeach

Clinton if the evidence justified it. Instead, they mainly used their opening statements to attack the process, attack Ken Starr, attack Newt Gingrich, and attack the Republicans generally. One hysterical Democrat accused us of attempting a coup d'état on the United States. Another called our hearing a "kangaroo court." A third likened us to Hitler's Nazi regime. One even suggested a correlation between these impeachment proceedings and the specter of slavery.

Beyond this disgraceful demagoguery, the committee Democrats maintained unanimity in their approach to the evidence:

- Not one Judiciary Committee Democrat addressed the fact that Clinton engaged in a pattern of lies and obstruction of justice to destroy Paula Jones' right to bring a sexual harassment lawsuit against him, even after the United States Supreme Court ruled that she had that right.

- Not one Judiciary Committee Democrat ever expressed any concern over Clinton's personal profit motive in destroying through lies Jones' right to recover monetary damages against him if his behavior warranted it.

- Not one Judiciary Committee Democrat said they would review the evidence and consider any of these allegations as grounds for impeachment if found to be true.

Not one Judiciary Committee Democrat demanded an accounting when the leader of their Party used his position of power to try and intimidate an unwilling and lowly female subordinate Arkansas state employee into having an unwanted sexual relationship with him.

For once on this issue, that White House spokesman was right. The refusal of any committee Democrat to back the resolution proved there was "unfair and unwarranted" behavior in our committee.

It just wasn't for the reason he suggested.

15

Circus Performers

With the full House of Representatives now gearing up to determine whether to authorize the Judiciary Committee's formal impeachment hearings, several moderate Republican congressmen suggested they might vote with the Democrats to limit the time and scope of the hearing. Speaker Gingrich summoned our Republican conference to a meeting on the eve of the floor debate:

Diary, House Republican Conference, October 7, 1998

Newt assured everyone that leadership "isn't twisting any arms. But before you vote with Howard Berman [senior Democrat on the House Judiciary Committee pushing for a limited review], I beg you to talk to the Republican members of the committee who voted unanimously for the inquiry."

At our last Judiciary Committee internal meeting, Henry Hyde closed the door on any inquiry expansion beyond Lewinsky. Now, before the entire GOP House conference, this ever-swinging gate popped back open with Henry repeating an earlier hint of some bombshell information that he could not share immediately. He also addressed the various concerns of some of our wobblier members:

"Should we agree to the Democrat demand that we hold hearings to adopt a definition of what is an 'impeachable offense'? No. Why should we have a hearing on whether to have a hearing?

"Every accommodation will be given to the president: the right to be present, the right to cross examine any witnesses, and so forth. The Democrats keep calling us unfair. I am almost a circus performer the way I'm bending over backwards for them. You can never do enough for them.

"Should we limit this inquiry to Lewinsky? No. If we do that, and then during the congressional recess Starr sends us information relating to Whitewater, Filegate, Travelgate, etc., we'll be hamstrung. Also, I won't agree to limit our review only to matters brought by the independent counsel. There are other areas I don't care to discuss now. They may come up later and they will deal with Clinton's fitness for office. If additional matters do come forward, and they will, then these are felonies and they must be reviewed. There are things I can't talk about now. You need to trust me. You will be there at the landing, and you will be very pleased."

Committee staff added fuel to the speculation fire when they passed out copies of a letter delivered earlier that day to Hyde and Conyers from Judge Starr confirming that additional matters "continue to be under active investigation and review by this Office. Consequently, I cannot foreclose the possibility of providing the House of Representatives with additional substantial and credible information arising from those investigations that William Jefferson Clinton committed acts that may constitute grounds for an impeachment."

Diary, House Floor, October 8, 1998

There has been great speculation last night and this morning as to how many Democrats will vote today for the Republican open-ended (no time limit) resolution authorizing an impeachment inquiry. News reports this morning project that scores of Democrats may defect and vote with the Republicans despite furious lobbying by the White House. According to some Democrat colleagues, Bill Clinton, Hillary Clinton, and Al Gore have all been working the phones. Hillary Clinton has reportedly threatened that any Democrat who votes for an inquiry will never get any help from the White House again....

10:47 a.m.: The Democrats are requesting we extend the debate from the scheduled one hour to eight hours. Henry just told me he will give them an extra hour in exchange for them making no additional procedural motions.

I see six Democrats standing over Bart Stupak (D-MI) working him over to get his vote for the Democrat alternative resolution. The same sort of intense lobbying is also focused now on Democrats Gary Condit (D-CA), Ellen Tauscher (D-CA), and Jim Turner (D-TX). [Democrat leader] Dick Gephardt and John Conyers are actively lobbying on the floor. Meanwhile, Speaker Newt Gingrich is silently watching the activity from his chair at the rostrum.

10:59 a.m.: Henry Hyde opened the debate with a unanimous consent request for doubling the debate time from one hour to two. Conyers asked him to double it again; Henry declined the request.

Shortly after the debate began, Republican Judiciary Committee counsel Jon Dudas said they had budgeted time for me to speak right after Mary Bono (R-CA). I was unprepared for this news. Henry told us at our last meeting that he would contact by last night those he wanted included in today's debate. As it turned out, his staffer did call the night before to tell me to get ready, but my intern taking the message forgot to pass it along.

While the debate on the floor continued, I went back to my office and cobbled together a speech quickly. I returned to the House floor and sat with Mary Bono. We were nervous. She decided to jettison her prepared remarks and hurriedly attempted a complete rewrite. As her time neared, she said she wanted to back out and offer her time to another member. I urged her to go forward. Our side needed an articulate woman who was not a lawyer to give our presentation more strength. She trembled a bit when she rose to address the chamber, but she did a great job.

Knowing I was next, I cleared my throat and took a deep breath. Instead of yielding to me, Henry moved "a call of the House." This is a procedural motion reserved usually for the final closing speeches on a very significant piece of legislation. It requires all House members to return to the chamber and record their presence on the voting machines. I breathed a huge sigh of relief because I assumed that Henry ran out of time and no longer needed me in the lineup. Addressing the entire House of Representatives (along with a large contingent of the senators who had come to our chamber to witness the historic debate) with almost no preparation held little appeal for me. I walked over to the committee staff and thanked them for getting me out of this situation.

"Oh, no," an aide told me. "Henry wants you to close the debate with him on behalf of the Judiciary Committee." My heart sank. He counted on me to get on base and I was barely prepared to walk to the plate. As the chamber filled with members, I went back to the Republican cloakroom and grabbed some scratch paper. I had 15 minutes to come up with something worthy of the moment.

When I returned to the House floor, there were no vacant seats in the vast chamber. Senators lined the back railing. Reporters and spectators jammed the visitors' galleries. I had never seen the House so crowded since State of the Union night.

The two senior Democrats on the committee, John Conyers and Barney Frank, closed the debate for their side. I didn't relish having to follow them. My heart pounded. Although I had spoken many times in the chamber, it was always to a nearly empty hall. Many of my Republican colleagues, especially my fellow freshmen, sent silent signals that they were rooting for me.

The moment came. Chairman Hyde yielded time "to the distinguished gentleman from California." The chamber was silent as I stepped to the microphone. It was an intimidating yet awesome sight to look over the lectern and see most of Congress looking back.

I departed from my notes to compliment both Conyers and Frank and express my respect for them. I think this caught the Democrats off guard because they expected me to launch into a tit-for-tat counterattack when I started.

I intended my brief remarks to impart a former judge's perspective in the midst of the highly charged battle:

Mr. Speaker: I start with the presumption that the president is deemed innocent of any allegation of wrongdoing unless and until the contrary is shown. Every reasonable inference that can be drawn in his favor must be drawn in his favor.

It is unfortunate that some of today's rhetoric suggests that this resolution seeks to give Congress carte blanche to inquire into the president's private life. Nothing could be further from the truth. However, it is both our purpose and our legal obligation to review any president's alleged constitutional misconduct within the framework of the Constitution and the rule of law. When serious and credible allegations have been raised against any president, the Constitution obliges us to determine whether such conduct violated his obligation to faithfully

execute the law. We must make this determination or else forever
sacrifice our noble heritage that no person is above the law.

This Congress must decide whether we will ignore allegations
respecting both the subversion of the courts and the search for truth.
I fear for my country when we no longer view perjury and obstruc-
tion of justice with opprobrium, but instead regard it as a sign of
political or legal finesse.

This House has an obligation to embrace the words of one of our
predecessors, Abraham Lincoln, who called on every American
lover of liberty not to violate the rule of law nor show toleration for
those who do. There is a difference between knowing the truth and
doing the truth. We have an obligation to both despite any political
discomfort it might bring. For as Justice Holmes once said, if justice
requires the truth to be known, the difficulty in knowing it is no
excuse to try. Let our body be faithful to this search.

I returned to my seat as colleagues greeted me with enthusiastic
applause from half of the chamber. The compliments of my fellow
freshmen were particularly gratifying, although I wasn't sure if their
kind words were for the message or for my delivering it without
fainting.

Gephardt (for the Democrats) and Hyde (for the Republicans)
then closed the debate. When the clerk tallied the votes, the House
approved the committee's Republican resolution to begin an
impeachment inquiry against President Clinton by a vote of 236 to
198. Despite heavy White House lobbying, *31 Democrats voted for*
the Republican version of the resolution. When one also considers the
votes cast for the Democrats' alternate resolution calling for a more
limited inquiry, a startling *429 of the 435 members of the House of*
Representatives voted for some form of an impeachment inquiry against
President William Jefferson Clinton.

For those who believed that the Clinton impeachment was a Republican partisan enterprise, you can blame your ignorance on the phony mainstream media and their hack pundits working as subsidiaries of the Clinton Propaganda Machine for propagating that lie.

16

Lipstick on a Pig

The day after my big speech and the vote to begin Clinton's impeachment hearings, I found myself face-to-face with the president. It proved an awkward moment for both of us. Clinton hosted a "Top Cops" ceremony for police bravery in the Rose Garden of the White House. Normally, I would have avoided the reception so as not to create discomfort, but with the president honoring one of my constituents—Los Angeles Police Officer Kevin Harley—I could not bypass his big day at the White House because of my tensions with Clinton.

Diary, The White House, October 9, 1998

In the White House Rose Garden, Attorney General Janet Reno offered brief remarks and then introduced a police union leader who showered Clinton with glowing tributes. During these speeches, I caught Clinton staring at me a few times, but he looked away each time I made eye contact with him.

After Clinton's speech, he walked over to shake hands with the congressional delegation present. When he reached me, I put out my hand, offered a greeting, and asked how he was holding up. He didn't look at me directly. Instead, he fixed his gaze on my forehead. "It's a great day for law enforcement," he said robotically, and then he moved on. It was weird.

After the uncomfortable encounter, I returned to the Capitol in time for our scheduled Republican Judiciary meeting. We had much work to do and precious little time in which to do it, especially since Henry kept telling reporters he wanted to abide by his "New Year's Resolution" to have our hearing done before year's end:

Diary, House Republican Meeting, October 9, 1998

Henry said we would do nothing before the November 3 congressional elections. Meanwhile, he said our staff was drafting an outline of potential articles of impeachment: "We will try to pick the best, most understandable, and the most 'saleable to the public' grounds for impeachment. When we present them, it will be an educational document for the public."

Henry confirmed that one of his subcommittees would hold a hearing under the direction of its chairman, Charles Canady (R-FL), on a scholarly review of historic constitutional impeachment standards. Henry said, "Its purpose is not to define an impeachable offense. Congress has never defined that standard in the history of the Republic. The Democrats' 1974 Watergate staff report on impeachment stated that 'the process does not lend itself to a fixed or rigid definition; the standard must be sufficiently flexible to meet individual circumstances and events, now and in the future.'"

Henry remained confident that once the public heard the whole story of Clinton's greedy motivation in the Paula Jones case (as opposed to the shibboleth that we wanted him impeached over an affair), the polls would change. However, even with that faith, he must have worried that his group of stuffy, pudgy, middle-aged white male Republican lawyers was no media match for the Democrats and their simplistic refrain that "it's about sex." The Democrats were raw, emotional, hip, and masters of slash-and-burn combat.

When they accused us of being a bunch of Puritanical stiffs on a sexual witch-hunt, our bland and monochromatic appearance before the cameras fed that image. Henry decided we needed to undergo a crash course in media charm-school training:

Diary, October 10, 1998

At Henry's request, pollster and message crafter Dr. Frank Luntz met with our group of Judiciary Committee Republicans. Dr. Luntz urged us to emulate a folksy approach and tried to teach us how to do it. Looking directly at me, he suggested we not sound so "lawyerly and judicial."

I didn't view it as my charge to fake folksiness or charm. I was there to do the biggest job of my life. That meant, at least for me, approaching Clinton's impeachment as a former prosecutor and judge, and not as a play-acting politician coached by handlers. Ignoring Frank's helpful advice probably gave me some feeling of anti-politician pureness of motive. I still believe that approaching it my way was noble. It was stupid, but it was noble.

• • •

After Judge Starr delivered his report in September, Newt tantalized us with how our expected big win in the November midterm elections would realign our country:

Diary, House Republican Conference Meeting, September 15, 1998

Newt said, "If we can take 250 GOP House seats in November [up from our current 228 members], the Democrats will crumble in two years on both incumbent retention and challenger recruitment efforts. If we go above 250, we will change the core balance of power in this country."

He added with disdain, "The generations of Washington and Lincoln are gone. Ours is represented by Bill Clinton."

By October, Speaker Gingrich had a laser-like focus: pass the federal budget, get his troops home to campaign for reelection, and increase our Republican majority on November 3. Each goal depended on the other. We couldn't leave Washington until we finished the budget, and we couldn't finish the budget until Newt and his leadership team negotiated a deal with Clinton. In order to do so, Clinton demanded compromises that increased federal spending in many areas. Newt's capitulation on these points inflamed our conservative base and ignited a growing rebellion in our ranks.

During these negotiations, Newt briefed us almost daily. He kept emphasizing how our leadership team killed many White House spending priorities (like proposed free hypodermic needles for drug addicts, school testing standards, statistical sampling on the 2000 census, and countless other items on Clinton's wish list). However, these victories did nothing to mollify many conservatives. They hammered Newt, and not Clinton, for signing off on other administration programs.

At his October 12 briefing, Newt pleaded for unity. Unmoved, conservative budget hawks criticized him harshly for making unavoidable compromises. Newt warned us not to go home and "trash" the budget. If we did, he predicted it would depress our voter base and hurt Republican candidates nationwide next month. "Compromise is a reality," he declared. "It is the cost of divided government. Clinton is a liar. If anyone in the country hasn't figured that out yet, then they never will. We need to get this budget passed, go home, and come back with a bigger Republican majority."

Newt still believed that Clinton's scandals would drag down the House Democrats on Election Day. He had been predicting confidently for months that November would bring us huge GOP gains. Always the history professor, he reminded us that in the last century presidents in the sixth year of an eight-year run averaged a loss of 30 House seats in the midterm elections, and that did not factor in Clinton's multiple scandals that he believed would increase our margin over the average. He renewed his longstanding prediction of a 30-to-40 seat GOP pickup.

In the end, Newt threw the dice. He leaned hard on his conference to accept a budget agreement that, for conservatives like me, had all the attractiveness of a pig wearing lipstick. Instead of digging in and rejecting Clinton's big-spending wish list, he conceded many points to forge a deal. With that, he staked his speakership on the promise of a more muscular Republican House majority returning in January to undo the devil's bargain to which he had agreed three months earlier.

• • •

Once our GOP leadership concluded a budget agreement with the White House, most House Republicans (like me) held their nose and voted for it. On that last night of session, I recorded one final diary entry from Washington before I flew home to face the voters for the first time as an incumbent congressman on the front lines of The Clinton Wars:

Diary, House Chamber, October 20, 1998

Our last recorded vote of the 105th Congress was on passage of the federal budget conference report. After casting my vote, I lingered for a while on the House floor while taking in the moment. Many retiring senior members had just cast their final vote after decades of service in the chamber. The anticlimactic nature of the scene struck me as odd. There were isolated handshakes and hugs, but for the most part no solemnity marked the moment. Most members treated this vote as any other: they entered the chamber when the bells sounded, cast their vote electronically with their voting card, and then they turned and walked out.

It has been a great thrill and privilege serving my community and my country in Washington. I don't know whether I will return next year. I am taking a pounding back home from my opponent. Republican registration in my district is now down to 34 percent and dropping. Some things I can't change, and a changing demographic is one of them. Also, there is no telling how my involvement on the House Judiciary Committee will hurt me on Election Day. We will see.

I shook hands with Speaker Gingrich and thanked him for all he had done for me these last two years. His reply was devoid of any sentimentality: "Go home and win," he said.

As I left the chamber for the last time before the election, I reflected on the irony. When I won my seat in Congress in 1996, I turned down Henry Hyde's repeated entreaties to join his controversial Judiciary Committee because it would put me on the wrong side of too many issues with my Democrat constituency. Later, I agreed to come on the committee to work on intellectual property issues. Instead, I inherited a high-profile position in the most bitterly partisan political battle of the twentieth century.

Following the 1998 congressional elections on November 3, Judiciary Committee members would return to Washington to make history. Chairman Hyde had a role for me to play in it, but if I lost reelection, then I'd watch that history unfold from my television set back home in Southern California.

• • •

The day after Congress adjourned, I flew home to California to battle for my House seat. My first event was a joint appearance with former President Gerald Ford. Once again, he brought along a bit of heartburn. In a recent *New York Times* opinion piece, Ford urged Congress to drop impeachment.

**Diary, Rogan for Congress Campaign Event with
President Gerald R. Ford, October 21, 1998**

Before the event, Ford and I chatted privately. He called
Clinton "disgraceful and dishonest." I asked if he ever dreamed
that a president in the White House could behave as Clinton
had and then have the American people greet his conduct with
indifference. "No," he said angrily, "and it's a disgrace."

Later, during the question and answer session at our
campaign reception, someone asked Ford if his recent op-ed
in the *New York Times* had generated positive feedback.
"Oh, my, yes," he exclaimed. He reiterated his position that
Clinton should not be impeached. The House should make
him stand in the well of the chamber and listen while a censure resolution is read aloud to him and with no rebuttal
right. "The unprecedented humiliation would be punishment
enough," Ford opined.

I listened politely—and silently—to Ford's comments.

• • •

I don't know if impeachment helped other Republicans nationwide,
but it was killing me in Los Angeles County. From the time I first
won my seat, I had worked the Democrat precincts of my district
assiduously. I knocked on their doors, made random phone calls
to constituents to see if they needed help, and held innumerable
town hall meetings and sidewalk office hours. I danced at their
weddings and bar mitzvahs, worshipped in their churches, handed
out flags to their Eagle Scouts and medals to their young academic
scholars. I painted over their graffiti, swept their sidewalks, walked
their dogs, raced their kids on scooters, and did anything else my
creative district staff dreamed up to show we cared.

Going into the 1998 election, our efforts paid off. After winning in 1996 by a mere 50.1 percent, we built up a comfortable 15-point lead over my competitor before impeachment heated up. Once the House began its debate over removing Clinton, that hefty double-digit lead evaporated almost overnight.

Diary, Tuesday, October 27, 1998
(One Week Before Election Day)

Ten days ago, my campaign was ahead 15 points. Last week my lead dropped to ten points; we were ahead only six points last night, and tonight we are only two points ahead. My staff is frantic. The Democrats in my district have rallied to Clinton's defense. I used to get support from about 30 percent of district Democrats; my latest poll shows I now get only a 10 percent crossover from them. If I lose, I will lose because I undertook a tough responsibility. I guess there are worse reasons for being defeated.

Diary, October 28, 1998

We cling to a bare two-point lead. I would hate being removed from the Judiciary Committee at this historic time, but it is in the Lord's hands.

I may have been calm, but alarm bells went off among friends over my predicament. Newt Gingrich, Majority Leader Dick Armey, and other colleagues offered to send more money. In the final days, I turned down most offers: more money at this point wouldn't help. We needed to turn out Republican voters and hold back the slide.

In his final phone conversation with me on election eve, Newt sounded glum. Gone now were his predictions of a 30-to-40-seat gain. Still, in suggesting a silver lining, he said, "Even if we lose you and four or five other heartbreak cases, we should still have a net gain of six House seats."

• • •

On Election Day, Newt didn't pick up those six extra House seats. Instead, Democrats knocked off five incumbent Republican congressmen and trimmed the number of Republicans from 228 to 223. The House GOP was now only six seats away from losing their majority. Gratefully, I was not one of our defeated veterans. I squeaked by with a bare 50.8 percent victory despite our state GOP gubernatorial nominee losing my county by a whopping 25 points.

I would return to Washington for the 106th Congress. However, I'd be returning to a city far different from the one I had left just two weeks earlier.

17

On Their Watch

"With the prospects that President Clinton will be impeached fading after last week's elections, the White House and congressional leaders are searching anxiously for an exit strategy [T]he Clinton camp has hardened its resistance to reaching a deal with the same terms it would have welcomed just a few weeks ago. Some emboldened Clinton confidants have gone so far as to argue against any concession, effectively daring the House to take an up-or-down vote. [Clinton] advisers are sensitive to the fear that [he] may grow cocky after the latest turn of events."

—PETER BAKER AND JOHN F. HARRIS,
WASHINGTON POST, NOVEMBER 9, 1998

T he ink had not dried on the newspaper headlines about the Republicans' electoral disappointment before leaders on both sides, along with the media pundits, pronounced impeachment dead on arrival:

"My analysis today would be either the Judiciary Committee doesn't pass [articles of impeachment], or, if they do, that there won't be the votes in the House to move it to the Senate. Since the election, I've talked to at least 100 members. Maybe three or four have brought up the impeachment question and all of them have brought it up in the context of how quickly we can get it over with."
—CONGRESSMAN BILL PAXON (R-NY), FORMER CHAIRMAN,
NATIONAL REPUBLICAN CONGRESSIONAL COMMITTEE

"The American people have certainly indicated in the polls that they don't see [the Lewinsky scandal] as an impeachable or dismissible offense."
—HOUSE APPROPRIATIONS COMMITTEE CHAIRMAN BOB
LIVINGSTON (R-LA)

"What impeachment? There aren't the votes to move impeachment if all we have in front of us is the information we have now."
—CONGRESSMAN MARK SOUDER (R-IN)

"As far as impeachment is concerned, it's about to go the way of the dodo.... Republicans should take Newt's belt and shoelaces away from him."
—JAY SEVERIN, REPUBLICAN STRATEGIST

"A nation that seems never to weary of seeing Newt Gingrich get his comeuppance watched him pile chips on the impeachment card and then let Hillary Rodham Clinton sweep them off the table. [America] wants a formal condemnation of Mr. Clinton for lying under oath and demeaning his office. But it also wants him to continue in office[.]"
—THE *NEW YORK TIMES*, NOVEMBER 5, 1998

"God, I'd like to forget all of this [impeachment business]. I mean, who needs it? We paid attention to the polls and the elections."
—HOUSE JUDICIARY COMMITTEE CHAIRMAN HENRY HYDE,
WASHINGTON POST, NOVEMBER 10, 1998

I was still sleeping after a late night of watching election returns when a predawn telephone call from Washington awakened me. On the phone was Kathryn Lehman, special assistant to Speaker Gingrich, who tracked me down:

Diary, Wednesday, November 4, 1998

Kathryn wanted to know "my read" on how the election results affected Newt's chances for reelection as speaker. I said I felt that Newt would get a lot of criticism but ultimately reelected if he fought for it. Although many of our troops will gripe about our losses, he is still the man who won our first Republican majority in 40 years, and yesterday won twice-reelected Republican majorities for the first time since the 1920s.

Kathryn agreed and lamented how some of our members who win reelection with over a 70 percent majority will attack Newt while guys like me who squeak out a 50 percent win will stand firm by him.

On the plane back to Washington the next day, I started wading through the stack of telephone messages from Republican colleagues lobbying for conference leadership changes. The biggest surprise came when close Gingrich ally and friend Bob Livingston (chairman of the House Appropriations Committee) declared his candidacy against Newt for speaker. In announcing his run, Bob said that the election results showed "the American people want more than politicians with good speeches. They want politicians with ideas."

The weathervane shifted quickly away from Newt. Congressman Matt Salmon (R-AZ) announced he would not vote for Gingrich. Even Chairman Hyde expressed uncertainty as to whether Newt would (or should) survive, and he gave the embattled speaker little encouragement. "Leadership takes credit when things go right,"

Henry told a Chicago press conference. "They ought to take the blame when things go wrong." Congressman David McIntosh (R-IN) circulated a white paper to Republican colleagues cataloguing Gingrich's failures to abide by true conservative principles.

Newt's inner circle took the Livingston challenge seriously. Within an hour of Livingston's announcement, my office received a fax from the speaker's office marked "CRITICAL," and attached a list of colleagues for me to call and plead Newt's case. Meanwhile, my staff reached me in Pennsylvania and said the speaker wanted me back at the Capitol immediately. I got in my car and headed back to Washington:

Diary, Friday, November 6, 1998

By the time I drove back to Washington, NBC News reported that Newt had pulled out of the speakership race and announced that he would resign from Congress. The news has stunned everyone. I am saddened beyond words. He has been a friend during my tenure in Congress. To see the architect of the GOP House majority dumped like this is hard to watch. He should be in the GOP pantheon; his troops have instead relegated him to the dustbin.

Within the hour, Newt's office called and asked me to dial in to a conference call with him:

**Diary, Conference Call with Speaker Gingrich,
6:41 p.m., November 6, 1998**

Newt sounded cheerful as he broke the news to us. "For the future of the House Republicans, it is better for me not to be a candidate for speaker. We need to purge the poison and get the bitterness out of the system. As long as I am there, the

news media will always use me as a target and not let Republicans get out their message. Looking to the 2000 elections, I'm not the person to bring the House together. I'm incapable of cementing that unity. It is important that Republicans pull together, or this White House will tear us apart."

After various members on the line pleaded for Newt to reconsider, he closed the call: "The House Republicans are my extended family. You have given me tremendous honors. I love you all." With that, the phone clicked dead.

• • •

It took only a couple of days for Bob Livingston to consolidate his victory. In the interim, Henry Hyde scheduled a conference call for Judiciary Republicans. He sounded deflated as he laid out a significantly abbreviated timeline for the impeachment hearing. We would call just one witness—Judge Starr—and only to have him outline his report. Both Henry's tone and message signaled that from here on we'd just be going through the motions:

Diary, Judiciary Republicans Conference Call,
November 4, 1998

"Congratulations to all of you on your reelections," Henry said. "Yesterday was a disaster. We need to resolve this matter. Sorry to intrude on your celebrations, but this turkey will be over by Christmas." Henry said he would send a letter to Clinton tomorrow asking him to stipulate to certain facts. "I won't release my stipulations to the press," he said. "If the press wants them, they can get them from the White House. I don't expect the White House to be of any help. We will be ready to proceed without their help.

"Once we finish with Starr's testimony on November 19, we'll have Dave Schippers and Abbe Lowell summarize the

evidence for the committee. Our theme will be that we will do what it takes to resolve this early."

Not wanting to leave his colleagues with a sense that our future efforts were meaningless window-dressings, or perhaps because Henry didn't want any of us becoming independent deal-cutters operating outside of his purview, he ended the call on a note out of rhythm with his earlier message:

"If you are talking to the Democrats, don't make any commitments regarding any 'deal' to wrap this up. There will be facts that come out that may change people's minds. Meanwhile, we'll get our Senate impeachment Managers [prosecutors] fitted for striped pants and cutaway coats."

That last sentence suggested, to the untrained ear, that Henry still held a belief that the full House might impeach Clinton. I certainly did not believe that would happen. Moreover, I don't think anyone else, including Henry Hyde, believed it, either.

• • •

Two days after the election, Henry Hyde released a press statement saying the election results would not deter the Judiciary Committee from completing its impeachment inquiry. Privately, however, his "do our duty" statement masked what was happening behind the scenes. Suddenly, from many Republican leadership sources, we were getting the word privately: *Make impeachment go away.*

In our meeting of Judiciary Republicans a few days after the election, Henry expressed his frustration: "National conservative leaders were calling us cowards before the election for not pursuing an impeachment inquiry aggressively enough. Now they are calling on us to cut and run."

Unrecorded in my diary, but vivid in my memory, are two calls I received from senior staff of both Speaker Gingrich and Speaker-designate Livingston. The calls came two hours apart, but the messages were identical: "The speaker doesn't want this to be the (last thing) (first thing) on his watch." I told Gingrich's representative that, for all practical purposes, Newt wasn't speaker any longer, and I told Livingston's representative that Bob wasn't speaker yet. And I told them both to be prepared for this ending up as the last thing/first thing on their respective watches.

18

No Adult Supervision

"The Chairman recognizes, as does the Judiciary Committee, that to be locked into a time limit to complete our review would be totally irresponsible and unwise."

—CHAIRMAN PETER RODINO (D-NJ), HOUSE JUDICIARY COMMITTEE, REJECTING A TIME LIMIT FOR HIS DEMOCRAT-CONTROLLED COMMITTEE TO INVESTIGATE WATERGATE

"No."

—CONGRESSMAN JOHN CONYERS (D-MI), HOUSE JUDICIARY COMMITTEE MEMBER, 1974, IN VOTING ON THREE SEPARATE OCCASIONS AGAINST A TIME LIMIT FOR HIS DEMOCRAT-CONTROLLED COMMITTEE INVESTIGATION OF WATERGATE AND REPUBLICAN PRESIDENT RICHARD NIXON

"No."

—CONGRESSMAN JOHN CONYERS, HOUSE JUDICIARY COMMITTEE MEMBER, 1974, IN VOTING AGAINST A PROPOSAL TO LIMIT THE SCOPE OF HIS DEMOCRAT-CONTROLLED COMMITTEE INVESTIGATION OF WATERGATE AND REPUBLICAN PRESIDENT RICHARD NIXON

After the election debacle, it looked like the fix was in. Holding majorities in both houses of Congress did nothing to deflect everyone's perception that Clinton and the Democrats won and that we lost. Grabbing three consecutive Republican House majorities after 40 years didn't save Newt Gingrich. When the victory margin didn't meet expectations, his troops fragged him. Between the pundits, the polls, and the politicians, all agreed that the voters wanted Congress to find a big rug and sweep Clinton's dirt under it—now.

Before that could happen, one detail remained. Shortly before the election fiasco, the House had passed a resolution directing the Judiciary Committee to conduct an impeachment inquiry against Clinton after the election. The obligation still existed even if the duty now wafted through the air like the summer stench of a nearby landfill. No doubt the House would (if it could) countermand that order in light of the election results, but that option didn't exist. The 105th Congress already had adjourned permanently unless the now-highly unlikely occurred and the Judiciary Committee passed articles of impeachment.

Republican Judiciary Committee members regrouped to discuss where we go from here. In his book *The Breach: Inside the Impeachment and Trial of William Jefferson Clinton*, Peter Baker of the *Washington Post* described our group as "distracted, disoriented, and demoralized, and [returning to Washington] to find virtually no leadership left in their Party and no energy left in their grand adventure." He described a scene that I remember well. As Henry Hyde explained our need to wrap up this inquiry quickly and get it behind us,

> Rogan spoke up. Nobody had more to worry about politically than he did. A freshman who had won his seat by just a hair two years earlier in a Southern California district that included the liberal bastion of Hollywood, Rogan survived a scare in the

election a week before. In his district, impeachment could easily spell the end of his congressional career before it really got started.

"If anyone understands the potential for fallout, it's me," Rogan told his colleagues. "I won 50.8 percent of the vote. If [the Democrats] are going to make an example out of anyone on this committee, it's me." Then he tried a joke to lighten the mood.

"In 1996, we weren't impeaching Clinton, and I only got 50.1 percent. In 1998, we are impeaching him, and I got 50.8 percent. So, obviously, this issue is a political winner!"

People around the table laughed, and tension was broken. If Rogan was still willing to press ahead, his colleagues thought, then they should be, too.1

Dave Schippers' account in his impeachment memoir of that pivotal discussion left me humbled by his comments:

Jim Rogan was the voice of courage: "My race for reelection was the one where impeachment was the major issue," Rogan said "A former senator once told me years ago to put honor above incumbency. I believe that."

Rogan was talking my language. One by one other Republicans agreed with him. From that moment on there was no question that my staff and I were associated with 21 of the most courageous and decent people on the American political scene. When I told my staff about the meeting, [investigator] Jeff Pavletic said, "Well, now it's up to us to be worthy of them." We had a new life and a new goal.[2]

1   Peter Baker, *The Breach: Inside the Impeachment and Trial of William Jefferson Clinton* (2000).

2   David Schippers with Alan P. Henry, *Sellout: The Inside Story of President Clinton's Impeachment* (2000),

• • •

The 37 Judiciary Committee members returned to finish their unpleasant business with Washington largely deserted. Most congressmen were still home for the holidays or globe-trotting on junkets. While our now-lame duck Speaker Gingrich packed his office, our incoming Speaker-designate Livingston busied himself contemplating the job he wouldn't assume until next year.

Although I didn't recognize it then, the timing of the Judiciary Committee's return to Washington was one of those historical accidents where a slight repositioning of circumstances might have allowed Bill Clinton to escape impeachment. The only reason committee members rushed back to town after the election was by pre-arrangement with the House Democrats, who had earlier demanded that we complete the inquiry by the end of the year. What if we had agreed to start the hearing after the new 106th Congress began in January? Alternatively, what would have happened if the entire House had previously agreed to return to Washington after the election instead of adjourning? Would the presence of some 400 additional congressmen in the Capitol (with most lobbying hard to end impeachment, albeit for different reasons) have made a difference? During these critical days, Gingrich was out but Livingston was not yet in. Would a consolidated, brawny speakership have rung down the impeachment curtain in the interest of political damage control?

Had any of these "what ifs" been in play when the Judiciary Committee returned to finish its work, Clinton probably would not have suffered anything more severe than a mild spanking. However, the stars under which we returned aligned otherwise.

• • •

November 3 might have left Clinton and his team elated and smug, but at least a few House Democrats understood Yogi Berra's maxim, "It ain't over 'til it's over." My friend and freshman colleague on the Judiciary Committee, Bill Delahunt (D-MA), himself a former prosecutor, called me. Along with Howard Berman (D-CA), Bill's earlier publicized "breakfast club" meetings with Republican committee members Lindsey Graham and Asa Hutchinson received press attention (and got both Republicans in trouble with Henry Hyde). Now Bill reached out to me in a similar vein:

Diary, November 11, 1998

Bill Delahunt called and said he wanted to have a "quiet, way off the record" talk. Given the election results, he doesn't want our committee to have to vote on articles of impeachment. He wants the committee to exercise its discretion and take a pass. He said Ken Starr is "dominated by real hard-chargers."

"My earlier efforts to forge a compromise with other Republicans on the Judiciary Committee didn't work," Bill said. "Lindsey Graham's and Asa Hutchinson's meetings with Howard Berman and me may have made Henry Hyde distrust them."

Bill said he wants to work quietly with me to reach a compromise—maybe a censure of Clinton instead of passing articles of impeachment. He doesn't believe there are enough votes in the House now to pass impeachment, and he's probably right.

I was noncommittal. I told Bill I'm always willing to listen, but I wouldn't do anything to undercut Chairman Hyde.

Bill warned me there was a precondition to any settlement or deal: "Clinton will *never* admit wrongdoing," he said. "He won't admit the stuff."

Although I never doubted Bill Delahunt's sincerity, I didn't take his overture too seriously for another reason: I didn't believe that he spoke with high-level White House authorization. Why? Over the previous months, and at both Newt's and Henry Hyde's request,

I spoke or met intermittently with two Clinton White House impeachment liaisons: former Congressmen Butler Derrick (D-SC) and Tom Downey (D-NY). My GOP leadership directed me to keep open a White House backchannel in the event our mutual interests later warranted forging a compromise short of impeachment.

Before I left Washington for the campaign recess, Tom Downey and I had scheduled a post-election lunch to assess the situation and see what could be done about it. Once we had the election results behind us, we had agreed to use that meeting to see if we could reach a possible compromise to avert impeachment.

After our GOP shellacking, I returned to Washington and spoke with Newt and Henry Hyde. With their blessings, along with the blessing of Bob Livingston (communicated to me through Henry), I called Tom to confirm our previously scheduled lunch date. Although Tom didn't know it, I would attend with authorization from my House leadership to negotiate a non-impeachment settlement.

Tom came on the line. He apologized and said that he needed to cancel our lunch. When I suggested an alternative date, he told me that we would have no further meetings. He said his White House contact instructed him to end our talks. When I asked why, he told me that his "principal" said the Republicans wouldn't dare impeach Clinton after their thrashing at the polls.

"I understand all that," I told him, "but remember that before the House adjourned last month, we passed a resolution ordering the Judiciary Committee to return to Washington after the elections and begin impeachment hearings. Those hearings are going to launch in a week or so despite the election results."

"Yes, I know."

"Tom, once those hearings start, if the genie escapes from the bottle, we might not be able to put him back."

"I know, but I have been directed by my principal to cut off all negotiations. I'm sorry, Jim."

Before we ended our call, I said, "Tom, I've got to know. Who's your principal that gave you this order?"

His answer stunned me: *Hillary Clinton.*

Of all the "what ifs" of the Clinton impeachment saga, this one remains the most ironic. Tom received his marching orders at a time when Newt Gingrich, Bob Livingston, and Henry Hyde all wanted to cut Republican losses and head for the exits.

A brief opportunity existed for Bill Clinton to avoid impeachment. His wife scuttled it. Her overconfidence proved to be more than a miscalculation. It became the reason her husband's legacy forever bears a tattoo.

• • •

Amid all this chaotic uncertainty, the House Republican conference met to bid goodbye to Speaker Newt Gingrich and to ratify Bob Livingston as our choice to replace him as speaker in the 106th Congress. Perhaps the most visionary speaker in congressional history said farewell in his own way:

**Diary, House Republican Conference Meeting,
Cannon Caucus Room, November 18, 1998**

In his farewell remarks to us as speaker, Newt Gingrich warned that, "The media in this city, along with the Democrats, will do all they can to convince you that you are losers." After going through a litany of GOP policy victories since capturing the majority in 1994, he acknowledged we lost more seats than we should have two weeks ago. "But lock this in your brains," he thundered. "You are the majority Party in the House. [Democrat leader] Dick Gephardt said this last election was 'a referendum.' He should know—he is the first Democrat leader in modern American history to have to turn over the speaker's gavel to the Republicans."

As the French say, *Le Roi est mort, vive le Roi*. It was time for Judiciary Republicans to get back to business—which now meant going through the bare motions to an apparently doomed impeachment hearing:

Diary, Judiciary Committee Republican Meeting, November 10, 1998

Henry Hyde said, "When we question Judge Starr, we need to focus on the facts, which we can establish through Starr's testimony and through the record that Dave Schippers will summarize. Dave will explain Lewinsky's role and then show Clinton's obstruction of justice when he told Lewinsky to sign a false affidavit in the Paula Jones case. Once he got her signature on the affidavit, he went to his Paula Jones deposition very cocky until he realized that Jones' attorneys had too much information. Meanwhile, the Democrats will use their time to attack Starr. Our answer is to remind people that if Starr was so unfair, Clinton could have ordered Attorney General Janet Reno to fire him."

• • •

On November 17, Republicans again met with Henry to discuss Starr's pending testimony before the committee:

Diary, House Judiciary Committee Republican Meeting, November 17, 1998

Henry spoke with great seriousness: "I want all of you to believe in what we are doing," he said. "This committee's action may be the only censure this man [Clinton] ever receives. Don't give up on the evidence. But we need to finish this by the end of the year. The new Congress will never

reconstitute us to continue any investigation of Clinton. We'll finish our committee work before December 7. Then the speaker can call back Congress if necessary to vote on any approved articles of impeachment."

Over these few months, Henry kept flip-flopping on the possibility of expanding our hearings beyond Monica Lewinsky to the point of sounding schizophrenic. Now, after accentuating the need to resolve the inquiry quickly, he raised the suggestion again:

Henry remains vague about discussing a possible inquiry expansion because he said someone in the room is leaking information to the press. He keeps asking us to "trust him" that he is working on something big. He thinks Ken Starr is trying to get imprisoned presidential pal Webster Hubbell to turn the state's evidence and testify that the $700,000 Clinton's friends paid to Hubbell for "consulting fees"—while Hubbell awaited prison surrender—was nothing more than "hush money."

"We're talking about Webster Hubbell being paid $700,000 for what?" Henry nearly shouted. "It's not treason; it's bribery!"

The Democrats sensed Henry wobbling back toward expanding our review, and he said that they issued him a warning: "The Democrats are demanding we confine the investigation to Lewinsky," he reported to us, "and they are threatening a walkout en masse if we go beyond those facts."

How curious. For months, House Democrats demanded that Judge Starr give them every piece of information he collected during his four-year investigation of multiple Clinton scandals. Now, on the eve of his scheduled appearance before the Judiciary Committee and their opportunity to cross-examine him, Democrat Leader

Richard Gephardt was telling reporters that committee Democrats would not stand for Starr raising any issues unrelated to Lewinsky. Members of the press should have probed these Democrats more deeply with a single follow-up question:

Why?

Why didn't House Democrats want to join us in a "let the chips fall" search for the truth? Why didn't they want Judge Starr talking about the serious and corroborated allegations that Clinton's own attorney general authorized him to investigate? Did it matter to any committee Democrats if any of these allegations were true? Why have a fit over opening the barn doors and airing out the Clintons' stall?

Were Democrats conflicted over the credibility of the combatants? I doubt it. On one side was Judge Starr (a law professor, former federal appeals court judge and former U. S. solicitor general), his staff of professional federal prosecutors and investigators, and the 14 fraud convictions they obtained during their ongoing investigation—including the conviction of a sitting Arkansas governor. On the other side was (forgive the harsh tone, but there is no polite way to phrase this) a president up to his neck in a swamp of scandals and who showed a recurring propensity for lying his way out of trouble. It was Democrat U.S. Senator and Congressional Medal of Honor winner Bob Kerrey (D-NE), and not favorite targets Ken Starr or Newt Gingrich, who called Clinton "an unusually good liar—unusually good."

Were Democrats secretly worried that the damaging information revealed might create political fallout for them? Perhaps, but after all, only days earlier they toppled their hated nemesis, Newt Gingrich. In addition, they had just picked up five key House seats; they continued clobbering the GOP in the public relations war over all things impeachment, and they had a two-year respite until the next election cycle. Besides, the voters already sided with the Democrats in expressing their fatigue and indifference to Clinton's perjury and obstruction of justice. Was it likely these same voters might suddenly turn giddy over Republicans dragging this out further?

Even assuming Starr's revelations kicked over enough rocks to lead a bipartisan Congress to boot Clinton from office, wouldn't that increase (rather than decrease) the Democrats' power? With Vice President Al Gore succeeding Clinton and running as the incumbent in the 2000 presidential election, wouldn't that strengthen the Democrats' political hand?

The committee Democrats had a stock answer to the big "why" question. In one shrill speech after another, they pooh-poohed Clinton's conduct and instead attacked Judge Starr as a modern day version of the obsessed Inspector Javert from *Les Miserables*—a rogue prosecutor engaged in the sexual witch-hunt of a man who did nothing worse than bumble into an affair and then lie to avoid embarrassment. After creating this false premise, they became aiders and abettors in the White House's four-year-long malicious character assassination campaign against one of the most respected lawyers and jurists of his generation.

If Judge Starr really was the out-of-control bullyboy that the Clinton attack machine branded him, why didn't Clinton's Attorney General Janet Reno fire him from the investigation for abusing his authority as the law permitted her to do?

The House Judiciary Committee Democrats or their leaders never answered that question, so allow me to do so for them:

Attorney General Janet Reno didn't fire Judge Kenneth Starr because of the vast evidence of corruption seeping from every crevice of the Clinton White House—almost from the day their bus arrived from Little Rock.

Do I overstate the situation?

Then what about Clinton's former Associate U.S. Attorney General Webster Hubbell, Hillary Clinton's former law partner who collected over $700,000 in "consulting fees" from Clinton friends while he awaited federal prison sentencing for stealing $400,000?

What about the White House giving Mrs. Hubbell a high-paying job while her husband sat in federal prison? Did that have anything to do with Hubbell's refusal to cooperate in the grand jury investigation? Consider the intercepted telephone call from jail between prisoner Hubbell and his wife:

Mrs. Hubbell: [White House aide Marsha Scott says that by Hubbell suing his former law firm, it makes it look like] you are opening Hillary up to all this.

Mr. Hubbell: Well, honey, I keep telling you. Sometimes you have to fight battles alone. You just can't worry about other people. I know what I am doing. If you don't want me to, I won't.

Mrs. Hubbell: No. I want you to. But I am the one that bears the brunt of this up here. I am the one that has to explain this to Marsha. She says you are not going to get any "public support" if you open Hillary up to this. Well, by "public support," I know exactly what she means. I'm not stupid.

Mr. Hubbell: And I spent Saturday with you saying I would not do that. I will not raise those allegations that might open it up to Hillary. And you know that. I told you that.

Mrs. Hubbell: Yes, but then I get all this back from Marsha, who is ratcheting it up and making it sound like, if Webb goes ahead and sues the firm, then any "support" I have at the White House is gone. I'm hearing the squeeze play.

Mr. Hubbell: So, I need to roll over one more time....

Mrs. Hubbell: No, I am just thinking out loud. That's an area where Hillary would be vulnerable. Not unless she overbilled [her law firm in Arkansas] by time, right?

Mr. Hubbell: No, you are talking and not listening. We are on a recorded phone. I am trying to explain . . .

Mrs. Hubbell: I've got to keep this [White House] job. I have to have the support of my friends at the White House to keep it. If anything happened, I need that to keep this job. When the election is over and things are better, I need to have done a good job and have friends there who will let me get a better job. To that extent, I need to worry about it. It is just like any other job you have, whether it is in the White House or wherever else it was. I don't mind it. It is just part of the game.

What about Bill and Hillary Clinton's Whitewater land invest-ment deal, where former Arkansas state court Judge David Hale testified that Clinton pressured him to make an illegal $300,000 loan to Susan McDougal, the Clintons' Whitewater business partner, who herself received a two-year prison sentence for Whitewater related fraud? What about McDougal accepting an additional 18-month prison sentence for contempt rather than answer two simple questions before the grand jury investigating Clinton's involvement in Whitewater? I'll bet that you never saw those "incriminating" questions in the mainstream press, so let me enlighten you. McDougal chose prison over answering these two straightforward questions:

1. Did you ever discuss your loan from David Hale with Bill Clinton?

2. To your knowledge, did Bill Clinton testify truthfully during your trial?

What about Clinton releasing McDougal from prison on his last day in office by granting her a presidential pardon, which allowed her to forever escape a judge's order to answer those two questions before the grand jury?

What about major Clinton donor Johnny Chung's statement that the Clinton White House was like a subway: "You have to put in coins to open the gates"? What about Chung donating $366,000 to the Democrat National Committee, a portion of which Chung later admitted came from China's military intelligence community, while seeking favors during 49 separate visits to the White House?

What about the Clintons renting out the Lincoln Bedroom in the White House to donors for at least $5.4 million in contributions to the Democrat National Committee during 1995 and 1996?

What about Clinton Commerce Secretary Ron Brown's alleged statement to a close business associate that Bill and Hillary Clinton approved the sale of seats on official government trade missions to donors giving at least $50,000 to the Democrat National Committee?

What about Charlie Trie's illegal contribution of $460,000 to President Clinton's legal defense fund, along with an additional donation of $220,000 to the Democrat National Committee, in exchange for 23 White House visits? What about Trie's private White House coffee with Clinton, where Trie brought a Chinese arms dealer as his guest while the U.S. and China engaged in sensitive global arms negotiations?

What about China obtaining top-secret U.S. missile technology through both theft and over-the-table Clinton-approved technology transfers that allowed China to modernize its nuclear missiles? What about the chairman of the aerospace company engaged in (and profiting heavily from) these Clinton-approved technology transfers being the single largest donor to Clinton's Democrat National Committee and to Democrat Party satellite organizations?

What about John Huang raising $3.4 million for the Democrat Party, his 65 White House visits in 1996 alone, and his later money laundering conviction trying to hide the donations?

What about Vice President Al Gore dining with poverty-vowing

Chinese Buddhist Temple monks and nuns who later showed up on reports as having donated over $100,000 to the Clinton-Gore reelection campaign through an illegal money laundering operation?

What about the Clinton White House having the FBI investigate loyal White House travel office employees, and then using the investigation as an excuse to fire the longtime workers so the Clintons could hire their cousin and her Arkansas friends to take over the operation?

What about the Clinton White House hiring Democrat Party operative Craig Livingstone to head the sensitive White House Office of Personnel Security, when Livingstone's only prior "security" experience came from working as a bouncer at a D.C. nightclub? What about reports that Livingstone improperly obtained and rifled through up to 900 national security background files on high-level former Republican administration officials? What about reports that senior White House figures, including Hillary Clinton, reviewed those files illegally and for political purposes?

What about investigating Clinton's and Vice President Gore's direct role in their "Citizenship USA" program, implemented to bypass background checks and grant rushed citizenship to over 1,000,000 aliens that the White House identified as likely 1996 Clinton voters? What about their granting citizenship to 75,000 aliens with criminal arrest records and an additional 180,000 aliens—all without standard FBI fingerprint criminal background checks?

What about the email traffic Dave Schippers and his staff uncovered between Clinton and Gore senior aides, who warned both Clinton and Gore personally that these efforts might be viewed as using the government to run a pro-Democrat Clinton voter mill? What about Vice President Gore's senior policy advisor Elaine Karmack writing to Clinton aide Doug Farbrother and warning him that "THE PRESIDENT IS SICK OF THIS [DELAY] AND WANTS ACTION. IF NOTHING MOVES TODAY WE WILL HAVE TO TAKE SOME PRETTY DRASTIC ACTION" [capitalization in original].

Although it wasn't before our committee at the time, is there anything about Clinton's post-impeachment conduct that gives those 1998 Judiciary Committee Democrats reason to apologize for slandering Judge Starr and his investigation of presidential corruption? What about those 140 pardons Clinton issued on his last day as president, many of which reeked of an exchange of executive clemency for money and favors?

What about Clinton commuting the sentences of 16 Puerto Rican terrorists responsible for over 100 U.S. bombings that left many dead and injured? Does it bother those 1998 Judiciary Committee Democrats that these terrorists never asked for the pardon and refused to renounce violence after Clinton released them? What role did these pardons play in Hillary Clinton's attempt to ingratiate herself with the Hispanic population in New York during her first Senate race? What about Clinton claiming executive privilege and refusing to turn over documents relating to this commutation even after Congress launched a bipartisan investigation?

What about Clinton's pardon of fugitive Marc Rich, a man who renounced his U.S. citizenship while on the run from the FBI for 17 years, after his ex-wife reportedly paid to furnish Bill and Hillary Clinton's presidential retirement home? What about her $500,000 donation to the Clinton Library, her $1,000,000 donation to the Democrat Party, and her steering $100,000 to Hillary Clinton's U.S. Senate campaign? What about the Clinton Justice Department's assistant U.S. Attorney assigned to prosecute Rich, who blasted Clinton for pardoning the biggest tax cheat in U.S. history? Was that Clinton Administration's career prosecutor also part of Hillary Clinton's declared right-wing conspiracy out to get her husband?

What about Clinton granting clemency to dope peddler Carlos Vignali, who served only six years of a 15-year federal sentence for trafficking 500 pounds of cocaine before Clinton freed him? What about Vignali paying $400,000 to Hillary Clinton's brother, Hugh Rodham, to lobby Clinton for clemency? What about Vignali's father contributing more than $150,000 to the Democrat Party while the clemency request was pending?

What about Clinton pardoning Almon Braswell for mail fraud and perjury while the U.S. Department of Justice and FBI conducted an ongoing federal investigation into new charges of money laundering and tax evasion? What about Braswell paying $200,000 to Hillary Clinton's brother, Hugh Rodham, to lobby Clinton for the pardon?

What about Clinton pardoning his brother Roger Clinton for his own federal narcotics conviction? What about those major drug dealers who paid Roger Clinton $250,000 to lobby his brother to pardon them as well? What about Roger Clinton collecting a huge fee and a Rolex watch from the Gambino crime family after they hired him to lobby his brother for yet another pardon?

What about Clinton pardoning Edgar and Vonna Jo Gregory for their bank fraud convictions after they contributed over $100,000 to Democrat campaigns, including Hillary Clinton's Senate race? What about the Gregorys then forgiving a $107,000 loan to Hillary Clinton's younger brother Tony Rodham after he lobbied Clinton for their pardon?

What about Clinton pardoning a group of Hasidic Jewish felons that stole $40 million from taxpayers? What about the connection between this pardon and the New York Orthodox Hasidic leaders who requested the pardon after delivering their community's votes for Hillary Clinton in her Senate race two months earlier by the lopsided result of 1,400 votes for her to 12 votes for her opponent?

What about Hillary Clinton's two brothers raking in $700,000 in fees for pardon lobbying of their presidential in-law while both brothers lived with the Clintons in the White House?

What about the Clintons moving out of the White House with nearly $600,000 worth of china, gifts, art, clothing, historical artifacts, and furniture belonging to the White House? What about them returning much of the loot after the U.S. Department of

Justice began a criminal investigation?

Of course, all of this piles atop Judge Starr's meticulous investigation showing Clinton's direct perjury, subornation of perjury, and obstruction of justice in Paula Jones' federal civil rights lawsuit against Clinton. Oh, and by the way: just before Starr testified before the House Judiciary Committee, Clinton agreed to pay Paula Jones $850,000 to settle her lawsuit against him.

You say you still see no reason to apologize to Judge Starr?

Then what about Bill Clinton signing a plea bargain with federal prosecutors on his last day in office, where he *admitted*—finally—that he lied under oath in the Paula Jones sexual harassment lawsuit? What about Clinton negotiating that plea bargain to avoid criminal prosecution after leaving the White House? What about Clinton surrendering his law license in exchange for federal prosecutors agreeing not to file felony charges against him? What about Clinton getting a five-year suspension of his Arkansas law license from the Arkansas Supreme Court and paying a $25,000 fine to avoid Arkansas courts disbarring him for his dishonesty? What about Clinton also surrendering his license to practice law before the United States Supreme Court to avoid our nation's highest court from disbarring him, too?

At the beginning of this recitation, I asked why the Judiciary Committee Democrats in 1998 fought a bloody war against the search for truth. The question was rhetorical; I've always known the answer. Theirs was a circle-the-wagons mentality. They chose defending the Clintons at all costs to ward off collateral political damage to the Democrat Party. As a former prosecutor and judge, their tactics and motivations disgusted me. As a partisan politician I understood and expected it, despite their Machiavellian extremism.

No, my real question isn't for those congressional Democrats who substituted self-serving and vicious hardball politics for defending the rule of law. My question is for the two-thirds of you out there who tolerated, enabled, and rewarded this behavior:

Why didn't you care?

19

Piñata Politics

On the eve of Judge Starr's highly anticipated testimony before our committee, Henry Hyde gave a welcomed adrenaline shot at our final GOP Judiciary members' strategy meeting:

Diary, Judiciary Republicans Meeting, November 18, 1998

After Starr testifies tomorrow, Henry Hyde told us he wants our investigators to depose additional potential witnesses: "We will vote on issuing subpoenas for them tomorrow if necessary," Henry said. His proposed new witnesses are:

- **Daniel Gecker, attorney for former Clinton aide Kathleen Willey, regarding attempts to influence Willey's testimony in the Paula Jones lawsuit;**

- **Nathan Landau, a major Clinton contributor, who supposedly tried to influence Willey into changing her testimony;**

- **Robert Bennett, Clinton's attorney in the Paula Jones lawsuit, regarding Lewinsky filing a false affidavit in the Jones case;**

- **Bruce Lindsey, Deputy White House Counsel and Clinton confidante, regarding Clinton's obstruction of justice in the Lewinsky matter.**

Confirming the possibility of extending the scope of the hearing beyond the Lewinsky materials, Henry assured us, "We will continue to actively pursue leads regarding bribery and campaign finance law violations," he stated.

Now that's what I wanted to hear. If Clinton broke half as many laws as Judge Starr claimed, he forfeited his right to the presidency and Vice President Gore needed to replace him. However, if Clinton greased the skids for nuclear missile technology transfers to China in exchange for laundered foreign campaign contributions, if he jammed through citizenship for thousands of criminal aliens, and if he helped bribe grand jury witnesses, he wasn't just a candidate for forced retirement. A warden needed to fit him for prison stripes.

Although Henry still promised to conclude the review before year's end, he appeared ready to throw some elbows by reserving the right to call witnesses other than Judge Starr. These new potential witnesses weren't earth-shattering names, but at least Henry now signaled his intent to do more than invite Judge Starr over, have him read his summary, let the Democrats beat him like a piñata, and then call it a day. His suggestion at our meeting delighted me, but my euphoria proved short-lived. Near the end of the meeting, someone asked Henry if our committee would summon or depose any major witnesses as opposed to the people he had just mentioned. He shook his head no.

"Not Lewinsky," he replied. "Not Betty Currie or Vernon Jordan either [Clinton's secretary and close friend, respectively, both of whom Judge Starr alleged to be part of the Lewinsky obstruction of justice]. I don't think we need

them. Besides, it's too risky to call these three. Jordan is very smooth. Monica would bring the focus back to sex and the Democrats would make her look like Starr's victim. Currie is a sympathetic and fragile looking woman, and she is also an ardent defender of Clinton."

Oh.

Once again, we were back to Lewinsky, but now it wasn't even the meat and potatoes of corruption in the Paula Jones case. It was Lewinsky Lite: toss a few collateral witnesses on the barbeque to give the aroma of doing something, but in the end, call no key witnesses because Henry signed off on a foolish pledge to end the hearings by a fixed date next month.

Mine wasn't the only balloon that Henry had just deflated. I glanced over at our chief investigator Dave Schippers. The old mafia hunter, seated in the rear of the room, looked increasingly agitated:

Dave Schippers suddenly blew his stack. He interrupted Henry's explanation of why the committee needed to stick to this abbreviated schedule and wrap up our hearings by December.

"Pardon me," Dave called out. "I probably have no right to say this and am out of line, but what the hell are you people doing? Don't you understand that my team is closing in on stuff that nobody else has seen? I'm not talking about Lewinsky. I'm talking about bribery. I'm talking about the Chinese military in the White House. The American people will want Clinton's tail. Christ, don't cut and run now!" Dave said he is on the verge of getting FBI reports that "will make Watergate look like child's play."

"Give me a little time to complete my investigation," Dave pleaded, "and I can blow that bastard out the door of the White House."

Henry again shook his head passively: "We have to keep on the schedule I just outlined. All that's great if you can get it, but that son of a bitch [Clinton] is charmed."

Meeting adjourned.

• • •

Shortly before 10 a.m. on November 19, I took my seat in the House Judiciary Committee. With the room jammed full of reporters and committee staff, only a handful of seats remained available for the public to watch the historic presentation of Independent Counsel Kenneth W. Starr kicking off the impeachment hearing against President Clinton.

Diary, House Judiciary Committee Meeting, November 19, 1998

Judge Starr entered the committee room from the majority side. He greeted me as he walked by. I was making notes at the time and wasn't looking up, so I didn't recognize him until he passed. He took his seat at the witness table smiling and nodding confidently to committee members.

At 10:15, Henry Hyde called the committee meeting to order, and then he recognized Bill Delahunt (D-MA), who made a motion to quadruple the amount of time scheduled for Clinton's attorney to question Starr (from 30 minutes to two hours). Henry denied the motion but granted Delahunt five minutes to argue his point. This was an unwise move on Henry's part. It opened up a 20-minute debate followed by a roll-call vote. In the first half hour of our live televised hearing, Henry's indulgence allowed the Democrats to take control of the proceeding.... I hope Henry doesn't make that mistake again.

Finally, Henry delivered his opening statement welcoming Judge Starr. John Conyers, ranking Democrat, followed with his own opening statement. Conyers used his time to rip Starr personally, accusing him of having no ethics, of threatening witnesses, and of being out to get Clinton. Starr sat stoically and never flinched throughout this diatribe. Once again, Henry failed to take control and allowed Conyers to blast away long after his five-minute time limit expired.

In what turned out to be a 12-hour marathon session, Starr remained composed and patient as he explained the evidence while defending both his conclusions and his ethics. In opening remarks, he laid out the facts uncovered during his investigation that showed Clinton had committed multiple impeachable offenses.

The Democrats never once addressed the substance of Starr's investigation or the evidence. Instead, they used their time to attack him incessantly. As Peter Baker and Susan Schmidt of the *Washington Post* reported the next day, "[C]ommittee Democrats and the president's attorney quickly transformed the nationally televised hearing into a daylong debate about Starr's conduct, rather than Clinton's. Hardly contesting the factual evidence Starr presented against the president, Democrats focused instead on how the independent counsel gathered it, assailing him as a 'federally paid sex policeman' who ran an unethical investigation."

Following our lunch break, Henry Hyde recognized Democrat counsel Abbe Lowell for 30 minutes of questioning. Lowell kept trying to paint Starr as part of some rightwing conspiracy in cahoots with Paula Jones' lawyers. Starr handled himself well. Then, at the end of Lowell's half-hour, Henry Hyde on his own gave Lowell an additional 30 minutes to assault Starr. I expressed my renewed frustration with

Henry to my seatmate Chris Cannon (R-UT). "The more the Democrats complain and make trouble," I told Chris, "the more Henry rewards them."

At the end of Lowell's second 30-minute mugging, he asked for yet more time to bash Starr. Unbelievably, Henry ignored Republican objections and granted Lowell's request. Committee Republicans right now are very displeased with Henry's overly indulgent attitude.

Following Lowell's questioning, Henry recognized committee members in order of seniority, with each receiving five minutes to question Starr.

Zoe Lofgren (D-CA) exploited her time by reading a speech that suggested Starr himself committed perjury. After going well beyond her time, she then started posing multiple questions to Starr all at once, and (along with Barney Frank chiming in) continued to interrupt his answers with additional questions. When Maxine Waters' (D-CA) turn came, she proved especially bitter and hostile. After also going past her five-minute limit, she refused to stop sniping and yield to the next questioner despite Henry Hyde's repeated admonitions. She grew so nasty that Henry finally punched the mute button on her microphone.

During my five minutes, I asked about the anomaly of the Democrats expressing "shock" at Starr's insensitive investigators swooping in and interviewing poor Lewinsky without any warning, but showing silent indifference to Clinton intentionally exposing his former intern to a five-year federal prison sentence by having her sign under oath a false affidavit in Paula Jones' lawsuit. I also asked about Clinton's deposition in the Paula Jones case where he claimed under oath not to remember ever being alone with Lewinsky in the Oval Office. I asked Starr the legal significance of a witness testifying under oath that he didn't remember something when in fact he did. Starr gave me the answer that I already knew:

It constituted felony perjury.

By the time committee members finished their questions and Henry recognized Clinton attorney David Kendall for his 30 minutes of questions, our unflappable witness had been in the hot seat some ten hours. Kendall followed the same partisan playbook: attack Starr personally and divert attention away from the founder of the scandal feast.

At the end of Kendall's 30 minutes, Henry on his own gave Kendall an additional 30 minutes to trash Starr. Republican committee members (again) groaned audibly with disgust at Henry's unilateral conduct, especially after subjecting Starr to this brutalization for over ten hours.

The long day ended with our chief investigator, Dave Schippers, finishing out the questioning. After walking through the evidence with Starr, Dave closed on a poignant note:

Schippers: You have been given a duty that you did not seek, and you've performed that duty to the best of your ability. Is that correct, sir?

Starr: I've certainly tried to do it to the best of my ability, and I'm proud of what we have been able to accomplish. I'm proud of my colleagues; they have become my friends, and they've worked very long and very hard under very difficult circumstances. But we're big boys. When we were accused of a political witch hunt [in our Whitewater prosecutions], we just took it. We did our arguing in court, and we proved to the satisfaction of a fair-minded jury with a very distinguished judge that the sitting Arkansas governor, along with President and Mrs. Clinton's business partners [Jim and Susan McDougal], were guilty of serious felonies. We had been listening month after month to, "It's a political witch hunt." That was unfair, but we learned that goes with this territory.

Schippers: How long have you been an attorney, Judge Starr?

Starr: Twenty-five years.

Schippers: Well, I've been an attorney for almost 40 years. I want to say I'm proud to be in the same room with you and your staff. Thank you.

When Starr concluded, Republican committee members and staff rose and gave him a prolonged standing ovation. I remained seated and did not join in the expression of congratulations. It wasn't because I didn't respect Starr's job; I simply felt it inappropriate to stand and applaud a testifying witness for his performance. However, he was tremendous. I've never been more impressed by anyone in my legal career.

Reflecting back on that long-ago tumultuous day, there is one thing I would do differently if I could relive the experience:

When Judge Starr finished his testimony, I would stand for him.

20

Street Justice

"To White House allies, the prospect of a Party-line [Judiciary Committee impeachment] vote . . . would reinforce the impression that the inquiry was a partisan exercise, taking some of the sting out of history recording Clinton as only the third president faced with the threat of impeachment."

—JULIET EILPERIN AND PETER BAKER,
WASHINGTON POST, NOVEMBER 21, 1998

Henry Hyde had faith that once Dave Schippers and Ken Starr went before the television cameras, the truth would remove the scales from the public's eyes, Clinton's poll numbers would reverse, and we could have a legitimate debate on impeachment. The morning after Starr testified, Henry reported that the committee received almost 3,000 emails soon after his testimony began, and they ran 60 percent to 40 percent against the independent counsel. However, by midnight, after he testified all day, the results flipped to show 70 percent to 30 percent favoring Starr. Henry hoped this signaled a breakthrough in public opinion about Starr and a willingness to listen to the true merits of the case.

Although unscientific, Henry's poll mirrored a CNN/Gallup/ *USA Today* survey to the extent their poll showed almost 70 percent of those watching Starr rated his presentation as "good" or "excellent." Unfortunately, their sampling also showed that very few people bothered watching the proceedings. Henry's early optimism was mislaid. Despite all the evidence against Clinton, public opinion didn't move. We took our best shot to show America the evidence, and America yawned.

After Judge Starr testified, I conducted a poll of my own. Like Henry's, mine was unscientific, but unlike his, mine had far greater reliability and its methodology was nearly foolproof. I walked around and asked Republican committee colleagues whether they thought we had enough evidence to impeach Clinton. Each agreed the evidence of perjury and obstruction of justice was overwhelming. Despite the daily national polls telling us what we must do to regain public favor, my empirical survey told me House Judiciary Republicans were poised to pass an impeachment resolution against the president.

My poll also detected traces of what one might call an "X" factor: hardening GOP spines from members fed up with watching six years of unrelenting and vicious attacks from Team Clinton's professional smear artists trying to destroy anyone who stood up to them. I'm no psychologist, but my ex-bartender radar detected the vibration of a sudden readiness among my colleagues to disregard public opinion and administer street justice to a bully.

With Clinton failing to address the evidence during Starr's testimony, Henry Hyde cut to the chase. He sent Clinton a list of 81 requests for admissions that gave him the chance to admit or deny each individual piece of key sworn evidence before the committee. Three weeks went by with no answer. Henry sent Clinton another letter stating, "The committee welcomes any facts that tend to dispute the factual assertions in the referral or that otherwise tend to establish your innocence of any of the allegations." Henry also invited Clinton to make any presentation he wished before the committee.

Clinton replied under oath to the 81 questions almost a month after he received them. Not only did he refuse to directly answer many of the straightforward inquiries, he again refused to identify any exculpatory evidence that would mitigate or disprove Starr's charges. Instead, he filled many of his responses with vague and ambiguous answers, claimed memory lapses, and (in some instances) pure gibberish.

For example, the first question posed to him was, "Do you admit or deny that you are the chief law enforcement officer of the United States of America?" This was not a trick question. The Constitution specifies that the president is the only federal public official charged with the responsibility to "take care that the laws be faithfully executed."

Instead of giving a simple "yes," Clinton offered this answer: "The president is frequently referred to as the chief law enforcement officer, although nothing in the Constitution specifically designates the president as such. Article II Section 1 of the United States Constitution states that 'the executive power shall be vested in a president of the United States of America,' and the law enforcement function is a component of the executive power."

His other 80 answers weren't much more insightful. After reviewing these responses, a disgusted Henry Hyde released this press statement:

> The [requests for admission] were made in order to allow the president to candidly dispute or affirm key sworn evidence before the committee by admitting or denying certain facts. Unfortunately, the president . . . has made it very clear he is going to stick with his reliance on bizarre technical definitions and legalistic defenses. Although given the opportunity to do so,

neither the president nor the Democrat members on the committee have sought to call a single witness, offer any exculpatory evidence or present any information that disputes the factual record. The committee will continue to welcome any exculpatory evidence from the president relating to the allegations that have been made against him, and will welcome an appearance by the president or his counsel for purposes of making a presentation to the committee. However, this will be the last opportunity for the president to provide the committee with his version of the facts before the committee evaluates the evidence and considers debating articles of impeachment.

As *Washington Post* reporters Eric Pianin and Guy Gugliotta wrote after Clinton filed his response, "Although the GOP's disappointing showing in last month's election seemed to doom the chances of presidential impeachment, what many members see as President Clinton's arrogance and lack of repentance have made it far more likely that the House will approve at least one article." Similarly, Alison Mitchell of the *New York Times* reported: "[T]he White House, using its own internal polling, began arguing that the force of public opinion was running so strongly with Clinton that the Republicans would never proceed with impeachment. 'The White House is so obsessed with polling that it can't imagine anyone else would ignore it,' said one Democrat strategist. So, when Republicans called Starr before the Judiciary Committee, the White House played for public opinion and sought to heap more discredit on a prosecutor already low in public standing. [Then, when Clinton answered the] 81 questions put to him by the committee, his answers seemed so evasive and legalistic that Republicans say that was a turning point. Many of the same moderates Clinton needs to woo saw the White House response as arrogant and were alienated by it."

The reporters were correct: if Bill Clinton really hoped to convince the House Judiciary Committee not to pass any articles of impeachment, one wouldn't know it by his approach. His continued stalling in conjunction with his brass knuckle tactics proved effective in tiring America of the whole business. However, his tactics also produced a side effect: for a president so consumed with his future legacy, he seemed bent on assuring that the word "impeached" made it into his official biography.

House Republicans may have misread the mood of the voters in November, but Clinton now misread the resolve of the Judiciary Committee Republicans to show an arrogant president that the polls be damned: No man is above the law.

• • •

During our impeachment hearings, Henry Hyde wanted to high-light the importance of protecting the justice system from perjury, as well as demonstrate the blatant double standard Clinton and his defenders now sought for the president:

Diary, Judiciary Republicans Meeting, November 18, 1998

As to the Democrats' repeated claims that perjury "is no big deal," that "nobody ever gets prosecuted for it," and that "everyone lies about sex," Henry said we will hold a separate hearing on the impact of perjury on the justice system: "We'll have federal judges and people convicted of perjury. We will produce women who are in custody right now for perjury or who have been convicted of perjury."

Now, as we prepared to use this next hearing to accentuate the destructive impact of perjury on the justice system, one of our GOP committee colleagues made headlines by minimizing it. The weekend before our scheduled perjury hearing, Lindsey Graham (R-SC) told an interviewer that he would not vote to impeach Clinton for com-mitting grand jury perjury if Clinton would "come forward and admit to the wrongdoing that I think is obviously there." Lindsey's shoot-from-the-hip comment didn't sit well with his colleagues, as he discovered at our next private GOP Judiciary meeting:

Diary, Judiciary Republicans Meeting, December 1, 1998

Before the start of our formal committee hearing, Bob Barr (R-GA) approached Lindsey Graham in our private conference room and took him to task for saying on national television that Clinton's grand jury perjury wasn't an impeachable offense if Clinton came forward, admitted his wrongdoing, and apologized.

"So," Bob taunted Lindsey, "if any criminal calls you and says, 'I'm sorry,' then he gets off the hook, right?" Lindsey tried to defend his position, but Bob wouldn't let up on him.

As the argument progressed, Bob (a former federal prosecutor) pulled out his dog-eared, heavily highlighted copy of the statutes to show Lindsey the applicable law. Lindsey waved him off. "Look, I already said it on TV," Lindsey said in frustration, "so I'm sticking by it." With that, he walked away from his still-fuming colleague.

At the day-long hearing, an array of federal judges, military leaders, a former U.S. attorney general, and leading law professors shared their views on the impact of perjury. Unfortunately, our otherwise scholarly discussion was punctuated with the emotional and histrionic outbursts of a Democrat-invited witness, Harvard Law School Professor Alan Dershowitz. He opened his presentation with a sweeping indictment of police officers everywhere and accused them of having been taught to commit serial perjury at their police academies. He then tossed America's prosecutors and trial judges into his conspiracy soup for knowing that they all lie and for allowing them to do so. From there he moved to the current impeachment debate. He alternated between defending Clinton and hurling insults at committee Republicans. His disrespectful rant prompted many of my GOP colleagues to walk out on his TV-orchestrated theatrics. The professor even brought along his own cheering section: a group of sycophantic Harvard law students who applauded his every point from their seats in the visitors' gallery.

Among Dershowitz's contributions to our previously decorous panel discussion were these unhelpful nuggets:

- "Now we are seeing incredible [Republican] hypocrisy introduced into the debate: 'Oh, we care so much about perjury. What a terrible thing perjury is.' The only reason the Republican majority on this committee cares about perjury is because they believe that President Clinton, their political opponent, is guilty of it."

- "[Committee Republicans] don't care at all about perjury by the police, as evidenced by their lack of attention to this problem."

- "When is the last time this committee has expressed concern about the rights of criminal defendants except when criminal defendants can show that the president is being selectively prosecuted? It's a sham."

When my turn came to question Dershowitz, I tried to lighten the mood with a smile. I told him that unlike my displeased colleagues now boycotting his testimony, I found his remarks therapeutic—because until I had heard from him, I had only my undergraduate grade point average to explain why I didn't bother applying to Harvard Law School. The audience laughed, but Dershowitz didn't appear to get my joke.

In calmer moments, Dershowitz warned the committee not to ignore this important "fact": prosecutors almost never file charges of perjury against people, and the false statements of which President Clinton is accused "would never even be considered for prosecution in the routine case involving an ordinary defendant." He said this was especially true if a defendant made statements "in a civil deposition about a collateral sexual matter later found inadmissible in a case eventually dismissed and then settled."

"On the basis of my research and experiences," he intoned, "I am convinced that if President Clinton were an ordinary citizen, he would not be prosecuted for his allegedly false statements."

Based on your research and experience, Professor Dershowitz?? He should have stuck around to hear the testimony of our next witness: Dr. Barbara Battalino.

The accomplished Dr. Battalino was an osteopathic physician, a board-certified psychiatrist, and an attorney. While working at an Idaho veterans' hospital, the doctor began a short-lived affair with a resident patient who was not under her care. Later, after they broke up, her former paramour filed a lawsuit against the Veterans Administration (VA), alleging the affair as evidence of hospital malpractice. With her family, her job, and her professional licenses on the line, she panicked. During her deposition in the patient's civil case against the VA, she denied the affair under oath while unaware that the plaintiff had secretly recorded their romantic encounter. When confronted with this evidence, she confessed. The court later dismissed the plaintiff's lawsuit.

What was the response of the Clinton Justice Department to Dr. Battalino lying under oath about sex in the civil deposition of a dismissed case? After the Clinton VA fired her, the Clinton Justice Department prosecuted her for perjury. On the day she appeared before our committee, she remained in custody while still serving her sentence.

I found this level of hypocrisy breathtaking, especially in light of the Democrats' year-long drumbeat that perjury regarding sex in a civil lawsuit was no big deal and it somehow doesn't count at all if the underlying case ends up dismissed (as happened in Paula Jones' case—before Clinton agreed to pay her $850,000 to settle her claims).

Contrary to Professor Dershowitz's authoritative claim, Dr. Battalino's circumstance was consistent with the Clinton Administration's record of responding to lying about sex in civil matters:

- As to the Democrats' unending and false refrain that "nobody gets prosecuted for perjury," on the very day of our hearing, 115 people were sitting in federal prisons around the country after being prosecuted and convicted for perjury in federal court proceedings.

- The Clinton Administration fired U.S. Postal Service supervisor Diane Parker for having sex with a subordinate employee. As the *Washington Times* reported, "Parker had been a model citizen. She was active in a local community group, had attended college and served in the military." None of that mattered to the Clinton Administration. After she lost her job for lying about the affair, the Clinton Justice Department prosecuted her, and she served a federal prison sentence for her perjury.

- The Clinton Administration kicked U.S. Air Force Lieutenant Kelly Flynn out of the military because she lied to her commanding officer about having an affair, even though she was not under oath when she lied, and no legal proceedings were underway.

I was most interested in hearing the committee Democrats explain their "nobody gets prosecuted for perjury" fantasy to Dr. Battalino and another panel witness, Pamela Parsons. In the 1980s, *Sports Illustrated* published an article claiming Parsons, then a successful women's basketball coach, was a lesbian. She denied the claim and filed suit against the magazine. In her civil deposition, Coach Parsons denied ever patronizing a gay bar. Later evidence proved this to be a lie. After losing her job, the U.S. Department of Justice prosecuted Parsons for perjury in 1984. She pleaded guilty and received a federal prison sentence.

I came to the perjury hearing with no notes or prepared questions, but as Dr. Battalino's story unfolded, this stunning differentiation so bothered me that I quickly sketched out a direct examination meant to highlight the flagrant double standard. When my turn came to ask her questions, Dr. Battalino and I had the following exchange, which made national headlines the next day:

Q. Dr. Battalino, your case intrigues me. I want to make sure I understand the factual circumstances. You lied about a one-time act of consensual sex with someone on federal property; is that correct?

A. Yes, absolutely correct.

Q. This act of perjury was in a civil lawsuit, and not in a criminal case?

A. That's also correct.

Q. In fact, the civil case was dismissed eventually?

A. Correct.

Q. Yet despite the dismissal, the Clinton Justice Department prosecuted you for this act of perjury; is that correct?

A. That is correct.

Q. During your prosecution, did anybody from the White House, the Clinton Justice Department, or any Democrat member of Congress show up at your trial and suggest that you should be treated with leniency because "everybody lies about sex"?

A. No, sir.

Q. Did anybody ever come forward from the White House or from the Clinton Justice Department and urge leniency for you because your perjury was "only" in a civil case?

A. No.

Q. Did they argue for leniency because the civil case in which you committed perjury was later dismissed?

A. No.

Q. Did anybody ever come forward from Congress to suggest that you were the victim of an overzealous or sex-obsessed prosecutor?

A. No.

Q. You lied when your lawyer asked you at a deposition whether "anything of a sexual nature" occurred; is that correct?

A. Yes, that is correct.

Q. Did anybody from Congress or from the White House come forward to defend you, saying that that phrase "anything of a sexual nature" was ambiguous, or it all depended on what the word "anything" meant?

A. No, sir.

Q. Doctor, you lost your medical license and your license to practice law. Your conviction precludes you from practicing law?

A. That is correct, sir.

Q. You also had a medical degree and license. You lost your medical license?

A. Yes. I am no longer permitted to practice medicine either.

Q. Did anybody from the Clinton Justice Department, the White House, or from Congress come to your sentencing hearing and suggest that perhaps you should simply receive some sort of censure?

A. No one came to my aid or defense, no.

Q. Has anybody come forward from the White House to suggest to you that in light of our present circumstances, perhaps you should be pardoned for your offense?

A. Nobody has come, no.

Q. If the United States Congress now decides that a public official sworn to uphold the law who lied under oath about sex should not lose his job, would you feel you were the victim of an unfair double standard?

A. Yes, I would.

Q. Mr. Chairman, I see my time has expired.

•••

While Henry Hyde tried to rush through the hearings, Dave Schippers and his team continued their investigation into allegations of Chinese campaign money laundering. As it turned out, this pursuit wasn't a fantasy. Columnist Paul Greenberg reported on December 1 that both the Clinton-appointed Director of the FBI and a senior Clinton Justice Department prosecutor reviewing the same evidence thought the allegations merited serious consideration: "When FBI Director Louis Freeh urged [Attorney General Janet Reno to appoint] another independent counsel to investigate the administration's campaign finance scandal, Reno moved swiftly. She immediately sought advice from another quarter. This time she appointed a respected prosecutor, Charles LaBella, to advise her. He reached the same conclusion that FBI Director Freeh had. Having had her fill of advice she didn't want to accept, General Reno decided to follow her own and not appoint an independent counsel. She now has dismissed the evidence. The key qualification for an attorney general in [the Clinton Administration] remains a willingness to let bygones be bygones. Janet Reno now has qualified abundantly. Having dropped this investigation, the attorney general assured all: 'We will continue to vigorously investigate all allegations of illegal activity.'"

Diary, Meeting in Chairman Hyde's Office, November 30, 1998

Dave Schippers updated us on his investigation into the Clinton campaign scandal. Dave said he learned that both FBI Director Louis Freeh and Justice Department prosecutor Charles LaBella wrote memoranda to Attorney General Janet Reno naming Clinton and Gore personally as targets of a criminal probe. These memoranda have not yet been released. Dave said his tentative plan is to issue subpoenas

to both Freeh and LaBella for the memoranda and subpoena the documents directly from both Bill Clinton and Attorney General Janet Reno. Dave spoke with LaBella, who told him that the Clinton Administration has LaBella "in their sights" because of the memo he drafted for Reno.

Henry told Dave he would have to "race against the clock to get the memos. If we get it, and the tip is true, then all bets are off. Otherwise, we proceed on just the Starr report."

"We probably have the votes in committee to send articles of impeachment to the House floor," Henry added, "but we don't have the votes on the floor to prevail. We might pick up a few Democrats, but we probably lose 20 Republicans. It will be the usual suspects on whom we can always count to cut and run on anything of substance or controversy."

Dave and his investigators continued fighting a recalcitrant Attorney General Janet Reno for these memoranda. Reno refused to turn over the documents, but in a meeting with Schippers mediated by Senate Judiciary Committee Chairman Orrin Hatch (R-UT), she agreed to let Dave read edited versions of the reports while she sat with him on condition that he not make copies or remove the documents. Dave later related the incident in his book:

I concentrated on the LaBella report. I soon realized that all the relevant information had been deleted, with page after page of blank space, up to nearly 20 pages at a time. I was disgusted. [Senator] Hatch, on the other hand, agreed that these redacted versions constituted "sufficient compliance" to protect Reno from a [congressional] contempt citation. Here we had it. More bipartisanship, of which the Republican senatorial leadership seemed to be the grand champions.

Later, when Dave won the right from a federal judge to read (but not copy or remove from the room) LaBella's report, he thought it contained enticing leads. As reporter Peter Baker wrote in his book on impeachment: "The memos suggested there was evidence of abuses and that the president and some of his close advisers engaged in a "pattern of conduct worthy of investigation." LaBella offered a stinging critique... of Justice Department officials resisting the appointment of a special prosecutor and urged a probe of the "entire landscape" of campaign finance. But the memos did not contain enough to accuse the president of specific criminal violations without more information."

Without more information. That is why Clinton's handpicked FBI director, himself a former FBI agent and federal judge, as well as career Justice Department prosecutor LaBella, wanted an independent prosecutor appointed.

Dave pleaded with Henry Hyde to proceed with an investigation into Clinton's China fundraising connection, and that we bring in both Freeh and LaBella to testify. This time, there was no Judiciary Republican roll call on the issue: Henry said no. He insisted that the House would not reauthorize our investigation if we went into January. Furthermore, he dropped all further consideration of issues surrounding bribery, Webster Hubbell, China, missile technology transfers, money laundering, and campaign finance violations. Our committee staff withdrew subpoenas for Freeh, LaBella, Clinton, Reno, and other non-Lewinsky players. Henry also pulled the plug on his previously announced expanded Kathleen Willey investigation. Our investigators already took the deposition of Clinton donor Nathan Landau regarding his attempts to get Willey to change her testimony. What was the result? Landau pleaded the Fifth Amendment over 70 times, including when asked questions like "Where do you live?", "What is your telephone number?", "Are you married?", and "What are the names of your children?"

"It was now clear that no boats would be rocked, no chances

taken," Dave Schippers later wrote. "We were going to have a nice, bland, friendly impeachment hearing."

Anticipating unhappiness among some of his committee members (like me), Henry asked a few of us to join him in a private meeting:

Diary, The Capitol, November 30, 1998

Chief counsel Tom Mooney called and asked me to come to Henry Hyde's office. When I got there, I joined Asa Hutchinson (R-AR), Charles Canady (R-FL), Mooney, and deputy Chief Counsel Jon Dudas. Henry wanted to discuss our impeachment inquiry and his earlier pledge to wrap it up by the end of the year.

"We all know that Bill Clinton is a world-class liar," Henry said. "The problem is that the clock is ticking, and we haven't much time left. America is tired of the whole thing. Ken Starr is a great man, but he spent too long—four and a half years—and he spent too much money on his investigation.

"Unfortunately, I'm in hurry-up mode. We have to keep our case to the basics: perjury, subornation of perjury, and obstruction of justice in the Monica Lewinsky matter."

That (as they say) was that. The other explosive issues were off the table. When the Judiciary Committee met to debate and vote on articles of impeachment, it would be about Monica Lewinsky and nothing else. For the rest of my time on the House Judiciary Committee, we never again discussed Clinton's potential criminal exposure in the other areas where he faced liability.

• • •

Despite Clinton's refusal to address any of the evidence compiled by Starr, his attorneys demanded four full days (32 hours) before the Judiciary Committee to argue against impeachment. Henry Hyde granted their request to appear, but because of his clock fixation, he collapsed their time to 30 hours spread over two days. (In comparison, Dave Schippers and Ken Starr's *combined* opening evidence presentations to the committee took about four hours). Henry warned the White House and committee Democrats that this would be the president's last chance to show committee members that Clinton was not guilty.

**Diary, Conference Call of Judiciary Republicans,
Saturday, December 5, 1998**

"When Bill Clinton's witnesses are through making their presentations," Henry said, "try not to ask questions unless you have a zinger. The White House's new goal is to drag out the time of these hearings and prevent us from voting on articles of impeachment by the end of the week. I have told them they will have 30 hours over two days to present their evidence, but no more."

Members complained that we couldn't turn over the hearing to the Democrats for 30 televised hours and not ask questions or respond to their shenanigans. Henry backed off his request: "We can cross-examine these guys, but I think it will be boring as hell. Just don't ask any questions that will come back and bite you in the neck."

In approaching the finale of the Judiciary Committee's impeachment hearings, the Democrats ratcheted up their efforts to substitute the nuclear option of impeachment with the wrist-slap of censure.

The latter was never something for which I would vote.[1]

I agreed with Professor John McGinness of the Cardozo School of Law, who wrote: "To put it simply, censure is unconstitutional. It flouts the separation of powers that is the keystone of our Republic. By allowing Congress to punish the president outside the bounds of impeachment, this precedent would establish a new avenue of legislative political assault against the Executive Branch of our Federal government. Any such action would weaken the presidency while permitting Congress to avoid its responsibility to render considered judgments on the integrity of our highest officers."

Censure was also a meaningless exercise because any future Congress could erase it from the history books with a simple majority vote. A Whig controlled Senate passed a censure resolution of questionable constitutional validity against President Andrew Jackson in 1834; Jackson simply refused to recognize it. When his fellow Democrats took over the Senate in 1837, their first act was to expunge the censure. There was no doubt that if we censured Clinton, an eventual Clinton-friendly House would vacate it, meaning (like Andrew Jackson's) the censure never happened. If Clinton offered a plausible rebuttal to the evidence against him, I would vote against impeachment, but under no circumstance would I vote for a censure resolution. As I said in many press interviews during this time, "The Constitution already has a built-in procedure for censure. It's called 'impeachment.'"

Henry Hyde felt he had to allow the Democrats to raise the censure motion in committee despite our shared belief that the remedy had no constitutional validity:

---

1   As I noted in Chapter 18, the House Republican leadership gave me authority to negotiate with Clinton's representatives (after the midterm election) a non-impeachment compromise. Censure would have been among the potential remedies had those discussions taken place. I had made clear to our GOP leadership that I would negotiate with the White House for a censure as a possible resolution, but if both sides agreed to move forward with it, I would not vote for censure on the House floor for the reasons explained in this chapter.

Diary, Conference Call, Republican Judiciary Members, December 3, 1998

"There will be blood on the floor," Henry warned, "if we deny the Democrats a chance to debate a censure motion in committee. We can announce that the first debate and vote will be on impeachment, and the second vote will be on their censure resolution. I will try to limit their time, but I must be liberal or else we will appear unfair.

"When this battle later moves to the House floor, we should fight any attempt to raise a censure motion during debate, even if our own leadership wants us to pass it. If the Democrats try to raise it there, I will object and raise a point of order that the motion is not germane. I expect the chair will sustain my point of order and then the Democrats will appeal the ruling of the chair. That's where we may lose Republican votes on the House floor."

Henry then called the GOP committee roll and asked each of us individually if anyone would vote for a censure resolution as opposed to impeachment. Only one member, Lindsey Graham (R-SC), said he would consider censure: "I will only vote for censure if Clinton comes forward and admits he committed perjury and obstructed justice," Lindsey said.

With or without a censure resolution, when we met again on December 8, we would begin the last phase of our committee's constitutional showdown.

• • •

I close this chapter with a quick story.

Near the end of our private Judiciary Republicans' meeting on December 1, chief counsel Tom Mooney whispered that he wanted to speak to me. We stepped outside the meeting room. He looked both ways and then he handed me an unmarked manila envelope.

"This material is *highly* embargoed," he said in a hushed voice. "The only other member of Congress who has seen this document is Chairman Hyde. He wants you to review it and propose any revisions." I tucked away the envelope and never let it out of my possession for the rest of the day. I didn't open it until I got home that evening.

Sitting at the kitchen table in my small Arlington townhouse, I unsealed the envelope and removed an unadorned five-page typed document. I couldn't help but exhale deeply when I read the first line:

> *"Resolved, That William Jefferson Clinton, President of the United States, is impeached for high crimes and misdemeanors."*

That night I sat at the table sipping coffee, reading each word carefully, and scribbling editorial suggestions throughout. The next morning, as I left to catch an airplane, I faxed back my revisions to Tom on a secure line and put away the original.

Beginning in November 2000, and for the next two decades, this document was been on display at the Smithsonian Institution in the American Presidency exhibition, nestled between George Washington's Valley Forge uniform and Abraham Lincoln's top hat.[2] Whenever I reflect on the electoral loss that I suffered in 2000 for doing my duty in this impeachment drama, I think about those pages bearing my handwritten notes and I remember where they resided.

And I hold my head a little higher.

---

2   At the conclusion of the Smithsonian's twenty-year exhibition of my memorabilia, I donated this and my other Clinton impeachment artifacts and records to Hillsdale College in Michigan.

21

No One Left to Lie To

"There's no question that the euphoria from the November election clouded Clinton's expectation about what would happen in the Congress with impeachment."

—LEON PANETTA, FORMER CLINTON WHITE HOUSE CHIEF OF
STAFF, DECEMBER 1998

O n the first morning of what promised to be a long week, I found myself the only Republican exercising in the House Members' Gym:

Diary, The U.S. Capitol, December 7, 1998

While working out, I chatted with a few of my Democrat House colleagues. Congressman Gene Taylor (D-MS) mentioned casually that if the House Judiciary Committee voted to send articles of impeachment to the floor, he would vote to impeach Clinton.

Bill Delahunt (D-MA) joined the conversation and said that we would look terrible in history if we impeached Clinton. I assured Bill that no matter what happened we would survive as a country even if it meant disappointing our liberal European cousins or our more liberal American history professors.

"But what about the stock market?" he interjected. "What will this do to the international markets and our economy?"

I put my arm around Bill's shoulder and smiled: "Billy, if the stock market dropped 6,000 points tomorrow, it would still be higher than its highest point on the last day you Democrats held a majority."

• • •

The two-day White House defense presentation before the Judiciary Committee began on December 9 and was led by Clinton lawyers Gregory Craig and Charles Ruff. I found both to be articulate advocates, even if their mission to persuade Republicans involved a very steep climb. Clinton's under-oath responses painted his lawyers into a corner. Clinton's need to avoid criminal liability forced Craig to argue that Clinton's testimony was "evasive, incomplete, misleading, even maddening," but not perjury. He insisted that Clinton never lied under oath—not a single time. When Charles Canady (R-FL) challenged that point by saying Clinton clearly lied when he testified that he couldn't remember being alone with Monica Lewinsky in the Oval Office, Craig held his ground. Canady retorted, "For you to contend today [that answer was] truthful is not credible. I don't see how anyone in this country could believe that was a truthful answer in light of all of the evidence that is before us."

Congressman Jim Sensenbrenner (R-WI) didn't have any more success in shaking Craig from his assertion. He asked Craig, "Let me get to the heart of the case: Did Monica Lewinsky provide false testimony to the grand jury?"

"We think," Craig replied, "in some areas, she provided erroneous testimony that is in disagreement with the president's testimony."

White House Counsel Charles Ruff echoed the same theme, arguing that Clinton testified truthfully before the grand jury. Alternatively, if committee members still believed that he lied, Ruff pleaded with us to find that such conduct under those circumstances still did not warrant impeachment. In his presentation, he offered a proposed compromise: Ruff represented that for the first time, Clinton would accept a congressional reprimand such as censure.

During the 30-hour presentation, the White House treated us to a witness parade featuring the opinions of sympathetic lawyers, retired government officials, academics, and even former Democrat Judiciary Committee members from the Watergate era. Each offered their opinion that Clinton's conduct did not merit impeachment. Meanwhile, the White House filed a 184-page brief in which his lawyers again attacked Starr while minimizing, disputing, or reinterpreting Starr's evidence against Clinton. One thing the brief didn't do was present any proof to refute the sworn claims from Starr's grand jury.

During Ruff and Craig's presentations, the Democrats scored some political victories. Former Governor William Weld (R-MA) appeared before our committee as a Clinton witness and urged the committee not to support impeachment. Congressman Amo Houghton (R-NY) became the sixth House Republican to announce publicly that he would not vote for impeachment. Later, another announced "no" vote, Congressman Peter King (R-NY), told an interviewer there were between 15 and 20 other Republicans "that I know of" who would join him in voting against impeachment, "and [that number] could go higher than that."

What did all of this mean practically? It meant that even if the Judiciary Committee passed an impeachment resolution, Clinton had sufficient bipartisan votes to defeat it on the House floor with relative ease.

• • •

At the conclusion of the two-day Clinton defense presentation, the committee gathered for the final summations of committee investigators Schippers and Lowell, and to then begin the final debate and vote on articles of impeachment.

Republicans on the committee loved and respected Henry Hyde deeply, and I counted myself in that camp. However, as our hearings neared the end, GOP members' teeth-clenching frustration with his continual bending over backward to accommodate hatchet-wielding Democrats took a toll on our patience:

Diary, House Judiciary Committee Hearing, December 10, 1998

Henry Hyde is a brilliant and wonderful man, but Republican committee members agree he has been an ineffective enforcer of the rules during this inquiry. He continues to entertain the Democrats' frivolous claims and allows them to speak both out of order and well past their time limits. On the other hand, he strictly enforces the rules against us. He looks great on television as a grandfatherly presence on the committee, but when things get hot, the rambunctious Democrats roll him easily.

Contrast that with the curmudgeonly Jim Sensenbrenner (R-WI) who sometimes takes over when Henry needs a break. Sensenbrenner brooks no nonsense from the Democrats. In times like this, I prefer to see him in the chair.

Dave Schippers closed our case by recounting the web of lies in which Clinton found himself ensnared: "The President has lied under oath in a civil deposition. He lied under oath in a criminal grand jury. He lied to the people. He lied to his cabinet. He lied to his top aides. Now, he's lied under oath to the Congress of the

United States [in his sworn answers to committee questions].

"There's no one left to lie to."

• • •

I tried to find a legitimate reason to vote against Bill Clinton's impeachment.

Part of it came from wanting to give Clinton that which every defendant in a criminal courtroom enjoys: a presumption of innocence until proven guilty beyond a reasonable doubt. Although the Constitution does not specify any particular standard of proof in an impeachment trial, many colleagues adopted the minimal "probable cause" standard in making their decision. I felt the president deserved the benefit of the highest legal burden of proof before we voted to oust him from office.

My wanting to vote against impeachment wasn't just motivated by a generous desire to indulge Clinton on every rational evidentiary inference. I also hoped to find an excuse to spare Clinton based on my own political self-preservation. Up to now, many Democrat voters in my district liked me, but they loved Clinton, and they loved him much more than they liked me— and in far greater numbers. Our polling showed their generally favorable opinion of me would downgrade rapidly if I supported articles of impeachment.

I was a young teenager when I first read President Kennedy's bestselling book, *Profiles in Courage*. Now, with decision time upon us, I re-read his chapter on U.S. Senator Edmund Ross, the Kansas Republican who bucked his Party and his constituency by casting the deciding acquittal vote in the 1868 impeachment trial of President Andrew Johnson. Ross later said that when he cast that fateful vote, "I almost literally looked down into my open grave. Friendships, position, fortune, everything that makes life desirable to an ambitious man were about to be swept away by the breath of my mouth." According to other published biographies,

Ross' premonition came true. Rebuked as a traitor for following his conscience, he was defeated in the next election. Upon his return home, he and his family suffered ostracism and eventual poverty. The abolitionist Republicans first drove him out of their Party, and later they drove him out of Kansas. Ross relocated to New Mexico and died a broken man.

I closed Kennedy's book feeling less than inspired.

No matter what happened, my personal situation was far better than that of poor Senator Ross. If I voted for impeachment, I might lose reelection, but since my landlord loathed Clinton, I knew I still had a roof over my head—at least until the Edmund Ross Memorial Posse drove me out of California and banished me to New Mexico and financial ruin.

I was in the fourth grade when I set my sights on becoming a member of Congress. After working 30 years to get here, I was in no hurry to leave—no matter how lovely the New Mexico sunsets.

• • •

I arrived at my Capitol office early on the morning of December 11, the day the Judiciary Committee began its final impeachment debate, without having told anyone how I might vote. Even though I never revealed my intentions in advance, the overwhelming evidence, coupled with Clinton's refusal to rebut any of it factually, left no doubt in my mind which way to go. The evidence showed Clinton mugged the rule of law to hang on to his job. I decided not to do the same thing to hang on to mine.

After I let myself in the back-office door, my chief of staff, Greg Mitchell, joined me and mentioned we were receiving thousands of emails, calls, and faxes because I was reportedly "undecided" on impeachment. Without tipping my hand, I told Greg, "There is a difference between *undecided* and *unannounced*."

My press secretary, Jeff Solsby, handed me a very complimentary op-ed by Paul Gigot in that morning's *Wall Street Journal*. I saw my picture alongside the caption, *Impeachment is GOP's Finest Hour*. Gigot wrote about my political predicament:

> The beauty of a debate as serious as impeachment is that it opens a window on political character. The phonies get sorted out from the fearless. The same commentators who denounce politicians as slaves to polls now call Republicans fools for ignoring them. A White House that won't cough without polling has been astonished by Republicans who act out of conviction. If anyone could justify running in retreat, it's Judiciary Republican James Rogan. His Pasadena district is just 38 percent Republican and becoming less so. Mr. Clinton easily carried his district twice. The White House has him on its list of members who may oppose impeachment, but the president shouldn't count on it. From the first, Mr. Rogan told me he'd vote his conscience come what may. All politicians say this, but few of them get to prove it so publicly. Mr. Rogan hasn't announced his conclusions. But the logic of his questions is that Mr. Clinton's lying before grand juries isn't harmless self-protection but is an assault on the civil justice system. The lying and obstruction in the Lewinsky case compound the felony. [H]istory will best remember those who stood for unpopular principle and voted for the constitutional form of censure called impeachment for a president who lied repeatedly and without remorse, even after he got caught.

When I finished reading, I put down the article. Jeff asked, "What do you think about it?"

It was great, I told him, except for one problem:

"Paul Gigot doesn't vote in my district."

22

Rag-Tag Remnant

The Judiciary Committee reconvened on Friday morning, December 11. Just before Henry Hyde began the final phase, I handed him a package wrapped with ribbon and a bow. He opened it and removed a brand-new walnut gavel. "Gee, that's beautiful, Jim," he exclaimed. "To what do I owe this lovely gift?"

Being a lifelong collector of historic political memorabilia, I had an ulterior motive for my munificence. "Because," I told him as I picked up his battle-scarred committee gavel that he used, "when these hearings are over, I want this one for my collection." He laughed, accepted the trade, and agreed to make the switch later when the debates ended. I suggested that he get some extra gavels and use them during the hearing to give his grandchildren.

"A great suggestion, Jim," he said with a sigh, "but my grandchildren don't seem to really care about such things." Henry later reconsidered, because the next morning a large box of gavels sat on the floor next to him. Throughout the day he removed each gavel from the box, tapped it a few times during the debate, and then he placed it in a second box. He ordered engraved metal bands for them and presented one to each Judiciary Committee member.

• • •

Since I was near the end of the seniority rotation, I wasn't due to deliver my summation until late morning. I worked on it until moments before Henry recognized me. I hoped to explain to both my constituents and to future generations the reason for my decision, announced now for the first time:

Our committee undertakes its task in an era where the deceitful manipulation of public opinion no longer is viewed as evil but as art. Propaganda once invoked images of dictators enforcing mind control over the masses. Now we readily bathe ourselves in spin, and we confer the degree of "doctor" upon those who administer the dosage. In this sobering hour, the time has come to strip away the spin and propaganda and face the unvarnished truth of what this committee is called upon to review.

First, this impeachment inquiry is not and never was a license to rummage through the personal life of the president of the United States. It is a gross distortion to characterize his present dilemma as only about sex. As Governor Weld said earlier this week, adultery is not an impeachable offense. The country needs to know that nobody on this committee seeks to make it so.

If that is true, then why are these unsavory elements of the president's private life now at issue? It is because the president was a defendant in a sexual harassment civil rights lawsuit. When Paula Jones' lawsuit reached federal court, after much consideration, the trial judge ordered the president to answer under oath questions relating to other subordinate female employees with whom he might have solicited or engaged in sexual involvement. This line of questioning was not invented to torment the president. These questions are routine and must be answered every day by defendants in harassment cases throughout the country.

Why is this so? It is because the courts want to see if there is any pattern of conduct that might show a similar history of either harassment, abuse, or granting or denying job promotions. It was in this context that the president first was asked questions about Monica Lewinsky, and it had nothing to do with Judge Starr, Speaker Gingrich, or any member of the Congress of the United States.

If lying now becomes acceptable in harassment cases because candor is embarrassing or because the defendant is just too powerful to be required to tell the truth, we will destroy the sexual harassment protections currently enjoyed by millions of women in the workforce. One cannot fairly claim to support the societal benefits of these harassment laws on the one hand and then deny the application of these laws to a defendant merely because he is a president who shares one's party affiliation.

Next, the Constitution solemnly required President Clinton, as a condition of his becoming president, to swear an oath to preserve, protect and defend the Constitution and to take care that our nation's laws are executed faithfully. That oath of obligation required the president to defend our laws that protect women in the workplace, just as it also required him to protect our legal system from perjury, obstruction of justice, and abuse of power.

Fidelity to the presidential oath is not dependent on any president's personal threshold of comfort or embarrassment. Neither must it be a slave to the latest polling data. Even more disturbing is the current readiness of some to embrace out of political ease a thoroughly bastardized oath so long as the offender expresses generalized contrition while at the same time rejecting meaningful constitutional accountability.

Consider how far afield these new standards would move us as a nation since our first president obliged himself to the same oath that now binds Bill Clinton to the Constitution. On the day that George

Washington became president, he pledged to our new country that he would ground the foundation of his public policies in principles of private morality. He said that by elevating an otherwise sterile government to the level of private moral obligations, our new country would win the affection of its citizens and command the respect of the world.

Most significantly, in his first presidential address, Washington presented himself not as a ruler of men, but as a servant of the law. He established the tradition that in America powerful leaders are subservient to the rule of law and to the consent of the governed.

Two hundred years later, in an era of increasing ethical relativism, it seems almost foreign to modern ears that the first speech ever delivered by a president of the United States was a speech about the relationship between private and public morality. George Washington was not perfect. He certainly was no saint. But soldiers knew his bravery on the battlefield, and his national reputation for truthfulness was unquestioned. Washington, a very human being with very human flaws, still could set by personal example the standard of measurement for the office of the presidency.

Today, from a distance of two centuries, Washington stands as a distant, almost mythical figure. And yet, President Clinton and every member of the Congress of the United States have a living personal connection to him. Like Washington, each of us took a sacred oath to uphold the Constitution and the rule of law.

There is no business of government more important than upholding the rule of law. A sound economy amounts to nothing beside it, because without the rule of law all contracts are placed in doubt and all rights to property become conditional. National security is not more important than the rule of law, because without it there can be no security and there is little left defending. And the personal popularity of any president pales when weighed against this one fundamental concept that forever distinguishes us from every other nation: no person is above the law.

Mr. Chairman, the evidence clearly shows that the president engaged in a repeated and lengthy pattern of felonious conduct—conduct for which ordinary citizens can and have been routinely prosecuted and jailed. We cannot wish or censure this away. With his conduct aggravated by a motivation of personal and pecuniary leverage rather than by national security or some other legitimate government function, the solemnity of my own oath of office obliges me to do what the president has failed to do—defend the rule of law despite any personal or political cost.

With a heavy heart, but with an unwavering belief in the appropriateness of the decision, I will cast my vote for articles of impeachment against the president of the United States, William Jefferson Clinton.

When I finished, I felt none of the angst or grief that Senator Edmund Ross felt 130 years earlier when he reflected on his Andrew Johnson vote. I hoped that my constituents would see I made my decision thoughtfully. But whatever their impression, trial judges are not hard-wired to worry about public opinion when making tough calls. We rule and then we move on.

That is what I did here.

• • •

After members' summations, Chairman Hyde recessed the hearing. During the lunch break, committee Republicans met privately with him in our conference room.

Diary, Judiciary Republicans Meeting, December 12, 1998

Henry Hyde told us, "I have never been prouder to have worked with so many people," and then pleaded with us: "Please try to stick together if it is morally possible for you, and don't vote for the Democrat amendments."

Lindsey Graham (R-SC) said he would vote against Article II relating to Clinton's deposition perjury. I asked if Lindsey would reconsider if we amended the article to include Clinton's false answers in his 81 answers submitted under oath to the committee. Lindsey agreed to support the article with this change, which would give us a unanimous GOP vote on Article II.

After lunch, our committee began debate on Article I (Clinton's grand jury perjury). While the committee hashed through the many amendments, some of us started getting phone calls from non-Judiciary Republican congressmen who remained nestled cozily back home in their districts during the holiday. Some now demanded technical changes to the various articles and threatened to withhold their vote on the House floor if we failed to conform to their wishes. It was a distracting nuisance and showed a lack of respect for our long hours of work on the committee. Since every vote mattered, we could ill afford to alienate these last-minute backseat drivers.

Newly minted Congresswoman Heather Wilson (R-NM), barely five months on the job and with no legal or judicial background, telephoned the committee from her home in New Mexico and demanded to speak to me. Wilson told me she wouldn't vote for the perjury article unless we divided it into separate articles so she could vote on each of Clinton's lies individually. At first, I thought she was joking. "We'll be here voting into the 21st century," I replied with a laugh.

When I realized she meant business, I explained that the precedents of impeachment going back to the 1790s never required that sort of specificity. Growing very curt, she cut off my explanation and delivered an ultimatum: make this change or lose her vote. I asked if she would be satisfied if I drafted an amendment that added language impeaching Clinton because he committed "one or more of the following" incidents of grand jury perjury (and then adding the laundry list of his lies). She paused for a long time before answering that she would accept the change.

I returned to the committee and advised Henry of her call. He grew very annoyed over her last-minute interference and with her meaningless demand, but he told me to draft the amendment to satisfy her:

The Democrats went ballistic over the last-minute amendment introduced at Heather Wilson's insistence. Barney Frank mocked it at length and likened it to the game show *Let's Make a Deal*. I replied that the Democrats, and not the Republicans, originally suggested the change. A groan from their side arose over my claim. To prove the point, I cited the exact language in Articles I and II from the Democrat-drafted Watergate impeachment articles against Richard Nixon. The Democrats demanded we follow the Watergate model now, I said, and that is what the amendment did.

After we finished the debate on Heather Wilson's worthless and extorted amendment, I pulled a committee staffer aside and told him, "Don't put through any more goddamned phone calls to me from these out of town members—and pass the word to everyone else."

. . .

As our debate neared its end, a reporter showed me a press release indicating that Clinton planned yet another "apology" address to the nation that he now scheduled only minutes before we voted on the first article. As Democrats filed out of the committee to listen to Clinton's remarks on a television in their back room, Democrat Howard Berman (D-CA) asked to speak privately with my seatmate Lindsey Graham. Berman now undertook, on behalf of the White House, a last-minute attempt to peel off any Republican votes he could find. They left together.

A few minutes later, Howard returned alone and took his shot with me. "Listen, Jim," he said, "this article is going to pass. The Republicans don't need your vote on this. Back in your district it would be a big help to you to vote 'no.' You don't need to be on this."

"Oh, Howard," I replied with a grin, "your sudden concern for my political health is really touching. I didn't know you cared— especially since you have already endorsed my likely opponent! Listen, since you guys are going to hammer me in the next election anyway, let a guy have a little fun while he's here."

Knowing my comment rang true, he smiled sheepishly. "You can't blame a guy for trying," he said, and then he returned to his seat.

Berman wasn't the only person that day to suggest I vote against impeachment. Earlier, one of the speaker's staffers asked me to step out of the committee to see Newt. When we were alone, Newt asked if I had seen the disastrous numbers in my district tracking polls regarding impeachment and my unlikely longevity as a congressman if I voted for it. When I said I had, he got to the point: "My job is to bring you home. We have the votes in committee to pass articles of impeachment. We don't need your vote. Everyone will under-stand." He never told me to take a dive explicitly, but his message was clear. He wanted to protect me and not lose a House seat on a vote that might be meaningful personally but irrelevant numeri-cally—and potentially fatal to maintaining our slender House GOP majority in 2000.

"Mr. Speaker," I told him, "if you wanted someone to ignore the facts, you shouldn't have appointed an ex-prosecutor and ex-judge to the committee." He again urged me not to commit an unnecessary sacrifice. I expressed gratitude for his concern, and then I chuckled as I reminded him, "With all due respect, I don't tell you how to be speaker. Please don't tell me how to be a member of the Judiciary Committee." I know in cold print those words sound harsh and disrespectful, but I didn't deliver them that way, nor did he receive them as such.

"Okay," he told me, "I just wanted to make sure you knew how we all felt about it."

• • •

With all the Democrats still in the back room watching Clinton on television, there was nothing for us to do but wait for them. Republicans filtered back to our conference room to watch his belated expression of remorse "for what our country is going through and for what members of both parties in Congress are now forced to deal with." He then said he was willing to accept a "rebuke" short of impeachment, but he still refused to admit any legal wrongdoing.

"What a pile of shit this is," one colleague muttered aloud. "This bastard's been lying, stalling, and throwing bricks at us for an entire year, including this morning! Now he's sorry for what the Congress is 'forced to deal with' because of his stonewalling. For the last year, including these last two weeks, he's been calling us fanatics dragging him through trumped up charges. Now he regrets our pain? Fuck him."

When Clinton finished his speech, committee members returned to their seats. Nine minutes later, Henry Hyde called up Article I for a vote.

The voting on Article I surprised me a bit. It was such a solemn and historic occasion, yet to anyone witnessing it without knowing its circumstances, it would seem like any other routine committee vote. There was no narration about its significance. It was just a vote like any other.

Since so much press focus had been on what I would do because of my precarious election situation, I wanted to be certain there was no mistake when I voted. When my turn came, I swung the committee's fixed amplification microphone in front of me, turned it on, and cast my vote so all could hear:

"Aye."

As Chairman Hyde cast the final vote on the Article, I remembered watching Chairman Peter Rodino make the same vote during Watergate 24 years ago. When Rodino voted "aye" on Article I of Nixon's impeachment, his voice cracked. Hyde showed no such emotion. He was all business.

It was over in a few minutes. At 4:25 p.m., the House Judiciary Committee passed Article I on a 21-to-16 Party-line vote. For the first time in American history, an elected president would undergo an impeachment vote in the chamber of the United States House of Representatives.

• • •

The night wore on as we debated Article II (perjury in the Paula Jones lawsuit) and Article III (obstruction of justice in the aula Jones lawsuit and in the Starr investigation). Article II passed at 6:30 p.m., with only Lindsey Graham breaking rank with the GOP and voting against it. This surprised me, since Lindsey promised earlier to vote for it if we amended it for him (we did). Howard Berman's last-minute lobbying must have swayed Lindsey back to his earlier expressed (and legally erroneous) opinion that perjury in a settled civil lawsuit wasn't a crime.

Almost three hours later, Article III passed on a straight Party-line vote. We still had one more article with which to deal, but because of the late hour, Chairman Hyde adjourned the hearing until morning.

It didn't take long for the hate email and angry phone calls to bombard my office from around the country. My staff confirmed that a disturbingly high percentage of them originated from my Southern California district. Fortunately, I was too busy to wallow in the unpleasant sentiments.

• • •

The next morning, Henry Hyde called an early private meeting of GOP committee members to discuss our internal dissentions over the language in Article IV, scheduled for a vote shortly. This article alleged abuse of presidential power and contained a medley of complaints against Clinton, many of which involved deplorable behavior not involving criminal violations of law. The article as proposed had four subparts:

1. Clinton made false public statements to deceive the public intentionally and conceal his misconduct;

2. Clinton lied to his cabinet and aides knowing they would repeat the lies on his behalf to deceive the public and buffer him from accountability for his conduct;

3. Clinton used the White House Counsel's office to make frivolous assertions of executive privilege, which is only available to protect constitutionally protected communications, and may not be used to delay and obstruct a federal criminal investigation and a federal grand jury;

4. Clinton refused to truthfully answer questions propounded to him by the Judiciary Committee (in the 81-question request for admissions), and in some of his replies he gave false, misleading, and perjurious answers.

During our meeting, it became evident that this article carried far more controversy among Republicans than did the other three:

Diary, Judiciary Committee Republican Meeting, 8:30 a.m., December 12, 1998

As we discussed Article IV, Henry said, "The problem with this article is that we now have five Republicans who will vote against it just because of section (3) alone." Henry said he also had problems with some of the article although Clinton's offensive overall conduct justified its passage. As we debated it further, we saw too many members prepared to vote against it due to various objections. A consensus developed to drop sections (1), (2), and (3), and proceed only on section (4)— the "81 questions" perjury. "This is a much cleaner way to proceed," Henry said approvingly.

As to the censure resolution the Democrats would introduce after we voted on Article IV, Steve Buyer (R-IN) suggested we put that debate off until the following week. His suggestion received no support. Everyone else wanted to complete debate on it immediately.

Tom Mooney ended our meeting by pulling a new survey out of his pocket. "Last night, ABC News did a poll: Voters agreed that the Judiciary Committee treated Clinton fairly by a 55 percent to 45 percent margin." I leaned over and whispered to a colleague, "Wait and see that poll tonight after we kill the Democrats' censure motion."

We returned to the committee room to complete debate on Article IV, which also passed on a Party-line vote (with Republican Congressman Chris Cannon absent). Just before the clerk recorded the final tally, Chris rushed into the room breathlessly and yelled out his request from the back of the room to record his vote. The sight of Chris bursting through the doors—out of breath, red-faced, and perspiring—and shouting his vote proved the only light moment of the morning.

With all four articles of impeachment adopted by the committee, Henry granted the Democrats' request to introduce their censure motion as their alternative to impeachment. It read as follows.

It is the sense of Congress that:

1.   On January 20, 1993, William Jefferson Clinton took the oath prescribed by the Constitution of the United States faithfully to execute the office of President; implicit in that oath is the obligation that the president set an example of high moral standards and conduct himself in a manner that fosters respect for the truth; and William Jefferson Clinton has egregiously failed in this obligation, and through his actions has violated the trust of the American people, lessened their esteem for the office of President, and dishonored the office which they have entrusted to him;

2(a)   William Jefferson Clinton made false statements concerning his reprehensible conduct with a subordinate;

2(b) William Jefferson Clinton wrongly took steps to delay discovery of the truth; and

2(c) In as much as no person is above the law, William Jefferson Clinton remains subject to criminal and civil penalties; and

3.   William Jefferson Clinton, President of the United States, by his conduct has brought upon himself, and fully deserves, the censure and condemnation of the American people and the Congress; and by his signature on this Joint Resolution, acknowledges this censure and condemnation.

Think about the vicious attacks Democrats leveled at Ken Starr and our committee Republicans for citing Clinton's lawbreaking, and then reread what *they* said about him: Clinton violated America's trust; Clinton dishonored the presidency; Clinton lied; for all these reasons, and because no person is above the law, *Clinton should be subject to criminal prosecution.*

Ken Starr should have sued them for plagiarism.

In arguing for censure, Sheila Jackson Lee (D-TX) distinguished it from impeachment, which she called "final and unappealable." That was one of my problems with censure: it was *never* final. As noted earlier, a simple majority of any future Congress could vacate the censure and strike it from the history books.

Diary, House Judiciary Committee Debate on Impeachment Article IV, December 12, 1998

When the attacks on the Republicans' motivations in opposing censure continued, Bob Barr (R-GA) grew irked. He shot back, "This isn't group therapy or a feel-good session. This is the Congress of the United States. We have a solemn duty here based on an oath that we took to uphold the Constitution. Let's do it. If you people believe that it is okay for the president of the United States of America to perjure himself, to lie under oath, and to make false and misleading statements under oath, then have the backbone to stand up and say so. But, let's not succumb to that siren song, that mirage in the desert of a censure."

After a few hours, and with no surprises, it was over. All Republicans voted against censure; one Democrat voted "no," and another voted "present." With that final vote, the committee rejected censure as an option. The Clinton impeachment inquiry authorized in October by H. Res. 581 ended. Chairman Hyde adjourned the

House Judiciary Committee sine die for the 105th Congress.

As I collected my papers, Majority Chief Counsel Tom Mooney signaled for me to join him in the Republicans' committee conference room. Tom (the only current Republican committee staffer who was there for Watergate) patted me on the back. "Well," he sighed, "twice in one life," referring to his previous Nixon impeachment experience. Then he reached into his jacket pocket and retrieved Henry Hyde's committee gavel that he had used since becoming chairman and for each of these historic votes. "Henry told me to give this to you," he said. "He told me you'd know why."

Henry's grandchildren might not have been sentimental over such things, but I knew that this and other impeachment relics deserved preservation. Like the original first draft of the articles of impeachment, the committee's roll call tally sheets, and other memorabilia I saved, today you can also see Henry Hyde's gavel at the Smithsonian Institution where it remains on display.

• • •

In my interview with former Judiciary Chairman Peter Rodino earlier in the year, he told me that after he voted for impeachment articles in committee against Richard Nixon, he went back into the chairman's office, closed the door, and wept like a baby. Make what you will of the contrast, but there was no similar sentiment following our vote. At the risk of sounding callous (which I often am), or insensitive to the historical ramifications of our action (which I never have been), there were no Republican crocodile tears shed for Bill Clinton's self-inflicted predicament:

> **"Come in, Jim!" a beaming Henry Hyde called to me through his open door as I walked past his small committee chairman's office [following the final vote on Article IV]. I congratulated Henry and Tom Mooney and told them how proud I was to have been on their team during this historic endeavor. Henry reciprocated with praise for my colleagues and me.**

A few straggling members joined us in the chairman's office. We embraced and shook hands. We knew we had made history together in these last few hours and we were proud of our work.

I watched as Henry executed his final duty: signing a letter to Speaker Gingrich and Speaker-designate Livingston. The opening sentence cut right to the point: "Gentlemen, I am writing to inform you that the Committee on the Judiciary has ordered favorably reported a privileged resolution impeaching William Jefferson Clinton, President of the United States, for high crimes and misdemeanors." He requested the speaker reassemble the House on Thursday, December 17, to debate and vote on whether to impeach Clinton.

Late that night, while sitting at my kitchen table, I recorded these observations in my diary. In a few shorts' weeks, the tables had turned dramatically:

> Following our unexpected loss of GOP seats on November 3, the Republicans came out of the election rudderless, and adrift. The Democrats were rightfully jubilant, congratulating each other, and had a confident psychological advantage. Why not? The national polls showed overwhelmingly that the public supported Clinton's job performance, opposed impeachment, wanted the matter dropped, and warned Republicans not to pursue it.
>
> After the election, both outgoing Speaker Gingrich and incoming Speaker Livingston wanted a quick "exit strategy" to end the impeachment inquiry for the sake of the Party.
>
> Everyone failed to consider that the GOP losing seats on November 3 may have, in a bizarre way, made passage of impeachment articles in our committee more likely for a few reasons.

First, the pundits and politicians never factored into their "this will go away" calculation that Judiciary Committee Republicans really believed in what we were doing despite the election results.

Second, with Gingrich deposed, but Livingston not yet in charge, a leadership vacuum existed at the top GOP ranks that might otherwise have exerted meaningful pressure on Hyde and his committee members.

Third, when the Democrats pressured Hyde to end the inquiry by the end of the year—and with Henry's acceptance of the demand—it meant the committee had to work through the Thanksgiving holiday season while the rest of Congress had left Washington and had returned home. We didn't have scores of poll-rattled and wobbly Republicans descending on us while voicing their woes about impeachment, which might have caused hesitant committee members to lose their nerve.

Fourth, Clinton dealt with our committee from a position of arrogance. When we sent Clinton our 81 questions to help expedite the end of the proceedings, he took his time replying. When he did respond, he returned a document containing answers that one of his aides described as "intentionally snotty." Big mistake: Clinton's under-oath answers in that document are now the basis for impeachment in Article IV.

Our dejected, rag-tag team withstood the attacks of committee Democrats and the White House. We will make our case that he deserved impeachment. Come hell or high water, we will endure the cost and the consequences.

My old friend Larry Arnn [president of the Claremont Institute; later president of Michigan's Hillsdale College] told me the other night that very few politicians ever get the chance to do something great for their country. He said this was a great thing for our Constitution, for the rule of law, and for the notion that no man is above the law. In the whole world, Larry reminded me that there were only 21 committee Republicans standing between Bill Clinton and justice.

I understood going into this that I have the most to lose. Every other committee member is in a safe district. My district is now solidly Democrat and heavily pro-Clinton. By taking a leading role in pushing for impeachment, I have drawn a big target on my back. But as Larry Arnn also reminded me, if I must lose my reelection, there is only honor in losing for a great constitutional cause.

If this means the end of my political future, I will always count it an honor to have been part of this noble effort.

23

Backlash

Until the eve of it actually happening, I never expected the House of Representatives to impeach President Clinton—despite the Judiciary Committee's recommendation. Many Republican members had already announced publicly that they either opposed impeachment or that they leaned heavily against it. On top of that, most of our leadership wanted it to go away because it was a demonstrable loser politically.

Now, slowly, the pendulum swung the other way. For the first time, non-Judiciary Republican House members evaluated critically the evidence presented before our committee. The more they looked, the more the dynamic changed. Inside my diaries I found a "call sheet" assigned to me on December 14, two days after the Judiciary Committee passed the impeachment resolutions. The sheet listed six moderate and undeclared Republicans for me to contact. My job was not to lobby them, but rather ask this question: Will you support the recommendation of the committee on impeachment? On every call I completed, the answer surprised me: Yes.

Diary, Tuesday, December 15, 1998

Tom Campbell (R-CA), a leader of the moderate Republicans, today came out in favor of Clinton's impeachment. This is a huge loss for the White House. Many of our undecided moderates look to Tom for guidance, so his action may

sway others who might otherwise have voted "no." For the first time, some reporters are speculating that the House might actually impeach Clinton. This stunning prospect, so unlikely only a few days ago, has taken on a life of its own.

Yesterday's *Washington Post* quoted a member of Clinton's inner circle as saying, "The first inkling that he could be in danger has begun to dawn on people at the White House. There's a greater amount of second-guessing about why we didn't take it more seriously." In his televised appearances today, Clinton looked terrible. He continues flailing about with more apologies while refusing to admit he lied.

As Judiciary Republicans prepared for the House debate, Henry Hyde broke down the impeachment issues into 25 parts and divided them among his committee members. My assignments included presenting an overview on Article I (perjury), the negative impact on all sexual harassment laws if Congress excused Clinton's lies in a sexual harassment lawsuit, and the precedent we would set if we failed to hold him accountable for perjury and obstruction of justice.

Diary, Judiciary Committee Republican Meeting, December 16, 1998

After passing out a final list of tasks, Henry told us to get ready: "Every fact must be covered. Each one of you needs to be an expert on your assigned area, but you also must be prepared to speak about any of the articles in general and every theme that winds through the articles."

Henry also assigned me to the "Truth Squad"—four GOP committee members who would remain on the floor during the entire debate to rebut immediately any Democrat mischaracterization of the evidence. Joining me on the squad are Bob Goodlatte (R-VA), Charles Canady (R-FL), and Asa Hutchinson (R-AR).

Putting the cart before the horse and signaling a new-found confidence that the House might actually impeach Clinton, Henry warned us about our demeanor: "When we win this thing, we all need to look somber and serious. Make sure there are no visible demonstrations of joy on the floor among our troops."

"The momentum is with us," Henry said, "and Clinton knows it."

Henry then related a rumor he heard earlier this morning at a leadership meeting: that Clinton planned to slow our advance by launching a missile attack against Iraq in a desperate attempt to halt the impeachment debate set for tomorrow. Many in the room (including me) looked around at one another smirking at his suggestion. "Henry's been watching too many movies," I whispered to a colleague. "Not even Clinton would pull a stunt like that." We chuckled quietly over the notion that Clinton would be so foolish as to replicate the plot of a recent Hollywood movie, *Wag the Dog*, about a president who started a phony war to shift attention from his sex scandal.

Then, unbelievably, with only hours to go before the final impeachment debate began, Clinton launched an air strike against Iraq. When news of this military assault reached us, our focus necessarily shifted to whether we needed to cancel tomorrow's scheduled impeachment debate. If we did so, we'd play into Clinton's cynical plan to kill impeachment by any means available.

Clinton understood at this time what most Americans did not. The House only had two weeks to vote on the Judiciary Committee's impeachment resolutions or they would expire on January 3 when we seated the new Congress. If that happened, impeachment was dead unless the House reauthorized the Judiciary Committee to begin the inquiry from scratch. The incoming 106th Congress promised five more Democrats and five fewer Republicans, making this prospect very unlikely. Given Clinton's win-at-all-costs history, we all knew his latest gambit was a last-ditch attempt to buy enough time to suffocate impeachment.

> When our meeting resumed, and after listening to news reports of the Iraq attack, I accused Clinton of putting soldiers' lives in jeopardy in a reckless effort to delay the impeachment vote. I argued for going through with the debate. Jim Sensenbrenner (R-WI) agreed, saying, "We don't stop elections during war. We shouldn't stop this, either."
>
> Steve Buyer (R-IN), an Army reserve officer, also concurred, saying he just called the Defense Department: "They confirmed there was no immediate threat today from [Iraq leader] Saddam Hussein. There is no threat today of any biological or chemical attack by Saddam. They said this attack was launched just as 'a response' for Saddam's refusal to cooperate weeks ago with United Nations weapons inspectors."
>
> On the other side, Lindsey Graham (R-SC) voiced the concern that we might lose moderate GOP votes by failing to cancel the debate. Joining him was George Gekas (R-PA), who grew emotional in his plea to halt the impeachment: "What if we suffer U.S. casualties?" he asked.
>
> "If we suffer *any* American casualties because Clinton put those kids in harm's way to fend off an impeachment vote," I replied harshly, "then this Iraqi raid should be grounds for a new impeachment article against this bastard."

We recessed our discussion to join an emergency session of the entire House GOP conference called by Speaker-designate Bob Livingston in response to the Clinton-created military crisis. The commander in chief's willingness to risk American military lives to avoid an impeachment vote caused a seething contempt for him to circulate through our conference ranks. In yet another ironic twist, instead of slowing the clamor for impeachment, his action pushed some outraged undecideds into the pro-impeachment camp.

**Diary, House Republican Conference,
The Capitol, December 16, 1998**

Bob Livingston began the meeting by telling us that tonight at 8:00 p.m., the secretary of Defense would brief all members on the House floor regarding the ongoing Iraq bombing.

"You all need to know that I have great reservations about bringing an impeachment resolution to the House floor while our service people are at risk," Livingston said. "However, we will determine as a conference whether to delay these proceedings."

Don Manzullo (R-IL) noted that Iraq had refused to cooperate four times this year with weapons inspectors and Clinton did nothing. "Why now?" Manzullo asked, and urged us to continue with the impeachment vote. Bob Barr (R-GA) agreed, saying the meeting with Secretary Cohen tonight would be a trap. "These guys will justify anything," he argued. A strong consensus developed not to surrender to Clinton's conduct. Overwhelmingly, our members want to proceed with the impeachment debate tomorrow.

We interrupted our meeting to watch Clinton's hastily scheduled address to the nation. In his speech, he said he took this action because Iraq's leader, Saddam Hussein, announced six weeks ago that he would no longer cooperate with the United Nations weapons inspectors.

Moments after Clinton finished, House Democrat Leader Richard Gephardt and his team flooded the airwaves demanding that Republicans halt the impeachment debate indefinitely: "It shouldn't come up as long as our troops are in harm's way," Gephardt insisted, suggesting that doing anything less was unpatriotic and harmful to our military.

Henry Hyde's measured reply spoke for most House Republicans: "Many who oppose consideration of articles of impeachment at this time are opposed to considering them at any time," he told the press. "These events should not be an excuse for turning away from our constitutional duties."

After watching Clinton's remarks, we resumed our Republican conference meeting:

> **After two more hours of discussion, Sonny Callahan (R-AL) made a motion to give Livingston the flexibility to delay the debate and vote. Livingston urged us to adopt the motion, and then he asked for Henry Hyde's opinion. "Despite the suspicious circumstances surrounding Clinton's action," Henry said, "maybe we should put this over for a couple of days. This would acknowledge the presence of our troops in harm's way, and then we can get on with our job."**
>
> **At Livingston's request, we passed the motion. "We will meet tomorrow on the House floor," Livingston said, "and we will pass a resolution supporting our troops. We will not initiate impeachment proceedings tomorrow. This will remain subject to the call of the chair. We may take it up in a few days."**
>
> **Majority Whip Tom DeLay announced that no whip count would be taken to determine who supported or opposed impeachment. He advised that there were not enough votes to impeach Clinton. "There are too many of you still undecided," he said.**
>
> **"Not for long!" someone called from the back of the room, which generated great laughter.**

At 8:00 p.m., we adjourned our meeting and walked upstairs to the House floor for the confidential military briefing. Clinton's

Defense Secretary William Cohen told us the attack on Iraq was a purely military decision. "Impeachment was never mentioned or considered" by Clinton, he said. "This decision to bomb was based solely on military necessity." His statement elicited disbelieving laughter on the Republican side. Under later questioning, Cohen admitted that Clinton made the bombing decision without consulting any member of the United Nations Security Council. "I don't know how [the Security Council members] will feel about it," he admitted.

Tom DeLay asked Cohen if there was any national security reason why the House should not begin the impeachment debate. Cohen declined to answer directly but said that right now the president needed broad bipartisan support. The Democrats stood and applauded that assertion.

After the meeting with Cohen, the GOP leadership put off the impeachment debate indefinitely. Another round went to Clinton—or did it?

• • •

From the time the Judiciary Committee adopted articles of impeachment on December 12, it didn't take long to get a taste of what would await those of us involved in supporting them:

Diary, Sunday, December 13, 1998

Following church services, I went to the bookstore in Pentagon City with Dana [my six-year old daughter]. As we held hands and browsed the racks, a well-dressed man in his late 30s or early 40s stormed up to me shrieking at the top of his lungs, "You make me ashamed to be an American! You're a traitor!" When he continued screaming in a combative and crazed fashion, my old bartender instinct kicked in. I slowly slid Dana behind me to protect her, and with my hand out

of sight, I curled my fist. If this lunatic made an aggressive move, I stood ready to knock him through the wall. Fortunately, he skulked away before it escalated any further. I was glad—I can't very well go around slugging every Clinton supporter in America.

When I mentioned the confrontation later to Tom Mooney, he sounded worried, but not over my encounter. He said that the police warned him about a "contract" someone put out to kill Henry Hyde, Bob Barr, and Lindsey Graham. The price is $2 million to kill Henry and $250,000 to kill either Bob or Lindsey. His news made me feel like I hadn't done my job satisfactorily. I had no hitman contract against me—just some chubby, screaming asshole in a bookstore.

Diary, Thursday, December 17, 1998

I walked back from the Capitol to the Cannon Building with Mary Bono (R-CA). Mary was distraught over the hate mail and angry calls she had received since voting a few days ago in committee to impeach Clinton. She said that the tabloid *National Enquirer* just published a false story that she had an affair during her marriage to Sonny. I tried to cheer Mary up by telling her that nobody reads or believes that trash.

"How would you feel," she asked me, "if the *Enquirer* wrote false stories about your sex life for everyone to read?"

Putting my arm around her, I said, "Mary, I keep sending the *Enquirer* false stories about my sex life. No matter how hard I try, I can't get them to print any."

The tabloid focus on the sexual indiscretions of Republican members of Congress was nothing new. Two months earlier, Larry

Flynt called a press conference and offered up to a million-dollar bounty to anyone coming forward with evidence of an illicit sexual relationship with House Republicans. I learned about the bounty when I entered the Judiciary Committee room and found my seatmate, Lindsey Graham, reading a news account of Flynt's offer. As Lindsey recounted the story to me, he looked up from the paper and in his soft drawl asked me, "Jim, do you really think a woman would sacrifice her virtue and her family name for a million dollars?" Candidly, I thought he was joking. However, the earnestness in his eyes told me otherwise.

Knowing he was the only bachelor in our group and suspecting there might be some old girlfriend story floating around that now made him uncomfortable, I thought I'd have a little fun. "Lindsey," I replied, "you're one of my best friends in Congress. You need to know something: for a million dollars, I'll turn you in."

The laughter I expected as a reaction didn't come. Instead, he studied me closely, almost as if he now took my measure as a friend and as a man:

"Jim," he asked, "would you really turn me in for a million dollars?"

Patting his back and returning the solemn gaze, I said, "Lindsay, for a million bucks I'll not only turn you in—I'll say I was the guy who did it with you."

Soon thereafter, I saw another colleague—we'll call him Joe (not his real name)—seated alone in the House chamber looking very despondent. I asked if everything was all right. After a while, he confided in me: "There's this woman. It's not what you think—we're just good friends. However, it's complicated and the relationship could be, well, misunderstood. She said Larry Flynt's people just called her and they know about us. They gave her an ultimatum: come forward and give us the story and we will pay you $250,000, or don't come forward, we'll print it anyway, and pay you nothing. She said she was calling me because she doesn't know what to do. My wife doesn't know about this. She'll leave me and take the kids if she finds out."

"Listen, Joe," I told him firmly, "get this through your skull. She didn't call for advice. She's giving you a head's up. She's going to give up her information. You need to go home and tell your wife. You can't let her find out about this in the press."

"But she'll kill me! She'll leave me and take the kids!" he cried.

"Goddamn it, Joe, get home and tell her."

The next day I saw Joe. He looked awful. Still in the same clothes from yesterday, with puffy red eyes and needing a shave, he nodded wearily and gave me a "thumbs up" sign when I approached. He said he took my advice. He went home and told his wife. As she packed her bags to leave, he sobbed and pleaded for forgiveness. Finally, as morning approached, she promised to stay, but only after he agreed to a long list of oppressive conditions.

"I bet you feel better about yourself now," I said. He admitted that he did, and that his confession had lifted a burden from his shoulders.

A week or so later, Flynt's exposé hit the newsstands. I was standing on the floor of the House that day when, through the corner of my eye, I saw Joe heading toward me down an aisle. Holding a rolled-up magazine in his hand, he approached and asked me if I had seen the exposé edition. I told him I hadn't. His face contorted as he spoke:

"I'm not even in the goddamn thing!" he snarled at me. "I went home and let my wife beat the living shit out me thanks to you and your goddamned advice!"

"But Joe," I said with the biggest smile I could muster, "you feel better about yourself!"

"Fuck you!" he barked, and then he threw the rolled-up magazine at me. It bounced off my chest as he turned and stormed out of the chamber. I followed him down the aisle and teased, "But, Joe! Remember! You feel better about yourself!"

I handled the scrutiny differently. One night a national talk show host interviewed me. He asked if Flynt's threat of exposure worried me—especially since I had something of a checkered youth. I looked directly into Camera Two with the red light and replied, "Larry Flynt, if you're watching, you need to know something. I bartended in strip clubs in Hollywood. I even worked as a bouncer in a porn theater. There's plenty of information's out there on me. Dig it up, Larry! Dig!"

Alas, nobody published any sexual stories about me (sensational or otherwise), no matter how hard I tried to promote the effort.

• • •

The day after Clinton's impromptu Iraqi air strike and our decision to delay the impeachment vote, Judiciary Republicans gathered for another strategy meeting. An announcement from the House floor interrupted our session:

Diary, Judiciary Committee Republican Meeting, December 17, 1998

As our GOP Judiciary meeting began, Republican Majority Leader Dick Armey (R-TX) announced over CSPAN that the House would lift the stay and proceed tomorrow with the impeachment debate. Speaker-designate Bob Livingston took the floor and echoed Armey's sentiment, saying the House could not close down its business indefinitely.

In an emotional blast at Republicans, Democrat Minority Leader Dick Gephardt again demanded that we hold off debating impeachment for as long as U.S. troops were in harm's way. The GOP leadership reiterated their intent to proceed tomorrow.

After Clinton depleted his bag of tricks with the last-minute missile attack, his risking the lives of American military personnel bought him nothing more than a measly 24-hour delay in facing the music.

Late that same evening, Speaker-designate Livingston called another House GOP conference meeting. In what proved to be an already exhausting, topsy-turvy week, nobody anticipated the next bomb about to drop:

> At our GOP conference meeting, I saw Bob Livingston, arms folded across his chest and looking pensive, standing alone and off to the side of the room. I walked over to Bob and said I needed to leave and get to work on my impeachment prep for tomorrow's showdown: "Is there anything else going on here of importance tonight," I asked unsuspectingly, "or can I take off?"
>
> Bob looked at me dolefully for a moment, and then he heaved a sigh. "Yeah, there is," he replied, "and I'm going to say it now. Stay for a few more minutes."
>
> Stepping to the microphone, Bob looked nervous as he began speaking. Referencing pornographer Larry Flynt's recent sex bounty, he told us, "I've been 'outed' by Larry Flynt." Bob then confessed that he had an affair some time ago and that Flynt planned to publish the details. Bob expressed deep remorse, but he said that this news would not intimidate him from doing his duty.
>
> [Fellow Judiciary member] Chris Cannon (R-UT) pounded his fist into his chair. "Damn these people in the White House," he growled.
>
> I collected my things and told Chris, "We don't have time for this shit right now. We've got too much work to do tonight."

As members jumped to their feet expressing both support for Bob and outrage over this latest smear, I grabbed my notebooks and slipped out the side door. Reporters (already tipped off about Livingston's revelation) mobbed me. One television reporter shoved her microphone in my face screaming, "Has he resigned? Has he resigned?" Unable to resist poking a little fun at the situation, I shook my head:

"No," I replied, "he hasn't resigned. Nor do I think he should resign. President Clinton should remain in office and allow us to proceed with our impeachment debate."

That unexpected answer caught the reporter off guard. After shaking it off, she shouted, "No! No! No! I'm not asking about Clinton! I'm asking about Livingston!"

"Oh, *Livingston*! I thought you meant Clinton. No, Livingston hasn't resigned, either." With that, I pushed my way through the crowd and went back to my office to continue debate preparation.

My final diary entry that night, written late in the evening of this long and harrowing day, closed with this observation:

> **There is great anger at Clinton tonight on the part of my Republican House colleagues. First, they believe he bombed Iraq and risked American lives to spare himself impeachment. Now, despite his denials, they blame him for this last-minute smear against Livingston. ABC News reporter Cokie Roberts revealed that the White House "shopped" the Livingston story to her for the last two weeks. Everyone now expects warfare on the House floor tomorrow.**

• • •

Long after both Bob Livingston and I left Congress, we met for lunch occasionally to catch up. At one such lunch he told me the rest of the story behind the Flynt smear.

A few hours before Bob stood in front of the GOP conference and revealed his affair, he received a call that President Clinton wanted to see him at the White House. At their private meeting,

Clinton told Bob matter-of-factly that enough was enough: Bob needed to shut down the impeachment process and kill it *now*. Bob told Clinton it was too late, and he couldn't stop it if he wanted. Clinton looked at him and said nothing for a few moments. Then, tight-lipped and nodding his head, he spoke one word: "Okay."

Bob headed home, but he hadn't traveled more than a few miles when his wife called on his cell phone with a question: "Why is an *Associated Press* reporter asking me to comment on your having an affair?"

Clinton and his team continued denying that they had anything to do with leaking the damning information on Bob's ancient indiscretion.

Good luck convincing Bob Livingston of that, and don't waste your time trying to convince me, either.

24

Earning Their Pay

"The House of Representatives . . . shall have the sole Power of Impeach-
ment"

—UNITED STATES CONSTITUTION, ARTICLE I § 2

On the morning of the House debate on the impeachment of President Clinton, I arrived at my Capitol
office well before dawn. After reviewing my notes
and thick resource binders one final time, I shut the door for a few
minutes of prayer. In reading some passages of Scripture, I wondered
if President Clinton, a fellow Christian, was doing the same thing.
This curiosity became stronger when I happened on Job 31:15: "Did
not He who made me make him? Did not the same One fashion us?"

Two sides locked in a bitter struggle, yet maybe praying to the
same God to watch over us and protect us. How irreconcilable at
first blush, and yet how remarkable. Abraham Lincoln had it right:
"I do not boast that God is on my side," he once wrote. "I humbly
pray that I am on God's side."

Diary, The U.S. Capitol, December 18, 1998

**Henry Hyde met with his team briefly in the Judiciary Com-
mittee conference room before the floor proceedings began.
He told us to pass the word on a key point: "I'm concerned
that after the vote on the final Article of Impeachment, our
members will rush from the floor and head to the airport
after adjournment. They need to know that after we vote
on the last article, we must remain to vote on the resolution
appointing House Managers [the prosecutors authorized by
the House to try the case before the U.S. Senate]. If we don't
have the votes on the floor to pass the Managers resolution,
it will destroy our ability to move forward.**

**"During debate, keep your demeanor solemn, serious and
persistent. Stick to the facts and law. Avoid taking the bait on
Iraq or censure. If the Democrats say something that requires
a response, keep it to ten seconds or so." Finally, in reference
to the Livingston revelation yesterday, Henry added gravely,
"If you're not convinced by now that these people in the White
House are evil, then I don't know how else to convince you."**

A few minutes after 9:00 a.m., Speaker Pro Tempore Ray
LaHood (R-IL) gaveled the crowded House floor to order.[1] Henry
Hyde began the formal presentation on behalf of the Judiciary Com-

---

1 Shortly before LaHood opened the session, I handed him one of the official House gavels
given to me earlier by Speaker Gingrich after I had presided over debate on another bill. I
told him that I collected historic memorabilia, and I asked him to use my gavel throughout
the impeachment debate and vote these next couple of days. He agreed, and he put the
podium gavel in a nearby drawer. He then took my gavel and used it throughout the day. At
the end of the lengthy session, I retrieved my gavel from him. We repeated the switch the
next morning. After he banged my gavel for the last vote during the impeachment debate,
I walked back to the speaker's platform, retrieved my gavel, and handed him back the one
resting in the drawer for the last two days. Along with some other impeachment memorabilia
that I wanted preserved for future generations, the gavel he used and returned to me that day
went on display in the Smithsonian Institution for two decades.

mittee Republicans. Standing in the well, the dignified chairman spoke of the importance of the rule of law:

> The question before this House . . . is not a question of sex. The matter before the House is a question of lying under oath. This is a public act, not a private act. This is called perjury. The matter before the House is a question of the willful, premeditated, deliberate corruption of the nation's system of justice. Perjury and obstruction of justice cannot be reconciled with the office of the president of the United States....
>
> We must decide if the chief law enforcement officer of the land, the person who appoints the attorney general, the person who nominates every federal judge, the person who nominates the [justices of the] Supreme Court, and the only person with a constitutional obligation to take care that the laws be faithfully executed, can lie under oath repeatedly and maintain it is not a breach of trust sufficient for impeachment. . . .
>
> The President is our flag-bearer. He stands out in front of our people, and the flag is falling. Catch the falling flag as we keep our appointment with history.

Minority Leader Dick Gephardt opened the debate for the Democrats, again using Clinton's deployment of force against Iraq as an excuse to halt the proceeding. His deputy, David Bonior (D-MI), ratcheted up the Iraq rhetoric, suggesting that the failure to halt impeachment showed the Republicans lacked both patriotism and concern for our troops overseas.

From there, it went downhill.

Throughout the marathon debate, the Democrats wafted between attacking our loyalty for seeking to oust the commander in chief during hostilities, pursuing a sexual witch-hunt against

Clinton, and using impeachment to "undo an election" to secure what we could not win at the ballot box.

This latter notion was particularly silly, since Clinton's removal guaranteed Democrat Vice President Al Gore's succession to the presidency. To show the constitutional fallacy of this claim in one of my presentations that day, I quoted Dr. Larry Arnn of the Claremont Institute:

> Elections have no higher standing under our Constitution than the impeachment process. Both stem from provisions of the Constitution. The people elect the president to do a constitutional job. They act under the Constitution when they do it. At the same time, they elect a Congress to do a different constitutional job. The President swears an oath to uphold the Constitution. So does the Congress. Everyone concerned is acting in ways subordinate to the Constitution, both in elections and in the impeachment process. If a President is guilty of acts justifying impeachment, then he and not the Congress will have overturned the election. He will have acted in ways that betray the purpose of his election. He will have acted not as a constitutional representative, but as a monarch, subversive of, or above the law.

I often quoted the writings of my old friend Dr. Arnn to vaporize the Democrats' impeachment rhetoric with constitutional logic. In fact, I must have quoted him too frequently. Soon after impeachment, Clinton's Internal Revenue Service audited him.

Although the historic impeachment debate began in a standing-room-only chamber, by the end of the first hour most members drifted away. During all 13 hours, I remained on the floor with our other "Truth Squad" members to correct Democrat misstatements and misrepresentations of the record. Near the end of the battle, I closed my portion of the GOP's case with a summary of why Clinton's conduct warranted impeachment:

Mr. Speaker, our Supreme Court characterizes perjured testimony not as trivial conduct, but as criminal conduct. This Congress must decide whether we will ignore allegations respecting the subversion of the courts, the search for truth, and the perjurious abuse of a young woman in a sexual harassment lawsuit. If we allow perjury to be viewed as a sign of legal finesse, we will be responsible for setting the standard that any future president may lie under oath for any personal convenience and may do it without regard to constitutional consequences. Under this perversion of the law, any president may commit perjury for reasons of self-interest and trample his constitutional obligation to ensure that our laws are executed faithfully. The Congress must not insulate from constitutional accountability those who repeatedly violate their oath.

The evidence against the president on this score is overwhelming, and so too is Congress' constitutional obligation. We must keep faith with our Founders' dream that they could raise, and we could sustain, a nation where no person is above the law.

• • •

Over the last few months, reporters kept asking me if Henry Hyde would appoint me as a House Manager in the event the House really impeached Clinton. The first diary entry I found relating to this speculation came three months before our impeachment vote:

Diary, September 15, 1998

Congressman Kevin Brady (R-TX) told me, "Two very high-up members of our GOP leadership told a handful of my Texas donors today that you are their first choice to lead the prosecution of Bill Clinton in a Senate impeachment trial." A week ago, some reporters told me they heard the same rumor that I was under consideration as a Manager if the House

impeached Clinton. I brushed off the suggestions, but privately I view the prospect as an overwhelming consideration.

Whenever asked, I always told reporters that I expected Speaker Gingrich and Chairman Hyde to choose senior members rather than freshmen for such a solemn duty. Still, as we moved closer to an impeachment vote, these press inquiries increased, which in turn made me wonder if I stood a chance of selection.

The speculation energized my congressional staff. Over the last few weeks leading up to the final vote, I rarely returned to my office without one of them asking if I had "heard anything" about becoming a Manager. Now, as we neared completion of the House's role, I remained certain my name was not under consideration.

When the House adjourned after ending our 13-hour marathon debate, a committee staffer handed me a nondescript thick envelope marked "Member's Personal Attention." Assuming it contained more debate research data, I carried it back to my office and tossed it on my desk. Meanwhile, my chief of staff Greg Mitchell rushed in: "Any word on the House Manager issue?" he asked.

I told him no and said that by this late hour I couldn't possibly have made the roster. "We're voting on the Managers' resolution early tomorrow morning," I said. "Henry must have selected and notified his Managers long before now." As I explained to Greg all the sensible reasons for my not being selected, I opened the envelope and removed a brief cover letter from Chairman Hyde asking me to familiarize myself, as soon as possible, with the contents of the enclosed publication. I removed from the envelope a booklet entitled *Procedure and Guidelines for Impeachment Trials in the United States Senate.*

Handing the letter and booklet to Greg, I asked, "Hmm. Do you think this means anything?"

Diary, The U.S. Capitol, December 18, 1998

Judiciary Chief Counsel Tom Mooney called me late tonight to confirm I received Henry's letter and the booklet. Tom said that Henry wants me as one of the prosecutors in the Senate if the House passes any impeachment articles tomorrow morning.

This is a very sobering duty.

In rereading this brief diary entry years after writing it, I am reminded of later stories portraying me as some sort of "reluctant warrior" doing the duty for which I was drafted, however distasteful the task personally. I always suspected someone in my reelection campaign planted that image trying to minimize the political damage back home. There was no truth to the characterization. Although I never asked to be a Manager, I wanted to be part of the trial team before the Senate because I believed in the mission. Besides, what old prosecutor worth his salt would shy away from strapping on his spurs for the biggest trial in American political history? Had Henry Hyde kept me off his list, it may have helped me retain my seat, but I would have regretted the exclusion for the rest of my life.

• • •

The next day, Saturday, December 19, it fell upon us to answer the question asked endlessly since the Lewinsky story broke a year earlier: Will the United States House of Representatives impeach President Clinton?

Diary, The U.S. Capitol, December 19, 1998

Minutes before Speaker Pro Tem Ray LaHood called the House to order, I walked outside and stood atop the House steps surveying the Capitol Plaza. The quietness and serenity

of the scene surprised me. Just a few reporters and protesters out there. On the south side of the Capitol, a long line of tourists waited silently for their turn to enter the building on this historic day.

The scene inside the House Chamber was anything but serene. By now, members filled all the seats and visitors packed the galleries above. U.S. Senators (voicing disbelief to each other over what was about to happen) lined the back rail. Above the speaker's dais, it was standing room only for the reporters when LaHood banged my gavel at 9:24 a.m. for the final round of debate. Henry Hyde asked me to lead off the GOP final summations, and I kept my presentation brief:

Mr. Speaker, the evidence is overwhelming, and the question is elementary. The President was obliged under his sacred oath to execute our nation's laws faithfully. Yet he repeatedly perjured himself and obstructed justice—not for any noble purpose, but to crush a lone woman's right to be afforded access to the courts. Now his defenders plead for no constitutional accountability for the one American uniquely able to defend or debase our Constitution and the rule of law.

When they are old enough to appreciate today's solemnity, I want my young daughters to know that when the last roll was called, their father served in a House faithful to the guiding principle that no person is above the law. And I want them to know that he served with colleagues who counted it a privilege to risk political fortune in defense of the Constitution.

Midway through the debate, LaHood recognized Speaker-designate Bob Livingston:

After expressing support for our case, Livingston addressed President Clinton directly from the House well and told him that his behavior damaged the country. With that, he called on Clinton to resign the presidency.

House Democrats jumped to their feet hissing and booing Livingston. Some banged their hands on the tables. Showing a fury that I've never seen before inside the chamber, the faces of many contorted into hateful looks as they screamed and shrieked at Bob, "You resign! You resign!"

Livingston waited silently for the clamor to die down. Sitting in the front row only a few feet from him, I saw no hint that he was about to detonate another live grenade. He raised his hand for silence, and then in a calm voice, he told the House:

I was prepared to lead our narrow majority as speaker, and I believe I had it in me to do a fine job. I cannot do that job or be the kind of leader that I would like to be under current circumstances. I will not stand for speaker of the House on January 6, but rather I shall remain as a backbencher in this Congress that I so dearly love for approximately six months into the 106th Congress, whereupon I shall vacate my seat and ask my governor to call a special election to take my place. I thank my constituents for the opportunity to serve them. I hope they will not think badly of me for leaving. And I thank my wife most especially for standing by me. I love her very much.

Livingston's words shocked everyone. Some Democrats who moments earlier shouted in wrath at him now had tears in their eyes. Republican members also had tears, but for many these were tears of rage.

"Now, you bastards, are you satisfied?" one Republican seated behind me shouted at the Democrats. Members began

rising and applauding as Livingston folded his speech and exited the House floor. The rustling notepads of reporters above me in the press gallery sounded like a swarm of bees.

As dazed members absorbed the stunning scene, LaHood next recognized Democrat Jose Serrano (D-NY), who typified the inflammatory spew Democrats hurled at Republicans throughout the debate. After accusing us of wanting to "overthrow the government," Serrano alluded to Livingston's sudden resignation:

> From day one, the Republican right wing wanted to get rid of Bill Clinton. From day one, they stood on him and tried to make him out to be the number one villain in this country. They were blinded by hate then, and they are blinded by hate today. This place is full of hate because of what they tried to do to our president. I grew up in the public housing projects of the South Bronx. I can tell a bunch of bullies when I see them. The bullies get theirs, and these [Republicans] are getting theirs, too.

In delivering this abusive speech on the heels of Livingston's emotional words, Serrano horribly misread the mood of the chamber. Dozens of furious Republicans now booed him and walked off the floor in protest of his intemperate remarks, which incited Serrano to increase his invective.

Fortunately, another Democrat had far greater political sensitivity, and it came from one that most Republicans disliked: Democrat Leader Dick Gephardt, who rushed down the center aisle and sought recognition. Apparently abandoning his earlier prepared remarks for the final impeachment debate, he spoke passionately, calling Livingston "a good and honorable man." He added, "I pray with all my heart that he will reconsider this decision." Republicans responded by giving Gephardt a standing ovation—the only time I ever saw that phenomenon.

As things calmed down, we returned to the final debate. Democrat John Conyers yielded time to Republican Chris Shays (R-CT) to speak against impeachment. Weeks earlier, Shays announced that he would vote "no" on impeachment. Then, as our committee produced the mounting evidence and Shays sensed the mood of the House shifting, he went on television and said he was "reconsidering" his position and demanded a private meeting with Clinton to "discuss it" (Clinton gave it to him). Basking in the sudden rush of media interest, Shays never missed a chance to agonize like Hamlet in front of TV cameras over his decision. Now he spoke on the floor against impeachment. Republicans sitting near me expressed their disgust with Shays—not because of his position (other Republicans also opposed impeachment and did so honestly), but for his sickening display of rank opportunism.

Toward the end, Democrats again tried unsuccessfully to raise their censure motion. The chair ruled their amendment was not germane to the impeachment resolution. The House sustained the chair's ruling.

With the last procedural vote completed, and all time for debate now expired, the moment arrived for the House to decide the question. I was down near the front of the chamber when Speaker Pro Tem LaHood opened the electronic roll for the vote on Article I of the impeachment resolution. As voting began, Democrats filed out of the chamber temporarily in protest over their inability to raise their censure motion as an alternative. "Let them go!" many GOP members called as Democrats filed out the doors.

While the votes continued trickling in on the first article, I busied myself lobbying undecided GOP members on Article III (obstruction of justice). To those who said they needed to "vote against something" for political reasons, I suggested they vote against Articles II or IV. My committee colleagues agreed with me that the perjury and obstruction of justice charges in Articles I and III were the two key components we needed to make an effective presentation in the Senate.

Congressman Ed Markey (D-MA), my Commerce Committee colleague, lightened my mood when he walked over and put his arm around my shoulder. "You know, Jimmy," he whispered, "truth be told, we all could be prosecuted for perjury." When I asked what he meant, Eddie smiled: "Because," he replied, "we Democrats all want the son of a bitch to go, and you Republicans all want the son of a bitch to stay."

When the tally board showed that the votes in favor of Article I reached 218 (a majority required for passage), applause burst from the visitors' galleries. Those Republicans on the floor trying to maintain an air of somberness looked up disapprovingly at the spontaneous demonstration. At 1:25 p.m., Speaker Pro Tem LaHood closed the roll on Article I. The final vote was 228 in favor and 206 against it. Not surprisingly, five Republicans joined with the Democrats and voted no. What was surprising [and quickly forgotten by most pundits when discussing impeachment later] was that five House Democrats voted to impeach Clinton.

For the first time in American history, the House impeached a popularly elected president.

When it was over, the balloting showed a split decision. The House impeached Clinton on Articles I and III, and defeated Articles II and IV.

Following the vote on Article IV, Chairman Hyde introduced a resolution naming the 13 House Managers to prosecute the case against Clinton before the United States Senate [Henry Hyde (R-IL), Jim Sensenbrenner (R-WI), Bill McCollum (R-FL), George Gekas (R-PA), Charles Canady (R-FL), Steve Buyer (R-IN), Ed Bryant (R-TN), Steve Chabot (R-OH), Bob Barr (R-GA), Asa Hutchinson (R-AR), Chris Cannon (R-UT), Lindsey Graham (R-SC), and me]. Meanwhile, Judiciary Committee staff rounded up each proposed Manager and asked us to assemble near Lafayette's portrait at the front of the House chamber to await further instructions.

After passage of the Managers resolution, committee staff led us downstairs to Room HC-5 for a press conference. After each of us made a brief statement, Capitol police escorted us to Room H219, the majority leader's hideaway office.

Inside the small private room, Henry Hyde sat on a couch awaiting our arrival. In front of him was a table on top of which rested two large blue leather folders bearing the gold seal of the House of Representatives. Inside the folders were Speaker Gingrich's just-signed original articles of impeachment.

According to custom, once all the House Managers gathered, we were to walk across the Capitol rotunda to the Senate where we would then advise them formally that the House impeached the president. Henry was in a hurry to accomplish our task, especially since live television cameras waited to broadcast our brief trek. He had us line up in seniority order and then he gave the signal for us to proceed.

"Wait," I called out as I broke ranks. "Mr. Chairman, this is history. We need a group photograph of the Managers with the articles of impeachment." Henry brushed off my suggestion by saying we had no photographer handy and that we had to get moving. Undaunted, I blocked the exit physically. "Respectfully, Mr. Chairman, I'm not moving from this doorway until we get a photographer up here." Although annoyed by my interruption, Henry gave in and directed a committee staffer to summon Dwight Comedy, the House's official photographer. When Dwight arrived, all the Managers posed with Henry and the articles on the table before us.

Our formal portrait with the articles had a small problem (unexplained until now)—a problem in which even the Managers didn't become aware until much later when it was too late to correct:

Our historic photo has one too many congressmen in it.

How did this happen? Like me, I presume the other Managers didn't learn of their assignment until the night before. Because of this, none of us knew the others that Henry selected until we all gathered for our post-impeachment press conference following the final vote. Elton Gallegly (R-CA) joined our initial assembly on the House floor, and then followed us to the Managers' press conference—he even spoke at it. At the time, the other Managers and I assumed Gallegly was on our prosecution team.

Weeks later, the Managers were in the midst of the Senate impeachment trial when Dwight sent over the proof of our picture. I noticed immediately that Gallegly was in our photo. I presumed he started as a Manager and then withdrew for some reason. Handing the photo to our chief counsel Tom Mooney, I asked him why Gallegly was no longer a Manager. Rolling his eyes, Tom said Gallegly *never* was a Manager: he was a *Manager wanna-be*. When we gathered to pose, Tom tried telling him politely the photograph was for Managers only. "Shh!" Gallegly whispered, and then shooed Tom away. I complained to Tom that he should have kicked Gallegly out of the picture.

Tom threw up his hands: "Hey, I'm only staff. He's a member. What the hell could I do?"

Like me, the other Managers were unhappy when they discovered Gallegly's invasion. To make up for it, on "Verdict Day" (the final day of the Senate impeachment trial two months later), we agreed to pose for a news photographer. As it turned out, our second portrait also proved deficient when one Manager—Ed Bryant— failed to show up for the shoot. Thus, we had two formal pictures taken of the House Managers during the impeachment proceedings. In the first, we had one guy too many, and in the second, we had one guy too few.[2]

After posing for the photograph, Henry instructed us to line up two-by-two in seniority order. Before the door opened, Henry cautioned us not to smile or look happy. "This is a serious and somber time," he admonished us. "No grinning or laughing." It was a good thing Henry reminded us of his wishes, because the general mood behind the scenes was anything but morose. We were (in all candor) satisfied with the result and the moment in which we now found ourselves created an air of electricity. The only gloominess I showed is what I faked for the cameras at Henry's insistence.

Holding the two blue leather folders that encased the momen- tous documents, Chairman Hyde ordered a staffer to open the office doors, and then he led our procession from the House wing of the Capitol to the Senate. The last time the House Managers traversed these same marble floors for this purpose was in 1868 when our predecessors delivered to the Senate the impeachment resolution against President Andrew Johnson.

---

2   In all, three posed photographs exist that depict all 13 House impeachment Managers. The first is the "Gallegly Error" photograph that I described—the one with one too many people in it. A few weeks after the impeachment trial ended, Congressman Ed Bryant's staffer took a second picture of all 13 Managers in the Judiciary Committee conference room. That photograph was more of a snapshot than a portrait. The photographer took it hurriedly and with no formality. It depicts television sets, chairs, random papers, and other such distractions scattered throughout the image. Finally, in March 2000, before the November election separated us forever, I hired a professional photographer to shoot a formal portrait of the 13 House Managers in the Judiciary Committee hearing room where we debated and passed the articles of impeachment. This third photograph is the one most often depicted in history books and is the one on display at the Smithsonian Institution.

Once our procession approached Statuary Hall, we saw huge crowds of tourists and reporters crowded behind the rope lines that marked our pathway. Many took photographs; all watched in silence. One could have heard a pin drop in the Rotunda. "This is too eerie," I whispered to Lindsey Graham, who agreed and called the moment "surreal."

Both the House and Senate Sergeants at Arms escorted us to the office of the secretary of the Senate, Gary Sisco, who greeted each of us individually. Reading from a prepared script, Chairman Hyde advised the Senate formally (through Sisco) that the House of Representatives impeached the president. Henry then handed Sisco the leather folders containing the signed articles of impeachment. Sisco received the folders on behalf of the Senate and then wished each of us a Merry Christmas. With that, we marched back to the House wing.

Returning to our chamber, I passed a group of senior Senate staffers congregating nearby and speaking excitedly among themselves. One said, "I can't believe it! They actually did it! What do you think the senators will do?"

I answered the staffer's question as I walked by:

"They'll get to earn their pay."

Minutes after we returned from the Senate, a House aide handed me a note that fanned my already mammoth cynicism about the Clinton Administration. Just after the House of Representatives officially impeached him, President Clinton suddenly ended his bombing campaign in Iraq.

In a day filled with shocks and surprises, that wasn't one of them.

Here I am with my beloved pal and colleague, Congressman Sonny Bono, 1997. A few months later, Speaker Newt Gingrich appointed me to a vacancy on the House Judiciary Committee created by Sonny's untimely death on a Lake Tahoe ski slope.

President Clinton and I shared a laugh at a St. Patrick's Day luncheon in the Capitol shortly after my appointment to the Judiciary Committee. Within weeks, neither of us would find much about which to laugh.

To my very good friend, Jim Rogan, with appreciation, for a great job on the Senate. Best wishes. Gerald R. Ford

Here is former President Gerald Ford campaigning for me. Look closely and you might see the bruises from where he twisted my arm with some last-minute blackmail.

For over a year, we Judiciary Committee members couldn't leave our offices without encountering a massive press gaggle awaiting us. Here, Congressman Asa Hutchinson and I conduct one of our countless impromptu live press conferences.

With ABC News reporter Linda Douglass and anchorman Peter Jennings (via earpiece from his New York studio) as the first copy of the Starr Report was made public to a waiting world audience.

Huddling with Congressman Jim Sensenbrenner, committee counsel Mitch Glazier, chief investigator Dave Schippers and Chairman Hyde during televised Judiciary Committee proceedings.

No flinching: I announce my decision to vote for President Clinton's impeachment. I knew when I gave this speech that it would likely end a promising political career—mine.

ROLL CALL NO. 2   **DATE** 12-11-98   4:25 PM

COMMITTEE ON THE JUDICIARY
HOUSE OF REPRESENTATIVES
106TH CONGRESS

Subject: ARTICLE I - IMPEACHMENT OF PRESIDENT WILLIAM JEFFERSON CLINTON

Present		Ayes	Nays	Present
	MR. SENSENBRENNER	✓		
	MR. McCOLLUM	✓		
	MR. GEKAS	✓		
	MR. COBLE	✓		
	MR. SMITH	✓		
	MR. GALLEGLY	✓		
	MR. CANADY	✓		
	MR. INGLIS	✓		
	MR. GOODLATTE	✓		
	MR. BUYER			
	MR. BRYANT			
	MR. CHABOT	✓		
	MR. BARR			
	MR. JENKINS			
	MR. HUTCHINSON	✓		
	MR. PEASE			
	MR. CANNON		✓	
	MR. ROGAN	✓		
	MR. GRAHAM	✓		
	MS. BONO			
	MR. CONYERS			
	MR. FRANK		✓	
	MR. SCHUMER			
	MR. BERMAN			
	MR. BOUCHER		✓	
	MR. NADLER			
	MR. SCOTT			
	MR. WATT			
	MS. LOFGREN			
	MS. JACKSON LEE			
	MS. WATERS			
	MR. MEEHAN		✓	
	MR. DELAHUNT		✓	
	MR. WEXLER		✓	
	MR. ROTHMAN			
	MR. BARRETT			
	MR. HYDE, Chairman			
	TOTAL	21	16	

Congressman Bill Jenkins reading the impeachment press; Lindsey Graham preferred to follow it on cable news.

Shortly before the House Judiciary Committee impeachment vote, I pose with my colleagues Lindsey Graham, Mary Bono, and Ed Pease in our conference room. The pressure from impeachment grew so intense that Ed suffered a heart attack because of it, and soon thereafter retired from Congress.

A piece of history I saved from the trash: the House Judiciary Committee Clerk's official roll call sheet on the first Article of Impeachment against the President of the United States. Today it is on display at the Smithsonian Institution.

A contraband photograph: as the entire House of Representatives voted on passage of Article One of the President's impeachment, I stood at the back rail of the chamber, slipped a camera out of my pocket, and snapped this shot. I broke one of the longstanding rules of the House (no photography in the chamber) for the sake of posterity, and then slipped out a back door before anyone could confront me over the breach.

Holding the live grenade: Chairman Henry Hyde and I examine the signed Articles of Impeachment. Clutching those documents gave me an eerie chill.

Reviewing the Original articles of impeachment against President William Jefferson Clinton on the Day he was impeached by House of Representatives. To my friend Jim Rogan with my admiration and esteem! Henry Hyde, Chairman, House Judiciary Com
Dec. 19, 1998

Just before we left for the Senate, all the House Managers posed with the Articles of Impeachment. As I explain in the book, there is one too many congressmen in this picture. Can you pick out the House Manager wanna-be?

That book in Paul McNulty's hand is the published proceedings from the 1974 impeachment inquiry against Richard Nixon. Here, Chairman Hyde listens to our staff debate how to apply those Nixon precedents in the Clinton case.

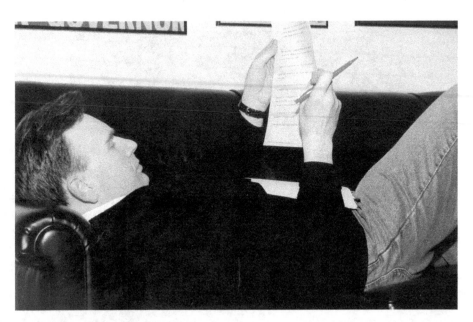

The end of a long road: my legislative aide Myron Jacobson snapped this photo of me about 4:30 a.m. as I lay on my office couch drafting my closing argument in the impeachment trial, scheduled for delivery later that day.

106TH CONGRESS—FIRST SESSION
United States Senate
Impeachment Trial of the
PRESIDENT OF THE UNITED STATES

ADMIT BEARER TO THE SENATE GALLERY

Sergeant-at-Arms United States Senate

DATE FEB 09 1999

A gallery ticket to the last day of the impeachment trial, autographed for me by Chief Justice William Rehnquist.

Once the Senate advised us they had reached a verdict, the House Managers gathered in the Judiciary Committee conference room that morning for our final meeting before the Senate announced its finding. We knew how the trial would end, but there were no tears. In fact, it was more like an Irish wake, with backslaps, hugs, laughs, and many Member and staffer requests for our autographs.

Unlike their son, former President George Bush and former First Lady Barbara Bush had no qualms about standing by me in a tough fight. They even hosted a fundraiser for me in Houston. At the end of the evening, President Bush slipped a $1,000 personal check for the campaign into my pocket. I still have and treasure the check; it's the only one from my race I didn't cash. I'll always be grateful to them for sticking by a guy getting pummeled for doing his duty as he saw it.

To: Our esteemed friend, Tim Roger.
A man of principle, who never faltered. G Bush & Barbara Bush

When impeachment ended, we House Managers were surprised to find ourselves with national celebrity status, at least among conservatives. Speaking invitations poured in from all over the country. Here I am addressing the 2000 Republican National Convention. What a great speech—all 90 seconds of it!

As we were: The only formal portrait taken of all 13 House Managers in the impeachment trial of President Clinton. I will treasure the memory and friendship of each of these men for the rest of my life.

Three weeks after leaving Congress, I returned to the Capitol once more for George Bush's inauguration. From my place on the presidential platform, I raised my camera as Bush stood to take the oath. Just then I spotted Bill Clinton look back at the Capitol dome during his last few seconds as president. The scene looked poignant, so I swung the lens toward him. When I did, Clinton looked over and spotted me. I clicked this hurried photo as Clinton gave me this Cheshire grin and a nod as if to say, "I'm still here—I finished out my term." I grinned and nodded back in acknowledgment. Despite the warfare, I guess we both walked away from the Capitol that last time in 2001 feeling like a winner.

PART TWO:
The Senate

25

Short-Circuit

"The Senate shall have the sole Power to try all Impeachments. When the president of the United States is tried, the Chief Justice shall preside: And no Person shall be convicted without the Concurrence of two thirds of the members present."

—UNITED STATES CONSTITUTION, ARTICLE I § 2

T he relationship between the United States Senate and the United States House of Representatives is complicated. With 435 members, the House drives Washington policy in an unending frenzy of activity. Its debates can be bare-knuckled and the majority rules. Also, with its entire membership up for election every two years, political control remains in flux, which leads to unending partisan battles. Contrast that to the Senate across the rotunda: with 100 members, a leisurely six-year term, and only one-third of the membership up for reelection every two years, the Senate is a rarified club whose preferences are comity and collegiality, not bloodying noses.

Collectively, House and Senate members are "members of Congress." They all earn the same paycheck and take the same oath of office. Still, there is no particular love between these first cousins. Senators as a whole view House members as inelegant riffraff (they'll deny they hold this view if you ask them, but their denial is insincere). The snobbery of the Senate toward the House can be insufferable. For House members, the most common manner of seeking revenge for the Senate's patronizing elitism is to run for the Senate, ostensibly to "show them I'm not one of them" and to "shake the place up." Alas, Mother Nature decrees that once the successful Senate candidate crosses the threshold of the Holy of Holies, their election transfigures the scrappy House member into a Magnificent New Creature bathed in unending sycophancy and a steady diet of pontificating on the Sunday news shows. Soon, memories of their hobo years in The People's House fade away.

Lest you think I exaggerate the strained relationship, consider these examples. First, there is the debate phenomenon. It is a violation of House Rules to refer in debate to the Senate as "The Senate." House members must refer to the Senate by the aloof and antiseptic term, *The Other Body* (I'm not kidding). Perfecting the ability to speak the phrase dismissively while showing simultaneous disdain pegs one as having future leadership potential, which in turn starts people talking about one's Senate potential. Call it Capitol Hill's version of the circle of life.

Second, there is the gymnasium phenomenon. In the House Members' Gym, congressmen lift weights, run on treadmills, play basketball, swim laps, and throw medicine balls while working up a respectable sweat. In the Senate Gym, senators recline on massage tables and get rubdowns. The handful of senators who like to exercise come over and use the House Gym, where they make a point to let House members know their presence in our gym shows their egalitarian spirit (diminished, of course, by their telling us about it).

Given this complex relationship, I could only speculate on how these august senators would react to 13 House Managers bursting into their domain and dropping articles of impeachment on their carpet. When we delivered the documents to their secretary near their empty chamber, I felt some disappointment in missing their collective grimace when facing the reality of having to soil their hands with this indelicate obligation.

• • •

After depositing the documents with the Senate, we returned to find the House chamber also vacant. Immediately after our last vote, House Democrats boarded chartered buses and raced across town to the White House. The just-impeached President decided to hold a pep rally on the South Lawn with his congressional friends. At their demonstration, Clinton and his leading supporters alternated between declaring themselves defenders of the Constitution and attacking us for holding him accountable to the Constitution. House Minority Leader Dick Gephardt called our impeachment vote "a disgrace to our country." Vice President Gore declared us filled with a "vitriol and vehemence that hurts our nation," and questioned how we could do this to the man who "will be regarded in the history books as one of our greatest presidents." For his part, Clinton put to rest any rumors that impeachment would bring about his resignation. He vowed to stay on the job "until the last hour of the last day of my term."

No Clinton-orchestrated attack was ever complete without going through the basic mambo steps: pro-Clinton hatchet men spew venom at their targets while accusing their targets of being venom-filled, and then lecturing everyone on the need to show greater civility. This day's rally stayed on the beat: Gephardt scolded, "We must turn away, now, from the politics of personal destruction, and return to a politics of values." Gore lectured that America must seek "the renewal of civility, respect for one another, and decency toward each other." Watching all this later on the news, I wondered how people like Ken Starr, Paula Jones, Kathleen Willey, Bob Livingston, Newt Gingrich, Monica Lewinsky (remember how White House aides tried to paint her as a lying, crazed stalker until she produced her DNA-stained proof?), and so many others felt while listening to Bill Clinton sermonize that day: "For six years now, I have done everything I could to bring our country together across the lines that divide us. It is something I have felt strongly all my life. We must stop the politics of personal destruction."

Pardon me while I retch.

Following this rally, a reporter cornered me in the Capitol and asked if the president's refusal to resign surprised me. I told her no. When pressed, I said there are two kinds of people who resign under such circumstances: people who have honor and people who have shame.

"Are you saying the president has neither?" she asked.

"I'm saying I'm not surprised by his decision. I think that was your question."

• • •

While the Democrats cheered Clinton at their rally, Republicans held an emergency conference to discuss the leadership vacuum created by Bob Livingston's sudden resignation a couple of hours earlier. It didn't take long for the jockeying to begin—and end. Members were still recording their votes in the chamber on Article I earlier this morning when outgoing Speaker Newt Gingrich pulled me aside. "Because you are not only my colleague but my friend," he said, "I want to tell you something friend to friend. If you want to elect a speaker who'll work 18 hours a day to build this majority, vote for Denny Hastert [Illinois Republican serving currently as chief deputy majority whip]. I have the greatest faith in him."

Now, as we returned from the Senate, staff directed us to the Capitol basement to join the GOP meeting in progress:

Diary, The U.S. Capitol, December 19, 1998

When I arrived at the GOP conference, outgoing Speaker Gingrich was at the podium urging us to proclaim immediately Denny Hastert as our new speaker-designate. With Gingrich's sendoff, it will probably clinch the deal for Hastert.

Within hours of Livingston's resignation, the competition to replace him as speaker was over without any shots fired. By overwhelming agreement, the GOP conference chose our well-liked chief deputy whip, a former football and wrestling coach, to lead the House. Coming out of nowhere, Denny Hastert would be our new speaker in the 106th Congress.

• • •

Seated at my kitchen table working round-the-clock, and barely visible to my children amid the fortress of file boxes and three-ring binders stacked around me, I spent the bulk of the Christmas and New Year holiday break reviewing all my materials on the Clinton case. I then drafted a 15-page, step-by-step Senate impeachment trial outline, mapping out every element of proof, the witnesses and exhibits needed to establish each element, and the suggested order in which to present them.[1]

Henry Hyde called our first post-impeachment House Managers meeting a few days after Christmas. For the first time, we discussed some of the issues that would face us in Clinton's jury trial before the United States Senate:

---

1 For the history buffs curious as to what a real trial against Clinton might have looked like, a copy of this first draft outline is included in the appendix of this book.

**Diary, House Managers Meeting, Judiciary Committee
Conference Room, The U.S. Capitol, December 29, 1998**

"This is the big one, boys and girls," Henry said. "The stakes
couldn't be higher. We are fighting for the presidency of the
United States. The rumor so far is that the White House
intends to put on a full-court defense in the trial. We need
to be prepared to cross-examine any witnesses they may call."

Henry said he heard that Clinton might make a motion
to dismiss the articles on the grounds that they do not state
an impeachable offense. "Clinton takes a big chance if he
makes that motion," he noted. "If he loses, then the Senate
is on record that his offenses are indeed impeachable."

Henry noted a hurdle we needed to surmount: the outgoing
105th Congress passed the resolution appointing us as House
Managers, but the resolution would expire with the termination of
that Congress. If the new 106th Congress did not reauthorize us,
five days from now we would have an impeached president with no
prosecutors empowered to try him before the U.S. Senate. Henry
did not take our reauthorization for granted:

Henry warned, "Our new Republican majority will be very
thin. We can't afford to do anything that would impact our
ability to get reauthorized." He said he would call personally the five returning GOP members of the 105th Congress
who did not vote for articles of impeachment and ask them
to commit to supporting a reauthorization of the House
Managers.

Henry announced that Manager Jim Sensenbrenner (R-WI)
would make our initial opening statement, and that Henry and
I would close out the opening statements. Henry also announced

the appointment of Managers Ed Bryant (R-TN), Asa Hutchinson (R-AR), and me to handle the fact presentations of the trial: "We are working hard to get Dave Schippers the right to cross-examine Clinton's witnesses on the Senate floor," Henry told us, "but the Senate is balking because Dave is not a member of Congress. If the Senate refuses to allow Dave the right to speak on the floor, then our three fact presenters need to be ready to cross-examine them." Henry assigned to Managers Charles Canady (R-FL), Lindsey Graham (R-SC) and Steve Buyer (R-IN) the job of showing that the articles articulated impeachable offenses. "This will be a tough area," Henry noted, "because the White House probably will move to dismiss on this issue." He then assigned Sensenbrenner and Bob Barr (R-GA) responsibility for handling general trial procedures (like objections); he charged Managers Bill McCollum (R-FL), George Gekas (R-PA), Steve Chabot (R-OH) and Chris Cannon (R-UT) with developing specific witness preparation for trial, including weighing the risks of calling particular witnesses.

I raised the issue of our using evidence still held in executive session. I felt it unfair to use materials against Clinton that nobody on his side could review. Hyde agreed that we needed to give Clinton's defense team access to any materials we used in trial.

Later, Charles Canady pulled me aside and told me he didn't think dividing witnesses with other Managers was a good idea. "Hyde put you, Bryant, and Hutchinson in charge of the fact presentation. You guys need to do it. We don't need 13 different guys jumping up throughout the trial. We need continuity."

While Canady spoke, I noticed Bob Barr walk over to Hyde, who then invited Barr to sit as they engaged in an animated conversation. Hyde kept shaking his head from side to side, and Barr kept pressing some point. After their ten-minute huddle, Hyde walked Barr over to Hutchinson, Bryant and me and told us, "Bob will be on your team, too. Bob's a former prosecutor."

I saw the Judiciary Committee senior staffers behind Hyde grimace. Hutchinson, Bryant and I exchanged worried glances. I knew Barr to be very smart, always well prepared, and a fearless soldier ready to charge any rampart. But he also earned (and seemed to enjoy) a reputation as a relentless attack dog against both Bill and Hillary Clinton. Just mentioning Barr's name caused a physical reaction from every congressional Democrats and from squeamish Republicans. If we hoped to pick off enough Senate votes in both of those camps to convict Clinton, I feared Barr's take-no-prisoners flamethrower approach might undermine that goal. My hesitancy was nothing personal against Barr, whom I respected and counted as a friend. If I had to pick anyone to watch my back in a foxhole, it would be him. Still, I felt his persona would work against us in trying to present a formal case as opposed to unleashing a partisan hurricane.

With Bryant's blessing, Hutchinson and I met with Hyde privately and explained our concern over a Barr backlash in the Senate. Hyde said that Barr was always a team player and had been pushing for Clinton's impeachment long before any of us. Then, looking remorseful, he confessed, "I let Barr talk me into it, but you are right. It will be bad for the team. I'll tell Barr he can't have a leading role because of his pit bull reputation. This is too important."

• • •

We discovered quickly that the Senate's sensitivities over Bob Barr were the least of our concerns:

Diary, Telephone Call from Judiciary Committee Chief Counsel Tom Mooney, December 30, 1998

Tom Mooney said Senate Republican Majority Leader Trent Lott called Henry Hyde today and said he wants the Clinton

impeachment trial to be a "one day trial," and that he doesn't want us to call *any* witnesses. Lott wants to hold this so-called "trial" in about two weeks. Henry Hyde is apoplectic at the news that Lott doesn't want the House Managers to be able to present our case. He said that Lott wants to tank Clinton's impeachment and make it go away.

My shock at this news grew deeper when Mooney said Lott also wanted to prevent any trial—one day or otherwise—unless two-thirds of the Senate agreed. This unheard-of requirement would give a bare one-third of the Senate the power to abort the impeachment trial.

Naturally, the Democrats and the White House wanted to bury Clinton's impeachment. Now our Republican Senate majority leader wanted to "expedite" the impeachment "trial" of the president by turning it into a witness-free, one-day farce. How could this be? For the record, the last Senate impeachment trial was in 1989 against a federal judge, Walter Nixon (whom the Senate convicted and removed from office, coincidentally, for lying under oath to a grand jury). Judge Nixon's Senate impeachment procedures stretched from May to November—and that didn't even include a full trial. The only other trial of an impeached president, Andrew Johnson, took almost three months. We all knew the senators, with their delicate sensitivities, didn't like that we impeached Clinton—but none of us contemplated them ditching the case, along with their constitutional responsibilities, in the ultimate display of poll appeasement.

After letting loose with a fund of expletives,

I said we should take a hard line and refuse to abide by such terms. We should show up in the Senate and announce our readiness to try our case. If Lott and the others try to gut it, we should refuse to proceed under their plan and walk out in protest. We should force Lott's hand publicly and not allow him to deal from the bottom of the deck behind closed doors.

I didn't make this suggestion recklessly. I don't think Lott can pull off his plan politically over our objection. Conservative Republicans will burn Lott down if they see him aborting the impeachment trial. It could cost him his leadership position if we fight him on this.

Henry said he took comfort that Senator Orrin Hatch (R-UT), chairman of the Senate Judiciary Committee, called and pledged to stand "shoulder to shoulder" with us. I said I wasn't sure what that meant—Hatch had just told reporters that since the Senate would never remove Clinton from office, censure remained the only option left.

Shortly after this call, Henry faxed me a copy of the two-page letter he fired off to Trent Lott. After criticizing Lott's suggestion to deny the House Managers and the president's counsel the opportunity to call and cross-examine witnesses, Henry wrote, "Perjury and lying under oath—even outside the scope of official duties—have played a central role in each of the [Senate's] four most recent impeachments. For example, in the impeachment trial of Judge Walter Nixon, you and 88 other Senators voted to convict and remove Judge Nixon because [he made] a materially false or misleading statement to the grand jury.... We are especially concerned by your proposal to forgo a trial if one-third of the Senate [agrees]. The Constitution requires a two-thirds vote on the ultimate issue of conviction and removal. The Senate's Rules and its impeachment precedents require only a majority vote to dispose of impeachment matters other than conviction.... I believe that a fair presentation of the evidence and a full defense by the president can be expeditious; we need not sacrifice substance and duty for speed."

Soon after receiving a copy of Henry's letter, Speaker Newt Gingrich called me from his home in Georgia:

**Diary, Telephone Call, Speaker Newt Gingrich,
December 30, 1998**

Newt said he was livid with Lott and asked what I thought
about the Senate leader's idea. I tore into the suggestion and
said I would not be a party to him tossing out our case. I said
we should show up in their chamber on the day appointed
and demand to present our case. If they refused, we would
walk out. Under no circumstance should we give Lott or any
other pantywaist Republican senator cover. If they want to
betray us, we must make them do it publicly.

Newt agreed strongly: "The Managers must be firm on
this. Henry Hyde cannot give in. This is about much more
than his reputation and his legacy. It is about the Constitution and the defense of it." Newt said that if Lott pushes this,
he will destroy his Republican majority in the Senate. I told
Newt that I thought our conservative base would torch Lott
if he forced this idea. Newt agreed that Lott risked losing
his leadership position if he tried. Newt volunteered to help
fire up our troops, suggesting we "unleash" Majority Whip
Tom DeLay [called "The Hammer" for his political hardball instincts] and get this story out to conservative editors,
columnists, and talk radio hosts. Newt then caught himself
and wondered aloud whether he should be involved, saying,
"I'm not there anymore."

I reminded him he was still there: technically, Newt
remained the current speaker and a member of Congress
until he resigned his seat formally or until the start of the
new Congress. "By the way," I added, "we may need to swear
you in to the new Congress so you can vote with us on reappointing House Managers. We've heard some of our anti-
impeachment Republicans might not stand with us." When
I told him that passing a reappointment resolution might

be a problem with some Republicans, Newt blew his stack:

"This is so fundamental that nobody—*nobody*—gets a free vote on this," he shouted. "If any member of our conference won't vote to reappoint Managers, we should drum them out of the Republican Party. Let them become Democrats and let Dick Gephardt become speaker. Let him then try to govern the House with a one-vote majority. This is traitorous. We must enforce a Party-line vote."

Newt singled out Congressman Chris Shays (R-CT), the Republican who made such a public spectacle over his opposition to impeachment and his ultimate embrace of Clinton remaining in office. "I heard Shays' wife now has a job working for the Clinton White House," Newt said. "Let these guys become Democrats if that is their game and make them show their true colors."

After this call, I took heart when a staffer handed me a message that Senator Rick Santorum (R-PA) wanted to speak with me. Elected to the Senate just two years earlier, Santorum had been a conservative House stalwart who appeared to be the rare exception to my senatorial hypothesis about new members breathing the ether in The Other Body. I felt sure that if anyone might go to bat for us with Trent Lott, it was Rick.

**Diary, Telephone Conversation with
Senator Rick Santorum, December 31, 1998**

I told Rick that Trent Lott was trying to sell us out and dump the impeachment case against Clinton. I said Lott was acting out of expediency in wanting to make a political headache just go away despite the evidence.

"Oh, the Leader would *never* do that," Rick said defensively.

The Leader would never do that? Oh-oh.

The more Rick defended Lott, the deeper my heart sank in realizing another good guy drank the Senate's collegiality Kool-Aid.

I told Rick I would recommend to Henry Hyde that we flatly reject participating in anything that resembled a one-day submission on the record that allowed the Senate to sidestep a public trial. I also made clear that I would vigorously and publicly object to any attempt by Lott to define impeachable offenses as a predicate to the Senate deciding whether to let us to try our case.

Rick said Lott was concerned about the upcoming 2000 Senate elections and Lott's fear he might lose Republican seats over this unpopular cause. As one facing defeat myself, I told him that I understood that concern, but our obligation was to the Constitution and not worrying about elections two years away.

Rick said he thinks Henry made a "fatal mistake" in appointing Bob Barr as a lead presenter. "Your case is dead on arrival in the Senate if Barr shows up to litigate," Rick warned.

By the end of the conversation, Rick sounded as if he had backtracked somewhat. He indicated he now had reservations over Lott's plan. He added that he was especially concerned about Clinton remaining in office if Juanita Broaddrick's 1978 rape allegation against him is true: "I wonder what kind of man we have in the Oval Office?" he asked.

"I'll tell you what kind of man we have in the Oval Office, Rick," I replied. "We have an impeached man in the Oval Office. And we need you guys to let us come over and show you why."

26

A Laughing Matter

"Most Republican senators want to dispose of these articles of impeachment. If there's a way of doing that without a show trial in the Senate, then that would be my preference."
—SENATOR MITCH MCCONNELL (R-KY) CHAIRMAN, SENATE
RULES COMMITTEE, *WASHINGTON POST*, JANUARY 1, 1999

"President William Jefferson Clinton today is the most admired man in America. Running second to Clinton is Pope John Paul II."
—THE GALLUP POLL, JANUARY 2, 1999

On Monday, January 4, 1999, in a meeting with the other House Manager presenters (Asa Hutchinson, Ed Bryant, and Bob Barr), I distributed copies of my 15-page draft trial outline. We spent the better part of the day going over it. They agreed to draft their own outlines with suggestions and improvements, and we would meet later to fashion a final outline to present to Chairman Hyde.

After our meeting broke that evening, I learned from press

reports that two more senators floated another Trent Lott-styled no-witness "trial" idea. Senators Slade Gorton (R-WA) and Joseph Lieberman (D-CT) proposed that both the House Managers and Clinton's lawyers make opening addresses, and then the senators could ask questions. After that, the Senate would permit dismissal of the case by a simple majority vote.

The morning after I got word of this latest bad idea, Senator Jon Kyl (R-AZ) called me to lobby for yet another version of Lott Lite:

Diary, Telephone Call with Senator Jon Kyl,
January 5, 1999

Kyl called urging support for the Gorton-Lieberman pro-
posal and asked for my impression of it. I blasted the idea
and said that I remained baffled by the Senate claiming they
were too busy to spend a fraction of the time on a presidential
impeachment that they spend routinely on the lowest-level
federal judicial impeachment. Kyl defended Gorton's idea,
saying, "I respect Slade Gorton. After all, he's a former state
attorney general."

I interrupted: "I'm not sure what kind of procedures they
have in Washington State, Jon, but I doubt that they allow
the jury to vote in advance of the evidence whether to have
a trial." Kyl had no reply to that point.

Later, Senator Jeff Sessions (R-AL) called our group to say he favored a trial, albeit a stripped-down version:

Diary, Telephone Conference Call with
Senator Jeff Sessions, January 5, 1999

Sessions thinks we should have a trial, but he warned that we
needed "to contain it to just the guts of the case. You guys

produced a magnificent record in the House, but nobody has read it. The record clearly shows that so-and-so did all he could to cover up for himself and Monica."

Sessions offered his own recommendations for the witnesses he thought we should call, and then specified the one we should not: Monica Lewinsky. He suggested we submit her testimony through a transcript.

Bob Barr agreed with Sessions that Lewinsky would make a poor live witness. I leaned the other way, saying that although calling her was a risky proposition, she would bring greater public scrutiny to the trial and perhaps force the senators to listen more carefully to the facts. After further discussion, we agreed to table the issue for now.

Later that afternoon, chief counsel Tom Mooney met with our team and said that Trent Lott just told Henry Hyde that he now wants the Senate's so-called "trial" to be a procedure where they limit our presentation to a "stipulation of the record." The Senate would not permit us to proceed any further. As expected, this news infuriated us. "Tell Lott that's a great idea—for an appellate court reviewing a trial that already took place," I replied.

"Whose side is Trent Lott on?" Bob Barr shouted.

Mooney told us that Lott was doing handsprings trying to circumvent our ability to prosecute the case. He wants it to go away and is apparently ready to do whatever it takes to pull the rug out from under us. He said Hyde planned to meet with Lott tomorrow morning to plead our cause and advise Lott that the Managers are unanimously opposed to his refusal to give us a chance to present our case.

By now, I had reached my fill of Trent Lott. I suggested that Hyde tell him that when we show up in the Senate, we will be there to try our case, and not to stipulate it away. He should also tell Lott not to worry about us wasting the Senate's precious time. We estimated that the entire impeachment trial would take us less than three weeks.

"One more thing, Tom," I added angrily. "Have Henry tell Lott that 'the record' is created during a trial, not before one."

• • •

At 8:00 that evening, Henry Hyde summoned a meeting of all the House Managers. He appeared uncharacteristically tense and distracted:

Diary, House Managers Meeting, January 5, 1999

Henry told us Trent Lott's newest "bipartisan" idea envisioned the senators voting up front on whether they felt Clinton committed a removable offense. If only one-third of the Senate voted no, there would be no trial.

Henry warned that despite our anger and frustration with Lott and other like-minded Senate Republicans wanting to avoid doing their duty, "Constitutionally and legally, the Senate calls their own procedural shots. Our only leverage is political. We can criticize what they create for us, but we can't do anything about it."

It got worse.

Next, Henry told us that Lott threatened to block all subpoenas and keep us from calling any witnesses if we made trouble:

Hyde said that Lott "reminded me today that the Senate has the power to approve or deny issuing any subpoena. This is another area where he is exercising control over us."

Looking more drained than I had seen him, Henry seemed resigned to the stunning notion that the Senate would force us into a "trial" without calling any live witnesses:

"Let me now give you my opinion, not as your Chairman, but as a fellow Manager," he said with a sigh. "In an ideal world, we would call our witnesses and have them tell their story. The problem is that all of our witnesses present problems for us. Betty Currie [Clinton's secretary] wants to find a way to defend Clinton. Vernon Jordan [Clinton's friend] is a slick operator. And as for Lewinsky, you don't know what you'll get from her. These people aren't our friends. We would have to use the grand jury transcripts to impeach all of them if they took the witness stand."

Henry's evolving position irked me. If we had to impeach the testimony of every Clinton friend on the witness stand with their prior testimony, then so what? When I prosecuted Crips and Bloods gang murderers in Los Angeles, I impeached almost every gang-banging witness I ever called. Since impeaching hostile witnesses is a commonplace trial technique, I said we needn't be afraid to confront them with their prior inconsistent statements.

Before finishing my unremarkable point, Henry spun in his seat and glowered at me. "I'm not *afraid* of anything," he snapped angrily, "and I'm not *afraid* to proceed, either." When I tried to diffuse the moment by assuring him that I never meant to suggest he was afraid personally, he wouldn't accept my retreat. "Well, *you* are the one who used the word *afraid*," he barked.

Always a model of courtliness and patience, Henry taking sudden umbrage at an innocent comment was out of character. Something was wrong. I dropped it without further explanation. A few minutes later, when someone else provoked him over another trivial matter, the floodgate opened. Henry shouted at us that we weren't prepared, and he accused us of not taking this awesome responsibility seriously.

When he finished venting, someone handed him copies of the

trial outlines we had prepared. I explained that we planned to work through tonight to cull our four documents into one and then present him the final outline in the morning. Henry sat quietly and reviewed the outlines as we assured him that his entire team of 12 was working round-the-clock shifts. Although it would be nice to know the rules and have time to prepare adequately, if necessary, we could cross the Rotunda tomorrow morning and try this case. All we needed was the Senate to unlock the front door and let us inside.

As Henry flipped through the pages, the tension in his face melted. By the time he finished, the old Henry was back. He shared with us the cause of his surliness: earlier tonight Lott told him to be ready to start the impeachment case before the end of this week—and he still won't tell Henry the procedural rules that will apply. Lott must have presumed the threat of forcing us to "trial" immediately would compel the Managers' to accept capitulation on his terms. Now, when Henry realized that we were ready to charge the gates of hell, he shook off any private fear of public embarrassment.

During the remainder of our meeting, we discussed further whether to call Lewinsky as a live witness or just introduce her grand jury testimony via transcript. After going around the table, our group agreed unanimously that if the Senate gave us the power to subpoena her, we'd bring her into the Senate and see how the drama played out.

Henry adjourned the gathering. As we stood to leave, he asked to meet with the case presenters separately:

Following our meeting with all the Managers, Henry met privately with Barr, Hutchinson, Bryant and me. Seated behind his desk, he lit a cigar and pointed to our outlines. "I didn't know how prepared you four were," he told us apologetically. "I should have had more faith in you." He sounded impressed—and grateful.

Twice during this private meeting, Henry said he wanted me to do the direct examination of Monica Lewinsky. He said he wants someone who can be gentle with her and handle her with kid gloves in front of the Senate.

I suspected Henry made the offhand remark as a way to signal his faith in me after upbraiding me in front of the other Managers. I nodded my thanks, but right now we needed to focus on getting witnesses before we started worrying about assigning witnesses.

• • •

The next morning, our presenter team met with chief counsel Tom Mooney and investigator Dave Schippers. Both updated us on Hyde's just-finished meeting with two leading Senate Republicans, Lott and Senate Rules Committee Chairman Mitch McConnell (R-KY):

Diary, House Managers Presentation Team Meeting, January 6, 1999

Tom Mooney told us that Hyde was very firm with Lott, telling him that House Judiciary Republicans fought a bloody battle in our committee and later on the House floor to pass the articles. Some of our Managers might lose reelection over it. Hyde warned that if Lott tried to force any of his "no trial" suggestions, some of the Managers might resign over it and refuse to participate.

According to Mooney, Lott then proposed yet another idea to avoid a traditional trial. Under his new plan, the Senate would:

- **Give the White House two or three days to respond to the impeachment articles;**

- Give the House one day to respond to the White House;

- Give the House two or three days to present a "justification" for having a trial with live witnesses; and then

- Give the White House the same amount of time to argue against a trial.

The Senate would vote on whether they wanted to have a trial and hear any evidence. If they opted for a trial, each side would get just one week to present their whole case.

Schippers said that Lott began the meeting by asking Hyde to decide which was more important to him: calling live witnesses to testify or having the Senate record their vote on the articles of impeachment. Lott's alternative made no sense. Why were these two obvious elements of an impeachment trial mutually exclusive?

Schippers said both Lott and McConnell insisted that Starr's report should constitute the entire "trial" record. They also take the position that they will not allow us to call any live witnesses unless 51 senators agree to it in advance. Even though Lott leads 55 Republicans, he suggested we can't count on his ability to round up a bare majority of votes to subpoena our witnesses. Also, if they do decide to grant us the "privilege" of calling live witnesses, Lott and McConnell both said they would not allow us to call Monica Lewinsky, Vernon Jordan, Betty Currie, or anyone else who has already testified before the grand jury!

Schippers pressed Lott, saying the Senate jurors needed to hear from live witnesses to gauge their credibility and demeanor before deciding whether to remove Clinton. Lott cut Schippers off with a dismissive hand wave, telling him, "I

don't care if your evidence shows Clinton shot and killed a woman. You'll never get the votes in the Senate to remove him."

When Schippers recounted Lott's words to us, he told us that Lott's comment "made me want to vomit."

We recessed our meeting shortly before noon so that we could rush over to the House floor and take the oath as members of the 106th Congress. As expected, the House elected Denny Hastert as the new speaker, and Dick Gephardt returned as minority leader. After the elections, Henry Hyde offered a resolution reappointing House Managers. Despite our earlier fear of GOP defections, the resolution passed on a mostly Party-line vote, with a handful of Democrats voting for authorization. Once again, the House directed us to prosecute Clinton's impeachment trial before the Senate in the newly constituted Congress.

Now all we had to do was convince the Senate to do their duty.

• • •

That same evening, Henry sent an urgent summons for his presentation team to meet in his office. After we gathered, he said that Lott and Democrat Leader Tom Daschle wanted us to meet with their appointed Senate "delegation," right now, in Lott's Capitol office. With no time to strategize beforehand, Henry led the way over to the Senate:

Diary, The U.S. Capitol, January 6, 1999

We arrived at Lott's office and found it empty. After waiting ten minutes, Senator Fred Thompson (one of the senators with whom we would meet) appeared and told us that the other senators were delayed. He said the other two Republicans on the delegation were Senators Ted Stevens (R-AK) and Pete Domenici (R-NM). When Thompson left the room,

Henry said with a smirk, "Ted Stevens. What a pompous and arrogant guy he is to deal with."

After half an hour, the three Republican senators arrived with their Democrat counterparts: Joe Biden (D-DE), Carl Levin (D-MI), and Joe Lieberman (D-CT).

In a tone suggesting hospitality, Thompson observed that we might all be more comfortable in a larger room. He led us down the hall to a small committee room, where the six senators took seats atop the circular elevated platform. They invited us to have seats at the witness tables underneath them. From this vantage, the senators looked down on us as if holding court within the Circus Maximus. Leaning over to Henry, I whispered, "All that's missing is a guy in a toga giving the signal to release the lions."

Henry chuckled quietly: "Be patient. The night's still young."

Republican Pete Domenici asked what the House Managers wanted to present beyond what was already in the grand jury transcripts. Before any of us could answer his question, he volunteered that no matter what we presented in our trial, "I assure you that the United States Senate will never cast the 67 votes needed for conviction." With that statement he again demanded to know what the House wanted to present for their consideration beyond what was already in the record.

Republican Ted Stevens nodded approvingly, adding, "What the House did was partisan. We are the Senate. We need to proceed in a bipartisan manner."

Stevens then stunned us by saying the Senate expected the Managers to formally present the articles of impeachment before their body tomorrow morning. After that, the Senate would advise Chief Justice William H. Rehnquist that they were ready to begin the impeachment "trial." He expected Rehnquist to arrive in the Senate tomorrow afternoon to

take his oath as presiding officer, and then Rehnquist would administer an oath to each senator to "do impartial justice" as jurors in the "trial."

Earlier this morning, Trent Lott threatened Henry that he would make us start the "trial" by the end of the week. Now, on Lott's and Daschle's behalf, Stevens said we'd be starting the historic "trial" tomorrow morning. Our Managers sat poker-faced and offered no objection nor showed surprise. In failing to do either, I felt that we disappointed some of our hosts in denying them their anticipated enjoyment of watching us panic.

Democrat Joe Lieberman said the Senate leaders on both sides asked their group of six senators [with whom we now met] "to act as pretrial judges. We are all concerned that this [impeachment trial] not impede the important work of the Senate in 1999."

Impede the important work of the Senate? Right now, the most important piece of work before the Senate was to do their constitutionally mandated task of deciding whether to remove a president and install a new one. Besides, getting these senators to butt out of the taxpayers' lives for a few weeks certainly wouldn't hurt the country. No matter: in dealing with senators, House members learn quickly that when appeals to duty and reason fail, try some old-fashioned ass-kissing.

Showing flowery deference, Henry said he respected greatly the prerogative of the Senate and their feelings. He told the senators we only needed about two weeks to present our case, and he pleaded with them to grant us that right. Following suit, Bryant thanked the Senate profusely for their statesmanlike efforts at bipartisanship before suggesting that our case had never received a full airing. We needed to show the senator-jurors the full picture, and the only way to do it effectively was with live witnesses.

Henry then called on me; his facial expressions signaled a silent plea to behave myself and preface my comments with additional Senate flattery. I managed to join in the chorus of adulation without gagging, and then I eased into my point:

> **I told the senators that Clinton has offered many apologies, but he has also denied every single factual allegation against him. Who is lying and who is telling the truth? The senator-jurors needed to see and hear the live witnesses and observe their demeanor under direct and cross-examination to determine credibility issues before delivering their verdict.**
>
> **Democrat Carl Levin said he wanted the Managers to brief him in detail on our entire trial outline and strategy. Republican Domenici interrupted and said the senators didn't have time to hear this now. When Levin ignored Domenici and renewed his demand, Domenici looked at me and mouthed silently the word "No" while moving his head from side to side. Seeing Domenici's cue (I wasn't sure if he was telling me not to trust the Democrats or he really just didn't want to hear it), I told Levin I couldn't provide that information because I left my notes behind.**

When I said I didn't have my order of proof outline, Asa pulled out his copy and held it aloft. Domenici interrupted and again said they didn't have time to listen to all of this. Levin ignored Domenici and asked Hutchinson to read it. Asa caught onto my silent body language and pulled back:

> **Hutchinson told the senators, "I'm reluctant to share this now."**
> **With that, Democrat Joe Biden flashed a beaming smile:**
> **"Hey, listen Asa," he said with oozing sincerity, "we senators here are all honor-bound that anything you tell us will**

never get out of this room. We wouldn't tell the White House your strategy. If anything, you guys are our congressional colleagues—those guys in the White House aren't! They don't dictate up here, we do. In fact, we will favor you over them in a close question because you are one of us."

At the end of Biden's soliloquy about how the Democrats wouldn't share any of this information with the Clinton White House, I wrote in my notes the impression his pledge left on me:

"*Snow job.*"

> **Republican Ted Stevens interrupted, saying that he also wanted Hutchinson to read it. Domenici said, "I guess I'm outvoted." Hutchinson began walking the senators through our entire proposed outline. Levin interrupted often, asking for more details. As Hutchinson read from our order of proof, the three Republican senators sat and listened. The three Democrats never stopped scribbling notes.**

Whenever I reflect back on the entire experience of President Clinton's impeachment, an indelible image comes from this meeting with these senators. It happened at the end of the session, which lasted over two hours. When Republican Ted Stevens echoed Domenici's earlier point—that the Senate would never convict and remove Clinton, no matter the evidence—I tried to shame away their breathtaking cynicism. Looking at those six senators seated above us, I appealed to their sense of duty:

> *Senators, before I came to Washington, I served for over ten years as both a prosecutor and a trial court judge. At the end of every trial, I always talked to the jurors about their impressions. Those thousand or more jurors always told me the same two things almost without fail. First, when they received their jury summons, most didn't want*

to serve. Second, once they took the oath to do impartial justice, they understood they now had a grave responsibility and they took that responsibility seriously.

Tomorrow, for only the second time in American history, the Chief Justice of the United States will enter your chamber. He will require 100 senators to raise their hands and take the oath to do impartial justice. In fact, if a senator refuses to take that oath, your body will not seat that senator as an impeachment juror.

At the same time that you are taking your oath tomorrow morning, tens of thousands of humble, ordinary Americans will take that same oath in courtrooms all across our country. I have to believe that the members of the world's greatest deliberative body will give that oath at least as much consideration as all the waitresses, bartenders, cab drivers, and janitors who will also take that oath tomorrow.

The senators listened politely. When I finished my story, Domenici, Stevens, Biden, and Levin exchanged brief glances with each other.

And then they laughed at me.

27

Fait Accompli

Apparently, the senators weren't bluffing about starting the Clinton impeachment "trial" the next morning.

As our evening meeting with their bipartisan group broke up, they instructed us to prepare to exhibit the articles of impeachment in the Senate the following day. "Exhibiting" is another impeachment tradition where the House Managers enter the Senate, stand in the well, and formally present the articles to their body. This triggers the start of the impeachment trial.

Chairman Henry Hyde asked his House Managers to assemble in the morning at the same Capitol office where we gathered a few weeks earlier for our procession to notify the Senate of the president's impeachment:

Diary, Room H219, The U.S. Capitol, January 7, 1999

Our Managers were in a jovial mood when we gathered despite the solemn event about to occur. We mocked the senators' continuing pomposity as they strut before the television cameras preening about protecting the dignity of the Senate. Henry said, "I've been practicing my bowing and scraping in anticipation of our entrance."

Just before we left, Trent Lott called Henry on the phone to float another "no witness trial" proposal. While Henry spoke with Lott, I circulated among our other Managers

and urged that we stand together, reject any proposal that amounted to a phony "trial," and refuse to proceed if the Senate blocked us from making our presentation. Most Managers agreed with me, but George Gekas shook his head in dissent. "Oh, we have to go over there and put on a case," he insisted.

At the appointed time, we began our procession back to the Senate. When we reached the center of the Capitol rotunda, House Sergeant at Arms Bill Livingood delivered us into the protection of Senate Sergeant at Arms Jim Ziglar, who escorted us to the main entrance door of the Senate. Police allowed press photographers to take pictures as we approached the Senate, but once we reached the door, the guards ordered that they stop. Senate rules forbid the taking of any photographs inside their chamber, and since the main doors have glass windows, Capitol police instructed them to lower their cameras. I heard one burly guard yell at an errant photographer, "Don't shoot toward that door, sir. I won't say it again."

Senator Strom Thurmond (R-SC), seated at the dais, presided in his capacity as president pro tempore. Now 96 years old, Thurmond was the oldest man in American history to serve. Knowing this would be Thurmond's last term, fellow Manager Lindsey Graham motioned toward his state's senior senator and whispered to me, "When old Strom retires, I'm gonna run for his seat and then come over here and raise holy hell!"[1]

Shortly after 10:00 a.m., Ziglar opened the Senate doors, stepped inside, and called to the assembled body, *I announce the presence of the Managers on the part of the House of Representatives to conduct proceedings on behalf of the House concerning the impeachment of William Jefferson Clinton, President of the United States.*

---

1   In November 2002, Lindsey Graham won election to succeed Senator Strom Thurmond, who retired from the Senate at age 100.

Hear ye! Hear ye! All persons are commanded to keep silent, on pain of imprisonment.

As we entered, a few Republican senators winked or smiled at us. Gazing around the room, I saw senators who had signed autographs for me three decades earlier when I was a boy sneaking into political dinners hoping to meet our nation's leaders. Now, pulsing with nervous energy and standing before them at the start of our prosecution of the president of the United States, it felt otherworldly.

At Thurmond's direction, Henry stepped to the podium, opened a thin black notebook, and started his presentation:

Diary, United States Senate Chamber, January 7, 1999

As Henry read the text of the articles, the Republican senators sat erect and listening attentively. That was not true for all the Democrats. Many cast their eyes downward looking grim. Democrat leader Daschle appeared to be in an especially dark mood. Newly elected Blanche Lincoln (D-AR) sat with her head cocked back, mouth opened, and she stared toward the ceiling. Pat Leahy (D-VT) closed his eyes, grimaced, and then buried his head in his hands while shaking it from side to side.

I started sizing up the chamber and thinking about what it will be like to stand here and prosecute the impeachment "trial." In contrast to the more cavernous House chamber, the Senate chamber is small—almost intimate. Still, I know presenting this case before the Chief Justice of the United States, all 100 senators, and on worldwide television will be very intimidating. We all hope to be up to the challenge.

When Henry finished reading the resolutions, President Pro Tem Thurmond said the Senate would notify us when to return and begin opening statements. As Ziglar escorted us out of the chamber, all the Republican senators rose from their desks. The Democrats at first remained seated: a few rose, and then more followed. The last senator to stand for us was Daschle, who never looked at us.

Unlike his respect-challenged minority leader, Senator Daniel Patrick Moynihan (D-NY) had no qualms about showing courtesy to the House Managers. He bounded from his chair and walked over to the doors. As we exited, he shook hands and shared a word with each of us. Aside from being one of the most brilliant members of the Senate, he proved himself one of the classiest.

• • •

Back on the House side of the Capitol, the Managers assembled in the Judiciary Committee conference room so Henry could brief us on his latest Trent Lott contact:

Diary, House Managers Meeting, January 7, 1999

Lott now says the Senate will ask questions about the Starr Report to the Managers and to Clinton's lawyers, and then they will vote on whether to permit us to take witness depositions. However, even if they grant us permission to take depositions, Lott said that doesn't mean they will let any of the witnesses testify [either in person or by deposition]!

Under Lott's newest plan, we'd spend an entire month before the Senate—not trying our case, but instead arguing back and forth with Clinton's lawyers about having a trial. Only after this meaningless theater would the Senate decide whether to hear from any witnesses. For my money, their answer to that question was a foregone conclusion. I didn't wait for Henry to finish his briefing before I started disparaging Lott and his idea. I told Henry we could no longer trust the Senate's Republican leadership, and that this was a trick to suck us into a no-witness sham proceeding.

When I finished, Henry looked down at the floor and made

a stunning admission: He said he just told Lott that he could live with this new plan.

Forgetting all protocol, and with an index finger jabbing the air in his direction, I blurted in frustration, "Henry, we can try this whole fucking case in three weeks! Instead, we're going to spend a month in the Senate debating whether we should have a goddamned trial? This is bullshit, Henry, and you know it."

He said nothing in reply. Other Managers voiced more tempered support for my regrettably inelegant resistance. Only George Gekas sided with Henry openly: he argued that Lott's plan gave us "a chance to show the Senate why the House impeached Clinton."

"I don't give a shit about showing the *Senate* anything, George," I snapped. "I want to show *America* why we impeached him."

As the heated debate continued, I recommended a compromise to Lott's month-long, meaningless gabfest. Since the Senate was so concerned about wasting their precious time or offending their pious dignity,

I suggested we take a day in the Senate to let both sides make their case as to whether to have a trial. After the Senate hears from the president's lawyers and from us, let them take an up-or-down vote on whether to have a trial: "I'd rather be told 'no trial' than to go through a pro forma proceeding where the Senate can claim they had a 'trial' before they acquit Clinton."

Charles Canady agreed: "Lott's proposal is a sham. We should let them vote for no trial if that is where they are headed, and then let it be on their head."

Asa Hutchinson also concurred, and he advised us that the Senate Republicans were currently meeting. "We need to let them know this latest proposal is unacceptable," he added.

We paused our discussion to watch live news coverage of Chief Justice William H. Rehnquist entering the Senate chamber. After taking his oath as presiding officer for the impeachment "trial," Rehnquist administered the oath to the senator-jurors to do "impartial justice" for the impeachment court. This presented some comic relief to our war-weary troops. Laughter rippled through our ranks watching the solemn pageantry of those who announced publicly their prejudgment of our case yesterday swearing sacred impartiality today. Candidly, I found the spectacle more disgusting than funny.

After we resumed our discussion, Trent Lott called Henry on the telephone. Henry relayed to Lott our combative sentiments. Lott responded by ordering us to submit our entire record of the case to the Senate if we wished it to be considered during our "trial"—and he told us we had just ten minutes to get it filed! Curses from our team filled the room as our staff scurried to box up our materials. In trying to calm his infuriated troops, Henry said, "The Senate leadership right now is in a chaotic state." As I surveyed our side rushing to beat a disgraceful deadline designed to kneecap our case, the chaos appeared to be with us, not them.

Later that afternoon, and long after we delivered the materials that they forced us to compile at the last minute, our presenter team gathered to discuss initial responsibilities. During this meeting, Hutchinson received a call from his brother, U.S. Senator Tim Hutchinson (R-AR). Tim said that neither Lott nor his chief of staff ever mentioned our proposal that we asked him to submit to the Senate Republican Caucus.

Soon after, Senator Rick Santorum called me:

Diary, Telephone Call with Senator Rick Santorum, January 7, 1999, 5:00 p.m.

Santorum said that Lott is proposing the senators have a bipartisan caucus tomorrow morning to adopt his latest

proposal: have the House Managers and the president's attorneys argue their respective cases for four weeks, and then the Senate will vote on whether to allow a trial with witnesses. However, the Senate will also entertain a White House motion to dismiss the case outright.

Santorum confessed that under Lott's plans, the House Managers should "assume that you will get no witnesses."

Trent Lott apparently stood nearby when Santorum told me this, because as my colorful response blared from Santorum's telephone receiver, Lott took the phone from him and came on the line with me:

Lott said he wanted to meet with all the House Managers at 6:00 p.m. tonight. "Jim, we want to give you your trial and let you call your witnesses," he told me. "So, let's all get together with your Managers tonight and show you that we aren't out to be the enemy. I should have just done this myself the first time instead of using intermediaries."

Did I just hear him correctly? After presuming Lott the boogeyman trying to scuttle our case, had all this been a misunderstanding from the start? With his personal assurance, I felt a sudden ray of hope.

Our staff rounded up the other House Managers for the meeting in our Judiciary Committee conference room. Before Lott arrived, I related my conversation to the group, along with Lott's assurance that he wants to make sure we call live witnesses. Manager Chris Cannon interrupted me:

"I just spoke to [Utah Republican Senator] Bob Bennett," Cannon said. "Bennett told me, 'You guys just lost. The Senate plans to kill off your hope of calling any witnesses.'" Manager Bill McCollum shared that he had just received the same message from Senator Mike DeWine (R-OH).

Fuming over Lott's apparent smoke blowing over the telephone, I renewed my motion that we should refuse to participate in any proceeding where the senators block us from calling witnesses. Bob Barr agreed and made a motion to give Chairman Hyde authority to tell Lott we would refuse to proceed without witnesses. Henry took the middle ground, saying we should take two days in the Senate to make our case as to why we need witnesses. "Otherwise," he feared, "we might appear to be sore losers."

• • •

Trent Lott and Rick Santorum interrupted our discussion when they arrived together at 6:15 p.m. After expressing his love for the House and claiming fond memories of his own days there, Lott lamented that the Senate is a more complicated body to lead:

> **"I want you to have a chance to put on your case," Lott told us. "But 'putting on your case' means opening statements and maybe some evidence. There is no guarantee that you will get any witnesses. Maybe you can get some witnesses later, but keep in mind you always face a motion to adjourn the trial from the Democrats."**

Some of the Managers didn't wait for Lott to finish speaking before weighing in:

> **Chris Cannon accused Lott of trying to get us to participate in a sham trial. Bob Barr snapped at Lott, "We don't hear you guys on TV telling everyone you are fighting for us to be able to call witnesses. All we hear is you Senate Republicans saying that we need to convince you that we need witnesses."**
> **Growing defensive, Lott shot back, "I'm not prepared to agree to fight for your right to call witnesses without justification. I'm doing my best to hold the line on our moderate**

Republican senators. They may vote against the articles of impeachment themselves if you keep pushing this witness issue!"

"Without witnesses," Bill McCollum interrupted, "Clinton stands no chance of ever being convicted and removed."

"At least you'll stand a chance to have your side heard," Lott replied.

When my turn came, I ridiculed Lott's position and reminded him that the Senate routinely spends months on judicial impeachments. I also reminded him that in Judge Alcee Hastings' recent impeachment trial, the Senate heard from 55 witnesses. I accused Lott of wanting us to come and argue why we should have a trial, and then he wants to call that argument the "trial."

Next, I explained why the White House and the Senate Democrats fight so hard against having any live witnesses called: with witnesses, the Democrats have no control over an otherwise preordained verdict of acquittal. "The Managers understand why the Democrat senators don't want witnesses," I goaded, "but why on earth are you Republican senators afraid of them?"

Finally, I told Lott that if he really was fearful that moderate Republicans would vote against impeachment articles out of revenge if we asked for witnesses, then Lott should reverse the order of his proposal: have us argue to the Senate why we needed witnesses for a trial, and then let the Senate vote. If the Senate refuses our request, we should announce that the Senate has rendered us unable to proceed and walk out.

Lott and Santorum shared a panic-stricken look. Santorum blurted, "If we did that, then you guys could leave

and say you never got a trial!" With that comment, both Lott and Santorum tipped their hand. Here, ultimately, was their plan: call their charade a trial and then let the history books record Clinton's acquittal after an impeachment "trial."

Lott distributed copies of his final "no-witness" trial plan. He asked us to review it, and then he and Santorum stepped out of the room to await our decision.

A glum-looking Henry Hyde said he was willing to go along with Lott's plan. Bob Barr spoke against it vociferously. I joined Barr in suggesting we return to the Senate to argue for our right to have a trial but refuse to cooperate with this plan.

Henry summoned Lott and Santorum back to the room. "I'm getting great resistance to your plan from my team," Henry told them, and then he repeated our willingness to come and argue for our right to have a full trial. Lott reiterated Santorum's earlier concern that if they agreed to this, and if the Senate later refused to give us witnesses, "you guys might later say there never was a trial."

There it was again. Stripped bare were all the earlier winks and nods about calling witnesses later in the "trial." Lott and Santorum stalked out of the room amid hostile comments from our team.

When our meeting ended, a tired Henry Hyde pulled me aside for a private talk: "If we ever get witnesses," he said, "and if the trial starts going our way, it will force Clinton to testify in person. Knowing Clinton, he might show up unexpectedly and with great dramatic surprise. We can't let him catch us unprepared, so I need you to get ready to cross-examine Clinton if he shows up in the Senate." I suggested that senior colleagues might get upset if he gave that high-profile responsibility to a committee rookie, but Henry proved indifferent to the concern.

I went home and sat at my kitchen table until dawn sketching out my initial preparation for the ultimate trial confrontation should it ever occur.

• • •

The next morning, our litigation team divided the impeachment case responsibilities. Ed Bryant took the Paula Jones portion of the case, the Lewinsky timeline, and Clinton's role as chief law enforcement officer; Asa Hutchinson would handle Clinton's obstruction of justice; I would prosecute the perjury; and Bob Barr would handle the closing. Our only disagreement came over how to handle Lott's plan: Bryant and Hutchinson now agreed with Hyde and Gekas that we needed to present ourselves before the Senate despite their intention to block witnesses. Barr and I remained steadfast that the Managers refuse to proceed under that circumstance.

Bill McCollum joined our meeting with new intelligence from the Senate: "[Senator Mike] DeWine just told me the Republican senators are caucusing right now. They're discussing openly how Lott's proposal is designed to make sure we never get to call any live witnesses."

"Well," Barr asked our two dissenting colleagues, "does that help change your mind?"

After our meeting broke up, I returned to my office and found Managers Lindsey Graham and Chris Cannon waiting for me:

Diary, House Office Building, The U.S. Capitol, January 8, 1999

Chris and Lindsey said they wanted to go to Henry Hyde and ask to have me named as vice chair of the Managers. "We need a strong voice to buck up Henry, who holds firm until the end and then caves in," Cannon told me. I urged them to suspend the idea because Henry will interpret this as insulting or as an attack on his authority.

Neither Cannon nor Graham intended disrespect to our Chairman. Both shared the same affection and esteem for him that we all had. I interpreted their message as a reaction to their deep frustration with Lott and the impending Senate GOP sellout, combined with Henry's fading stamina to engage in intra-party warfare.

"We're getting fucked up and down on this Senate deal," Chris raged. He agrees with Barr and me about refusing to proceed if the Senate won't let us try our case. On the other hand, Lindsey thinks we need to take a more political tack and try to develop the "Jane Doe" testimony[2] before the Senate because it shows Clinton's pattern of evidence obstruction. Lindsey thinks this aspect of the case will capture the press' attention and increase pressure on the Senate to allow live witnesses.

While we met, the Senate Republicans and Democrats concluded a rare bipartisan joint caucus. Gathering in the stately Old Senate Chamber, the senators approved unanimously a plan to start the formal impeachment "trial" without telling the Managers in advance whether they would allow us to call witnesses. After their 100-member group hug, they fanned out to announce the way things would be.

Senator Phil Gramm (R-TX) called and interrupted my meeting with Cannon and Graham. He said he was on his way over to my office to explain the "bipartisan" Lott-Daschle agreement the senators just unanimously adopted. Gramm said that he was with Senator Ted Kennedy (D-MA), who was ready to start making the rounds to House Democrats to explain their plan.

---

2   The "Jane Doe" issue involved the grand jury testimony of other women making sexual assault allegations against Clinton (like Juanita Broaddrick and Kathleen Willey), and how Team Clinton tried to pressure and threaten them into silence.

Cannon, Graham, and I called House Majority Whip Tom DeLay at home. We expressed to Tom our fear that Henry would surrender to this Lott-Daschle 'no witness' fraud, and that Phil Gramm was on his way over to pitch the plan to us. We asked for Tom's advice on how to handle Gramm.

When I mentioned that Gramm (his fellow Texas Republican) was hawking the proposal with Ted Kennedy, DeLay blew up: "This is bullshit! He's been co-opted by Kennedy and is getting snookered." DeLay told us to challenge Gramm to be "the Tom DeLay of the Senate and be a champion for the House to call live witnesses to present your case."

"When you say it like that," DeLay said with a laugh, "that'll really piss him off!"

A few minutes later, Gramm barged into my office and took a seat without saying hello. He told us the Senate had just agreed to give each side 24 hours to make their respective case without calling any witnesses. After that, the Senate would let us know if they would allow witnesses. In trying to paint the rosiest scenario, he told us this was a "good deal" because "the Democrats now realize you can make opening statements and say what you will, and they can't do a damned thing about it." Gramm begged us not to take the position that we needed witnesses to make our case. Then, with a finger raised dramatically in the air, he told us stiffly, "You have a constitutional duty to present your case."

"*We* have a constitutional duty?" Cannon fired back in fury. "*You* have the constitutional duty—and you're shirking it." I told Gramm that the Senate was doing nothing more than trying to protect itself from an unpopular task and leaving the House Managers holding the bag. I renewed all the reasons why we needed live witnesses to prove our case: Clinton never stood a chance of conviction in the Senate without public opinion moving, and the public wouldn't listen to the Senate proceedings without the drama of live witnesses.

Gramm listened quietly, but there was nothing left to say. He didn't come over to negotiate. He came to tell us the Senate had decided the issue, and they had done so with a 100-to-0 bipartisan vote.

• • •

The Senate continued pretending to dangle the potential for witnesses before us while coaxing us deeper into the quicksand. This was all for public consumption. Once we started down this path, I knew that the Senate, the media, and the history books would forever call this farce an impeachment "trial." Gramm delivered Lott and Daschle's ultimatum in a homey Texas drawl, but perhaps it might have been more appropriate for him to say it in French:

Fait accompli.

28

Reformed Drunks

"Do you solemnly swear that in all things appertaining to the trial of the impeachment of William Jefferson Clinton, president of the United States, now pending, you will do impartial justice according to the Constitution and laws, so help you God?"
—OATH GIVEN TO EACH SENATOR AS IMPEACHMENT TRIAL JURORS. ADMINISTERED BY CHIEF JUSTICE WILLIAM H. REHNQUIST, UNITED STATES SENATE CHAMBER, JANUARY 7, 1999

The House Managers *"realize that the press and the public have consigned them to the waste bin of history. Their only vindication is bringing other people down to their level."*
—SENATOR JOSEPH BIDEN (D-DE), THREE DAYS AFTER SWEARING TO DO "IMPARTIAL JUSTICE" AS A CLINTON IMPEACHMENT JUROR, AND FOUR DAYS BEFORE THE START OF THE IMPEACHMENT TRIAL, *CHICAGO TRIBUNE*, JANUARY 10, 1999

The House impeachment Managers have *"fallen into the black pit of partisan self-indulgence."*
—SENATOR ROBERT BYRD (D-WV), THREE HOURS AFTER SWEARING TO DO "IMPARTIAL JUSTICE" AS A CLINTON IMPEACHMENT JUROR, AND SEVEN DAYS BEFORE THE START OF THE IMPEACHMENT TRIAL, SENATE CAUCUS SPEECH, JANUARY 7, 1999

"It is almost as if the Hand of Providence reached down into our historic chamber."

—SENATOR JOHN WARNER (R-VA), CONGRATULATING HIS
COLLEAGUES ON ADOPTING A BIPARTISAN "NO WITNESS"
PLAN FOR THE CLINTON IMPEACHMENT TRIAL, *WASHINGTON
POST,* JANUARY 10, 1999

T he weekend before the start of opening statements in our no-witness "trial," I watched a news interview with one of our "impartial" sworn "trial" jurors:

Diary, Sunday, January 10, 1999

Senator Tom Harkin (D-IA) told a reporter that our case against Clinton is "a sham partisan action and a pile of dung." He made this statement after taking an oath three days ago to do "impartial justice" in the case and before we presented any evidence. This is outrageous. The Senate should block Harkin from sitting as a juror on the case, but it will never happen. Senate rules do not provide for challenges to these so-called "jurors." Each senator decides for himself whether he can fulfill his oath of impartiality.

In any other courtroom in America, the judge would boot a self-disqualified juror like Harkin off the panel and consider holding him in contempt. Welcome to the Senate, where collegiality reigns supreme. None of his colleagues on either side of the aisle raised a protest over Harkin's oath abrogation.

Earlier, Trent Lott asked Asa Hutchinson and me to join a conference call with Republican senators who (like me) were making the rounds on the Sunday morning news shows. I later learned that Lott invited me on the line because he feared I might veer "off message" during my TV interview and attack their process.

Along with a couple other House Managers, I dialed in to the senators' call. Not surprisingly, the senators preferred we listen to them and not the other way around:

Diary, Conference Call with Republican Senators, Saturday, January 9, 1999

Lott instructed his senators to explain in their TV interviews that they set up a "fair and bipartisan process to get to the truth."

"In fact," Lott crowed, "Democrat partisans said we could never reach a bipartisan agreement. Well, we did!"

"Of course," added Lott, "the Senate will determine later if any witnesses are called." Then, in an apparent effort to pander to the House Managers on the line, he said, "You know, the more the White House and the Democrats scream 'no witnesses,' the more I wonder what they are afraid of."

In light of that comment, I asked Lott if that meant he was now reconsidering his "no witnesses" position. He offered no answer. Another senator spoke up to break the intervening silence:

Orrin Hatch (R-UT) said, "When we go on these shows, we senators need to say that if there are going to be any witnesses, the House needs to show a very compelling reason to call them." Olympia Snowe (R-ME) agreed with him, as did John Chafee (R-RI).

Chafee complained that calling witnesses "could take us into February!" Then, after congratulating his colleagues on fashioning a bipartisan agreement, he said, "We [sena-

tors] should remember that we won. We need to be cautious that we don't rub it in their faces [referencing the House Managers]."

They won? Don't rub our faces in it? Did this magoo not know—or care—that House Managers were on the line? Orrin Hatch's response to Chafee's victory dance gave me no additional sense of comfort:

"How happy we are to be unanimously marching down the road to justice!" Hatch echoed.

When an opening in their self-congratulatory discourse occurred, I objected to their take on the process and again discussed the importance of calling live witnesses. My comments hung in the air like an unwelcome odor.

Only Senators Mike DeWine (R-OH) and John Ashcroft (R-MO) backed me. "We have a responsibility to pursue the truth," said Ashcroft. "If witnesses are appropriate to get to the truth, then they need to be there."

"What if it was the White House that wanted to call witnesses instead of us?" Asa Hutchinson asked. "What would be the Senate's response then?"

After another long pause, Trent Lott responded meekly to Asa's pointed query:

"We would let them call every single one they wanted," Lott admitted.

At the end of the call, Lott asked me, "So, Jim, what are you going to say on your show tomorrow if you get asked about our plan?"

"Who knows?" I replied with a snicker. "I guess you'll have to watch the show."

Not long after the conference call ended, Lindsey Graham phoned me at home. "I just spoke with Trent Lott," Lindsey volunteered. "He said, 'Your friend Rogan is very smart—and very dangerous.'"

• • •

The next morning, at ABC News' Washington studio, an intern escorted me to the green room to join Senators Orrin Hatch (R-UT), Olympia Snowe (R-ME), and John Breaux (D-LA), all of whom were scheduled for a separate interview segment on the show:

**Diary, ABC News Studio, Washington, D.C.,
Sunday, January 10, 1999**

Hatch seemed especially worried about what I might say regarding the Senate's bipartisan trial procedures. He also expressed his deep concern over Bob Barr being one of our House Manager presenters. Hatch said Barr wouldn't be effective because the senators view him as a lightning rod.

Hatch put his arm around my shoulder and asked if he could speak to me privately. We walked out in the hallway together. "I'm on your side," he said (despite his joining in the senatorial chorus approving Lott's plan). Then Hatch hit me with an unexpected request:

"I'm seriously thinking of running for president in 2000," he told me. "Having smart and respected fellows like you on my side would make a big difference. What do you think? Do you think I could do it, and do you think you could support a guy like me?"

Taken aback by the unexpected plea, I smiled: "Orrin, ask me that question later—after you vote in the Senate on

whether we get to call witnesses."

Oblivious to the backhanded shot I took for him not backing us on witnesses, he replied, "Great! When this is all over, come by my office and get together with me on this. I really want to talk to you about it."

Walking away, I shook my head in amazement. I liked Orrin Hatch—then and now. In fact, he came to my district and campaigned for me when I first ran for Congress. However, asking someone to help make you president while you stab him confirmed my view that breathing the Senate air for too long can seriously distort one's judgment.

• • •

On Monday, January 11, Henry Hyde met with fellow Managers McCollum, Bryant, Hutchinson, Barr, and me in his conference room. He made an abrupt announcement: "Bob Barr is now off the presentation team. He'll remain a House Manager, of course. I'm replacing Bob with Bill McCollum."

Showing signs of accumulating stress, our usually gracious leader dumped Barr perfunctorily, and he did it with Barr seated at the table with us. To make it worse, Barr had received no advance warning. Henry then turned to McCollum and spoke as though Barr was not in the room. "Barr is probably pissed off at me," Henry said, "but he needs to know that it is an honor for him to be selected as a Manager."

I didn't know what to make of the bizarre situation. Looking over at Barr, he appeared more hurt than angry, but his tone never showed either emotion: "I'm here to serve this effort in any way you ask me, Mr. Chairman," he replied stoically. Throughout the rest of the so-called "trial," Barr made good on his pledge. If he harbored any residual disappointment, it never showed.

I had been one of several Managers who had lobbied Henry privately not to give Barr a key role in the mission. However, by the end of our Senate warfare, I regretted my role in advocating for his demotion. Of all our Managers, nobody showed up each day as consistently ready for run toward the gunfire as did Bob.

When the impeachment "trial" ended, I confessed to Bob my role in his demotion. I told him that I regretted taking that position, and I apologized to him privately.

Bob, now I'm apologizing publicly.

• • •

Diary, Presentation Team Meeting, House Judiciary Conference Room, Monday, January 11, 1999

Henry advised our group that I would conduct Clinton's cross-examination if he testified. He then assigned our roles for opening statements: we would begin late Thursday, and he wanted us to finish them by Friday afternoon.

Leaving the meeting, reporters who knew about my new responsibility surrounded me. Looking into the TV cameras, I did everything I could to taunt Clinton into testifying: "Mr. President, a trial should be a search for the truth. Look who's on our witness list. It isn't our golfing buddy. It isn't our best friend. It isn't our personal secretary. It isn't our chief of staff. It isn't our former intern. Mr. President, we want to hear from *your* golfing buddy, *your* secretary, *your* chief of staff, *your* best friend, and *your* former intern. If you're telling the truth, Mr. President, then what do you have to hide? Just come to the Senate, tell everyone your story, and then I'll ask you some questions about it. You're a Rhodes Scholar, Mr. President. I was expelled from high school. Surely you aren't afraid of me."

A reporter asked if I was geared up to cross-examine Clinton with any special plan in mind. Sure, I replied: "I always have a theory when preparing to cross examine a defendant. This case is no different."

"What's your theory for Clinton?" the reporter asked.

It's basic, I said: If Clinton comes to the Senate and testifies, he'll answer questions from his lawyers. When they finish, I'll get up and cross-examine him.

The reporter gave me a blank look. "That sounds pretty basic. But what's your *theory*?" I felt my eyelids narrow, which they often do when my countenance hardens, as I replied:

"My theory is this. When I'm done asking those questions, one of us will be destroyed."

Oh.

In a lighter moment, another reporter asked if I planned to carry any good luck charm to the "trial." I pretended to hesitate as if reluctant to share a secret. That, of course, only whetted her appetite. Not being superstitious, I had no plans for any special trial hoodoo, but I decided to have some fun with the pack. I concocted a story quickly about my faux talisman:

> **I whispered my answer in confidential fashion: "I intend to bring *The Brown Beast* into the Senate." Jumping on this, the reporters demanded to know what or who was The Brown Beast.**
>
> **The Brown Beast was a nickname that I had just made up on the spot for my battered old lawyer's litigation briefcase. I bought it the day before I became a deputy district attorney 15 years ago. After using it throughout my entire career, the briefcase had so many holes worn through the leather that I had to close the gaps with slabs of unsightly brown electrical tape wrapped around the outside to keep it together.**

My old briefcase was in such deplorable shape that my wife Christine threw it in the trash twice (I rescued it from the dumpster each time). Now, suddenly, the thought of carrying that duct-taped eyesore into the Senate chamber amused me as a silent protest against the puffed-up dignity of its members.

The reporters then pleaded to see The Brown Beast, so I led a large delegation of them to my office to view my just-created legend. After perching the old bag on my desk with faked reverence, I stepped back so photographers could shoot the dilapidated and caved-in remnant.

I told the reporters that The Brown Beast and I have one more trial left in us. One of them asked if I planned to carry The Beast during the trial for luck.

"No," I replied sharply, "not for luck. I don't believe in luck. I believe in tradition."

After hyping the joke, my press secretary Jeff Solsby insisted I had to use The Beast during the "trial." On the first day of opening statements, when I passed the phalanx of news photographers and reporters outside the Senate, I heard one of them yell, "There it is!" Dozens of camera lenses trained on the shabby briefcase. The next day, someone handed me a copy of the *Washington Post*. The lead story above the fold began as follows:

When Rep. James E. Rogan (R-Calif.) learned he would help conduct the impeachment case against President Clinton in the Senate this month, he knew he had to break out The Brown Beast. A tattered leather briefcase held together with brown duct tape, the bulky bag belonged to Rogan when he brought cases against gang members in Los Angeles in the 1980s. The briefcase was retired when he was first elected to Congress in 1996, but it's been resurrected since Rogan got back into prosecution work in recent days.

People started sending me various newspaper clippings from around the world with pictures of me carrying The Brown Beast into the Senate. The Beast and I even made the cover of a national magazine. Only Jeff Solsby and I knew that each day I carried The Beast into the Senate, it was filled with nothing but my personal Bible (to flatten out the bottom) and lots of crumpled newspapers to make it look filled. To top it off, a few weeks after the impeachment "trial" ended, an archivist from the Smithsonian Institution visited me and put together a list of impeachment "trial" relics the museum wanted me to donate some day. Near the top of their want list was my battered briefcase—with the original duct-tape left intact!

From the dumpster to the Smithsonian: talk about carrying a gag too far!

• • •

That weekend, Henry Hyde summoned a few Managers to his office for an impromptu meeting. I arrived to find a collection of Republican senators there: Jim Bunning (R-KY), Jon Kyl (R-AZ), Arlen Specter (R-PA), and Jim Inhofe (R-OK). Phil Gramm (R-TX) participated in our discussion by teleconference:

Diary, Meeting in Chairman Hyde's Office, January 8, 1999

Arlen Specter asked me, "Why would you want to call these witnesses live?" I replied that being a former prosecutor himself, Specter knew how important it was in trial not to stipulate away the testimony of key witnesses, especially when credibility issues would determine the outcome. I told him that if he were in our shoes, he'd never agree to that. Specter rubbed his chin in thought for a moment, and then he grinned.

"That is how I always felt about *my* witnesses," he answered, "not *someone else's* witnesses."

"Look, we're your friends," Jon Kyl told us. "But we don't represent the Senate. Let's cut to the chase. The mood of the Senate is this: every Democrat will vote against your calling witnesses. Some Republicans also believe it would be the worst possible mistake to allow the House Managers to call witnesses sympathetic to Clinton. And all of us are concerned about wasting time and preserving the dignity of the Senate."

Henry Hyde replied, "What you are suggesting is not a trial. It is a bastardized process. We have guys who are ready to try this case, but what you want is not a trial. You view us as rehabilitated drunks. You admire what we are doing, but you don't want us to hang out in the lobby too long."

The meeting produced no change in the Senate's adopted procedures. If we agreed to participate, we would start the "trial" with no witnesses and be forced to hold out hope that the senators might later change their minds (a hope that, by now, only a buffoon would contemplate).

Diary, Saturday, January 9, 1999

I spoke with fellow Managers Chris Cannon and Bob Barr, both of whom remain furious over the Senate's announced procedures. We still agree that Henry Hyde must tell Trent Lott to give us a real trial or else the House Managers should refuse to participate.

As far as Cannon, Barr, and I were concerned, the only recourse to the Senate's dirty deal was a full-fledged mutiny. We again lobbied our Manager colleagues to stand firm in demanding that the Senate let us try our case properly or else tell them to take their bipartisan screw job and shove it where the senatorial sun doesn't shine.

Diary, Sunday, January 10, 1999

I spoke on the phone with [Manager] Bill McCollum. I asked
if he would support Barr, Cannon, and me in urging Henry
Hyde to tell Lott we would refuse to proceed to trial unless
the Senate changed their rules.

Bill's earlier sympathy for that idea had waned. "We
really have no choice," he told me. "We *have* to appear before
the Senate to make our case. I know how you feel. If we end
up getting screwed by the Senate, you'll sure be able to say,
'I told you so.'"

This was an unwelcome sign. When I made my original motion
that we refuse to participate in a trial if the Senate blocked our witnesses, all of the other Managers (except George Gekas) agreed with
me. In the ensuing days, as the Senate forced our hand with their
unanimous "no-witness" resolution, our Managers' rebellion ranks
dwindled. Hutchinson, Bryant, and now McCollum had joined
Hyde and Gekas in accepting our fate.

Looking back, once Henry Hyde told Lott we would abide by
the Senate's terms, and when we couldn't convince our Chairman to
reverse himself, everyone else's opinion became superfluous. Henry
had already settled the issue for all practical purposes. It just took a
while longer for the inevitable to sink in.

Early Monday morning, just 72 hours before scheduled opening
statements, Henry called me at home. He said that Speaker Hastert
told him that Chris Cannon and I planned to call a press conference
to blast the Senate process and then announce our resignations as
House Managers. Henry asked if this was true. I replied that the
rumor was false, and that he should know that Cannon and I would
never abandon ship on him. Henry apologized, saying, "I didn't
think it was true, but I wanted you to know the rumor is out there."

My disgust with the Senate aside, I never once considered resigning as a Manager:

Diary, Monday, January 11, 1999

During our telephone conversation, Henry said he needs me to enter this trial with my heart in it. "I know you feel we are getting rolled by a Senate that has prejudged the case, and by Trent Lott, who only wants to protect his people at our expense. But I need to count on you to go forward with enthusiasm. This is the only chance we get to tell America what a son of a bitch this guy Clinton really is."

I told Henry to have no concern. Despite my misgivings, I know Henry depends on all of us. I will present my portion of the case to the utmost. Henry has been too good to me and my level of affection for him is too great to do anything other than to give this my very best.

Thus, the House Manager mutiny failed. As the record now shows, we "tried" the case on the Senate's terms. The Senate refused to allow us to call a single live witness. There was no direct or cross-examination. This scripted procedure preordained the exoneration of President Clinton. It was not a "trial" in any sense of the word. Yet today, every history book and public account records that Clinton "won" an acquittal after a Senate impeachment "trial."

As we used to say in Congress, I rise to a point of personal privilege. To my dear friend and former comrade-in-arms Bill McCollum, I say this with respect and deep affection:

I told you so.

29

"Have a Good Trial"

"Senator Richard J. Durbin (D-IL), who appeared with Senator Rick Santorum (R-PA) on Crossfire last week, said he believes Santorum and every other senator will at least make an effort to be impartial."
—*WASHINGTON POST*, JANUARY 6, 1999

As opening statements loomed, the House Managers and our Judiciary Committee staff labored feverishly. None of us had sufficient time to prepare, which was the senators' intent. They wanted us to go away and, barring that, to fall flat on our faces. By now, it wasn't just a constitutional principle to us. It became a personal principle, too. We weren't going to give them the smug satisfaction of watching us flail in their chamber.

Our team had toiled around-the-clock in shifts for weeks. Now only one shift existed, and we all worked it. Things like sleep and meals became intermittent annoyances. Manager Charles Canady's wife, Jennifer, delivered their first baby, little Julia, in a Florida hospital that week. Charles had to phone in his love. I hadn't spent any meaningful time with my wife and young daughters for months. The pace grew more frenetic with each passing hour. We *had* to be ready.

Diary, Wednesday, January 13, 1999

On the eve of beginning the "trial," I have been working on my opening statement for the last 23 straight hours. I'm not close to being done. Aside from completing this task, I have an even bigger concern: prepping my cross-examination of Clinton if he shows up in the Senate this week. Further, Henry Hyde asked me to be ready to present one of the closing arguments, which might come as early as this Saturday.

Later that evening, Henry asked our presenter team to meet him in his office to go over some last-minute details:

Henry confirmed a rumor we had been hearing all day. He told us, "The Senate is requiring that we draw up a complete list of the witnesses we wish to call. The Senate will treat the entire list as a single motion, and they will cast an 'all or nothing' vote on our entire list."

Why did the senators now decree that all potential witnesses be lumped into a single up-or-down vote? They used it as additional leverage to blackmail us: either roll over, or face a total shutdown of our ability to present competent evidence to prove our case. Whispered warnings from self-proclaimed "friendly" senators peppered my ears for the rest of that afternoon:

- "Tell your Managers not to put anyone on your list that is too controversial, or we'll have to vote down your entire list."

- "Tell your Managers to pare down your list to just a few people or we'll have to vote down your entire list."

- "For God's sake, tell your Managers not to put anyone on your list whose testimony might offend the dignity of the Senate or we'll have to vote down your entire list."

As we now discussed how to handle this latest Senate hurdle, Henry volunteered an unexpected opinion: *He no longer wanted us to call any live witnesses in the Senate.*

This sudden capitulation floored me. "However," he added quickly, "I will not impose that opinion on all of you." We nodded to Henry out of respect, and then we treated the remark as though we had never heard it. We resumed our discussion on which witnesses to add to our list.

Monica Lewinsky's lawyers have advised our staff that they will not produce her as a witness voluntarily. We will have to compel her attendance with a subpoena. Ed Bryant still thinks we need to call her even though her testimony "could be a keg of dynamite" that blows up in our face. Asa Hutchinson favors calling Clinton pal Vernon Jordan, whom Clinton lobbied to find a job for Lewinsky in New York after she ended up on Paula Jones' witness list.

Our discussion drifted toward throwing a surprise Hail Mary pass—adding an unexpected name to our list of witnesses we wanted subpoenaed:

Henry, Ed Bryant, and I want to add President Clinton to our witness list. Only Asa Hutchinson balked at this suggestion and urged caution. After further discussion, we compromised and agreed not to try to force a subpoena on Clinton. Instead,

we will ask the Senate to invite Clinton to testify as a witness in our case-in-chief.

"Well," I joked, "this will certainly shake up an otherwise laid-back day in the Senate."

Diary, Opening of the House's Case Against President Clinton, United States Senate Chamber, Thursday, January 14, 1999

The day has arrived. I stayed up all night and have been working feverishly all morning polishing the opening statement I will deliver this afternoon. I handed my extensive speech revisions to my staff at 11:15 a.m. with instructions to deliver the final reading copy to me in the Senate. I wanted to walk through the Capitol plaza alone for a few minutes to decompress.

Chairman Hyde instructed us to be on the Senate floor at 12:30 p.m. sharp. Chief Justice William H. Rehnquist wants to greet the House Managers at 12:45 p.m. in The President's Room, which is just off the Senate floor.

"The Chief Justice wants a ceremonial handshake with the Managers and to say a few words to us," Henry told us the night before. "He read that Chief Justice Salmon P. Chase greeted the House Managers and the president's lawyers at the opening of Andrew Johnson's impeachment trial in 1868, and he wants to do the same. The Chief is a stickler for tradition, and he is also a stickler for promptness—so be on time," he warned.

With about an hour to kill, I walked around the Cannon Building to clear my head, and then I returned to my office for a few quiet minutes to myself. I stretched out on my

couch and flipped through my desk copy of Oswald Chambers' "Precious Bible Promises" to read some encouraging Scripture verses before going to the Senate for the historic showdown.

Shortly after noon, I grabbed my newly-christened Brown Beast and headed for the Senate. As I walked through Statuary Hall alone, I thought of the House Managers in 1868 as they trod this same path to begin America's only other presidential impeachment. How could one not be filled by the history and significance of the moment?

Or, so I thought. Near the Rotunda, fellow Manager Jim Sensenbrenner caught up with me. As we walked together, Jim seemed wholly unimpressed with it all. At least outwardly, Jim appeared to view this occasion as just another day at the office.

When Jim and I entered the Senate chamber a few minutes before 12:30, it was empty except for a few staffers and technicians doing last-minute equipment checks. I staked out a seat at the Managers' semi-circular black Formica table located by tradition on the Democrat side of the aisle (an identical table for Clinton's lawyers was on the Republican side). The space is so tight that I can't back my chair away from the table without hitting a senator's desk.

The Senate Sergeant at Arms assigned to our Managers the Senate's "Marble Room" as our field headquarters. Perhaps only the Senate Gymnasium rivals the Marble Room as a private haven for senators. Nobody enters either temple without membership in the world's most exclusive club. The senators surrendered their regal hideaway reluctantly, and its loss probably created additional incentive for them to kick us out of the Senate faster. In my first book, *Rough Edges: My Unlikely Road from Welfare to Washington*, I described the House Managers' invasion of their palatial sanctum:

It wasn't the first time that uninvited pests had invaded the Marble Room.

A hideaway lounge next to the United States Senate chamber, the Marble Room has an inviolate Senators Only rule. In the 1800s, senators permitted clerks to enter, but only to shoo away the bats hanging from the fixtures. During the Civil War, when Union troops billeted inside the Capitol, the Massachusetts Sixth Regiment seized the Marble Room and used it as a meat locker. Soldiers covered the cold tile floors with smelly hams and bacon slabs while the Senate doorkeeper begged them not to grease up the walls and furniture.

Aside from flying parasites, national rebellions, and other such nuisances, the Marble Room remained the exclusive domain of the senators—until we showed up.

In 1999, they grudgingly relinquished their beloved sanctuary to the thirteen Managers selected by the United States House of Representatives to prosecute the impeachment trial of President Bill Clinton. For six weeks, it became our war room. Doubtless most of the grumpy senators would have preferred a return of the bat infestations. Only Senator Joe Lieberman (D-CT) showed good-natured patience about the temporary displacement. He complained playfully to me that we'd taken away his area to do push-ups between roll call votes.

The beautiful room, so large and splendid, soon became a bustling center of nervous activity:

Diary, The U.S. Senate Marble Room, January 14, 1999

Chairman Hyde called together the Managers to go over the final schedule for today. After Henry introduces the Managers, Jim Sensenbrenner will present a brief overview,

and Ed Bryant will explain the Paula Jones connection. Asa Hutchinson will outline Clinton's obstruction of justice, and I will finish by showing Clinton's grand jury and deposition perjuries.

Henry asked Ed Bryant to lead our group in a prayer before we began. Everyone bowed their heads as Ed committed our efforts to the Lord.

Bryant, Hutchinson, and I all ordered charts for our respective presentations. Their charts awaited them when we arrived in the Marble Room. While Bryant and Hutchinson went over their visual aids, committee staff made frantic calls to the printer because he forgot to send my charts with the others. The printer rushed them by air to D.C., where a police escort waited at Reagan National Airport to speed them to the Capitol.

With neither charts nor final speech yet delivered, I had little to do but sit and observe the buzzing activity backstage in our last few minutes before we started. The gruff Sensenbrenner, a 20-year House veteran who served as a Manager in the 1989 impeachment trial of Judge Walter Nixon, showed no nervousness. He seemed almost bored. Bryant looked serious and focused as he spread his large charts across the floor and studied them on his hands and knees. Hutchinson paced while reviewing his speech notes.

At 12:45 p.m., we filed out of the Marble Room and walked a few dozen feet to the President's Room, which Chief Justice Rehnquist now used as his impeachment court chambers.

Henry studied us with a quizzical expression and then he shook his head: "No, no, no! This won't do! Get in seniority order!" We looked like an unrehearsed chorus line trying to remember a complicated dance step as we figured out who needed to stand where. Finally, with Henry's sense of protocol satisfied, Senate Sergeant at Arms Jim Ziglar opened

Rehnquist's door and announced us. We entered single file.

Until this moment, I had never been inside the President's Room, which tourist brochures name as the most ornate space in the Capitol. Living up to its reputation, it resembled a miniature Versailles Palace. The room shone in golden splendor with floor-to-ceiling mirrors, a tiled marble floor, and exquisite fresco paintings by the great Italian artist Constantino Brumidi (1805-1880), whose exquisite works grace the Capitol's rotunda and corridors. Presidents dating back to James Buchanan have used this room. Abraham Lincoln enjoyed holding court there, telling jokes and stories to senators and congressmen while he signed bills and lobbied for his legislative priorities. It was in here that Lincoln received word from General Ulysses Grant that Confederate General Robert E. Lee wished to discuss Civil War surrender terms. Lyndon Johnson signed the 1965 Voting Rights Act here, and later presidents have used it on Inauguration Day to sign their first official acts.

Entering a room vibrating with such history and beauty made the sight of the lone man standing inside it look misplaced. He wore baggy, unpressed slacks and a rumpled sport coat. Gangly and awkward in appearance, his head cocked sideways as if he suffered from a neck injury, his teeth were long and mildly tobacco-stained, but his smile was wide and friendly as he shook hands with each of us. If Chief Justice Rehnquist looked out of place in these lavish surroundings, it didn't appear to bother him.

When House Manager Chris Cannon met the chief, Chris said, "Please don't be too hard on us. We're all out of practice and have been for a long time."

Rehnquist replied with a laugh, "So am I, for almost thirty years!"

After Rehnquist shook our hands, we filed out and headed next door to the Senate's Marble Room, now designated as the House Managers' bivouac during the impeachment "trial." Henry chased us down the hallway and into there. "Come back, everyone!" he called. "The chief justice wants to address us! You guys left too soon!" We had forgotten that the chief wanted to impart traditional words of wisdom, so we reversed direction and headed back to his chambers. Henry stopped us again before we reached the door: "No!" he hissed. "In seniority order and single file!" Once again, the bumbling chorus lined up before we reentered.

Rehnquist still stood in front of the desk and with the same cocked head and friendly smile. We shuffled in again and formed a semicircle around him. Henry bowed to him slightly but regally as if to signify our readiness to receive the chief's words before embarking upon this grave constitutional journey for only the second time in history. Rehnquist never stopped grinning as he made individual eye contact with each of us before he addressed the group:

"Well," he said, "have a good trial."

Silence. Fifteen seconds. Thirty seconds, maybe longer. Awkward stillness filled the room. Rehnquist remained mum (but still grinning). The Managers looked at each other.

Congressman Lindsey Graham (R-SC), standing next to me, whispered, "Hey, Jim, do y'all think that all?"

"I think that's all, y'all."

Henry bowed again, and we filed out of the room.

Because I was the last man to reach the door, I found myself facing President Clinton's attorneys as they now entered to receive the chief's precedent-keeping pep talk. I held the door for them. The last one in line, Lanny Breuer, shook my hand and asked, "What did he tell you guys?"

"It's too deep to explain, Lanny. Listen carefully and soak it in. You'll remember it for the rest of your life."[1]

The Managers returned to the Marble Room nervously awaiting our cue to begin. Across the room, I heard a sudden eruption of panic among some staffers. "There's no ELMO!" one of them shouted. "ELMO" was the overhead projection system we had been told would be available, and upon which we had based our visual aids.

Senate Sergeant Jim Ziglar, who briefed us yesterday on how ELMO worked, asked to speak with us: "[Democrat] Senator Robert Byrd this morning, out of the blue, objected to the use of ELMO on the Senate floor to project any 'still' images like your charts," he told us. "Senator Lott is respecting Byrd's wishes."

"Jim, let me get this straight," I said. "Byrd says it's okay if we show video clips on the ELMO television monitors, but not still images on the same monitors. How does he justify this difference? It makes no sense."

"Go figure, Congressman," Ziglar replied apologetically. "I don't know. I'm really sorry."

We all were angry at this last-minute change and imposed without any logical reason. By now I expected the Senate to pull such shenanigans, so I had prepared for multiple eventualities. If, at the last minute, the Senate blocked the video clips I planned to use, I was ready with ELMO charts. If they yanked ELMO, I was ready with charts on an easel. If they took those, I had planned to use transcribed Clinton testimony by having a staffer sit in a mock witness chair and read Clinton's answers to my questions.

---

1   I wrote in greater detail about my later relationship with Chief Justice Rehnquist in my book, *Shaking Hands with History* (2020).

Hutchinson, Bryant, and I chased down Henry Hyde to ask that he demand Trent Lott rescind his latest surrender to the Democrats. "In 1974, do you think the Democrat majority would have let the Republican minority dictate this in a Richard Nixon impeachment trial?" I asked our chairman.

Looking exhausted, Henry begged off lobbying Lott on our behalf. In fact, he gathered all the Managers around and shared an additional detail that tweaked us even more:

> **With just two minutes before our scheduled start time, Henry told us, "Senator Byrd came up to me a few minutes ago and said he wanted my promise that there would be no salacious language uttered on the Senate floor. I gave Byrd my word. I hope this promise doesn't affect any of your presentations."**
>
> **"Well, Henry," I chimed in, "I'm sure glad I didn't give Byrd my word. I'm planning on dumping all kinds of salacious shit on the Senate floor for two straight hours."**
>
> **Everyone laughed at my wisecrack—everyone except Henry. I had to reassure him I was just kidding.**

A deputy sergeant at arms poked his head inside the Marble Room: "Excuse me, gentlemen," he said somberly. "It's time." With a mutual nod to each other, we walked onto the Senate floor and stood by our assigned seats at the House Managers' table. The hands on the large clock over the Senate entrance read 1:03 p.m. when Chief Justice Rehnquist appeared in the doorway behind Ziglar.

> **The senators rose at their desks as the Chief Justice, clad in a black robe with gold bands embroidered on the sleeves (an affectation he adopted after seeing a similar robe in a Gilbert and Sullivan play) entered the chamber and took his seat at the dais. He picked up the traditional ivory gavel, rapped it, and called to order the U.S. Senate as a court of impeachment against a sitting president for the first time in 130 years.**

"It's show time, folks," one Manager at our table whispered.

By now, I was too preoccupied with getting my speech text and charts to focus on the awe of the moment. I labored on my draft for days, and my reading copy still wasn't in my hands.

After Senator Lott made some preliminary motions, the Chief Justice recognized "Mr. Manager Hyde." Henry introduced the Managers by teams and shared briefly with the senators what each team would present. As Jim Sensenbrenner kicked off his overview of the House's case, Rehnquist leaned back in his chair. Because the dais is so high, Rehnquist could see only the back of the speakers' heads, so he rarely looked at the speakers directly. Instead, he watched them on a video monitor positioned on the floor near his feet.

By the time Asa Hutchinson began his presentation, I still didn't have my speech or my charts in hand. I called my office repeatedly seeking my revised copy. "We're still having computer and printing problems, but don't worry!" they assured me. "You'll get it in time."

Sinking into a high-backed chair in the Marble Room (now strangely deserted and quiet), I reflected on how some things were out of my hands. No charts, no speech, and a year's worth of angry Hollywood-based constituents telling me to kiss my political career goodbye. Shortly before the Judiciary Committee vote to impeach Clinton, we ran a poll in my district: the results confirmed that if I voted to impeach Clinton, 75 percent of the voters said they would never vote for me again. That figure contained a significant chunk of Republican voters.

Now that I was prosecuting Clinton, that number was probably up to 85 percent.

I thought about all of this as I now sat alone. What a dichotomy: Clinton and I both devoted our lives trying to get to Washington.

After committing perjury and obstructing justice, favorable opinion polls and a complicit Senate guaranteed the president would keep his job. Because I helped call Clinton to account for violating the law and his oath of office, I expected to lose mine. Suddenly feeling intense weariness from days of sleep deprivation, I closed my eyes. Asa's piped-in voice soon faded as my mind drifted—until an assistant jolted me back to reality.

As Asa neared completion of his argument, my staffer Myron Jacobson arrived. He didn't have my speech with him (the computer problem still was not resolved), but Myron was in a near panic over something else: "Your charts just arrived from the airport," he told me. "Half of them are missing!" We went through the chart stack quickly and made an inventory of what was absent so I could work around them.

Asa finished his address at 5:00 p.m., and I still had no reading copy of my speech—or half of my charts. Fortunately, Chief Justice Rehnquist declared a brief recess, giving me time to rush back to the Marble Room and call my office: "I'm up next. I need my speech right now."

"It left here 15 minutes ago," a staffer replied. "Jeff Solsby is driving it over. It should be there by now." There still was no sign of my press secretary.

Here I was: missing charts, no speech, and minutes to go. I'm doing one of the two major presentations against the president of the United States. The Chief Justice of the United States is presiding. The entire United States Senate is my jury. The world is watching on live TV. This is the most important speech of my life, politically, constitutionally and personally. Strangely, despite all this, I felt very little anxiety.

Why? I'm not sure, but maybe my cumulative level of irritation and disgust with the Senate overrode any normal sense of panic.

When I surveyed the room of senators at that moment, I no longer saw statesmen. I saw lots of timid politicians putting in the fix to protect Clinton and their own hides. On this occasion, they didn't make me nervous. They made me scornful.

Our Republican senators wanted to dump the case for fear of electoral reprisals, while the Democrats wanted to dump it to protect their Party leader. They all joined in bipartisan league to destroy our case. Knowing that the people occupying the seats in front of me maneuvered out of sheer political expediency, my disdain for their behavior probably deadened what should have been a serious case of pre-speech stage fright.

As for the missing speech, reporter Geraldine Baum shared the rest of the story in the *Los Angeles Times* the next morning:

Rules are rules, and they nearly left Rep. James E. Rogan speechless. Rogan, a House prosecutor, spent the day making last-minute revisions on the text of his remarks on a laptop computer that his staff says is older than dirt. But he had technical problems, forcing him to head into the historic moment empty-handed while his staff struggled to make a printout.

With 20 minutes [to go], Jeff Solsby, Rogan's press secretary, hitched a ride to the Capitol, bolted up the Senate steps, and got to the door of the chamber minutes before Rogan was to take the floor for the most defining moment of his congressional career.

"You need to fill out this card," the deputy sergeant at arms told Solsby sternly, asking him to complete a form before allowing him to pass the documents to someone on the Senate floor.

"But I'm Mr. Rogan's press secretary and this is his speech and I have to give it to him," Solsby pleaded.

"You need to fill out this card," the sergeant at arms said sternly.

[A] sympathetic comrade on the Senate floor relayed the 100-page speech to his boss literally seconds before Rogan went to the well.

Rogan has been taking every precaution to ensure that things went right for his "fifteen minutes," including resurrecting what he calls The Brown Beast. Fortunately, for Rogan, there are no rules governing tattered accessories in the chamber.

Go ahead and laugh at The Brown Beast's mojo if you want, but the speech made it into my hands at the last possible moment.

As the Chief Justice appeared in the doorway to signal the resumption of proceedings, senators took their places in the chamber. Just then, Myron rushed onto the floor carrying a three-ring notebook. "It just got here now," he said breathlessly.

There was no time to review the speech for accuracy. I placed the notebook on the lectern, hoping all the pages were in proper order.

I took a seat at the front of our table and started scanning the gallery for one face in particular. Earlier in the day, I called Speaker Hastert's office and told his staff I needed a ticket for my wife Christine to watch my speech. "Sorry," his aide told me. "Tickets are limited. We've given those away, so I'm afraid you're out of luck."

This was the last straw. "No, I'm afraid *you're* out of luck," I barked into the receiver. "If my wife doesn't get a ticket to watch my opening statement, then you can tell the speaker to get his ass over to the Senate and deliver the goddamn speech himself." With that, I slammed down the phone.

Now, as I looked into the galleries and didn't see Christine up there, I grew furious and started cursing Denny Hastert under my breath.

"Hey," one of the Managers whispered to me as Rehnquist called the Senate to order, "someone's trying to get your attention." He pointed to the gallery above the Democrat side, where I saw Christine standing in a row of spectators waving and smiling. She gave me a thumb's up sign, blew me a kiss, and then she took her seat.

I exhaled.

With only seconds left, Henry Hyde patted my arm. Speaking in a fatherly tone, he told me that what I was about to do was for history. "You'll remember this speech for the rest of your life," he said. "I'm very proud of you. Someday your children will see it, and your grandchildren, and your great-grandchildren."

As I thanked him for the last-minute encouragement, he added with a wink: "So don't fuck it up!"[2]

I was still chuckling over Henry's unexpected language when Chief Justice Rehnquist called on me:

> **The Chief Justice announced, "Mr. Manager Rogan is recognized." I walked to the lectern positioned in the center of the well and looked around the chamber. The first person I saw looking back at me was Senator Edward Kennedy (D-MA). I had a momentary flashback of cutting school as a boy in 1971 to wait outside the old KGO TV studio in San Francisco to shake Senator Kennedy's hand and get his autograph. Now, almost three decades later, here we were.**

---

2   In the 2004 first edition of my first book, *Rough Edges*, I recounted this story and quoted Chairman Hyde as saying, "Don't screw it up." Since Henry was still alive and serving in Congress at the time of that book's publication, I sanitized the quotation to avoid causing him any political embarrassment. With Henry's death in 2007, I now correct the record.

I took a breath and began: "Mr. Chief Justice, distinguished counsel for the president, members of the United States Senate...."

Notwithstanding the intimidating nature of the surroundings, within moments I forgot all the distractions. The only real anxiety I felt came each time I turned the page of my speech text. Since I had no time to review the draft handed to me, I had to hope that whatever was on the next page was what was supposed to be there.

Despite all the hitches, the chart and videotaped portion of my two-hour presentation came off without incident. The only minor hiccup came when Myron Jacobson (my staff assistant handling the charts during my speech) displayed Chart #13. This chart defined "Sexual Relations" as given to Clinton during his Paula Jones deposition. The original chart I prepared for the Senate was supposed to show a sanitized version of the definition eliminating graphic language. When the chart I ordered turned up missing, the Judiciary Committee rushed to print a replacement chart. However, the chart they made bore the actual definition.

When Myron displayed to the Senate the new Chart #13 on live television, the first thing I saw were billboard-sized words like "anus," "groin," and "breasts." Remembering Henry's pledge to Senator Byrd's sensitivities, I signaled for Myron to remove the chart. Instead, I read into the record a cleaned-up definition.

By the way, that evening Myron asked if I would autograph Chart #13 and let him keep it as a memento. If the Smithsonian ever wants it for their archives, they'll have to talk Myron out of it.

In the final moments of my presentation, after laying out the evidence, I addressed the television camera directly rather than the senators to make my pitch to America for the Senate to give us witnesses:

The president has denied all the allegations set forth in these impeachment articles. Who is telling the truth? There is only one way to find out.

On behalf of the House of Representatives, we urge this body to bring forth the witnesses and place them all under oath. If the witnesses can make the case against the president—witnesses who, incidentally, are his employees, his top aides, his former interns and his close friends—if all of these people in the president's universe are lying, then the president has been done a grave disservice. He deserves not just acquittal, but he also deserves the profoundest of apologies.

But if they are not lying, if the evidence is true, if the chief executive of our nation used his power and his influence to corruptly destroy a lone woman's right to bring forth her case in a court of law, then there must be constitutional accountability. And by that I mean the kind of accountability the Framers of our Constitution intended for such conduct, and not the type of accountability that satisfies the temporary mood of the moment. Our Founders bequeathed to us a nation of laws, not of polls, not of focus groups, and not of talk-show habitués. America is strong enough to absorb the truth about their leaders when those leaders act in a manner destructive to their oath of office. God help our country's future if we ever decide otherwise.

I finished my speech at 6:59 p.m.—one minute before my two-hour time limit expired.

After the Senate recessed for the day, one of our enthusiastic committee staff members exclaimed, "You guys are putting on a great trial! A great trial!"

While thanking him, I thought to myself, "Don't you get it? This isn't a trial. There are no witnesses. The jury is fixed. The acquittal already is in." Despite weeks of arguing this procedure was a sham, the nuance now was lost even on our staffers. He saw the same thing the country saw, and what the Senate knew in advance everyone would see once we showed up and participated:

He saw a trial.

30

The Voodoo Eye

We started our portion of the president's so-called "trial" on Thursday; the Senate ordered us to conclude our case presentation by Saturday. Two days: what a joke. Rookie DA's prosecuting public drunkenness misdemeanors get more time to make their case.

On the second "trial" day (January 15), I stayed away from the Senate chamber while other colleagues made their presentations, working instead on a closing argument draft. I didn't return to the Senate until the third day's session.

Notes Taken on Senate Floor During Impeachment Proceedings Against President Clinton, Saturday, January 16, 1999

It was surprising to find the Capitol so quiet this weekend morning, with only a handful of tourists roaming about a building where legislators now determined a president's fate. Just a few senators were present when I entered their chamber. Senator Bob Kerry (D-NE) said I did an excellent job in my opening statement, adding with a laugh, "I'm very glad I'm not in trouble and that you aren't prosecuting me." Other senators came over to offer bipartisan congratulations for my first day's effort: Joe Biden (D-DE), Bob Smith (R-NH), Connie Mack (R-FL), and Bill Frist (R-TN).

One of our committee staffers said I didn't appear nervous during my opening presentation. I replied that I was surprised how little nervousness I felt at the time. "Henry Hyde told me he wasn't nervous either," the staffer said. "And he told me why. Mr. Hyde pointed to the senators and said, 'These guys represent states. They represent mountains and streams. I represent people. Why should they intimidate me?'"

In this final day of making the House's case against Clinton, our presenters will focus on whether the president's crimes warrant removal from office. Right now, I'm sitting with Lindsey Graham, who will speak next. He keeps asking me if he should "lighten up" his presentation "to keep these fellows awake."

• • •

Lindsey is now making his presentation. He got a chuckle in the chamber (the first since we started; probably the last) when he referenced a U.S. Supreme Court case. He said he didn't know how he might have voted on it had he been a justice on the Court, and then quipped that there was no danger of that ever happening. Even Rehnquist laughed at that comment.

A couple of times during Lindsey's presentation he said things that raised unhappy eyebrows from his Manager colleagues. The first was when he reminded the senators that he voted against the impeachment article in the House accusing Clinton of perjury. Lindsey said people reasonably might lie to protect themselves from embarrassment. He excused Clinton's perjury by saying maybe he was "surprised" at the deposition when asked about Lewinsky.

This claim is incorrect. Clinton was not "surprised" by the question. He knew that Lewinsky was on the Paula Jones witness list more than a month before he testified. That's why Clinton and Lewinsky engaged in a lengthy scheme to hide gifts and keep their relationship secret.

Lindsey suggested (again) it was a "very high and terrible burden we have to overcome" for the Senate to convict Clinton. When Lindsey made that comment, Manager Steve Chabot leaned over and whispered to me, "I wish he'd quit saying that. The president's lawyers will shove that down our throats."

Some observations of the senators on the floor: most of them appear to be listening. Tom Daschle (D-SD) wears a perpetual scowl. Harry Reid (D-NV) is reading papers. Blanche Lincoln (D-AR) scans the room from side to side continually and appears not to pay attention. Rick Santorum (R-PA), Rod Grams (R-MN), Pat Leahy (D-VT), and Ben Nighthorse Campbell (R-CO) all look bored.

For some creepy reason, Democrat leader Tom Daschle started (as we used to say when I prosecuted gang cases) "mad doggin'" me. This led to moments of childish behavior admittedly more appropriate for the school playground than the United States Senate chamber:

During the proceedings today, I've noticed Daschle staring at me many times and always with a very sour look. When I've looked over and caught him staring, he doesn't look away— he just keeps staring. I smile and then look away to be polite.

Later that afternoon:

Almost every time I've looked over at Tom Daschle, he's still staring at me. This is too eerie. Not wanting to be rude, I've looked away rather than stare back. But in the last few minutes, I've glanced over three times to see if he is still staring and I've caught him doing it each time.

Okay, tough guy, I know the rules of this game—hey, I wasn't the oldest of three brothers for nothing. When we were kids, I played "Stare Down" with my siblings Pat and Johnny until a white film clouded over my unblinking corneas. If Daschle really wanted to rumble in this sandbox, he was messing with the stink-eye world champion:

That's it. Daschle did it to me again. The hell with him. This time, I shot back a cold stare and maintained it until *he* looked away. He must think this silliness intimidates me. If I didn't flinch from gang murderers when I prosecuted them, I certainly won't be rattled by some pampered senator.

First, I upended Senate dignity by bringing over The Brown Beast. Now Daschle forced me to unveil The Voodoo Eye. I doubt if it spooked the minority leader much, but it was the best I could come up with (short of mooning him).

As Manager Charles Canady wrapped up his speech, I suggested to Asa Hutchinson and Ed Bryant that we have lunch with Bill McCollum (our fourth presentation group member) to strategize over our witnesses list. Asa whispered, "Oh, is Bill in our group for that? I think just the three of us should talk about it."

Bryant and Hutchinson then complained to me about Bill's earlier presentation where they said he mentioned repeatedly things like "underwear," "kissing her breasts," and "touching her genitalia." They said the references were gratuitous and noted that the rest of us avoided such things in our presentations.[1]

---

1   I was not on the Senate floor that day and did not hear McCollum's speech. While writing this part of my book, I went back and read the transcript of McCollum's address to the Senate. In his 90-minute speech he mentioned "genitalia" and "breasts" in a few brief sentences buried in the middle of his remarks. He mentioned "underwear" once. McCollum did not base any significant portion of his speech on these indelicate words, nor were they the focus of his overall presentation.

At their request, we met without Bill to discuss witness responsibilities. Ed wanted to take charge of Monica Lewinsky; Asa wants Betty Currie and Vernon Jordan. I volunteered to take the lesser witnesses since I'm already responsible for prepping a closing argument and for Clinton's cross-examination.

The Managers completed their presentations on behalf of the House of Representatives that afternoon. After Rehnquist adjourned the Senate for the day, we returned to the House side of the Capitol for a meeting:

Diary, House Managers Meeting, January 16, 1999

Henry Hyde thanked each of us for making excellent presentations in the Senate. He said he now wanted to revive our "Truth Squad" that we had used during the House debate as a "Rapid Response Team" to any untrue points Clinton's lawyers make.

Henry added that there would now be a period for senators to ask us random questions, so we all "needed to get ready and prepare for anything." Also, he revealed that the Senate has decided not to give us any rebuttal time following the White House's case. "They are telling me this was a mistake they made when they set their schedule," he noted ruefully. "But they made it and they won't correct it now."

As to our witness list we are still discussing, Henry suggested that we "stick to just three or four witnesses and get ready to be outmaneuvered. Any witnesses we get are all friends of Clinton's, and they will all act as if they have been coached by Lawrence Olivier." He warned again that "the fewer witnesses you guys add to your list, the better. It gives us a better chance of getting any witnesses."

Steve Buyer said that Orrin Hatch came over and told him today that we were all doing a great job. "I always believed in you guys!" Steve quoted Hatch as saying enthusiastically. Buyer's report provoked laughter around the table. Just days ago, Hatch suggested the Senate either dismiss our case or, as an alternative, avoid all witnesses.

Although Henry Hyde surrendered ground on the Senate's "no witnesses" stance, he drew the line in one respect. Some Republican and Democrat senators now suggested they might invite Clinton into the Senate chamber, allow him to testify or make a speech, and then deny us the right to cross-examine him.

"If the United States Senate lets Clinton come down but limits his appearance to making a speech with no cross-examination," Henry warned, "then we'll boycott the damned procedure. Otherwise, we'd just be props sitting in there."

"What's the difference?" I whispered to Chris Cannon. "We're props sitting in there now." Chris nodded in agreement.

With the Senate adjourned for the weekend, I did something I hadn't done in a few months. I threw out the unopened morning newspaper, turned off the TV and the phone ringer, and Christine, the girls, and I took a trip to the Washington National Zoo. But even there my presence proved conspicuous. I probably had more people staring at me than at the albino gorilla. It was bad enough that my district's voters were furious with me. Now I saw that even the local zoo had a vigorous pro-Clinton constituency.

When I returned home that evening, I found a document on my fax machine with snippets of supportive calls, emails, prayers, and letters coming in from across the country. It was a tonic to read these heartwarming messages. When I called Jeff Solsby later to see how much hate mail came in during the same period, his reply didn't surprise me: "I can't count that high." He did share some good news, however:

I was down to an average of only 12 death threats a day.

• • •

The brief family time I took that weekend made me miss another eyebrow-raiser from one of our Managers:

Diary, Sunday, January 17, 1999

On one of the Sunday news shows, Asa Hutchinson said he based his obstruction of justice case against Clinton only on "circumstantial evidence," and he couldn't say with certainty that we'd get a conviction if he presented the same evidence to a regular jury in a courtroom. Several phone messages from other Managers awaited me regarding Asa's comment. The consensus was that this had been an unwise position to take and that the White House would use it against us.

Most people think circumstantial evidence is an inferior form of evidence. This is a false perception. Under the law, circumstantial evidence is just as valid as direct evidence. In fact, we make hundreds of judgments each day solely on circumstantial evidence. For instance, as motorists, we drive through busy intersections on green lights. Why? Because that green light is circumstantial evidence that the driver's light in the opposing direction is red and that he will stop, even though we can't see the opposing red light. That's why, under the law, circumstantial evidence has just as much weight as direct evidence. As to Clinton's obstruction of justice, we had plenty of direct and circumstantial evidence, and it all led to only one reasonable conclusion. We may not have had surveillance video of Clinton breaking into the cookie jar, but there were plenty of telltale crumbs covering his mouth.

• • •

With our presentation concluded, President Clinton's counsel presented their case when the Senate proceedings resumed:

Notes Taken on Senate Floor During Impeachment Proceedings Against President Clinton, Tuesday, January 19, 1999

I sat with Henry Hyde at the Managers' table just before the start of the session. At their table, Clinton counsel David Kendall smiled broadly as he chatted with Democrat senators. Kendall's grin irked Henry, who pointed it out as he said to me, "Don't be fooled by that smile. I bet those guys are plenty nervous right now."

I've seen lots of false bravado in courtrooms over the years. Kendall's grin didn't look contrived. The Senate adopted rules guaranteeing a favorable White House result, all while doing backflips to shut us down. Why shouldn't he smile?

At 1:00 p.m., Chief Justice Rehnquist began today's session. His clothes are still rumpled; wisps of disheveled hair cover his balding head, and his necktie sticks out under the back of his shirt collar. In a Senate filled with blow-dried and coiffed peacocks, Rehnquist's total disregard for his slovenly appearance is refreshingly unpretentious and endearing.

The Chief introduced White House Counsel Charles Ruff, who spoke while seated in his wheelchair. I had difficulty hearing much of his speech, although I sat a short distance from him. When Ruff began by saying that he could not match the "eloquence" of the House Managers, Henry Hyde leaned over and whispered to me, "Ah, now the velvet ice pick is out!"

In a very tough speech that lasted more than two hours, Ruff referred to our case as "a witch's brew" and "prosecutorial fudge-making." He urged the Senate to reject our call for witnesses and claimed that there was no need for the Senate to determine anyone's credibility. Further, he challenged us by saying that since there was no basis for the House to impeach Clinton, there was no basis for the Senate to convict and remove him. Finally, Ruff claimed that even if the Senate found the allegations against Clinton were true, none of them warranted his removal from office.

While Ruff plowed through these now-familiar arguments,

I leaned over and asked Henry Hyde if he ever woke up at night and regretted that we impeached Clinton. He shook his head from side-to-side.

"Neither have I," I replied, "but I bet there have been plenty of nights when Clinton awoke and regretted it."

"Unless he's brain dead," Henry muttered.

Although I thought Ruff's presentation was both professional and compelling (at least from Clinton's perspective), the Senate's attention span waned noticeably, probably from the boredom of having to listen for a few days to the merits of a case they had decided long ago:

We are now 45 minutes into Ruff's speech, and many senators on both sides of the aisle look droopy-eyed. Don Nickles (R-OK) is almost asleep in his seat. Harry Reid (D-NV) keeps dozing off; as his chin hits his chest, he whips his head back reflexively. Steve Buyer and I chuckle each time he does it. Rod Grams (R-MN) struggles to keep awake. Evan Bayh (D-IN) can't stop yawning.

Ruff didn't wrap up his rebuttal until 3:30 p.m. When he announced that he was concluding his presentation, I heard Senator Chuck Schumer (D-NY), a diehard Clinton supporter, whisper to Senator Mary Landrieu (D-LA), "Thank God."

After Ruff finished, Lott moved to adjourn for the day so members of Congress could attend a bizarre opera later that evening. Despite suggestions from members of both parties that he reschedule, President Clinton insisted on delivering his annual State of the Union message to a joint session of Congress that night while in the middle of his impeachment.

Many congressmen questioned the propriety of Clinton's planned speech tonight. I have no doubt that the Democrats will turn it into a pep rally for him. Some of our Republican members have declared they will boycott the speech despite Speaker Hastert asking his troops to attend and be respectful.

I didn't want to attend, but I felt it more important to show respect for the office of the presidency than to indulge my natural preference to keep away. However, once Clinton got rolling, my negative personal reaction to him made it hard to separate the man from the office:

Notes from President Clinton's State of the Union Message, The U.S. Capitol, January 19, 1999

When Clinton isn't taking credit for our agenda, he is proposing massive spending plans, and pledging to pass out tax dollars to almost every sector of society. After he rattled off his laundry list of giveaways, I asked rhetorically if he left out anyone.

    "Yeah," answered Frank Wolf (R-VA) angrily, "the military."

"And midgets," snickered Dana Rohrabacher (R-CA).

Clinton keeps taking credit for many of the GOP's policy ideas that he and the Democrats opposed in the last election. His intellectual dishonesty is breathtaking. Many Republican congressmen seated in the chamber are laughing and mocking his hypocrisy. Personally, I'm disgusted listening to this. He has no shame.

After sitting through this weird evening spectacle, I almost looked forward to returning to the cartoon courtroom down the hall. At least in the Senate we didn't have to sit politely and pretend we were glad to be there.

• • •

I invoke my author's prerogative to end this chapter with a collateral story.

At the end of the Senate "trial," Henry Hyde invited a *Time* magazine photographer inside our House Managers conference room to photograph one of our strategy sessions. However, she didn't get the first behind-the-scenes shots of us at work. Her competitor at *Newsweek*, Pulitzer Prize-winning photographer David Kennerly, beat her to the punch. I lobbied hard to get Kennerly this scoop, and it had nothing to do with loyalty to his publication.

A month earlier, on the last day of the House Judiciary Committee's debate and vote on impeachment, our committee room was more jammed than I had ever seen it. Press photographers almost were on top of us (and each other). A middle-aged bearded photographer wearing a chest full of cameras and press badges standing around mentioned to me during a break that he also lived in Southern California. "Hey, how about letting me come back when this is done and get some exclusive pictures of you guys working on the impeachment trial?" he asked me after breaking the ice with generic conversation.

"Sorry," I replied, "but we haven't let any photographers in the back room with us." As I nixed his request perfunctorily, I noticed the name emblazoned on his press badges: David Hume Kennerly. When I saw it, I started a conversation with him intentionally designed to make him wonder if I was a kook:

"I have a congressional office in California," I told him. "It's in Pasadena."

"Oh. That's a nice place," he replied.

"I have lots of pictures on my wall. You should come and see them sometime."

"Oh, uh, Okay. Sure." Kennerly looked as if he wanted to get away, but I became more intense in my chatter, forcing him to talk with me further.

"And some of them are autographed," I told him. "In fact, some are inscribed to me."

"Yeah, Okay, that's nice. Well, I'd better get back to—"

"Some are even from presidents, like Lyndon Johnson, Richard Nixon, Ronald Reagan, and Gerald Ford."

"Uh, okay, well—"

"I'm especially fond of the Gerald Ford picture. It says, *To Jim Rogan, with best wishes, Gerald R. Ford*. He signed it when he first became president."

By now, Kennerly looked as if he heard *The Twilight Zone* theme riffing in the background. After stringing him along a bit more, I completed the story for him:

In fact, this picture of President Ford was his first official portrait taken after he became president in 1974. I was only 16 years old when I got it. I really wanted him to sign it, but I knew if I mailed it to the new president, some staffer would just run it through an autopen machine and send it back.

Then I read in the newspaper that Ford had just appointed a young guy as his official White House photographer and granted him unlimited and unprecedented Oval Office access. So, I wrote the photographer, sent him the picture, and I asked him to do me a favor—bring it into the Oval Office and have Ford sign it for me.

That photographer followed through and sent it back autographed. I never forgot that Ford's photographer, David Hume Kennerly, did this for me. So here we are, 25 years later. And before this is over, Mr. Kennerly, I'm going to repay that debt and get you inside to photograph the Managers at work.

Making that promise to Kennerly was easy. Delivering on it proved to be a heavy lift. Judiciary Committee Republicans had a standing rule during impeachment: any one of us could veto another's request to allow outsiders into our meetings. Earlier, a few Managers requested permission for their district newspapers to take pictures, but Steve Buyer always objected. He felt our discussions should remain secret, and if we did it for one we'd have to do it for all. Steve even vetoed a request from Henry Hyde to allow the chairman's own hometown photographer into one of our meetings. Once I made the pledge to Kennerly, I knew I'd have to get Steve's approval. Given his history of blocking all requests, including Henry's, this would be a tough sell.

At our next Managers' meeting, I made a point to sit alongside Steve. Before the session began, I mentioned casually that President Ford's former photographer now worked for *Newsweek* and asked if he could come back and shoot some pictures of the House Managers. As expected, Steve offered a polite rejection.

Suddenly, I spun in my chair, grabbed him by the shoulders, leaned in close to his face, and shouted as if possessed, "Goddamn it, Steve, I owe this guy a favor! I've owed it to him for 25 years! You've *got* to do this for me, Steve! You *can't* say no! Please, Steve!

Please! I'm begging you! Steve—*I need this favor!*"

The element of surprise worked. A stunned Steve gave me the same look Kennerly had given me earlier in the committee room (that I must be off kilter).

"Okay, Jim, if it's that important to you."

Twenty-five years after Dave Kennerly had President Ford sign that picture for me, the opportunity came to repay a great guy for a big favor. When I look at that old Ford photo today, I remember the look in Steve Buyer's eyes when I launched my surprise offensive—a look that told me he thought someone in a white coat should come and drop a net on his overstressed colleague from California.

31

Life Support

"The Republican members of the House Judiciary Committee . . . [have]
been labeled zealots by many Democrats and accused of carrying out a
vendetta against a duly elected president. Political analysts have blamed
them for the Party's poor performance in last November's midterm
elections. But by yesterday afternoon, the 13 GOP prosecutors from the
House had achieved a measure of vindication, pushing their perjury
and obstruction-of-justice charges against President Clinton farther
than all but a few politicians imagined was possible a few months ago.
Standing one after another in the well of the Senate for three days, the
Managers apparently made a strong enough case to persuade senators
not to summarily dismiss the charges."
—JULIET EILPERIN, *WASHINGTON POST*, JANUARY 17, 1999

Despite Ms. Eilperin's perception, the House Managers did not feel vindicated by the senators. We felt mugged by them.

Since the Senate still refused to give us time to rebut Clinton's case when his lawyers finished their presentations, we tried to strategize a way around their rule:

**Diary, House Managers Meeting,
Wednesday, January 20, 1999**

Bill McCollum suggested that if the Senate won't let us rebut Clinton's case, we should "work in" our rebuttal when we make our argument for live witnesses. Everyone agreed, and Henry Hyde instructed us to squeeze it in our later presentation. He also said we should weave in rebuttal during the upcoming session where we answer questions from senators.

As for our earlier idea to subpoena President Clinton as a witness before the Senate, that notion grew more watered down as each day passed:

Henry Hyde read his letter to the Senate leaders suggesting they "invite" Clinton to address the proceedings, and if Clinton accepted, "We would welcome the opportunity to participate" in questioning him. George Gekas felt we shouldn't even send a letter asking permission to participate. Instead, he suggested we just put out a press statement that we would like to be included if Clinton showed up.

This anemic letter didn't demand or request that the senators subpoena Clinton. It didn't even seek his sworn testimony. Henry's letter only said that if the Senate let Clinton show up and bloviate unchallenged, it would sure be nice if we could be a part of the hoedown.

As far as I was concerned, my colleagues could prettify this "invitation" all they wanted. If Clinton showed up, I resolved privately not to sit and listen to him prattle endlessly and then beg leave of the senators to "participate" in a polite exchange. I'd do the job Henry Hyde assigned to me: cross-examine Bill Clinton, even if I had to get up from my seat, interrupt the proceedings, and dare him directly on live worldwide television to answer my questions.

• • •

The next day, the White House lawyers continued their presentation and, as usual, they alternated between defending Clinton and attacking us.

Notes Taken on Senate Floor During Impeachment Proceedings Against President Clinton, Wednesday, January 20, 1999

Building upon Ruff's earlier assault that the House's impeachment of Clinton was "partisan" and "unfair," Clinton lawyer Gregory Craig now argues that the charges leveled against Clinton weren't "specific." That argument sounded hollow, since these allegations were spelled out in a 400-page Starr Report, its thousands of pages of appendices, and a 200-page House Judiciary Committee Report.

And so it went. As others had done before him, Craig picked through our case and offered hairsplitting definitions to rebut the allegations against Clinton: "To the extent that we have relied on overly legal or technical arguments to defend the president from his attackers, we apologize to you and to the American people," he said. "But to accuse us of using legalisms to defend the president when he's being accused of perjury is only to accuse us of defending the president. We plead guilty to that charge, and the truth is that an attorney who failed to raise these defenses might well be guilty of malpractice."

Craig conceded that Clinton's answers during the Paula Jones deposition may have been evasive and incomplete, but they couldn't be perjury because Clinton didn't "reaffirm" his entire testimony before the grand jury.
    During a break, I chatted with my state's senior senator, Dianne Feinstein (D-CA). As a fourth-generation San Fran-

ciscan, I told her I wanted to say hello to my former mayor. Dianne was very gracious and asked me where in San Francisco I grew up. When I told her the Mission District [a hardscrabble blue-collar and heavily immigrant neighborhood] she grinned. "No wonder you're so tough," she said.

In contrast, my state's junior senator, Barbara Boxer (D-CA), looks like she can barely contain her disdain for me. When I say hello as we pass in the hallways, she gets a tight-jawed look and says nothing.

I took no personal umbrage at Senator Boxer's obvious irritation with me. The press had touted me as a possible GOP challenger to her reelection campaign (in my very liberal home state, the likelihood of my challenging her successfully was *very* remote). More likely, she had another reason for her coldness: she and the Clintons were in-laws. Boxer's daughter Nicole married Hillary Clinton's younger brother in a 1994 White House wedding. I suspect that in her eyes, and quite understandably, my participation as a House Manager was not just political. It was personal, too.

• • •

The next day, the president's lawyers continued their case. Clinton's private attorney, David Kendall, argued in a three-hour address that Clinton never tried to get Monica Lewinsky to lie or file a false affidavit.

Former Senator Dale Bumpers (D-AR), a longtime Clinton ally who retired from the Senate only three weeks earlier, returned to close out the president's defense. After a lengthy introduction dripping with homey sentiments, he drew out his saber: "How do we come to be here? We are here because of a five-year, relentless, unending investigation of the president. Javert's pursuit of Jean Valjean in *Les Miserables* pales by comparison."

After spending most of his time bashing Ken Starr and the

Managers, Bumpers closed in praise for his former colleagues: "You have taken a solemn oath to be fair and impartial. I know you all. I know you as friends and I know you as honorable men. And I am perfectly satisfied to put [the verdict] in your hands, under your oath." Given the stampede of senators stomping on their "impartial justice" oath every time a TV camera pointed in their direction, I wondered how Bumpers could say that with a straight face, or how the senators could sit nodding their enthusiastic approval of his sentiments without any semblance of embarrassment.

• • •

At our next Managers meeting, Henry told us that tomorrow's Senate session would begin with the senators asking questions to both sides.

Diary, House Managers Meeting,
Thursday, January 21, 1999

"The questions will bounce between the Republican and Democrat sides without any time limits," Henry told us. "So, this will be our only 'rebuttal time.' It will also be our last shot to overcome the polls and the bullshit. History is on our side. Don't fret over the movement against us in the polls or the Democrat spin."

Ed Bryant reported to us that Senator Tim Hutchinson (R-AR) called and said moderate Republican senators "are getting very shaky. They want to fold" and end the impeachment proceedings.

Henry Hyde lamented, "They know if they vote to shut us down without giving us any witnesses or any rebuttal time, it will look like Holy Hell for them when they go back home and face their GOP base."

We returned to the seemingly unending debate over what witnesses to request:

Ed Bryant argued strenuously for placing Monica Lewinsky on our witness list. "All the other witnesses are in the White House's pocket," Ed said.

Henry Hyde, still resistant to the idea, interrupted Ed's plea: "Yeah," said Henry, "and so are her lawyers."

Dave Schippers mentioned that Lewinsky's lawyer told him earlier that she would not appear without a subpoena, but he felt Ken Starr's office would force her to submit to an interview. In her agreement with Starr's office to avoid prosecution, she promised to cooperate with ongoing investigations.

• • •

At the end of this meeting, Henry asked Ed Bryant to lead us in another prayer. When Ed finished, Henry requested that we keep our heads bowed so he could add an "addendum": "Lord, please be with us. We are doing this for our nation's kids. How can we raise them with the example of William Jefferson Clinton in the White House?"

I tossed in a gratuitous "amen" to Henry's addendum, but in truth I didn't vote to impeach Clinton to avenge my kids, nor did I run for Congress to police his personal life. Whether he had one affair or a thousand of them was of no moment to me. Besides, as an ex-bartender from Hollywood's Sunset Strip, I'm hardly a stranger to female temptation. However, I did care deeply about the precedent his conduct set for future chief executives who might later commit the same felonies for reasons weightier than testosterone.

Why is this notion of precedent so important? When the Founders wrote impeachment into the Constitution as the remedy against those who commit "high crimes and misdemeanors," they never defined that phrase. The definition comes from *precedent*, i.e., the previous House of Representatives impeachments. Whenever the House decides certain conduct is (or is not) impeachable, that becomes the precedent, or the standard, for future impeachments. Had the House failed to impeach Clinton just because of the tawdry subject matter underlying his crimes, any future president committing perjury, suborning perjury, or obstructing justice with far more destructive motives could point to the *Clinton Precedent* and claim his conduct was not impeachable.

Yes, I know the polls showed that most of you hated Clinton's impeachment, and that you hated us for doing it. But take this with you: because we impeached him, today you live in a country where every future president is on notice that perjury and obstruction of justice are one-way White House eviction notices—as long as a future Congress has the spine to stand up to such behavior.

I was glad to have Henry Hyde and Ed Bryant end our meeting in prayer. By now, we needed Divine intervention. Still, I would have settled for a favorable uptick in the daily tracking polls.

• • •

The next day, we returned for the senators' questions to both sides. In typical fashion, they refused to tell us the rules in advance. It didn't take long to see how they put in "the fix" even for this portion of the sham proceeding. The first question went to us. The second question went to Clinton's lawyers to rebut what we just said, which gave them the perpetual final word as this pattern repeated itself.

Diary, U.S. Senate Floor During Impeachment Proceedings Against President Clinton, Friday, January 22, 1999

The White House scripted their planted questions with the Senate Democrats beautifully. Meanwhile, Republican senators refused to ask *any* of the questions we submitted.

Yesterday, a Senate GOP staffer told us to give them the five questions we most wanted posed to us. The staffer later told us our Republican senators "rejected" *all* of our questions, and instead they gave us five different ones and said that we should prepare to answer these instead. Then they never asked us *any* of the questions for which they told us to prepare.

Some of these guys were real bastards.

• • •

There wasn't any choreography in the way we handled the dozens of queries senators threw our way:

Generally, once a senator asks a question of our team, we look around the table at each other. Usually a silent nod or an "I'll take this one" was all that went into deciding who approached the lectern and responded to it.

Our lack of orderliness sometimes came back to bite us:

We received a tip that Trent Lott was about to ask all the ex-prosecutors on our team whether each of us would be comfortable presenting this case in a courtroom. Those of us who were ex-prosecutors agreed that each of us would speak about 45 seconds.

When the question came, Ed Bryant jumped up to answer it first. He talked for over five minutes and never really answered the question. The other ex-prosecutors started grumbling as Ed kept talking.

"Slip Ed a note and tell him to sit down," one of them said. When Ed finally ended, Asa walked up and tried to answer the question directly. Chief Justice Rehnquist stopped him

by announcing our time had expired. The rest of us felt we lost an opportunity to pound home this point.

During this daylong Senate interrogation, Henry Hyde answered almost no Senate questions, but he didn't hesitate to express irritability if he didn't think we were scoring sufficient points:

> Steve Buyer is answering a senator's question now. I think he is doing a good job, but Henry thinks he isn't. Henry just complained to me, "He's over-answering the question!" A few minutes later, as Buyer kept going, Henry dropped his head to his chest and blurted, "Oh, Jesus Christ!"

Henry wasn't the only irritable person in the chamber that day. Some of our Senate colleagues were less than, well, senatorial with us:

> A staffer told me he overheard Senator Joe Biden (D-DE) call Bob Barr an "asshole" after one of Bob's answers. Mary Landrieu (D-LA) throws her pencil onto her desk and huffs in disgust with each of our answers.
>
> Senators Barbara Boxer (D-CA) and Carl Levin (M-MI) sat directly behind me during the afternoon session. As the House Managers answered questions, she hissed and heckled us, and continued complaining about us loudly.
>
> Later, after I finished answering a question on sexual harassment laws, I returned to my seat to find Boxer barking questions to me directly (in continued violation of the Senate's rules to "keep silent upon pain of imprisonment." She demanded to know why I kept talking about the Paula Jones lawsuit when a judge dismissed that case. I replied that the ultimate settlement of the case was irrelevant to the perjury and obstruction of justice. She was undeterred, telling me, "This case is over."

"Barbara," I'd love to discuss this with you," I said, "but I'd sure hate to see the sergeant at arms arrest you for not shutting up. Why don't we continue this some other time?" I turned away from her. She left the chamber for the rest of the session.

• • •

Diary, U.S. Senate Floor During Impeachment Proceedings Against President Clinton, Thursday, January 21, 1999

Shortly before resuming the "trial" this afternoon, Senator Orrin Hatch asked to speak with me privately.

"I have always been a proponent for the House Managers," he said, "but you need to know something. There are a lot of moderate Republican senators who are ready to jump ship on you guys." Hatch proposed that the Senate dismiss our case, "but with the Senate recognizing the 'validity' of the House vote to impeach Clinton, and also find that the House's vote to impeach him was the highest form of censure."

I told Hatch that such a vote was nothing more than a repudiation of our case, especially since the Senate had not yet allowed us to present any evidence. Further, I told him the House Managers didn't need the Senate to "validate" the House's action. It stood alone based on the record. Just then, Chief Justice Rehnquist entered the chamber to begin proceedings, so we followed him inside.

Once the session started and we heard the chaplain's daily prayer, I told Henry Hyde and Tom Mooney about Hatch's latest proposal. Mooney shrugged and said that Hatch tried to peddle this idea a month or two ago. He said that Henry looked dismayed when he heard it. "They just want this thing to go away," he replied. "They want to shove it under the rug."

Hatch's renewed activity in pleading for us to scuttle the ship should have signaled that something was up. It didn't take long for the torpedo to surface. The next morning, Senator Robert Byrd (D-WV), the dean of the Senate Democrats, issued a press statement saying he would move to dismiss the case outright.

Diary, U.S. Senate Floor During Impeachment
Proceedings Against President Clinton,
Thursday, January 22, 1999

After word filtered out of Byrd's plan, his fellow Democrats rushed out of the chamber to tell the waiting reporters that the Senate needed to follow his lead. Senators Chris Dodd (D-CT) and Charles Schumer (D-NY) today declared that the House Managers' case "is over," and that the White House did such a wonderful job that to continue any further would just "embarrass" the House Managers.

Many Republican senators now are coming over to tell us privately that we're through. They want us to agree that they should vote to dismiss it. I told those with whom I spoke that we are not quitting and that they need to hear the witnesses and evidence. I told Orrin Hatch today that if he and his fellow Senate Republicans want to dismiss our case without hearing any evidence, they should do it publicly. We were not conceding anything without a fight.

Later that afternoon, I recorded these observations:

Senate Republicans are meeting with their Democrat coun-terparts right now to work out their exit plan. We hear they

will propose letting us rebut what Clinton's lawyers said, but they will hear from no witnesses. I urged our Managers to reject this proposal. The prosecution of a trial requires both witnesses and rebuttal time.

Unfortunately, Henry Hyde says he likes the Senate's new plan: "We could avoid the problem of all Clinton's friends coming in as witnesses to bury us," he told his Managers. "We could go on TV in the Senate and hammer Clinton for a few hours. That might not be a bad idea."

In frustration, I shot back at Henry: "The polls aren't moved by us hammering Clinton. The only chance we have to change this dynamic is to call witnesses and get people listening to the evidence."

A tired Henry Hyde doesn't want to fight any more. He now is concerned any attack will "offend" the Senate. I see no reciprocal concern from them for the continuing insults they rain upon us as representatives of the House.

The next morning, our dejected Managers met to discuss the unraveling situation:

Diary, House Managers Meeting, The Marble Room, Saturday, January 23, 1999

Henry Hyde said the Senate will vote on Robert Byrd's dismissal motion on Monday. "We're not dead yet," he said as he began the meeting, "but we're on life support."

Henry thinks we will survive Byrd's dismissal motion. Despite all their threats, he doesn't think a GOP-controlled Senate can vote to dismiss the case outright without even a semblance of a trial.

Now ready to ring down the curtain, Henry again urged his fact team (McCollum, Hutchinson, Bryant and me) to narrow our witness requests:

Diary, House Managers Meeting,
Thursday, January 21, 1999

"Don't try and call any witnesses unless there is a reasonable chance that they will help us," Henry pleaded. "All those pro-Clinton witnesses like Betty Currie and Vernon Jordan will not help us. They will screw us. And Lewinsky is a ticking time bomb."

"However," he added with a sigh, "this judgment on witnesses remains with the fact team."

After further discussion, we decided to file our motion for witnesses on Monday, but we will not identify them until the Senate requires it.

Declining to identify our witness want-list publicly was not strategic. We still were arguing about what names to put on it. Hanging over our head was the senators' constant warning that submitting a "controversial" list meant no witnesses.

Diary, House Managers Meeting, The Marble Room,
Saturday, January 23, 1999

Bob Barr urged us to add Clinton pollster Dick Morris[1] and former Clinton aide Kathleen Willey to the list. "Morris will show Clinton's bad character and his motive to lie," Bob said.

---

1   Dick Morris, Clinton's former political consultant and pollster, told Clinton that polling data revealed he could not survive politically any admission of perjury or obstruction of justice. Clinton replied, "Well, we'll just have to win, won't we." Morris interpreted this to mean Clinton would do whatever it took to defeat the allegations.

"Willey will show Clinton engaged in a pattern and practice of obstructing justice."

Asa Hutchinson said that adding Willey is a bad idea. "If we start deleting from our witness list the Vernon Jordans of the world and start adding the Kathleen Willeys, we'll look terrible." Asa finally came around to agreeing to add her to our list: "I will support listing her as a witness," Asa said, "if we limit her testimony to the subject of trying to get her to file a false affidavit."

Only yesterday, a vacillating Henry Hyde acted very nervous about our forcing the witness issue in the Senate. Today, he throws caution to the wind. He says he wants to call them all: "If the Senate doesn't give us our witnesses," Henry declared, "it will make this proceeding more of a sham than it already is."

Near the end of our meeting, Henry reversed his earlier declaration that the "fact team" would decide the witness issue; he now proclaimed by fiat that the "witness debate" was over and we would submit to the Senate the following names: Monica Lewinsky, Kathleen Willey, Sidney Blumenthal, White House Chief of Staff John Podesta, and (maybe) Dick Morris. Henry nixed listing Betty Currie, Vernon Jordan, and any of the "Jane Doe" witnesses.

As Dave Schippers predicted earlier, when we sent word to Lewinsky's attorneys that we wanted an interview, they claimed they had no obligation to produce her. At our request, Judge Starr's team filed a motion to compel her cooperation. Only after a federal judge ruled that Lewinsky's immunity agreement required her to answer our questions did she agree reluctantly to meet with us.

Word leaked of our upcoming Lewinsky meeting The Senate Democrats demanded we cancel any planned interview, claiming it violated their rules. In a two-page reply, Henry Hyde told them we did not need their blessing:

**Letter from Henry Hyde to Senate Democrat Leader
Tom Daschle, January 23, 1999**

"The Managers, who represent the House of Representatives, retain powers separate and apart from the Senate. The Managers are not . . . an office or subset of the Senate. The Managers . . . may conduct activities, such as further investigation, that are not specifically authorized by the Senate [Any claim to restrict us from interviewing witnesses] would be an unconstitutional infringement on the prerogatives of the House."

Diary, Sunday, January 24, 1999

Ed Bryant reported to me on his interview with Monica Lewinsky. He called her poised and articulate, and he thinks she would do well as a witness.

Ed said he didn't cover much ground regarding the details of her possible testimony in order to avoid the inevitable accusation that he tried to get her to change her story. However, she did volunteer that she is still a Clinton "fan," and she thinks he is a "good" president who should not be removed from office.

The day the Lewinsky story first became public, Clinton embarked on a full-scale destruction campaign against his young former intern and paramour. To his White House operatives, Clinton "slut-ified" Lewinsky, portraying her as a sex-crazed "stalker" hounding their poor leader. He did this so his henchmen would leak these slurs to the media.

Clinton exploited her, dumped her, exposed her to possible felony prosecution, and then he prepared to sacrifice her in the incinerator of public character annihilation. Despite all this, Monica Lewinsky remained a "fan" of this "good" president.

Go figure.

After hearing Ed Bryant's report, I wasn't sure what was worse: not getting witnesses or getting them.

32

Exit Strategy

We had been in the foxhole too long.

For more than a year the mainstream press, the Democrat National Committee, the White House and their congressional allies, and even factions within our own Republican Party pounded away on us continually. Combined with a year's worth of too many sleepless nights, too many missed kids' birthday parties and dance recitals, too many pizzas gobbled hurriedly during late night strategy sessions, and far too many arrogant senators, it was bound to happen. The House Managers were tired: we were tired of the press, tired of the senators, and now growing tired of each other. At our next Managers' meeting, tensions rose as we bickered over the final witness list:

Diary, House Managers Meeting,
Wednesday, January 25, 1999

Asa demands we call Vernon Jordan; Bryant insists we call Betty Currie. I want to call all of them and more, and especially Clinton. Meanwhile, Henry Hyde (again) doesn't want us to call any witnesses.

When Lindsey Graham renewed the idea of calling Kathleen Willey, Charles Canady shot down the notion of "going down that path" and bringing in a witness who claimed on television that Clinton groped her.

"What's the difference?" Bob Barr snapped. "We'll be attacked anyway no matter what witness we call, so we shouldn't be concerned about being attacked if we bring in Willey."

"That isn't what I was saying," Canady retorted.

Barr cut him off: "I didn't say it was—don't be so defensive."

Even after Henry steered us back to business, the tenor sounded more like squabbling than strategizing:

Bryant wants to limit our witnesses to Lewinsky, Jordan, Currie and John Podesta (Clinton's current chief of staff). "Why not add Blumenthal?" I asked. "Why not add Dick Morris? Why not add—"

"I don't want us to call Vernon Jordan!" Barr interjected. "He has too much charisma and he has the confidence of too many senators."

"But we need to put him on the list," interrupted Hutchinson, "for P.R. reasons. Otherwise, everyone will ask why we dumped him at this late stage. If we only go with Monica, they'll accuse us of putting the focus on sex. With Jordan, we can put the focus on Clinton's obstruction of justice."

By now, nothing would launch me into irritability orbit faster than hearing a colleague still wringing his hands over "protecting" the sensitivities of the Senate. I was sick of mollycoddling people bent on cutting our throats:

Asa said, "We don't want our conservative senators in there to repudiate us. We need to respect the Senate's prerogative. It's better to lose this thing with 51 votes than to lose it with 40 votes."

Ed Bryant agreed: "We don't want to offend the senators. We still have many friends over there."

With friends like these senators, I'd rather have enemies. As it turned out, I wasn't the only one fed up with the apprehension of stepping on senatorial toes. Chris Cannon erupted after Ed's and Asa's plea for caution:

"Since we aren't going to get a conviction in the Senate anyway," said Chris, "we should just list all our witnesses. We should demand our right to a fair trial. Let's show the voters that these senators are nothing more than quislings and cowards!"

With the Senate treating us like a piñata, I said that we should assert our constitutional prerogative and demand to try this case properly—or not try it at all. However, if the other Managers disagreed with holding out for a full trial, I said we should call their bluff and just list two witnesses: Monica Lewinsky and Bill Clinton.

Henry Hyde jumped into the fray: "No!" he said emphatically. "Then the focus is only on sex!"

"So far, we've prepared to present our entire case without focusing on that subject," I replied.

This went on until Henry, for the second time in two days, pulled rank and rang down the debate curtain. Naming Ed Bryant as the captain of the witness team, he told Ed to make the call. Ed picked Lewinsky, Currie, Jordan, Podesta, and Blumenthal for our witness list. I then suggested if our group didn't want to add Clinton's name to that list, we should make a formal "request" that the Senate call him. "Let's put the burden on the White House," I said, "and give America the specter of Clinton refusing to testify." Henry nodded in silent agreement.

We paused our discussion to watch a live news report that Senator Joe Lieberman (D-CT), one of the few moderates on the Democrat side we hoped to impress with the evidence, wanted the Senate to dismiss the case. We expected this from Robert Byrd; we didn't expect Lieberman, who had earlier denounced Clinton in a powerful Senate floor speech, to join him. Henry shook his head at this latest disappointing news. As much as I liked and respected Joe Lieberman, I felt that he had orchestrated this with the White House for maximum press impact.

Diary, U.S. Senate Floor During Impeachment Proceedings Against President Clinton, Monday, January 25, 1999

As expected, Senator Robert Byrd (D-WV) made his motion to dismiss the impeachment charges. Surprisingly, he offered no argument on it.

Chief Justice Rehnquist recognized Manager Charles Canady to lead off our presentation against the motion.

Henry Hyde closed for our side, noting wryly: "The Constitution requires a trial, not an exit strategy."

At the end of the session, Henry asked to meet with Ed Bryant, Asa Hutchinson, Bill McCollum and me for one final discussion on the witness list. Henry reminded us of the senators' earlier threat: if we turned in a witness list of more than three names, or too many controversial names, we'd get none. After running through the pros and cons again, Dick Morris, Sidney Blumenthal, and Monica Lewinsky became the consensus picks. Once Henry left the room, Asa renewed his lobbying effort to swap Morris for Vernon Jordan. After much cajoling, he prevailed.

For better or worse, our final roster of proposed deposition witnesses listed only three names—and none of them was William

Jefferson Clinton.[1]

In our formal motion asking the Senate's permission to depose Lewinsky and Jordan, we summarized the tangle of lies and evidence obstruction spun by Clinton in his mania to obliterate Paula Jones and her lawsuit against him. We laid out how Lewinsky's and Jordan's testimony directly rebutted Clinton's claim, first made in the House Judiciary Committee and now repeated in the Senate "trial," that he

- never encouraged Lewinsky to file a false affidavit;

- never encouraged Lewinsky to conceal the gifts he had given her;

- never lied when he denied having a "sexual relationship" with her;

- never instructed his secretary, Betty Currie, to retrieve his gifts given previously to Lewinsky and to hide them under her bed from Paula Jones' lawyers;

- never had any "understanding" with Lewinsky that the two would lie under oath;

- never helped Lewinsky get a high-paying New York City job in order to gain her cooperation in his efforts to shut out Paula Jones.

The motion outlined how Clinton and Jordan used Lewinsky in a bungled scheme to encourage Lewinsky's perjury, and how Clinton bought her continuous cooperation with a high-paying job after she became a witness in the Paula Jones case:

---

1   At the very end of the House Managers' formal "Motion for the Appearance of Witnesses at a Deposition" filed in the Senate on January 26, 1999, we "petitioned" the Senate to "request" the testimony of President Clinton, which (of course) the Senate refused to do.

1. After their sexual relationship ended, Lewinsky wanted Clinton to find her a job. Clinton shuffled the burden onto his pal Vernon Jordan, a mega-wattage D.C. attorney. Long after Clinton promised her help, and before Jones' attorneys signaled that they knew about Lewinsky, she complained to Clinton personally that Jordan wasn't doing anything for her. However, once Lewinsky's name appeared on the Jones witness list, Jordan shifted into overdrive to get Lewinsky a high paying job in New York City.

2. When Lewinsky and Clinton discussed that the Jones lawyers identified her as a potential witness, Clinton instructed Lewinsky to contact his secretary, Betty Currie, if she received a subpoena. He suggested Lewinsky use previously concocted lies to deny their relationship if questioned. Clinton then said she could "avoid" testifying by signing an affidavit for the Jones lawyers that would have to contain a perjured denial regarding their relationship for her to avoid testifying.

3. On the day Jones' lawyers subpoenaed Lewinsky, she told Vernon Jordan of the development. Jordan took her in his chauffeured car to see an attorney he picked for her to meet. En route to seeing the attorney about submitting the false affidavit, she discussed the subpoena with Jordan, the Jones case in general, and his ongoing job search efforts for her.

4. The Jordan-recommended attorney prepared an affidavit for Lewinsky that denied any sexual relationship with Clinton. Lewinsky testified that Jordan helped her edit the affidavit before she signed it. Jordan later recalled only telling her to "consult her attorney" if she had concerns about its content.

5. When she later met Clinton in the Oval Office a few days after Christmas, he gave her additional gifts. She reminded him that the Jones lawyers' subpoena required her to turn over any gifts from him. She asked if she should hide all of his gifts to her or give them to his secretary Currie to hide. Clinton told Lewinsky, "Let me think about that." Later that morning, Currie called her and stated, "I understand you have something to give me," or, "The president said you have something to give me." Lewinsky put into a box all of the gifts that Clinton gave her. Currie came to Lewinsky's apartment, retrieved the box, and then she took the box home and hid it under her bed.

6. After Lewinsky told Jordan that former confidante Linda Tripp may have learned of her relationship with Clinton through copies of Lewinsky's notes to him that Lewinsky kept at her home, Jordan told her to "go home and make sure [the notes] aren't there," i.e., go home and get rid of the notes. She destroyed them at Jordan's direction, even though Jones' attorneys subpoenaed the notes previously.

7. On January 6, 1998, Lewinsky picked up the draft affidavit prepared by the Jordan-recommended attorney. The affidavit she signed falsely denied that she and Clinton had a sexual relationship. Since Clinton told her he didn't need to read her affidavit, she called Jordan to go over it. She told the grand jury that getting Jordan's approval of the document was the same as having the affidavit "blessed" by Clinton. She said Jordan helped massage the affidavit, including his suggestion that she remove a statement that implied she once had been alone with Clinton. She then signed the affidavit under penalty of perjury declaring she "never had a sexual relationship with the president." That same day, Jordan spoke to Clinton and reported on his continuing efforts to land a job for Lewinsky.

8. After she signed the false affidavit, Lewinsky called Jordan to say a job interview he set up for her went "very poorly." Jordan told her "not to worry." He then contacted the chairman and CEO of the company and asked him to "make things happen." The company re-interviewed Lewinsky and then hired her.

9. Upon learning of Lewinsky's employment, Jordan called Betty Currie and asked her to tell Clinton, "Mission accomplished" in getting her a job. Later that evening, Jordan reported to Clinton personally of his success in procuring employment for Lewinsky.

10. With Clinton now confident that Lewinsky's false testimony was secured, Clinton went to his own under-oath deposition in the Paula Jones case a few days later and lied with impunity. At that deposition, an attorney read a portion of Lewinsky's affidavit to Clinton in which she denied having a "sexual relationship" with him. The lawyer asked Clinton whether the statement was true and accurate. Clinton replied, "That is absolutely true."

• • •

Earlier, I had abandoned my short-lived assignment to prepare the cross-examination of Bill Clinton. Once the writing on the Senate wall showed their intent to gut our ability to call any live witnesses, this sham "trial" was essentially over. Public opinion wouldn't move without live testimony, and without that shift, Clinton never would show up and testify. With our deposition motion now filed, I changed my focus from questioning Clinton to deposing Sidney Blumenthal.[2]

---

2   From the time Chairman Hyde first assigned me the job of Clinton's cross-examination, my work schedule magnified. Each night at 2 a.m., I stopped my general trial preparation to work on my Clinton questions until 4 a.m. I then took a catnap before resuming regular trial preparation. In writing this book, I found my original (and very incomplete) draft Clinton cross-examination notes. This document barely touched the surface of where I wanted to go in confronting Clinton. However, for those interested, I include it in the appendix of this book to give the reader a flavor of how the confrontation might have looked.

Had it been solely my call, Blumenthal probably wouldn't have made the three-witness cut. However, the Managers all agreed we needed a witness whose testimony represented just one example of Clinton's witness tampering, and Blumenthal fit that bill.

On the day the Lewinsky story exploded, Clinton sought out White House aide Blumenthal to tell him that he rebuffed Lewinsky when she made sexual demands on him, and then Clinton went on to trash Lewinsky to him. Clinton painted her as a "stalker," and said she "threatened" to lie and tell others that they had an affair. He claimed that Lewinsky told him that if she could force an affair with him, then people wouldn't view her as a stalker anymore.

Why would Clinton make this pitch to Blumenthal as opposed to some other aide? It was Machiavellian. Nicknamed by his press friends and White House colleagues as "Sid Vicious" because of his reputation for leaking harmful personal information about political enemies to the mainstream media, Blumenthal was Clinton's designated hitman to smear and destroy Lewinsky publicly. Beyond that, Clinton knew the grand jury might later subpoena key aides. He wanted to use them as conduits for spreading false information to the grand jury investigating him.

Diary, U.S. Senate Floor During Impeachment Proceedings Against President Clinton, Tuesday, January 26, 1999

Ed Bryant filed the House Managers' formal motion to depose three witnesses. Bill McCollum led off our presentation. While he spoke, Senator Barbara Boxer (once more seated behind me) started heckling again: "Oh! He's just wasting the time of the Senate!" she complained.

McCollum's speech also drew an unexpected bipartisan critique:

Just as he had done to Steve Buyer recently, Henry Hyde started griping about McCollum, saying, "Bill takes too long to make his point." As Bill continued, Henry passed me a note: "We are planning to reserve time for rebuttal, right?"

Later, with McCollum still talking, Henry ordered a junior committee staffer to walk to the lectern and tell Bill to sit down.

Fortunately, Bill concluded before Henry forced the visibly uncomfortable staffer to give Bill the hook.

I thought Bill did a good job, so I didn't take Henry's complaint seriously. Besides, having been on Henry's bad side myself more than once recently, I just figured it was Bill's turn in our drained chairman's crosshairs.

After Bill finished, we presented our remaining arguments: Ed Bryant advocated for taking Monica Lewinsky's deposition, Asa Hutchinson did the same for Vernon Jordan's, and I made the case for Sidney Blumenthal's.

As Chief Justice Rehnquist recognized Clinton attorney David Kendall to oppose our motion, Henry Hyde waved me over to join him. Still perseverating over poor Bill McCollum, Henry complained,

"I don't want Bill McCollum to be part of the rebuttal. He goes on too long. I want you, Asa, and Ed to handle the rebuttal."

I passed a note to Ed explaining Henry's order. Ed slipped it into his folder. I don't know if he read it. As the White House lawyers wound down, I walked over and asked Ed how he anticipated lining up our rebuttal.

"First will be me, then Asa, then Bill, and then you," he replied. Before I could ask him about the note, Henry summoned me back to his seat.

"Bill's not rebutting, right?" Henry asked me. When

I replied that Ed said Bill was still in the lineup, Henry erupted. "Oh, Christ!" he barked in a voice loud enough for nearby senators to hear. He started moving from one chair to the next, sliding his large hulk along the length of the table trying to reach Ed. When he got close to where the rest of our lead presenters sat, he called out to McCollum, "Hey Bill—I don't want you using too much time on rebuttal. I want these guys up there," he said while waving his finger at Asa, Ed, and me. It was embarrassing and Bill looked hurt. When rebuttal started, Bill spoke briefly and then returned to his seat.

Still grumbling from the far end of counsel table, Henry said aloud, "I need to take more control of this thing."

By the end of the afternoon, Henry's annoyance at Bill started to give way to a newfound irritation with Ed Bryant—for failing to implement his earlier order.

After my reply to the White House arguments, I presumed I did satisfactorily, since Henry didn't start passing around notes about me (at least this time).

At the end of my presentation, Senator Rick Santorum (R-PA) walked over and congratulated me. "You may have just saved the day for your side," he said. "Some of our moderates [the GOP senators balking at our calling witnesses] wore expressions as if to say, 'Oh! Now I get it!'"

Later, Senator Larry Craig (R-ID) approached me and touted his plan for videotaping the witness depositions so that live witnesses in the Senate would be unnecessary. I panned that idea: "There is no substitute for live witnesses testifying in a trial for jurors to judge their credibility," I told him.

During the break in the late afternoon, Senator Joe Lieberman (D-CT) visited with me. We talked about the first time each of us met President Clinton. I shared with him the story of my meeting Clinton in 1978 when I was a college student and when the future president was Arkansas attorney general. Lieberman had me beat. He told me that back in 1970, then-law student Clinton volunteered as a campaign worker in one of Joe's earlier state races.

"To tell you the truth," he said with a sheepish grin, "I really don't remember him from back then, despite all the press reports to the contrary!"

"After he became president," he added, "I was at the White House for a reception. The president grabbed my hand and introduced me to a head of state, saying, 'Here's the man who got me into politics!'"

"Joe," I told him, "it sounds like you are still trying to wiggle out of that accusation!" Lieberman laughed.

• • •

Diary, House Managers Meeting, Friday, January 27, 1999

Henry Hyde talked about our upcoming closing arguments. Given the futility of our effort, Henry said, "I want everyone on our team to participate. Nobody will be on the bench for this." Then, trying to buck up our spirits, he began rallying us with great seriousness, "We're told by everyone we can't win. They said the same thing about the men at Valley Forge and the Alamo."

Lindsey Graham got a big guffaw when he chimed in, "I think they were right about the Alamo!"

Henry joined in the laughter, and then he replied, "Other than Santa Anna, I don't remember the names of any of those other Mexican soldiers—and don't tell me Jose!"

In response to the few of us left who still argued for taking the fight to the senators, Asa Hutchinson warned that if we complained too much about the inevitable, we might offend the Senate. Lindsey Graham and Jim Sensenbrenner agreed with him.

We might offend the Senate? As Ebenezer Scrooge said, "I'll retire to Bedlam."

33

The Three Amigos

Notes from the U.S. Senate Floor, Clinton
Impeachment Trial, Wednesday, January 27, 1999

Once Chief Justice Rehnquist gaveled the session to order,
the first issue presented was Senator Byrd's motion to dismiss. As expected, it died on a straight Party-line vote, with
only Democrat Russ Feingold of Wisconsin crossing over.
Everyone got a chuckle when Democrat Barbara Mikulski
voted accidentally to defeat Byrd's motion. She blushed as
she jumped to her feet to correct it. I called out from my seat,
"I object!" which lightened the mood momentarily.

Next, the Senate voted to allow the three depositions
taken that had been the subject of so much heated discussion.

Following the defeat of Byrd's motion, and trying to put
the best light on our floundering ship, our Judiciary Committee staff distributed talking points to the press: "The

White House hoped to convince the Senate to drop the case. It has failed to do so because the facts cannot be ignored." Even a politician like me, desperate to make lemonade from this barrel of impeachment lemons, had a hard time parroting that line to reporters while maintaining a straight face.

Now that the Senate deigned to allow us to take a few depositions, the House Managers sought to have Chief Justice Rehnquist preside over them. If Rehnquist declined, then we wanted another federal judge to do it. I especially wanted a judge for Blumenthal's deposition given his penchant for claiming executive privilege during his earlier grand jury testimony. However, the senators insisted on having their own members "preside" over the depositions, which promised to further politicize the process.

That afternoon, Henry Hyde summoned me to his office:

Diary, Thursday, January 28, 1999

When I arrived at Henry's office, he handed me one of his fat Montecristo cigars. As we both puffed away, he showed me a copy of Senator Orrin Hatch's latest "trial" dismissal proposal.

Hatch's newest plan contemplated the Senate adjourning the impeachment "trial" forever because there weren't the votes to convict and remove Clinton (predetermined, of course, before a single witness testified). Hatch apparently wanted the Senate to create a new extra-constitutional sanction that he called "Impeachment Without Removal from Office." Hatch declared it "the highest form of condemnation, other than removal, which can be imposed by the Congress" on Clinton.

Henry asked me what I thought about Hatch's new scheme. "It's horseshit," I said. "It's the Senate waving the white flag for us."

"I knew you'd say that," he replied with a smile. "That's what I told Orrin, too."

Henry took a call just as I stood to leave for my live television interview at CNN. Henry stopped me: "The Senate's going back in session in five minutes," he said. "It sounds like they are going to ratify their 'no live witness' deal, with no further input from us. Shall we go over to watch?"

"No, thanks," I replied. "If I'm going to get screwed any more by senators, I prefer it be in absentia."

After doing a round of interviews at various networks, I returned to CNN for an evening appearance on *Larry King Live*. I was finishing in the makeup room when Senator Mitch McConnell entered. Settling into the chair that I had just vacated, he pointed to me and told the cosmetician, "You'll need a lot more makeup than that to make Rogan look pretty."

"I don't have Mitch's chiseled features," I told her. "When you make him up, let me know if you'd like to borrow my chisel."

• • •

The senators scheduled our three witness depositions back-to-back: February 1 (Lewinsky), February 2 (Jordan), and February 3 (Blumenthal). For each interrogation, the responsible managers prepared outlines with questions in the left column, and any previous answers in the right column as an easy reference in case anyone started backtracking or claimed a sudden memory lapse.

On the morning of the Lewinsky deposition, Ed Bryant and I met early at the Capitol to review his 85-page outline of questions and answers. Asa begged off attending today's proceedings because he wanted more time to prepare for Vernon Jordan's interrogation tomorrow

Diary, Deposition of Monica Lewinsky, Mayflower Hotel, Washington, D.C., February 1, 1999

Capitol police drove Ed Bryant and me to the Mayflower Hotel. I couldn't believe the zoo outside. Television camera crews, satellite trucks, reporters and onlookers packed the entrance so tightly that we couldn't get inside. The police brought us to the rear of the hotel and escorted us to the tenth-floor presidential suite.

The suite has two bedrooms and a conference room now converted into a mini-television studio for Lewinsky's deposition. Security told us the bedroom to our right as we entered was reserved for the House Managers; the one at left was for White House attorneys.

I joined Clinton's attorneys David Kendall and Cheryl Mills for a cup of coffee before Lewinsky arrived. We all agreed that a long vacation was due when this "trial" ended. Senators Chris Dodd (D-CT), Patrick Leahy (D-VT), Mike DeWine (R-OH) and John Edwards (D-NC) joined us (the Senate tasked Leahy and DeWine with presiding over this morning's deposition). The mood was amicable. Leahy talked about skiing in Vermont while Edwards (a new senator on the job less than a month) said he still was trying to learn his way around the Capitol.

At 8:50 a.m., Lewinsky arrived at the suite with her attorneys Plato Cacheris, Jake Stein, and Sidney Jean Hoffman. Upon entering, Lewinsky stepped inadvertently on the presidential seal etched into the floor. When she looked down and saw her foot in the middle of it, she flinched away as if startled. Bypassing the House Managers completely, she walked directly into the White House counsels' room and greeted each of them warmly.

I stood chatting with Pat Leahy and Jake Stein when

**Lewinsky came over. She shook hands with Leahy enthusi-
astically and lauded his congressional service. "I hope you
get through your parent-child bill," she told him. "That is
very important to my family."**

**In contrast, when Stein introduced us, she shook my
hand perfunctorily. I offered to get her a cup of coffee. She
declined politely, but in a voice that signaled she was all
business with me.**

At DeWine's suggestion, everyone took seats. I sat on one side
of the table near Bryant. Across from us sat Leahy, DeWine, and
White House counsel Cheryl Mills and Nicole Seligman. I suspect
it was no accident that the White House fronted their two junior
female lawyers for this deposition, while lead lawyer David Kendall sat to the rear of the room. To my far right and at the head of
the table sat Lewinsky with her three attorneys. To my left was a
makeshift spectator gallery where various senators and staff sat in
chairs packed together.

**Shortly after 9:00 a.m., the video cameraman gave the
signal to begin. DeWine and Leahy read from prepared
statements, and then Stein tried to set ground rules by
saying he expected that Bryant would ask no questions
about his client's sexual activity with Clinton. Seligman
then objected to the manner in which the House Managers
provided notice to White House counsel for the deposition.
While Bryant played defense, I caught both Seligman and
Lewinsky's attorney Hoffman share a knowing grin over
their clearly orchestrated disruption.**

The Senate warned us in advance that the deposition "proctors"
DeWine and Leahy would cut off our questions at the four-hour
mark. This initial delay wasted almost half an hour. From that first

shared grin between Seligman and Hoffman, it became clear to me that the fix was in between these two camps.

> **When Bryant asked Lewinsky about her first meeting with Clinton, Cacheris objected to our asking questions regarding any subject matter contained in her prior grand jury testimony. In exasperation, Bryant replied that if that was the case, then we might as well all go home.**
>
> **"Sounds good to me," said Lewinsky.**
>
> **Cacheris renewed his objection to any questions relating to her prior testimony. DeWine ordered the session to go off the record. He and Leahy huddled as they reviewed the Senate resolution authorizing the deposition. During their whispered discussion, I overheard DeWine say, "We've got to resolve this, Pat." Twice Leahy expressed his concern that any questions already covered in the grand jury might create for Lewinsky "a perjury trap."**
>
> **After another wasted ten minutes, and while still off the record, DeWine advised Lewinsky she must answer Bryant's questions. "I know you have done it many times," he told her, "but you'll have to tell your story." Lewinsky sighed heavily and dropped her head downward.**
>
> **Later, when DeWine called a break, I spoke privately in the back of the room with Senator Fred Thompson (R-TN), one of the observers. When I told him of the apparent collusion between the Lewinsky and Clinton lawyers, Thompson said he noticed it, too. He dropped his voice and whispered to me, "I'd let a few friendlies in the press know about that."**

Lewinsky stuck close to her previous grand jury testimony. Meanwhile, her attorneys never missed a chance to object and run out the clock.

Lewinsky's attorneys again objected to the form of Bryant's questions. Meanwhile, Bryant complained to the senators about her attorneys objecting continually. After going off the record and discussing the dispute, DeWine and Leahy couldn't agree to a resolution. They caucused in the rear of the room with the four other senators present: Fred Thompson, Arlen Specter, Chris Dodd, and John Edwards. Soon DeWine called back all counsel. He said the Senate consensus is that Cacheris can continue objecting to Bryant's questions, but they asked Cacheris to keep his objections "brief" so as not to "clutter the record."

Lewinsky's non-cooperation was no surprise. What did surprise me was how often Ed Bryant, the consummate gentleman, avoided multiple opportunities to pin down her story. In addition, he appeared unaware of (or unable to see) what I saw: Whenever Lewinsky started offering anything above generalized responses, Cacheris reached under the table and tapped her arm while Hoffman made off-camera "chopping" motions with her hand, which were all designed to signal Lewinsky into silence.

At the next break, Bryant huddled with our committee staff and me in the back room. He complained that Lewinsky is not cooperating. I told him about Cacheris' arm-taps and Hoffman's "chop" signals whenever Lewinsky started giving meaningful answers, and that Fred Thompson and Mike DeWine also saw it, too. DeWine told me that he wants Bryant to start objecting on the record to the behavior.

We all agreed the White House and their attorneys coached Lewinsky heavily. Before the grand jury, she portrayed herself as vulnerable and charming—to the point where grand jurors offered advice for her future. That was not the Lewinsky that we met. This cunning woman was clearly

doing all she could to be unhelpful to us. Bryant agreed that he needed to be more aggressive in his questioning and not let her wiggle out of her answers quite as easily.

Despite her reluctance to cooperate, Bryant forced Lewinsky to validate her previous grand jury testimony of Clinton's plan to have her lie under oath in Paula Jones' lawsuit:

Q. In the context of your telephone conversation with the president on December 17, did you understand that you would deny your relationship with the president to the Jones lawyers?

A. Yes, correct.

Q. In fact, you did deny the relationship to the Jones lawyers in the affidavit that you signed under penalty of perjury; is that right?

A. I denied a sexual relationship.

Q. The president did not in that conversation, or any other conversation, instruct you to tell the truth, correct?

A. That's correct.

Q. Prior to being on the witness list, you both spoke about denying this relationship if asked?

A. Yes. That was discussed.

Q. He would say something to the effect that—or you would say that—you—you would deny anything if it ever came up, and he would nod or say that's good, something to that effect; is that right?

A. Yes.

At one point Bryant struck a raw nerve with his witness. Lewinsky bristled when he characterized her relationship with Clinton:

Q. Let me shift gears just a minute and ask you about the first so-called salacious occasion.

A. Can you call it something else?

Q. Okay.

A. I mean, this is *my* relationship.

Q. What would you like to call it?

A. It was my first encounter with the president, so I don't really see it as my first salacious—that's not what this was. An encounter, maybe?

Q. Encounter. You had several of these encounters, perhaps 10 or 11 of these encounters; is that right?

A. Yes.

After the lunch break, we resumed the deposition with Senator John Edwards replacing Leahy as the Democrat proctor. Instead of leaving, Leahy took a seat in the rear of the room. With everyone ready to begin, a hitch developed: the video and lighting technicians had not returned from lunch. From the back of the room, Leahy cracked to Edwards, "John, when I presided, we had lights—another example of the seniority system at work!"

The afternoon session mimicked the morning one. Other than ratifying her previous grand jury testimony, Lewinsky remained unaccommodating. When Bryant's time expired, Edwards and DeWine recognized the White House lawyers for their four-hour reserved block of questions. It didn't take Team Clinton four hours to make their points; it took them about four seconds. Nicole Seligman turned to the witness: "Ms. Lewinsky," she said, "on behalf of the president, we'd like to tell you how very sorry we all are for what you have had to go through." With that, the deposition concluded.

Lewinsky and her entourage left the Mayflower quickly. As the House Manager team met in our back room to compare notes, Mike DeWine wandered in and called the deposition a "disaster," saying it should never air before the Senate.

• • •

That night, after returning to the Capitol, I closed out the day's diary notes with this harsh assessment:

Monica Lewinsky is not the vulnerable young waif the media portrays. She struck me as sophisticated, snotty, and spoiled. I saw nothing endearing about her. She was in the hip pocket of Clinton's attorneys from the moment she walked into the Mayflower Hotel.

I didn't like her. Under the circumstances, I'm sure her impression of me wasn't any more charitable.

• • •

The next day, Congressman Asa Hutchinson teed up his deposition of presidential pal Vernon Jordan. By the time I arrived for Jordan's deposition, the players already were gathered and ready to begin.

Like yesterday's Lewinsky encounter, Clinton's lawyers started the deposition by lodging objections. After ruling on them, Senator Fred Thompson administered the oath to Jordan. From the start, Jordan answered Asa's questions with continued touches of arrogance. For example, when Asa asked Jordan about him taking Lewinsky to an attorney appointment, Jordan corrected Asa: "I took Ms. Lewinsky from my office [to see the lawyer] in my law firm's *chauffeur-driven car*."

Oh, brother.

As expected, Jordan answered each question carefully. He gave answers designed to protect Clinton and himself. Other than disputing Lewinsky's testimony that implicated him in the obstruction of justice charge, he gave Asa nothing but attitude, even when Asa tripped him up with previous inconsistent testimony. Lewinsky told the grand jury that Jordan took her to breakfast at the Park Hyatt on December 31, 1997 during the height of the ongoing job search to keep her happy and quiet. According to Lewinsky, Jordan told her during this breakfast to go home and get rid of the subpoenaed notes between her and Clinton. In his own grand jury testimony, Jordan denied meeting her for breakfast and having this conversation. Asa confronted Jordan with his American Express receipt from that morning:

Q. Is this a receipt for a charge that you had at the Park Hyatt on December 31?

A. That's an American Express receipt for breakfast.

Q. And is the date December 31?

A. That is correct.

Q. Does it reflect the items that were consumed at that breakfast?

A. It reflects the items that were paid for at that breakfast.

Q. Does it appear to you that this is a breakfast for two people?

A. The price suggests that it was a breakfast for two people.

Q. And the fact that there are two coffees, there is one omelet, one English muffin, one hot cereal, and can you identify from that what you ordinarily eat at breakfast?

A. What I ordinarily eat at breakfast varies. This morning, it was fish and grits.

Q. Ms. Lewinsky, in her testimony, referenced what she ate, which I believe is confirmed in this record. Do you now recall a meeting with Ms. Lewinsky at the Park Hyatt on December 31, 1997?

A. If you would refer to my testimony before the grand jury when asked about a breakfast with Ms. Lewinsky on December 31, I testified that I did not have breakfast with Ms. Lewinsky on December 31 because I did not remember having breakfast with Ms. Lewinsky on December 31. It is clear, based on the evidence here, that I was at the Park Hyatt on December 31. So I do not deny, despite my testimony before the grand jury, that on December 31 that I was there with Ms. Lewinsky, but I did testify before the grand jury that I did not remember having a breakfast with her on that date, and that was the truth.

When asked if this receipt also refreshed his memory on telling Lewinsky to "go home and make sure the notes aren't there," Jordan replied, "I'm a lawyer and I'm a loyal friend, but I'm not a fool," and "the notion that I said to her 'go home and destroy notes' is ridiculous."

Diary, Deposition of Vernon Jordan, February 2, 1999

During the break, I left to use the restroom. While washing my hands in the cramped lavatory, Vernon Jordan entered and positioned himself in front of the door. As I tried to leave, I said politely, "Excuse me." He didn't move to the side so that I could leave. He pretended not to hear or see me despite my repeated requests for him to make room for me to leave. He still didn't move, even as I squeezed and wiggled between him and the door.

What an asshole.

• • •

Despite his newfound misgivings, Henry Hyde passed out copies of a letter he sent to Trent Lott asserting our right to call witnesses.

Now, behind closed doors, he told us that Senators Orrin Hatch (R-UT) and Susan Collins (R-ME) were floating yet another proposal to end the "trial." There was nothing new in that revelation, but Henry left me exasperated (again) when he suggested (again) that it might be time to throw in the towel and go along with their plan:

Henry said, "The senators want out of this. Personally, I don't have any problem with Hatch's or Collins' proposals since we don't have the 67 votes we need in the Senate to convict Clinton. Under their 'adjourn the trial' suggestions, the Senate will hand us our hat. That is better than them giving us the proverbial stick in the eye, which we are about to get if we don't go along. We are up against a stacked deck. We always were. Now we have guys like [Alabama Republican Senator Richard] Shelby calling us to the press 'a corpse.' I expected this from the Democrats, not from the Republicans, and I resent the hell out of it."

Asa Hutchinson said he would prefer live witnesses, but under the circumstances, we should drop our call for live witnesses and try to play the videotaped depositions.

Once again, I advocated my "all or nothing" approach and made a motion that we demand live witnesses. Otherwise, I urged that we announce that we were "unable to proceed" and walk out of their chamber. If the Senate refused to give us a real trial, we should quit this sham proceeding.

Manager Steve Buyer disagreed with me:

> **"Under Susan Collins' plan," Buyer said, "the Senate would adopt 'findings of fact.' Our goal should be the vindication of the House's impeachment vote...." Buyer disagrees with Hatch's plan that the Senate should adopt the findings and then simply adjourn. He thinks we should press for a vote in the Senate on 'findings of fact,' and then let them vote down the articles of impeachment without a trial.**
>
> **Hyde agreed with Buyer, saying he wants the Senate to adopt favorable findings of fact, which he feels will vindicate us. "I don't care what they do on the articles of impeachment," Hyde now said. "Our legitimacy is not in question. We impeached the bastard."**

Charles Canady backed up my position that we needed to demand a trial and force the Senate to reject the demand:

> **"The senators 'acceding' to impeachment or 'recognizing' that the House impeached Clinton is an insult to the House of Representatives," Canady said. "Our goal must be to present a convincing case for conviction. It is bad for the Constitution and bad for the country if the Senate deems Clinton's conduct as consistent with the presidential oath of office."**

Canady's strong appeal accomplished what my own saber rattling could not. Henry Hyde throttled back on the stick. Acknowledging Canady was right, Henry conceded:

"Our first responsibility is to present our case and advocate for 67 votes. If the senators want to go on an excursion, that is their business. If they cut and run, they might be surprised to learn they haven't protected their own asses." However, he disagreed with Canady's statement that getting the Senate to "accede" to the impeachment articles was meaningless. Henry thinks that will go down in the history books as the Senate vindicating Clinton's impeachment.

The House Managers voted. A majority agreed to push for live witnesses only. Then, as if in contradiction to the vote just taken, a different majority of Managers also voted to push for playing the videotapes if the Senate refused our live witness demand.

Lindsey Graham wrapped up the meeting by sharing this insight:

Senator Slade Gorton (R-WA) called Lindsey to tell him there were less than 51 Senate votes to convict Clinton on the perjury article. Gorton, a former state attorney general, called Clinton's perjury in a federal civil rights lawsuit "trivial" and indicated a majority of his colleagues agreed. Gorton said the Democrats have a bigger problem because the House Managers had made their case on the obstruction of justice.

I liked Slade Gorton, but if the president of the United States used his position of power to sexually harass Gorton's daughter and then he lied about it under oath to crush her claim in court—all while his goon squad portrayed her as trash to a laughing world press corps, I wonder how "trivial" Gorton would view Clinton's perjury.

• • •

A few days before taking Blumenthal's deposition, Lindsey Graham called me at home with a personal request:

Diary, Friday, January 29, 1999

Lindsey wants to participate in deposing Blumenthal and to keep his participation a secret until the deposition. He wants me to question Blumenthal regarding Clinton lying about Lewinsky to him. Lindsey then wants to jump in and cover Blumenthal's alleged leaks to the press of damaging background information about others.

Lindsey hates Blumenthal and frequently rips him in committee and in interviews. He said Blumenthal reciprocated by calling reporters both in Washington and in Lindsey's South Carolina district trying to drum up unfavorable stories about him.

I agreed to Lindsey's request for a couple of reasons. First, I liked the element of surprise. I heard that Blumenthal was preparing for my questioning by watching tapes of my examination of committee witnesses and doing practice questions and answers with White House staff. Lindsey's surprise presence may throw Blumenthal off his rehearsed game. Second, Lindsey really wants to do this.

Later that day, I had another offer of assistance from an unexpected source. Dick Morris, Clinton's former political consultant, called me and said he felt responsible for Clinton's presidency, so now he wanted to help me:

Dick Morris said he heard me say something nice about him on TV the other day, so he wanted to call and thank me. He added that when I run for reelection in 2000, he wants to

help. "I don't charge for political advice anymore," he told me. "I can't because of my contractual obligations. So I just help my friends for free. I think of you as a friend."

Morris said he and his wife wanted to give me a nugget about Blumenthal before I question him. With that, he put Elaine on the line. She told me that Blumenthal fears a perjury rap.

"Ask him directly if he ever took the raw notes of Clinton's private investigator, Terry Lenzner, about Lewinsky and Ken Starr's deputies and turned them over to the editor of the New York Daily News." She said she knows for a fact that he did.

• • •

When I took Sidney Blumenthal's deposition, he reiterated his grand jury story of how Clinton portrayed himself (once the story leaked) as a victim. Clinton told Blumenthal that day that he was guilty of nothing more than being a Good Samaritan "ministering" to young Lewinsky—the sex-crazed stalker hounding him.

One surprise came out of Lindsey Graham's additional questioning: when Lindsey asked Blumenthal about participation in any White House efforts to smear people, Blumenthal denied under oath that he ever leaked derogatory information about Lewinsky, and he also denied he ever called her a stalker to any reporter. He claimed to have no idea how the media attributed these slurs to him.

**Notes from Deposition of Sidney Blumenthal,
United States Capitol, February 3, 1999**

During Blumenthal's deposition, Senate proctors John Edwards (D-NC) and Arlen Specter (R-PA) conferred frequently over objections to Lindsey's questions, which often came on the grounds that they lacked specificity.

When Lindsey tried to ask Blumenthal a question

regarding Kathleen Willey, the White House objected. A lengthy off the record debate ensued among Senators Specter, Edwards, Chris Dodd, Pat Leahy; White House attorneys Lanny Breuer and Emmett Flood, and Lindsey and me. Leahy and Dodd argued that even asking about Willey opened the door to all sorts of irrelevancies. I reminded them that Lindsey limited his question to the pattern and practice of White House obstruction. The group of senators then asked everyone to leave the room while they conferred further.

When we returned 15 minutes later, the proctors allowed Lindsey's question. Blumenthal denied any White House wrongdoing. "We never discussed the personal lives of any of these women," he declared.

An unexpected comedic moment occurred later that afternoon, when Senator Chris Dodd (D-CT) and I chatted during a break:

"So," Dodd asked me privately, "what do you think of old Sidney?" I replied that he seemed like a gentleman at the deposition despite his reputation for viciousness.

"Everybody hates him," Dodd chortled, "especially the press!" When I asked why, Dodd replied, "Because he's a prick!" and then he roared with laughter.

"Hey, do you know why Clinton worked so hard to bullshit Sidney on his Monica story?" he asked me. "He had to! Sidney is close to Hillary. Clinton knew he had to sell his story to Sidney so that Sidney could sell it to Hillary!"

Dodd kept laughing as he continued: "Shit! Bill didn't want any more lamps thrown at him that night! He had to get his story straight or he knew Hillary would become the Lorena Bobbitt of the White House!"[1]

---

1   In the event future generations of readers do not recognize the name Lorena Bobbitt or her contribution to pop culture, they can research independently how she exacted revenge on her sleeping, philandering husband.

Our theory that Clinton lied to Blumenthal to use his aide as an obstruction of justice pawn suddenly seemed mild by comparison.

34

"That Will Never Do"

"The notion that Sidney Blumenthal is peripheral in the impeachment trial of Bill Clinton was dispelled Saturday morning, as Representative James Rogan showed the senators a remarkable piece of videotape. The tape showed Blumenthal in a closed-door deposition unsurpassed in demeaning the character of his chief. The president's duplicity had forced his faithful servant to describe Clinton falsely impugning the character of Monica Lewinsky in order to save himself. Democrat senators are too bonded in support of their twice-elected president to look anew at the case against him. Nevertheless, even the restricted videotaped view of witnesses shows that this is far more sinister than an adult participating in adultery and then lying about it."

—COLUMNIST ROBERT NOVAK
THE *CHICAGO SUN-TIMES*, FEBRUARY 8, 1999

Afticer taking Sidney Blumenthal's deposition, Lindsey Graham and I returned to the House Judiciary Committee's conference room to brief our colleagues and join a discussion in progress over (what else?) witness strategy.

**Diary, House Managers Meeting,
Wednesday, February 3, 1999**

**Lindsey reported that Senator Mike DeWine still insists there
are not enough votes in the Senate to get any live witnesses.
"You'll get 40 votes at best," DeWine told him, and that he
urged us to ask for none. Further, DeWine keeps saying that
Lewinsky's deposition "hurt us" and that we should ask to
play only the depositions of Jordan and Blumenthal.**

Lindsey's comments lit a fire under our vacillating chairman.
Henry Hyde returned to a confrontational mood with the Senate,
if only for a moment:

**"We can't compromise ourselves to save the Senate's chest-
nuts," Henry declared. "We have to ask for live witnesses.
They will have to deny us our witnesses."**

**Asa Hutchinson disagreed: "We have to be logical to get
what we want. We need to work with the senators." He said
that based on his intelligence [which was good, considering
his brother Tim was a U.S. Senator], "it is most likely they
will adopt a rule giving us one live witness—Lewinsky, and
then let us play the other two depositions."**

**Bill McCollum argued that we should ask for all three
live witnesses, and if the senators refused, then we should ask
the Senate to let us show excerpts of the videotaped depositions. Sensenbrenner agreed with that idea.**

In combination with others who agreed with them, these
Managers reeled Henry back to the path of less resistance. We few
remaining members of the Defiant Caucus were outvoted. The
majority adopted Asa's idea of asking the senators to give us one
live witness and then seeking their permission to play the remaining

videos. Henry warned that even this minimalist approach might bomb with the senators:

> According to Henry, Senator Jon Kyl (R-AZ) said there is sentiment among his colleagues to prevent us from playing any video excerpts, even in our closing arguments, because the senators created those videos solely for their personal "education."
>
> "That shows you how rotten those fellows are over there," Henry said in disgust.
>
> Henry also reported that a cabal of GOP senators is still trying to fashion a dismissal deal. "Orrin Hatch just faxed to me yet another new plan," he reported. "It would involve adjourning the trial permanently and with the Senate making 'findings' that Clinton failed to uphold the law and gave false and misleading testimony. After that, Hatch suggests the Senate will 'recognize' and 'accede' to the impeachment articles." Henry didn't think it would pass because Hatch only had about six other senators with him on that plan.
>
> "We can't take a position on this," Henry said quietly, "but my heart would not break if this passed. It would validate us."

Once again, I felt compelled to disagree with my beloved chairman. I took a position on Hatch's plan in raw language. Sounding like an annoying broken record, I again urged that our job was to show the Senate why the House of Representatives, with five Democrat House members joining, impeached the president. If they didn't want to hear the evidence, let history record their dereliction as we're walking out the door.

• • •

Senator Orrin Hatch's unending cut-and-run strategies were, by now, old news. Asa Hutchinson's information was not. He felt Blumenthal perjured himself in his deposition, and he said that he might be able to prove it.

Asking to meet with Lindsey and me privately that night, Asa told us about one of his Arkansas connections, Michael Mushaw, who told Asa he had a series of lunches with Arkansas political columnist and Clinton apologist Gene Lyons. At these luncheons, Lyons allegedly boasted to Mushaw and others that Lyons' close friend Blumenthal often passed along negative information about Monica Lewinsky and other Clinton "troublemakers."

The next morning, Henry Hyde summoned Asa, Lindsey, and me to his office to discuss this new Blumenthal revelation:

**Diary, Meeting with Chairman Henry Hyde,
Thursday, February 4, 1999**

We discussed how (and whether) to track a possible perjury investigation against Blumenthal for denying he ever passed along negative information concerning Lewinsky. Henry doesn't want House investigators pursuing it. "It was a Senate deposition, so Senate investigators should be the ones to investigate it," he said. He wants Lindsey Graham and me to explore this issue further with Senator Arlen Specter (R-PA), who presided over yesterday's deposition. He said Specter already knows there may be information forthcoming to show Blumenthal lied.

Henry then shared a new surprise: he said an "unnamed senator" was told by a reliable source at the Department of Defense that every telephone conversation of President Clinton's was tape-recorded by the White House Communications Agency—including his calls to Vernon Jordan, Sidney

Blumenthal, and his 55 calls to Monica Lewinsky. He said that when Ken Starr subpoenaed all tapes from the White House, their attorneys responded that the White House did not possess any. Starr now has learned that the White House "parsed" the subpoena because the Department of Defense, not the White House, technically "possessed" them. Starr is now trying to get them from DOD.

"Ken Starr is going to indict the shit out of the people who played games with him on the subpoena," Henry stated. "This revelation is too late to help us in our trial, but if this is true, it could be dynamite. Starr doesn't want to give these to us when he gets them. He wants to save them for his grand jury."

While in this meeting, Henry's secretary passed me a note. Senator Arlen Specter (R-PA) called the committee office and asked to meet with me right away. Lindsey Graham and I walked across the Capitol to discuss these developments with him:

**Notes, Meeting with Senator Arlen Specter,
Senate Dining Room, 12:30 p.m.,
Thursday, February 4, 1999**

We found Senator Specter eating alone at a corner table in the Senate Dining Room. After his recent heart bypass surgery, the lunch platter before him surprised me: a high fat helping of fried eggs, bacon, and fritters. While he ate, we briefed him on Asa's lead regarding Gene Lyons.

Acting secretive, Specter told us to follow him to his private Capitol hideaway office. There he placed a call to Lyons directly and asked him if Blumenthal ever provided him with such information. Lyons denied it.

After leaving Specter, Lindsey and I tracked down Mushaw's number in England and called him. He contradicted

Lyons' denial and confirmed Asa's earlier information.

This sudden Blumenthal revelation so engrossed me that I forgot my obligation to present the argument before the Senate asking them to play Blumenthal's deposition. A staffer grabbed me and said my turn was only minutes away. Running onto the Senate floor, I got there just in time for Chief Justice Rehnquist to recognize me to make the case.

While the senators held a roll call vote on whether to play the three videotaped depositions, Henry Hyde called a team huddle:

Diary, House Managers Meeting,
U.S. Senate Marble Room, Thursday, February 4, 1999

Henry spoke with Senate Majority Whip Don Nickles (R-OK), who again reiterated the votes "aren't there" for live witnesses. Majority Leader Trent Lott told Henry that the Senate wants to play the deposition excerpts on Saturday, and then hear closing arguments on Monday.

Henry said he expected the Senate to give us three hours on Saturday to present our case with the videotapes. He told Asa and me to take the first two and a half hours: "Use everything you can from Paula Jones to today. Help these senators get over their allergy to the facts." He then said we should reserve the last half hour for Ed Bryant and Lindsey Graham to make the rebuttal argument. "These are the guys to throw into the fray," he said. "They can do the best job."

As for Monday's closing arguments, Chris Cannon urged Henry to scuttle the idea of having 13 different Managers make 13 different speeches: "Let's limit the closing arguments to the few Managers who know how to do it," Chris urged.

Henry smiled and replied, "You're a team player, Chris. Senator Nickles also thinks it's a mistake to let all 13 Man-

agers speak. I don't care what he thinks. I want each Manager to be a part of this final effort."

When we returned to the Senate floor, the roll call on depositions was still in progress. Sitting at his desk behind me was Senator Evan Bayh (D-IN), just sworn in as a new senator a month earlier. His father, Birch Bayh, once occupied that same desk for 18 years (from 1963 to 1981).[1]

I walked over to Evan Bayh's desk and slipped him an envelope. I smiled and told him, "I took these pictures almost 25 years ago. I thought you might like to have them." Bayh thanked me and opened the envelope as I walked away.

I had given Bayh two photographs of his late mother, Marvella Bayh, which I took when I was a teenager. At the time, his father was preparing for a presidential run and Mrs. Bayh made a campaign swing through San Francisco on his behalf. Sadly, she died of cancer at age 46 shortly thereafter.

A few minutes later, Evan walked over to the Managers' table and gripped my hand. "Jim, I appreciate this," he said with emotion in his voice. "You know, we lost her 20 years ago this year. She and I were very, very close." His voice drifted off, and he returned to his desk.

---

1   Coincidentally, after I left Congress and became a partner at Venable Baetjer Howard & Civiletti, I recruited former Senator Birch Bayh to our law firm. He and I became very dear friends, and our habit of spending too much time telling political war stories and not enough time billing clients became such a problem that the firm management wanted to separate us from our adjoining offices. A wonderful gentleman in every sense of the word, Birch died at age 91 on March 14, 2019.

• • •

Although agreeing to allow us to play excerpts of the three videos, the Senate refused, by a lopsided 70 to 30 majority, to allow the testimony of any live witnesses. Despite the Senate holding a Republican majority, they also refused to pass a resolution "requesting" that Clinton appear and testify voluntarily.

During one of the roll call votes, a man in the spectator's gallery stood and shrieked, "For God's sake, get on with the impeachment vote!" As security guards hustled him out of the chamber, I leaned toward White House Counsel Charles Ruff and quipped, "Hey Chuck—I see you make your law clerks sit in the galleries!" That drew a rare smile from him.

• • •

As the phony trial neared its conclusion, and at the end of another long session, Majority Leader Trent Lott rose to make his customary end-of-day motion to adjourn. This ritual was our nightly signal to grab our stuff, rush back to our offices, and prepare for the next day's ordeal. Once Lott began making his motion, the other managers scooped up their files and hurried from the Senate chamber. I remained behind because I was busy making notes. As I was both distracted while writing and thinking we had finished for the day, I wasn't paying attention when the White House lawyers sprang a trap. Once my team fled on Lott's cue, Clinton lawyer David Kendall sent a written motion to the desk demanding that the Senate order the managers to give the White House, by tomorrow morning, every quotation from every witness that we intended to use in our upcoming closing arguments. We had no advance notice of this motion, and Clinton's lawyers apparently timed it for when they expected our absence. It happened so fast that Kendall's brief comment to the Senate was over by the time I came out of my stupor and realized skullduggery was afoot.

Just as Kendall's sleight-of-hand drew my attention, our Judiciary Committee's chief counsel, Tom Mooney, burst through the Senate doors and threw himself into the chair next to me. "You need to get up and respond to this motion!" he barked.

"Motion? I don't even know what the hell the motion is, Tom. I just caught the last few words of it. It sounded like Kendall just asked for something crazy, like maybe copies of our closing arguments in advance. Was that it?"

Clarification was not an afforded luxury. Before Tom could answer, Chief Justice Rehnquist called upon me to offer the managers' reply. Tom grabbed my shoulders and heaved me out of the chair, pushing me toward the lectern while sputtering, "No time to explain. Besides, you're a politician. Since when do you need to know what's in a bill to make a speech about it?"

I approached the lectern hesitatingly, still unsure of what had just happened or what Kendall had just demanded. I glanced up at the robotic camera mounted above the chamber's entrance as it swung into place and pointed at me directly, which was a glum reminder that my upcoming response would be beamed to a live worldwide television audience of untold millions.

Oh, well.

"Mr. Chief Justice, distinguished counsel for the president, and members of the Senate," I began, drawing out each word slowly to buy a few extra seconds to formulate something to say. I told the Senate that Mr. Kendall's motion (whatever it was) was unprecedented—unheard of in any trial except for one known instance. It happened many years earlier, when an experienced defense attorney demanded an advance copy of a rookie deputy district attorney's closing argument in a Los Angeles County criminal trial. Because she was a new lawyer, the deputy DA assumed the request was fair and so she raised no objection. The trial judge, future California Supreme Court Justice Otto Kaus, called the lawyers to the bench. Tired of watching the experienced defense attorney take repeated advantage of a greenhorn, Judge Kaus told the prosecutor, "Young lady, when opposing counsel demands to know in advance what is in your closing argument, I believe the appropriate legal response is to tell him, 'It's none of your damned business.'"

With that, and in deathly stillness, I returned to my seat.

"Can you say that on the Senate floor?" asked Tom, his forehead now beaded with perspiration.

"We're about to find out."

Apparently, the answer to Tom's question was "yes." After a heart-thumping few moments of tomblike silence, the guffaws of Senators Strom Thurmond (R-SC) and Robert Byrd (D-WV) broke the tension.

And Kendall's motion, whatever it was, failed.

• • •

Even though the senators did everything they could to scuttle the impeachment trial from under us, on the first day of trial they announced with fanfare that they had voted to give us permission to use their *Senators Only* restroom adjacent to the chamber. Such munificence.

The day after the Kendall motion, I took advantage of their largesse during a recess. While washing my hands at the sink, Chief Justice Rehnquist (also permitted the use of this sanctum sanctorum) sidled next to me at the adjoining basin. We greeted each other as he soaped up.

I learned at the start of this sham trial that generally accepted court rules are in flux during Senate impeachment proceedings. In essence, there are formal rules—until the senators decide to break them, and then the rules vanish. Still, a sacrosanct rule in any trial is the prohibition of *ex parte* communications, meaning that the judge and a lawyer involved in the case shall have no private discussions unless all parties are present or until the case concludes. Rehnquist broke that rule with me as we washed our hands alongside each other. However, given the Senate's continued disregard of their own rules and their fixation on rigging the trial in Clinton's favor, who was I to correct him?

"Mr. Manager Rogan," he said, "were your ears burning last night? I was talking to my dinner companions about how you handled Mr. Kendall's motion yesterday. I told my friends that you appeared to have no notice of it."

"I thought that was obvious, Mr. Chief Justice."

"And yet, without any notice, you pulled out of the hat a quotation right on point that came from an obscure judge in an obscure trial. I told my friends that it was amazing, and that you must be a walking *Bartlett's Quotations* or something. I really was quite impressed."

He was still rinsing his hands. I had already dried mine and now held open the door to leave while he finished his story. With his compliment concluded, I smiled and nodded my thanks. Stepping outside the bathroom, I replied, "Well, of course, Mr. Chief Justice, you presume that was a *real quotation*."

As the chief justice's mouth went slack and his eyebrows arched, I let go of the door. It swung closed in front of me.

A couple of minutes later, I stood outside the Senate chamber with House Manager Asa Hutchinson. I was reading a document inside the three-ring binder I held when Asa nudged me. "Come on Jim," he said, "there's the chief. He's ready to get started." Rehnquist stood near us while putting on his robe, which was our signal to take our seats.

When I saw the chief, I couldn't resist compounding the prank. I flung open the binder dramatically and pretended to practice for Asa an upcoming impeachment speech. In a stentorian voice loud enough to catch the chief's attention, I intoned with mock solemnity, "And, as Abraham Lincoln once said—"

I looked over at the chief (now staring at me with a look betraying deep suspicion). I winked at him, closed the binder, and walked into the chamber.

Asa took a seat next to me at the House managers' table. "What's with the Lincoln quote?" he asked.

"Nothing," I replied. "I'm just driving a nice guy crazy."

• • •

The end was near.

Diary, Friday, February 5, 1999

The Capitol is quiet today I spent hours holed up in my office drafting my remarks for tomorrow, when Asa Hutchinson and I will deliver what Henry Hyde called the House Managers' "de facto closing argument" before the Senate. The technical closing argument will come in a few days when Henry plans to have all 13 Managers give brief summations.

This morning I went to the House Judiciary Committee's conference room. Asa was there already watching videotapes. Lindsey Graham joined us later. Asa is nervous. He has over 60 video segments of Jordan and Lewinsky he wants to play, and he said doesn't know where to pare it down.

We agreed that I would open our presentation with a half-hour Monica Lewinsky "teaser." Our committee press secretary, Paul McNulty, thinks all the television networks will carry this presentation live since it will be the first time America gets a chance to hear Lewinsky tell her story. I will then present a factual overview from the Paula Jones trial to the day Lewinsky appeared on the Jones witness list. Asa will then take over and present the case for Clinton's obstruction of justice. When he finishes, I will close with the evidence of Clinton's perjury.

Asa and I both feel horribly ill prepared. The Senate just gave us the unedited video tapes today. We must synthesize the case into a three-hour video and speech evidentiary pre-

sentation, and it must be ready by tomorrow morning. Asa, Lindsey, our entire committee staff, and I are seething over the senators once again stacking the deck and denying us the proper time to make a decent presentation.

Meanwhile, Lindsey remained focused on the potential Blumenthal perjury issue. Aside from Asa's earlier lead, Lindsey learned that journalist and author Christopher Hitchens went public and described a lunch with Blumenthal last March. In an affidavit executed under penalty of perjury, Hitchens swore that, "Mr. Blumenthal stated that Monica Lewinsky had been a 'stalker' and that the president was 'the victim' of a predatory and unstable sexually demanding young woman. Referring to Ms. Lewinsky, Mr. Blumenthal used the word 'stalker' several times. I have personal knowledge that Mr. Blumenthal recounted to other people in the journalistic community the same story about Monica Lewinsky that he told to me."

As CNN reported later that day:

Hitchens also suggests Blumenthal may have been involved in a campaign to discredit the allegations of Kathleen Willey, the White House volunteer who claims President Bill Clinton made unwanted sexual advances toward her. During his deposition, Blumenthal was asked whether there had been strategy sessions regarding Willey in the wake of her *60 Minutes* interview in which she alleged unwelcome sexual advances by the president. Rep. Lindsey Graham asked, "Did anyone ever discuss the fact that Ms. Willey may have had a checkered past?"

"No. Absolutely not. We never discussed the personal lives of any woman in those meetings," Blumenthal responded.

Capitol Hill sources told CNN that Hitchens contacted House Judiciary Committee investigators through his lawyer after seeing media accounts about Blumenthal's deposition.

Diary, Saturday, February 6, 1999

Yesterday, I worked at the Capitol all day and night drafting my presentation. By mid-afternoon, I reconnected with Asa Hutchinson and Lindsey Graham to compare notes.

After that meeting, I stayed in my office until 5:00 a.m. working on my speech. This morning I drove home for a 90-minute nap and a quick shower, and then I returned to the Capitol to make the final edits. I finished the draft only moments before leaving for the Senate chamber.

Notes from U.S. Senate Floor, Saturday, February 6, 1999

What I really needed this morning was some sleep, and not a major presentation before the Senate. I got to their chamber at 9:45 a.m. and joined the other House Managers for a meeting in the Marble Room. In preparing my address for today, I had no time during the night to make any meaningful study of the deposition videotapes. I only had time to read the transcripts, mark the areas I wanted to use, and have our staff flag the relevant sound bites. I'm hoping it will all match up when I speak, but there was no time to check it.

Our press secretary warned me that all the news networks planned to carry my speech live since it was the first time the public could see and hear Monica Lewinsky. However, given the emotions in the chamber over Scott Bates' shocking death last night, I felt it would be unseemly to launch into an immediate attack against Clinton. [A few hours earlier, a car struck and killed Bates, the Senate's longtime reading clerk.] When I began, I spoke slowly and quietly and tried to be understated. Instead, I decided to let the video snippets do the talking for me.

I did the initial half hour introduction and then yielded the floor to Asa to lay out the obstruction of justice case. Behind the scenes, Asa looked frantic—until he began. Then the cool prosecutor in him appeared. He had too much material and had to make cuts as he went along. As he neared the end, he wanted more time, but I couldn't yield it to him. I still had to present the case for Clinton's perjury.

When Asa finished, I reclaimed the floor and argued the perjury evidence, jettisoning heavily from my prepared text as I went along. When I reached the final ten minutes of my time, I tossed out everything remaining and cut directly to the video of Dr. Barbara Battalino's testimony before the House Judiciary Committee. The Clinton Administration prosecuted and jailed Dr. Battalino (after having her disbarred as an attorney and having her medical license revoked) because she had a consensual sexual relationship and then lied about it in a civil case. The video of my questioning her in our committee hearing deconstructed the long-held Clinton defense strategy of repeating the mantra that "nobody gets punished for lying about sex in a civil case."

As the tape played, I could tell most Democrats in the chamber had never seen it before—and they looked very uncomfortable watching it now. It won't win us a conviction, but it shows (again) the disproportionate criminal treatment suffered by anyone not named William Jefferson Clinton.

When I concluded, Henry wanted to meet and discuss final argument assignments for Monday. Assembling all the Managers, he said he wants all 13 Managers participating in closing argument. I think he feels guilty that a handful of Managers carried the bulk of the impeachment. Yet, as he talked about having so many speeches made, he started having second thoughts.

When he asked my opinion a few days ago, I told Henry

having 13 different speeches in ten-to-15-minute chunks was a lame idea. Now I reversed course: "The fix is already in with these senators," I said. "Nothing we say will change it. You should let each Manager tell America why they participated in Clinton's impeachment." Henry agreed and added that the final four closers would be Asa, Lindsey, himself and me.

Senator Rick Santorum (R-PA) interrupted our meeting. When he said he wanted to give us "advice," some of us started grumbling. We all liked Rick, but he was there to do Trent Lott's bidding.

"You guys did a great job playing those videos," Santorum gushed at Asa and me. "For the first time, our Republican senators are listening to the facts and thinking that having witnesses is valuable."

I interrupted Santorum: "Rick, if your colleagues now find the videotapes so enlightening and valuable, why don't you go back and tell them there's much more where that came from. Go back and make a motion to open this up to live witnesses and to have a real trial."

Suddenly, Rick's demeanor turned dour: "Oh, that will *never* do," he replied.

I had heard enough. "If you won't make that motion," I snapped at him, "then get the fuck out of here."

Some Managers laughed and jeered at Rick, who grew quite flustered. "I was just trying to be helpful," he said. "If you don't want my advice, then I'll leave." Henry tried to assuage Rick's feelings as other Managers continued heckling him. Rick bore the brunt of our frustration over the Senate's Republican-led sellout of our case.

There was one bright moment in an otherwise unpleasant day for me, or at least I thought so at the time:

Before I left the Senate floor tonight, Senator Phil Gramm (R-TX) approached me with his hand outstretched. "I don't know if you'll get beat for reelection in 2000, but if you do, it won't be for a lack of bullets in your gun." Gramm pledged that he would do a fundraiser for me in Dallas with his own donors and raise money for me.

Over the next couple of days, Gramm repeated the offer boldly in front of both his GOP Senate colleagues and in front of my fellow managers. A few months after the impeachment "trial" ended and the Clinton Machine targeted me for defeat in what became the most expensive political assault against a congressman in history, I left many telephone messages for Phil Gramm asking for the help he promised so publicly.

I'm still waiting for him to return my phone calls.

35

We Happy Few

"If you care to read the articles of impeachment, you won't find any complaints about President Clinton's private sexual misconduct. You will find charges of perjury and obstruction of justice, which are public acts and federal crimes. If you agree that perjury and obstruction of justice have been committed, and yet you vote down the conviction, you . . . have reduced lying under oath to a breach of etiquette, but only if you are the president."

—HOUSE JUDICIARY COMMITTEE CHAIRMAN HENRY HYDE,
CLOSING ARGUMENT TO THE SENATE, FEBRUARY 8, 1999

After 14 bloody months of political thermonuclear warfare, our finale would be the closing arguments. Here was my opportunity to summarize—for future generations—my reasons for embarking down this road. It also was my best chance to explain the importance of protecting the rule of law to my pro-Clinton, Hollywood-based, and now deeply embittered constituency. Despite their current fury over my participation, I hoped that my speech might convince some of them that having a congressman who put defending the rule of law ahead of political survival might not be such a terrible thing.

Considering this promised to be the single biggest speech of my entire life, and knowing that my great-grandchildren might one day watch it on some modern version of *The History Channel*, my nonchalance on the eve of the great event remains a mystery to me:

Diary, Sunday, February 7, 1999

Tomorrow are the closing arguments in Clinton's impeachment "trial." Early this morning I left all my notes, books, and review materials at my congressional office. As for tomorrow, I think I will just extemporize. I'm too burned out on this subject to come up with anything original. Instead of prepping all day, I drove home and spent the entire day with Christine and our girls.

• • •

The next morning, as the House Managers gathered, an animated Lindsey Graham urged Henry Hyde to ask the Senate to reopen Clinton's obstruction of justice evidence and continue the Blumenthal investigation. Henry Hyde listened to the request politely, and then he brushed off the suggestion.

**Diary, House Managers Meeting, Monday,
February 8, 1999—Closing Argument Day**

"Under the Senate Rules, we'd need [Democrat Minority Leader Tom] Daschle's OK to reopen," Henry said. "Without it, we'd get slapped down by the Chief Justice."

I suggested asking a liberal Republican like Arlen Specter to make a motion to suspend the rules. Henry just shook his head, saying, "Arlen Specter is really good in the windup, but he often forgets to throw the ball."

As an alternative, Henry proposed sending a joint letter to Trent Lott and Tom Daschle asking them to reopen the evidence. "Put it in their laps," Henry said.

As far as I know, Henry never sent such a letter.

Henry gave us the final lineup for our closing arguments. He doesn't know if the Senate will hold their deliberations in public. "If they open their debate, we will need to remain in their chamber," he said. "Let's hope they close it." He expects the Senate's roll call vote on whether to remove Clinton from office to occur on Friday. "We will all need to be present for that," he said gloomily. "We are going to lose. When this is over, the press will be all over us. After the Senate votes, I think we should just stand up and leave."

A staffer interrupted and said it was time to begin. As we all stood, Henry had one final instruction for his Managers: "Go unburden yourselves on the Senate."

Notes from the U.S. Senate Floor During the
Clinton Impeachment Trial, Monday, February 8, 1999

Lindsey Graham is still trying to collect more Blumenthal affidavits, holding out hope that it will buy us a delay in the Senate. He is wrong. No delays are forthcoming no matter what he finds. News stories now are leaking about Clinton raping a nurse (Juanita Broaddrick) in 1978. There are more allegations of perjury from his witnesses, etc. All are brushed aside. The Senate wants the "trial" over. They want Clinton acquitted no matter what additional evidence surfaces, and they want us gone.

Chief Justice Rehnquist gaveled the session to order, and then he recognized one of our senior House Managers, Jim Sensenbrenner, to make the first closing statement. By prearranged schedule, six Managers would do their closing arguments; when they finished, the White House would argue for three hours, after which we remaining Managers would close the case.

I still had no speech prepared. I planned to extemporize my closing argument. A few of our committee staffers approached me in the Marble Room while Sensenbrenner spoke. "We are so glad you are speaking near the end of the lineup," one of them told me. "Chairman Hyde said earlier he is really counting on you."

For the second time during impeachment, I showed up planning to wing it only to have "Henry's counting on you" guilt laid at my feet. I didn't believe I could deliver a decent speech now if I wanted to do so. Between fatigue and writer's block, I had nothing left to say. I don't know whether Henry was really counting on me for anything, but I felt obliged to respond as if he were.

I hurried back to my office in the Cannon Building, closed the door behind me, turned off the television, and told my staff not to disturb me. A couple of hours later, I still stared at a blank legal pad. Feeling a surge of panic, I knelt in silent prayer for some guidance. After a few minutes, calmness returned—and a new motivation got my pen moving across the paper. I decided not to tailor my remarks for either the senators (on its face a waste of time) or the massive television audience. Instead, I wrote for great-grandchildren that might be born long after I am dead. If one of them ever wondered why I sacrificed my life's ambition to battle for a lost cause, these words would be my answer from the grave.

I rushed back to the Senate and arrived as Asa Hutchinson gave his fifteen-minute closing argument. This left little time for reflection since the schedule had me following him. I wandered into the Marble Room to catch my breath and steel my nerves. The voice of a commentator coming from a nearby television caught my attention: "These House Managers don't care about Bill Clinton the man," he intoned. "They don't care about what impeachment has done to him or to his wife and daughter."

"You son of a bitch," I snapped at the image on the television screen.

One of our young staffers walked over and turned it off. "That's just one guy talking," he said, trying to console me.

Maybe so, I replied, but he was saying what millions of Americans believed, and that frustrated me deeply. Suddenly, my "answer from the grave" speech no longer appealed to me. Within moments, I had drawn a big black "X" across every page of the first half of my prepared text.

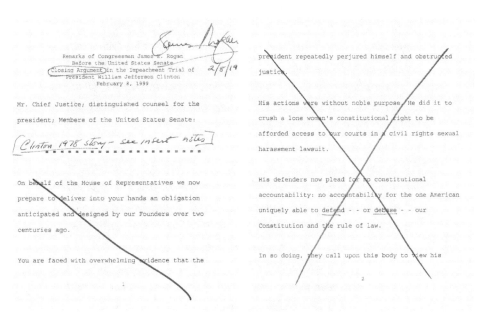

The first two reading copy pages of my intended closing argument in the Clinton impeachment trial, February 8, 1999. A television commentator's overheard claims caused me to "X" out most of my prepared speech moments before its scheduled delivery. (Author's collection)

"Congressman," a guard said, "you're up."

When Asa concluded, Chief Justice Rehnquist recognized me. Carrying my now-obliterated speech, I walked to the podium and extemporized much of my remarks. I now had a focused purpose: addressing the false but pervasive notion that none of us cared about the personal toll of impeachment:

Mr. Chief Justice, distinguished counsel for the president, members of the Senate:

For me, perhaps the most poignant part of this case came on the day former Senator Dale Bumpers addressed us in defense of President Clinton.

The thing that touched me most about his presentation was when he talked about the human element of what this impeachment proceeding has meant. It touched me because it reminded me that appreciation for this difficulty is not limited solely to the Democrats in this chamber. I am a House Manager and a Republican, but that was not always the case. I used to be a Democrat. Being a House Manager in the impeachment of President Clinton has been especially difficult for me, and I would like to tell you why.

Twenty years ago, in December 1978, I was finishing my last semester of college and I had just applied to law schools. I was waiting for my application to be accepted somewhere. That month I was a delegate in Memphis to the Democratic National Midterm Convention. At that time, President Carter was halfway through his term and he was not very popular with the Party faithful. Among the Memphis delegates that year was a great deal of sentiment that a current member of this body should challenge Carter for renomination.

When I spoke those words, I looked to the rear of the chamber at Senator Edward Kennedy (D-MA), who leaned back in his chair smiling and nodding at me. He was perhaps the only person in America who knew where I was going with this story.

The delegates to that convention had an overwhelming desire to see Senator Ted Kennedy run for the presidential nomination. In retribution for his popularity, the Carter White House froze out Senator Kennedy from all the proceedings. He was not invited to address the convention and his name appeared nowhere in the program. To correct this snub, the delegates did something on their own initiative. For their scheduled policy workshop on health care, the delegates invited Senator Kennedy to fly out that day and address them. He came that afternoon and left Memphis as soon as he finished speaking.

I had gone to a workshop earlier that morning where President Carter appeared personally. Only 200 or so people came to hear him. In contrast, Senator Kennedy's workshop had to move to a larger auditorium because over 2,000 people came to hear him.

Kennedy kept nodding his head and continued grinning. His smile grew when I said he outdrew President Carter's audience ten-to-one.

As I said, Senator Kennedy came, he spoke, and then he left. However, I stayed even though most people left when Senator Kennedy did. I stayed because I wanted to meet the young fellow moderating the program. He fascinated me. He was bright, articulate, and in control. He didn't look much older than I, and here he was already the attorney general of his state, and now the governor-elect.

After that workshop, I walked up to the moderator and introduced myself. He spent the next fifteen minutes encouraging me to go to law school and stay active in politics.

His name was Bill Clinton.

I never have forgotten that day twenty years ago when then-Attorney General Clinton took time for a young fellow with an interest in the law and politics. And I have never forgotten in recent years the graciousness he has shown my wife, my children, and me when we have encountered him.

This has been a very difficult proceeding for me and for my colleagues. Our presence here isn't out of personal animosity toward our president. It is because we believe that, after reviewing all the evidence, the president of the United States obstructed justice and committed perjury. He has violated his oath of office; in so doing, he sacrificed the principle that no person is above the law. Personal considerations cannot control under those circumstances.

It was here that I picked up the remainder of my prepared remarks:

Up until now, the idea that no person is above the law has been unquestioned. Yet, this standard is not our inheritance automatically. Each generation of Americans ultimately has to make that choice for themselves. Once again, it is a time for choosing. How will we respond? By impeaching the president, the House of Representatives made that choice. It went on record as saying that our body would not tolerate the most powerful man in the world trampling the constitutional rights of a lone woman, no matter how obscure or humble she might be.

We refused to ignore presidential misconduct despite its minimization by spin-doctors, pundits, and, yes, even the polls. The personal popularity of any president pales when weighed against the fundamental concept that forever distinguishes us from every nation on the planet: No person is above the law.

The House of Representatives jettisoned the spin and the propaganda. We sought, and we have now presented, the unvarnished truth. Now it is your unhappy task to make the final determination: face the truth and polish the Constitution, or allow this presidency, in the words of Chairman Henry Hyde, to take one more chip out of the marble.

The Constitution solemnly required President Clinton, as a condition of his becoming president, to take care that the laws be faithfully executed, and to swear an oath to preserve, protect, and defend the Constitution. That oath of obligation required the president to defend our laws that protect women in the workplace, just as it also required him to protect the legal system from perjury, abuse of power, and obstruction of justice. Fidelity to the presidential oath is not dependent upon any president's personal threshold of comfort or embarrassment. Neither must it be a slave to the latest poll.

How important was this oath to our Founders? Did they intend the oath to have primacy over the shifting winds of political opinion, or did they bequeath to us an ambiguous Constitution that was meant to roll with the punches of the latest polling data and focus groups? The Constitution gives us that answer in Article II, Section 1. It says, "Before he enters on the execution of his office, he shall take . . . [an] oath." The oath is then prescribed.

The fact that a person is elected president does not give him the right to become president, no matter how overwhelming his vote margin. Votes alone do not make a person president of the United States. There is a requirement that precedes obtaining the power and authority of the presidency. It is the oath of office. It is swearing to preserve, protect, and defend the Constitution. It is accepting the obligation that the laws are to be faithfully executed.

No oath, no presidency.

It is the oath of office, and not public opinion polls, which gives life and legitimacy to a presidency. This is true no matter how popular an elected president may be, or how broad his margin of victory. The Founders did not intend the oath to be an afterthought or a technicality. They viewed it as an absolute requirement before the highest office in the land was entrusted to any person.

The evidence shows the president repeatedly violated his oath of office. Now the focus shifts to your oath of office. The president hopes that in this chamber the polls will govern. On behalf of the House of Representatives, we entreat you to require that the Constitution reign supreme. For if polls matter more than the oath to uphold the law, then yet another chip out of the marble has been struck....

The evidence shows clearly that the president engaged in a repeated and lengthy pattern of felonious conduct—conduct for which ordinary citizens can—and have—lost their liberty. This simply cannot be wished or censured away. With his conduct aggravated by a motivation of personal and monetary advantage in the Paula Jones lawsuit, the solemnity of our sacred oath obliges us to do what the president regretfully has failed to do: defend the rule of law, and defend the concept that no person is above the law.

On the day the House impeached President Clinton, I said that when they are old enough to appreciate the solemnity of that action, I wanted my little girls to know that when the roll was called, their father served with colleagues who counted it a privilege to risk political fortunes in defense of the Constitution. Today, I am more resolute in that opinion.

The last words I ever spoke to the United States Senate in the Clinton impeachment proved (regrettably, at least from my standpoint) prophetic:

From the time I was a little boy, it was my dream to serve one day in the Congress of the United States. My constituents fulfilled that dream for me two years ago. Today, I am a Republican in a district that is heavily Democrat. The pundits keep telling me that my stand on this issue puts my political fortunes in jeopardy. So be it. That revelation produces from me no flinching. There is a simple reason why. I know that in life dreams come and dreams go, but conscience is forever. I can live with the concept of not serving in Congress. I cannot live with the idea of remaining in Congress at the expense of doing what I believe to be right. I was about 12 years old when a distinguished member of this body, the late Senator Ralph Yarborough of Texas, gave me this sage advice about elective office: "Always put principle above politics; put honor above incumbency." I now return that sentiment to the body from which it came. Hold fast to it, senators, and in doing so, you will be faithful both to our Founders and to our heirs.[1]

---

[1] Back in my office that afternoon, I lamented that I didn't deliver the "my answer to history" speech on why I voted to impeach Clinton. My recurring griping became something of a joke to my staff. They started referring to my originally planned speech as the "Lost Closing Argument." Left under wraps all these years, I now reproduce it in the Appendix as I wrote it originally.

**Diary, United States Senate Impeachment
Trial of President Clinton, Monday,
February 8, 1999—Closing Argument Day**

**As I neared the end of my closing argument, I noticed Demo-
crat Senator Robert Byrd focused on me intently as I spoke
about the constitutional issues. I made eye contact with him
several times, and each time he appeared pained. I think he
loathes Clinton for the shame he brought to his office and
to our country. Still, there is no doubt in my mind that Byrd
will vote to acquit. These Democrats all will choose Party
loyalty first in Clinton's sordid attack on the rule of law.**

**When I finished, I took my seat at our counsel table. My
manager colleagues offered whispered kudos, all of which I
appreciated.**

Chairman Henry Hyde concluded the presentation for the
House Managers. He grew emotional as he paid homage to us.
When he spoke these words, many of his Manager colleagues grew
misty-eyed along with him:

> As to the House Managers, I want to tell you and our extraordi-
> nary staff how proud I am of your service. For myself, I cannot
> find the words that adequately express how I feel. I must use
> the inaudible language of the heart. I have gone through it all
> by your side—the media condemnation, the patronizing edito-
> rials, the hate mail, the insults hurled in public, the attempts at
> intimidation, the death threats, and even the disapproval of our
> colleagues—which cuts the worst.

> You know, all a congressman ever gets to take with him when
> he leaves this building is the esteem of his colleagues and his
> constituents and we have risked even that for a principle, for our

duty, as we have seen it.

In speaking to my Managers, of whom I am interminably proud, I borrow the words of Shakespeare's *Henry V* as he addressed his little army of longbowmen before the Battle of Agincourt. He said:

> *We few, we happy few, we band of*
> *brothers*
> *For he that sheds his blood with me*
> *shall be my brother*
> *And gentlemen in England, now*
> *abed, shall think themselves accursed*
> *they were not here*
> *And hold their manhood cheap while*
> *any speaks that fought with us.*

To my House Managers: your great enterprise was not to speak truth to power, but to shout it. Now, let us all take our place in history on the side of honor, and let right be done.

When Henry finished, the Clinton impeachment "trial" ended. The Senate recessed. Tomorrow they will undertake their deliberations in secret.

I appreciated the number of senators on both sides who congratulated me. Paul Wellstone (D-MN) shook my hand and told me I was one of the bravest men he knew. Ironically, senators who treated us as if we carried into their chamber a communicable disease now wanted the Managers to autograph their trial mementos. Even Senate institutions like Strom Thurmond collected our autographs.

Senator Ted Kennedy walked over. Still grinning broadly, he shook my hand and told me what a great job I did. We talked for about ten minutes. He told me that the first time he ever met Bill Clinton was at that Memphis meeting I

had mentioned. While we talked, I pulled a picture from a folder that was taken of Kennedy and me back in 1971 when I was in the eighth grade. He was amazed to see it and took it around the chamber showing it to every senator within arm's reach.

Kennedy led me off the Senate floor and sat with me at a table in the lobby outside the Marble Room. After signing autographs for my daughters, he wrote down his phone number and invited my family to visit him, saying he wanted to show us his family mementos in his office.

• • •

It was time to go.

I followed Henry Hyde and the other Managers into the Marble Room to collect our things. When we entered, our waiting committee staff gave us a thunderous ovation. They made us feel like returning heroes. Everyone knows we will not win, but given the jubilant celebration, a passerby might think this was the winner's circle.

Our task is now complete. The senators will decide President Clinton's fate and they will decide in his favor. That is a foregone conclusion, but it does not matter. We stood for the Constitution. The senators will judge the president; the House Managers leave their chamber content to let time and history judge us.

• • •

In death penalty criminal trials, judges used to give the jury the so-called "Lingering Doubt" instruction, which orders them not to condemn a defendant to death if they have any lingering doubt of guilt. If I ever had any subconscious lingering doubt about Clinton's impeachment, an evening visit to my local ice cream parlor erased it.

Near the end of the Senate "trial," I enjoyed a rare family dinner at home. Later, we walked to our local Baskin Robbins ice cream parlor in Fairlington, located just a few miles from the Pentagon. As my daughters ate their ice cream, I slumped into a chair trying to keep my eyes open while battling complete exhaustion. One of my girls snapped me back to consciousness when she pointed to a man standing at the counter. "Look, Dad," she said. "There's a soldier."

"That's not just a soldier," I told her. "He's what we call a general."

While explaining the significance of his position, I looked back and saw the erect officer studying me. He walked over and interrupted our discussion: "Excuse me, sir, but are you Congressman Rogan?" When I said yes, the general's eyes narrowed and, in an emotionless voice, said, "Sir, you are impeaching my commander in chief."

Given his stern face and the gravity in his tone, I didn't know if he was going to curse or punch me. All I remember is that my respiration increased as I stood and answered him: "Yes I am, general."

Studying me for what seemed like eternity, he spoke these words: "My commander in chief is not fit to lead the men and women of the United States Armed Forces." With that, he handed me his business card: "My name is General [X]," he continued. "If you would like to report this conversation tomorrow morning to the secretary of Defense, I will be honored to resign my commission in the United States [military]." The general saluted me, said goodnight, and walked out the door.

After he left, my wife Christine came over to me. "That conversation looked awfully intense," she said. I related the story to her of what had just occurred. When she asked his name, I tore up his business card and threw it away. I never told Christine or anyone else the identity of the unsmiling warrior who approached me that remarkable night.

And I never will.

36

The Heart of the Founders

"The President, Vice President and all civil Officers of the United States, shall be removed from Office on Impeachment for . . . high Crimes and Misdemeanors."
—UNITED STATES CONSTITUTION, ARTICLE II § 4

"The question is, does this rise to the level of high crimes and misdemeanors? I say yes. There's no question President Clinton gave false testimony under oath more than once."
—DEMOCRAT SENATOR ROBERT C. BYRD, WHO THEN VOTED
FOR CLINTON'S ACQUITTAL ON ALL CHARGES

"To me it is clear that the president lied when he testified before the grand jury. I conclude he lied in the civil deposition."
—DEMOCRAT SENATOR CHARLES SCHUMER, WHO THEN VOTED
FOR CLINTON'S ACQUITTAL ON ALL CHARGES

"Clinton brought shame and dishonor upon the office of the president. The conduct at the heart of the charges is deplorable."
—DEMOCRAT SENATOR DIANNE FEINSTEIN, WHO THEN VOTED
FOR CLINTON'S ACQUITTAL ON ALL CHARGES

*"Simply put, [Clinton's conduct] was disgraceful, and possibly illegal....
For those who love this country, it demands outrage."*
—DEMOCRAT SENATOR HERBERT KOHL, WHO THEN VOTED FOR
CLINTON'S ACQUITTAL ON ALL CHARGES

*"History should, and I suspect will, judge that Clinton dishonored the
highest office in our American democracy."*
—DEMOCRAT SENATOR RICHARD BRYAN, WHO THEN VOTED
FOR CLINTON'S ACQUITTAL ON ALL CHARGES

Eighty-four percent of Americans believe Clinton committed impeachable offenses.
—CBS NEWS POLL, RELEASED THE DAY *AFTER* CLINTON'S
ACQUITTAL.

Seventy-three percent of Americans believe Clinton committed perjury.
—CNN/GALLUP/*USA TODAY* POLL,
RELEASED THE DAY *AFTER* CLINTON'S ACQUITTAL.

I shall refer to the Senate's executive session discussion on the articles of impeachment by using the shorthand word "deliberations," even though by its use I give more respect to their chore than is deserved. To say jurors are "deliberating" on a verdict evokes images of citizen-jurors approaching their task with unbiased and open minds. These senators weren't citizen-jurors; they were poll-driven politicians. Nobody who was there believed the senators gathered to deliberate seriously. They gathered to preen and blather before reaching preordained verdicts.

While the Senate "deliberated," the House Managers suddenly found themselves with something we hadn't experienced in well over a year: spare time. We also returned from the battle to find we had acquired a sort of celebrity status, at least in the short term, among conservatives. This came as a complete and welcome surprise, since all we had heard for over a year was that everyone hated us and that we had destroyed the Republican Party.

Diary, Tuesday, February 9, 1999

The U.S. Senate began their deliberations in the Clinton impeachment behind closed doors. This has been my first real day of rest in a very long time. Colonel Oliver North, a respected conservative champion, called me one of his heroes and insisted that I join him tonight on the inaugural broadcast of his new MSNBC television interview show.

Before Ollie's show aired, I accepted a last-minute invitation to drop by a reception at the Mayflower Hotel, hosted by the Claremont Institute for U.S. Supreme Court Justice Clarence Thomas. Dr. Larry Arnn, president of Claremont and an old friend, brought me into the private reception. Oddly, when I arrived, everyone treated me as if I were a guest of honor. When I met Justice Thomas, he greeted me warmly. "I sure watch you on TV a lot lately," he chuckled. "How's your hate mail running?"

At the banquet, Larry seated me at the head table near Justice Thomas. When emcee Pat Sajak introduced me, the applause grew to cheers, and then the audience rose to its feet. It was overwhelming and unexpected. I accepted their praise on behalf of all 13 House Managers.

Diary, Wednesday, February 10, 1999

This afternoon former U.S. Education Secretary Bill Bennett called me. He wrote a lengthy op-ed for the *Wall Street Journal* that ran today in which he called the Managers heroes. He invited me to a dinner at his home on February 20 with conservative radio talk show pioneer Rush Limbaugh. He wants to gather other conservative icons to thank the House Managers for our service. Regrettably, I can't attend. I have to be home in my district every possible day between now and November 2000 trying to convince my constituents not to throw me out at the next election.

The applause and approbation were all nice, but I had an even more meaningful reality check come my way during the Senate's three days of, ahem, deliberations.

From the first day we arrived in the Senate, there was an unnoticed ritual performed before the start and finish of the sessions. Each morning the Senate Sergeant at Arms, Jim Ziglar, put our nameplates on display at our table. At the end of session, he collected the nameplates in a cardboard box. These nameplates were nothing fancy. Your neighborhood trophy shop would sell them for a few dollars. After our closing arguments, I decided to keep my nameplate as a souvenir. "I might as well get something out of these guys for our effort," I told Asa Hutchinson as I put my nameplate into my briefcase.

The next day, my legislative assistant Myron Jacobson asked me, "Did you take your nameplate from the Senate chamber?"

"Yeah, I took it as a souvenir. Why?"

"They just called. They want it back."

This was the final straw. After treating us horribly for two months, now the senators wanted to begrudge me a cheap nameplate.

Myron interrupted my vulgar reply: "I think you might want to return it," he said. "They need it back because the Smithsonian wants it for their collection."

The Smithsonian. For the first time, the full historical import of our involvement landed like a roundhouse to the jaw. Of course, I always understood intellectually the significance of impeachment, but this Smithsonian revelation was the first time it connected with me emotionally. Suddenly, all the threats and bruising we endured throughout this bloody process didn't seem so bad.

It's a good thing Myron didn't communicate my initial reply to the Senate's request for the nameplate return. As it turned out, diplomacy paid off. At my suggestion, Ziglar made a second set of nameplates and used them the day we all returned to receive the Senate's verdict. Now the Smithsonian could have one trial-used set of nameplates, and each of us would receive the other set. On his own, Jim took the favor an extra step. He had custom framed the original nameplates in shadowboxes matted with pictures of us addressing the Senate and original gallery tickets from the first day of the "trial." On top of that, the Senate later gave us our leather trial chairs complete with an engraved brass plate on the back signifying its historical import.

• • •

The Senate met in closed session for three days. When Henry Hyde received word that the end of their gabfest had arrived, he called us together.

Diary, Last Day of the Clinton Impeachment Trial, Friday, February 12, 1999

Henry Hyde summoned all the House Managers to our Judiciary Committee conference room at 10:15 a.m. He said the senators wanted us to return in an hour. Their deliberations

would be finished by then and the Senate would vote on the articles of impeachment. After the Senate reached their verdict, Henry wanted us to regroup for a final press conference in the House Judiciary Committee room.

"When this is over," Henry pleaded, "have a tone of conciliation. Don't show any anger. Let's keep our chins up high."

Paul McNulty, our press spokesman, said our message should be whether the White House wants to pursue "reconciliation or revenge." I interrupted him, joking that, "Since Clinton has already threatened reprisals on me, I find 'revenge' is working great for my fundraising!" The laughter broke the tension.

When we ended our meeting, committee staff and other congressmen came in and deluged us with autograph requests. We sat for over half an hour signing copies of the impeachment committee reports and the Congressional Record for everyone who asked.

$$\bullet \ \bullet \ \bullet$$

Shortly after 11:00 a.m., we made our final procession to the United States Senate Chamber.

As we walked through the Capitol Rotunda, photographers lined our path taking pictures. As I write this, we are assembled in the Senate's Marble Room. Everyone's mood is upbeat, happy, and proud of our effort. We expect the Senate's vote at any time.

Technically, the Senate considers the Marble Room part of their chamber, so their rules forbid any photography inside it. However, given the historic nature of a presidential impeachment and the seemingly fluid nature of Senate "rules," I often snuck in my camera to memorialize these moments by hiding it in my briefcase. Getting it into the Marble Room was easy, but taking pictures in there proved chancy. Whenever I took a picture, the camera flash bounced off a large mirror in the room near the door, and it always caught the attention of the deputy sergeant at arms stationed outside. Each time he saw it, he came in the room looking for the contraband camera. In now divulging this information, I am keeping my fingers crossed that the statute of limitations has passed for my breach.

We're waiting in the Marble Room for the senators to finish their deliberations. Henry Hyde is patiently signing volumes of the Congressional Record and other souvenirs. The Managers continue giving autographs to senators, their staffers, and to each other.

Chuck Ruff, counsel to President Clinton, wheeled himself into our temporary headquarters. He congratulated Henry and me on our efforts, and we shared a few jokes as we talked about the history we had made together.

While we wait, Hyde is still signing autographs, Jim Sensenbrenner is asleep in a chair, and Steve Chabot is reading the newspaper. Bob Barr is sitting near a corner window away from the rest of his colleagues. He looks very dejected.

Around noon, the Senate chamber doors flung open and a rush of senators flooded the lobby. The debate is over; one senator told me there would be a 15-minute break before they reassemble and vote on the articles of impeachment.

Senator Joe Biden (D-DE) came over to me and slapped me on the back. "Joe, it won't be the same starting my mornings without you!" I said. He put his arm around my shoulder and told me, "You guys did a hell of a job. I want you as my lawyer if I am ever in trouble." It was a gracious comment from a guy I enjoyed getting to know.

• • •

Minutes before this final act in the historic drama, I noticed that the door to the President's Room was open. Chief Justice Rehnquist sat at Lincoln's desk in his shirtsleeves and with his sport coat draped over the back of his chair. He was signing various items of impeachment souvenirs for senators, House Managers, and the president's lawyers. I was the last person there, so when he finished autographing my few mementos, I told him that in a few months I intended to call him at the Court and invite him to lunch, and that I knew he would accept.

He replied in a playful tone, "Mr. Manager Rogan, you sound awfully confident. What makes you so sure that I'll accept?"

"Because, first, you're an impeachment scholar. You wrote a book on Andrew Johnson's impeachment, which means that you're dying to know what's been going on behind our closed doors. I'm the guy who can tell you, but I'll only tell you over lunch. And second, I know about your card game on Lincoln's desk. You can buy my silence by accepting my invitation."

On that last point, Jim Ziglar had told me that soon after the start of the trial, Rehnquist asked him for a deck of cards to help fight boredom while he remained stuck in the President's Room during recesses. Jim went to the Senate Gift Shop, bought a deck of cards, and gave it to the chief. A day or so later, Jim entered the President's Room and found Rehnquist and his law clerks playing poker. Cards and piles of dollar bills lay scattered across Mr. Lincoln's desk. Jim straightened up: "Mr. Chief Justice," he said, "this is the United States Capitol. As Senate Sergeant-at-Arms, I am responsible for administering the law here. Gambling is illegal in the Capitol. I'm going to leave now and return in a few minutes. When I return, well, I think you understand." When Jim reentered the room a few minutes later, the money had disappeared and the chief justice, with the expression of a little boy caught filching cookies from the jar, returned the deck (which Jim kept as a souvenir).

I doubt if my "impeachment scholar" bait and my tongue-in-cheek poker blackmail made any difference to my luncheon invitation. Still, as I turned to leave, the chief called my name. I turned and looked back at him.

"Don't forget to call me," he said.

• • •

We awaited the signal to take our seats in the chamber. As expected, spectators packed the galleries overhead.

Senator Evan Bayh (D-IN) came over and thanked me again for giving him the photographs of his late mother the other day. His seatmate, Senator Blanche Lincoln (D-AR), heard me say I had twin daughters. She told me she has infant twin boys. "My girls like younger men," I told her. "Bring them by if they grow to be good providers."

Other senators lined our table congratulating us; this camaraderie continued until Trent Lott asked all of his colleagues to take their places behind their desks. In the doorway stood Chief Justice Rehnquist, wearing his robe and ready to begin. I hurried to the clerk's desk and grabbed two of the Senate's official roll call tally sheets. I used them as a contemporaneous checklist while the senators cast their votes on both articles.

Rehnquist entered the chamber, took his place in the presiding officer's chair, and gaveled the Senate to order as a court of impeachment for the last time.

Trent Lott advised the chief that the Senate had completed its deliberations and was prepared to vote on the articles of impeachment. I looked up and saw the reporters in the press gallery (above the dais) leaning far over the rails straining to get a view of the House Managers directly below them.

As the clerk called the roll, each senator stood at his or her desk to answer "guilty" or "not guilty" on each article. When we had our first Republican defection on Article I alleging perjury—John Chafee (R-RI) voted "not guilty"— Chris Cannon whispered to me, "The yellow bastard."

As the roll continued, nine more Republicans joined Chafee in finding Clinton not guilty of perjury in his Paula Jones deposition: James Jeffords (VT), Olympia Snowe (ME), Susan Collins (ME), Slade Gorton (WA), Arlen Specter (PA), Ted Stevens (AK), Richard Shelby (AL), Fred Thompson (TN), and John Warner (VA).

When I heard Thompson vote not guilty, I blinked in surprise. Was this the same Fred Thompson who warned me a few months earlier about how "dirty" Clinton and his team were, that they "do whatever it takes to win," and that neither Clinton nor his team would tell the truth? Hmmm.

When Fred Thompson unexpectedly voted "not guilty" on the perjury article, Ed Bryant (a fellow Tennessean) looked stunned. "He's a good man," Ed whispered to me, "but this will hurt him back home."

Time proved Ed wrong about the vote hurting Thompson back home. He never returned to face the voters for reelection. When ex-Senator Thompson ran for president in 2008, nobody remembered his "not guilty" vote other than author Ann Coulter, who blistered him for it during his brief White House campaign.

• • •

Arlen Specter's "not guilty" vote provided unintentional comic relief to the House Managers:

After much public handwringing about how "unfair" it was that the Senate won't allow us to call live witnesses to prove our case (never mind he voted for the procedural rule that blocked us from getting the witnesses), Specter announced his verdict. He said the ancient Scottish Common Law allowed the verdict of "not proven," and that was his vote. The Senate parliamentarian advised him that the U.S. Senate does not recognize Scottish law. Under Senate rules, Specter's options are "guilty," "not guilty," and "present."

Today, when the clerk called Specter's name to record his vote on Article I, Specter stood and replied, "Not proven, and therefore not guilty." The chuckling Managers whispered to each other comments such as "What a horse's ass," and "He thinks he can have it both ways."

I suspect this is Specter's calculated attempt to appease both his GOP base ("I did this to protest these senators refusing to give the poor House Managers a real trial to prove their case.") and the majority Democrats in his home state of Pennsylvania ("I voted not guilty on Clinton's impeachment."). I guess Specter thinks this tactic shows political acumen. The House Managers viewed it as both foolishness and cowardice.

From that day forward, the House managers and our staff always referred him as *Arlen Specter (R-Glasgow)*.

Watching the senators cast their respective votes from my seat in the chamber, I saw different dynamics in play:

Some senators (like Barbara Boxer) stood and proclaimed their "not guilty" verdicts boldly and leaving no doubt about their loyalty to Clinton. Others (like Robert Byrd) looked and sounded embarrassed and ashamed when they recorded their vote.

It took 14 months to go from *The Drudge Report's* first revelation about Monica Lewinsky to the Senate's impeachment vote. It took the Senate as many minutes to find Bill Clinton not guilty of perjury.

"On this Article of Impeachment," said Chief Justice Rehnquist, "the Senate adjudges that the respondent, William Jefferson Clinton, president of the United States, is not guilty as charged in the first Article of Impeachment."

When Chief Justice Rehnquist announced the verdict, there was no reaction anywhere in the chamber. Without any fanfare, they moved to the vote on Article II. The clerks called the roll once again. Each senator rose at their desk and proclaimed their vote. By a vote of 50-50, Article II went down to defeat. The Republican senators finding Clinton not guilty of obstruction of justice were John Chafee (R-RI), Susan Collins (R-ME), Jim Jeffords (R-VT), Olympia Snowe (R-ME), and Arlen Specter (R-Scotland).

Both articles required a two-thirds vote to convict. President Clinton won; we lost. Neither came as a surprise—the results were preordained before we ever set foot in the Senate chamber last month.

• • •

Fittingly, the last official words in the Senate's Clinton proceedings came from the man who spoke the least during the long ordeal—our frumpy-looking but intellectually elegant chief justice:

More than a month ago, I first came here to preside over the Senate sitting as the Court of Impeachment. I was a stranger to the great majority of you. I underwent the sort of culture shock that naturally occurs when one moves from the very structured environment of the Supreme Court to what I shall call, for want of a better phrase, the more 'free-form' environment of the Senate. [Laughter.]

Our work as a Court of Impeachment is now done. I leave you with the hope that our several paths may cross again under happier circumstances.

Trent Lott presented Rehnquist with a plaque, "The Golden Gavel Award." Lott explained that the Senate tradition is to present the award to every freshman senator who presides over the chamber for more than 100 hours. "I'm not sure you quite reached 100 hours," Lott told him, "but it is close enough."

Without missing a beat, Rehnquist brought down the house with his reply: "It sure seemed like it."

After a committee of senators escorted the chief justice from the chamber, the sergeant at arms escorted the Managers out the way we first entered over a month ago—down the center aisle. We left the Senate chamber amid the blinding flashes of press cameras and lights. As we neared the Rotunda, scores of tourists and staffers behind the rope lines began to cheer and applaud for us. It was a heart-warming moment.

We returned to the Judiciary Committee room for our final press conference. Henry Hyde read a prepared statement, and then Managers came forward to speak. Ed Bryant and Asa Hutchinson complimented the senators. When Bob Barr and Steve Buyer started blasting the Senate, Henry whispered to me, "Please go up there and fix that."

Biting my tongue, I made this brief comment: "We did our constitutional duty. If nothing else, the American people saw political leaders who stood for conscience and principle and not for the polls." After that, I slipped away before the press conference ended.

Our press office conscripted me to do over a dozen TV news interviews in the Russell Building. When I finished, I felt physically and mentally drained. Walking out of Russell onto the street, the biting cold wind added to my feelings of sheer exhaustion. I may not have felt like a beaten man inside, but anyone seeing my hunched over and shivering figure might have thought otherwise.

As I neared the bottom step, a reporter running to catch up with me called out from the building's entrance: "Congressman Rogan—Just one follow up question, please!" I stopped as he trotted toward me.

"Okay," I said to myself in utter fatigue, "I can answer one final question."

With the Capitol dome floating over his shoulder, and with his pad and pencil ready, the reporter asked the final question I faced during this entire drama:

"Why did you guys impeach the president?"

If not for the earnestness on the reporter's face, I might have thought this a joke in bad taste. Before I could respond with some curt remark, something behind the reporter caught my eye. Outside on Constitution Avenue between the Russell Building and the Capitol stood a young girl and her parents bundled up in winter clothing. She looked about 11 or so. I saw the trio earlier that morning. Now, here they remained, many hours later and braving the terrible weather. The girl's cheeks looked red and chapped under her woolen cap. For the first time, I saw the sign she had been holding all day. It read:

The Hearts of the Founding Fathers Live in the House Managers.

Feeling a sudden lump in my throat, I suppressed the surge of emotion before the newsman saw any sign of it. Pointing to the girl and her placard across the street, I told the reporter, "That's why."

He looked at the girl and her sign, and then he turned back to me: "I don't understand," he said.

Pushing my cold hands back into my pockets, I turned and walked away.

That last reporter on that last day still didn't understand why we impeached the president of the United States. According to all the polls, neither did most of America.

I wrote this book so people like that reporter might comprehend what a young girl holding a sign on a cold Washington afternoon understood many, many years ago.

37

Two Asterisks

"The White House stumbled yesterday in its effort to walk away gracefully from the impeachment drama. The New York Times quoted anonymous advisers to Clinton saying that his appetite had been piqued by his desire to make the Managers who prosecuted the case in the Senate pay for their vote to impeach him."

—*WASHINGTON POST*, FEBRUARY 12, 1999,
THE DAY OF CLINTON'S SENATE ACQUITTAL

"Coming from a majority Democrat district carried by President Clinton, Congressman Jim Rogan will be Target One of the Clinton-Hollywood vengeance machine."

—MORTON KONDRACKE, *ROLL CALL*, FEBRUARY 15, 1999

At the end of the impeachment saga, a friend told me that history would be kind to the House Managers. "I doubt it," I replied. "I know who writes the history books."

Five years after the impeachment drama ended, former President Clinton opened his presidential library in Arkansas. Katharine

Seelye, who covered this 2004 grand opening for the *New York Times*, described the Clinton Library exhibit dealing with impeachment:

> Parts of the [exhibit] text, such as "character assassination," "politics of persecution," and "rumors and accusations," are highlighted in yellow. And it asserts: "The impeachment battle was not about the Constitution or rule of law, but was instead about a quest for power that the president's opponents could not win at the ballot box." Ralph Appelbaum, who designed the exhibits, called Mr. Clinton "our editor in chief, our curator in chief and even our art director at times. This is the way the president wanted to see his legacy defined," he said.

There you have it; Bill Clinton's impeachment resulted from persecution by my fellow fanatics bent on undoing an election. The National Archives let Bill Clinton, at taxpayers' expense, dictate those victimization verses personally and with no mention of minor details like his perjury, subornation of perjury, or obstruction of justice. Clinton isn't the first president to use his library as a temple of self-aggrandizement, but this borders on Orwellian propaganda. So much for "history."

As for the so-called "politics of retribution," try this on for size:

Diary, October 13, 1999

I had lunch with Congressman Chris Cox (R-CA). He told me that he recently visited with his old Harvard classmate, Susan Estrich, a major Democrat Party insider and Michael Dukakis' 1988 presidential campaign manager. Estrich told Cox she spent several days with Clinton in the White House during impeachment. One day she was with him for more than two hours in the Oval Office as he watched the impeachment proceedings, and he was full of profane threats.

He kept saying, "Fuck them—Fuck them! They're all fucking me, so I'm really gonna fuck them." She described him as a very angry and bitter man bent on personal revenge."

For the record, Clinton's language and attitude as related to Professor Estrich didn't shock me. First, as one raised by a long-shoreman grandfather, I can detonate expletives trumping anything in Clinton's vocabulary. Second, some infernos are hard to extinguish, and I'm sure suffering an impeachment is one of them. However, even if Clinton's rant to Estrich during the throes of impeachment is understandable, his ongoing, righteousness-laden denials are not. In 2010, more than a decade after impeachment, Professor Ken Gormley interviewed Clinton three times for his book, *The Death of American Virtue*:

Clinton makes clear, to no surprise of longtime observers of the 42nd president, how aggrieved he continues to feel over the whole episode, unspooling a stream of choice invective about his accusers. In Clinton's telling, the head of the House impeachment team, Henry Hyde, is a "bitter right-winger" and "hypocrite." [Clinton said] "The House Managers were disgraced. They ran a partisan hit job run by a bitter right-winger, Henry Hyde."

Clinton closed his interview series with Gormley by boasting,

"Yeah, I will always have an asterisk after my name, but I hope I'll have two asterisks: one is, 'They impeached him.' The other is 'He stood up to them, and he beat them like an old yard dog.'"

Indeed.

President Clinton denied every impeachable allegation brought against him and orchestrated the attempted destruction of anyone demanding his accountability to the rule of law. After their deck-stacked "trial," the Senate validated his denials by acquitting him of perjury and obstructing justice. But these 100 senators didn't write the last chapter in the Clinton impeachment saga. That came two years later, and it bears Bill Clinton's personal autograph. For those visiting tourists—past and future—to the Clinton Library, let me highlight the postscript missing from his exhibit displays.

On January 19, 2001—his last day as president—in a deal with federal prosecutors to avoid criminal charges, William Jefferson Clinton signed a plea bargain in which he *admitted* giving false testimony in the Paula Jones case. This was the same charge for which I prosecuted him and that most Americans believed his vehement denials throughout the impeachment and "trial." He admitted his lying under oath based on the very same evidence upon which 55 United States Senators voted "not guilty."

Independent Counsel Robert Ray would have filed a federal criminal indictment against Clinton had the outgoing president not signed a plea bargain admitting his crime. According to Professor Gormley, "Ray was prepared to indict Clinton after he left office if he did not agree to admit that he made false statements about Lewinsky under oath and accept disbarment. Ray had to be 'cajoled' by a colleague into signing off on the final deal. President Clinton would never fully grasp how close he came to being indicted," Gormley concluded.

After Clinton signed his criminal plea bargain, the United States Supreme Court suspended him from practicing before their Court. He resigned his Supreme Court law license to avoid the stigma of having our nation's highest Court vote to disbar him, which they were about to do. The United States Supreme Court ordered that Clinton's name "be stricken from the roll of attorneys admitted to the practice of law before this Court." Further:

- Clinton accepted a five-year suspension of his Arkansas law license. This allowed him to avoid the stigma of having the

Arkansas Supreme Court vote to disbar him, which they were about to do;

- Clinton agreed to pay an additional $25,000 fine;

- Clinton admitted he violated his ethical obligations as a lawyer under the Rules of Professional Conduct by giving false testimony;

- Clinton agreed not to seek reimbursement for his legal fees; and

- Clinton admitted that his false testimony violated Judge Wright's discovery order in the Jones case.

Meanwhile, soon after the Clinton Senate "trial" ended, the federal judge before whom Clinton testified in the Paula Jones case found him in contempt of court for lying during his under-oath deposition. Judge Susan Webber Wright castigated Clinton for giving "intentionally false" testimony, saying, "[I]t simply is not acceptable to employ deceptions and falsehoods in an attempt to obstruct the judicial process," and that his conduct "undermined the integrity of the judicial system." She levied a monetary fine on Clinton and ordered him to pay an extra $90,000 in legal expenses resulting from his dishonesty. These fines were in addition to the $850,000 Clinton paid to Paula Jones to settle her lawsuit.

Diary, May 18, 2000

Jon Dudas, deputy chief counsel of the House Judiciary Committee, told me that Independent Counsel Robert Ray will indict Clinton when Clinton leaves office on January 20, 2001. Jon said Ray's office called and said they had a request

for information from Bob Barr's office. They asked if they could defer answering requests for production of information unless the request came from Chairman Hyde's office. When told that Hyde agreed to their request, Ray's representative then asked Jon to have Henry Hyde write to Ray and ask for the same information Barr requested.

When asked why, Ray's representative said, "So we can start educating the public on the reason why Clinton needs to be indicted."

There you have it. Two independent prosecutors appointed by Clinton's own attorney general saw it. The judge before whom Clinton testified saw it. The justices of both the United States Supreme Court and the Arkansas Supreme Court saw it. Even a shivering little girl standing outside the Capitol holding a sign on that last day saw it. Yet not a single Democrat U.S. Senator (nor ten of their Republican buddies) saw it—not one of them.

Why should they see it? To this day, Bill Clinton still doesn't see it *even after he admitted it.*

Had Bill Clinton not committed felonies during his presidency, he wouldn't have that "asterisk" attached to his name that galls him. Neither Kenneth Starr nor the House Managers are to blame for that asterisk.

None of this probably matters. As the years roll by and memories dull, Bill Clinton and his legions of apologists in the mainstream media and their cohorts in academia will all record it the other way around.

That's too bad for anyone who thinks the truth matters.

• • •

Like Bill Clinton, I have a similar asterisk attached to my name.

During the impeachment drama, CBS News anchorman Dan Rather interviewed me. He started not with a question, but a statement, "You and Bill Clinton have something in common: when both of you die, the first sentence of your obituaries will have the word 'impeachment' in it."

"We don't have that in common," I replied quietly. When Rather asked me to explain what I meant, I said, "Because I won't be ashamed of it."

• • •

Two weeks before Clinton signed a plea bargain with federal agents to avoid prosecution and prison, I left the United States Capitol for the last time as a congressman. Clinton and his supporters made good on their threatened vengeance. I had lost my 2000 reelection campaign decisively because of my role in his impeachment. My term of office ended on January 3, 2001.

Bill Clinton said he wanted history to record after his name that "second asterisk," and I'll be the first to give it to him. He did indeed beat me "like an old yard dog." Still, when I walked out of that majestic building on my last day there, I remembered a quote I read as a boy attributed to the 1930s actress Carole Lombard: "When you fight for what you believe in, the end result doesn't matter. You've already won."

By that timeless standard, this beaten old yard dog left Congress a winner.

· APPENDIX 1 ·

Fan Mail

(And Some Others)

IMPEACHMENT VOTE, 1998 –1999

You are an arrogant, offensive asshole. You must be a horrible individual in your personal life. I am ashamed you are my representative. I have no faith in your intelligence nor integrity. You are not a man of honor. Your serious, grave, overblown rants during your presentation had me actually laughing at my television. You are doing a piss-poor job as a congressman, so please resign. You are a damned hypocrite who has put the interests of the right wing above the interests of your nation. God damn you, sir.
—KEITH MEREDITH, PASADENA, CA

You are a joke! That steely-eyed, righteous stare is really funny. You are insane and a dupe. The American people watch pomposity and you define the word. No good will.

—MARYANNE BRUDER, PASADENA, CA

Although you are unworthy of the pleasure, I hope you enjoy your last term in office. After you slither off into obscurity, your remaining legacy will be a stain on American history and a lifelong source of shame for you. Your behavior is reprehensible.

—SCOTT ZENZ, GLENDALE, CA

Dear Non-Representative Rogan: After this is over, you may wish to restructure your career path. Judge to politician to what? Trash collector? If you had ever been approached by a lewd young woman with knee pads and flashing ardent innuendoes, I am certain you would have fainted, just as I am sure you and your wife were virgins when you married.
—MARGERY MACKENZIE, SOUTH PASADENA, CA

Have you had anal intercourse with anyone? Have you had oral intercourse with anyone?
—ROBERT A. SCHULTZ, LAKEVIEW TERRACE, CA

I have never been so strongly angered toward an elected official as I am toward you. Resign your seat in the House, you petty political bastard. You don't seem to understand how democracy works, but you will clearly learn when you are voted out of office in 2000.
—MICHAEL GURNIS, ALTADENA, CA

Dr. Flores and I are most unhappy with your presentation at today's vote to impeach President Clinton. How absurd, how trivial, how trite, how obnoxious, how silly, and frankly how stupid you are? If you haven't guessed it by now we are pissed.
—DR. EARL SHERBURN AND DR. FLORENCIO FLORES,
GLENDALE, CA

We will remember! Please don't respond to this letter. Seeing your name upsets me too much, and it makes me sick.
—SALLY CULLMAN, SOUTH PASADENA, CA

You are a coward and a disgrace to the American people. What a disgrace you have brought to our country, and you have done it with such zeal, one can only wonder how you can be so hateful.
—MRS. JUNE JACOBSON, BURBANK, CA

You will never know how happy I was to hear a man on CNN call you "dead meat on a hook." There are groups willing to donate millions of dollars to be rid of you. The American people never forget threachary [sic]. Benedict Arnold lives on, The Maine lives on, Pearl Harbor lives on, the Rosenbergs live on, and now you will live on in infamy.
— DONALD REGIS, TUJUNGA, CA

I am appalled by your phony rectitude, as if you were some kind of judge or high priest. You put on a phony act to cover your ass. You are a mealy-mouthed hypocrite hiding behind unctuous pronouncements, afraid to come out and say you hate Clinton's filthy guts. You are a lilly-livered phony. I know whereof I speak. I am a disbarred lawyer, but I still work in a large law office doing research. If I hadn't been disbarred, I would be tempted to run against an ass-kissing boy scout like you.
— JOHN C. URSPRUCH, PASADENA, CA

If we were in other countries, we would all right now, all of us together go down to Washington and we would stone Henry Hyde to death! We would stone him to death! [Crowd cheers] Wait! Shut up! Shut up! No, shut up! I'm not finished. We would stone Henry Hyde to death, and we would go to their homes [the House Managers], and we'd kill their wives and their children. We would kill their families.
— ACTOR ALEC BALDWIN, *LATE NIGHT WITH CONAN O'BRIEN*,
NBC, DECEMBER 11, 1998

I retired with over 8,000 hours of combat and combat support flight time. I am thankful I will not have to fly into combat with the nagging thought that my reason for being there was to divert attention away from the deeds of a commander in chief whom I no longer trust. When President Clinton lied under oath, he lost his honor and integrity. When he lied to me, he lost my trust. I applaud your decision and your vote.
— WILLIAM V. WELLS, JR., LT. COLONEL, U.S. AIR FORCE (RET),
PASADENA, CA

Your courage, integrity, conviction and commitment to do what is right, despite unwarranted and unjustified pressure from polls and critics, has been a great lesson to my seven-year-old son. I have pointed out you and your colleagues to my son and have explained to him that doing what is right is not always easy. I told him it requires one to be brave and honest in the face of adversity. You have made these difficult lessons easier for him to understand.

—JOHN J. LIBONATI, RESTON, VA

I think you did especially well in your presentations in the proceedings. You spoke clearly and with strong conviction. Your thoughts were intensely focused, and each word carried its weight. I was very impressed by the substance of your argument, your delivery, and your obvious patriotism. You certainly demonstrated that you are a believer in Edmund Burke's famous words about the necessity of being a leader of one's constituents, not just a follower. You did your duty as you discerned it. I have no doubt that your conscience is clear. What more can be expected of a true representative of the people?

—U.S. SENATOR ROBERT C. BYRD (D-WV)

You performed your duty properly and well. I hope you can come back to see us in Plains.

—FORMER PRESIDENT JIMMY CARTER, PLAINS, GA

POST REELECTION DEFEAT, 2000

Clean your desk out you miserable fucking piece of shit. Go back to the gutter you climbed out of.

—J.R. LOMPROS, SHERMAN, IL

Got beat pretty bad didn't you fucker??? See what happens to lying assholes like yourself?

—MARK JAGER (VIA EMAIL), EARTHLINK SUBSCRIBER

You led the wild charge, and you lost your scalp!! Actually, you lost your ass. [It] could not happen to a more deserving zealot/despot. You can now take your place in the political bone yard. Bon voyage.

—GEORGE FRIEDMAN, VALLEY VILLAGE, CA

You brought your own demise on yourself by your extreme vindictiveness and hate. Go see a psychiatrist.

—TALMON MAGER, SEATTLE, WA

We don't get mad. We do get even when you joined the blowjob police. You fucked up trying to destroy the Clintons!!! Now you can go back to ambulance chasing.

—E. CORTEZ, POMONA, CA

Congratulations! Most people have to wait to get justice in the next world, but you got justice in this world.

—LORNA NEUNEKER, LAGRANGE, IL

I wrote you before protesting your embellished arrogance against President Clinton. Well I said then I hope with sincerity the good people in your district will VOTE YOU OUT. It appears they did thank God. Good riddance to another arrogant Republican!

—DANIEL R. WILLIAMS, AMERICAN TAXPAYER,
CROSS PLAINS, TN

You should have been impeached for your arrogance—but firing you was good enough for me. Adios forever.

—UNSIGNED, PASADENA, CA

Your 15 minutes of impeachment fame cost you your job. GREAT!!!!!! It's what you deserve.

—WALTER ZADAN, WILLIAMSBURG, VA

As a strong supporter of President Clinton, you can only imagine how happy I am that you were defeated!!
—JERRY L. HODSON, ANDERSON, IN

Well the elections are over and perhaps it is time to reflect. What have we learned? Perhaps one lesson is regarding hubris and that heady feeling power can engender. I assume that you now understand that no matter how self-righteous and sanctimonious you felt, you misread the will of the people. I assume the people who chose you to represent them have now pointed out the error and misassumption under which you so foolishly deluded yourself.
—JOEL M. LIEBOWITZ, PH.D., A PSYCHOLOGICAL CORPORATION, LOS ANGELES, CA

A measure of a man's quality is the hatred he attracts in pursuing a just action. It is to your everlasting credit that you could reasonably anticipate the flow of money from Hollywood and the vituperation from the media that would follow inevitably, but that you went ahead and did what had to be done. You performed in the finest tradition of public service.
—PETER AND PAULINE CHAPMAN, WINSTON-SALEM, NC

I admire you so much for your outstanding work in Congress, and for having the backbone to stand up for what is right regardless of the consequences. I am sure your grandparents who raised you are in Heaven looking down and are very proud of the fine man you have become.
—LUCILLE HOGSETT, ALBUQUERQUE, NM

You were the voice of courage. Thank you. You are and have been in my prayers.
—HENRY R. MAHSHIE, TARPON SPRINGS, FL

I admire you as a congressman willing to put his constitutional responsibility before his tenure and livelihood, and as a man not afraid to challenge the most powerful man on the planet when he violated our nation's laws. God bless you and your family. I will tell my children and grandchildren you stand with other great Americans.

—JIM KINNU, FOUNTAIN VALLEY, CA

I know you were Target #1. I read somewhere about the millions of dollars being spent on both sides in your district. Although I did not personally favor impeaching Clinton, I thought that you and Asa Hutchinson were the "class acts" on the Republican side. You are a man of character and ability. I wish you the very best in the years ahead.

—FORMER U.S. SENATOR THOMAS F. EAGLETON (D-MO),
1972 DEMOCRAT VICE PRESIDENTIAL NOMINEE

President Bill Clinton Cross-Examination Outline

The Unfinished Draft of Congressman James E. Rogan, January 1999

AUTHOR'S NOTE:

I started this preliminary draft after Chairman Henry Hyde assigned me the task of cross-examining President Clinton in the Senate impeachment "trial." Once the Senate blocked our ability to have any live witnesses, I knew Clinton would never show up and expose himself to my examination, so I abandoned my preparation and moved on to other responsibilities.

Had there been any reasonable chance President Clinton might appear, these notes would be far more comprehensive and polished. Still, I offer this very incomplete document to give future historians a glimpse into what a confrontation might have looked like between President Clinton and a former gang murder prosecutor determined to make him answer questions directly, and who would not have accepted nonresponsive or evasive dodges. I designed the questions to draw out answers that banged another nail into a political coffin—and I was prepared for it to be either his or mine.

It was not to be. Because the entire United States Senate turned cartwheels to shield President Clinton from constitutional accountability, I never posed any of these questions to him.

Perhaps one day someone else will.

Draft Cross examination of President Bill Clinton – Senate Impeachment Trial January 1999

James Rogan House Manager

Draft #1

Seriousness of Perjury

- Support the obligation of a witness under oath in a judicial proceeding to tell the truth, the whole truth, and nothing but the truth.
- What does "tell the truth" mean to you?
- What does "tell the whole truth" mean to you?
- What does "and nothing but the truth" mean to you?
- Do you have any quarrel with the law that makes perjury a serious crime?
- Do you agree that our judicial system can only succeed if citizens are required to tell the truth in court proceedings.
- What happens to our judicial proceedings if witnesses may lie with impunity for personal or political reasons?
- Do you believe that an alleged victim of sexual harassment is entitled to have the truth, the whole truth, and nothing but the truth from witnesses testimony given under oath?
    - Does the fact that the testimony is in a sexual harassment lawsuit make the obligation of truthful testimony less significant?
    - Does the fact that the testimony is in a federal civil rights case make the obligation of truthful testimony less significant?
- How would you characterize the character of a defendant in a sexual harassment lawsuit who lied under oath to defeat a woman's claim of harassment in the workplace?
- Do you draw a legal distinction between perjury in a civil deposition, and perjury before a grand jury conducting a criminal investigation?
    - Do you have any quarrel with a recent federal appellate court decision which stated:

      [W]e categorically reject any suggestion, implicit or otherwise, that perjury is somehow less serious when made in a civil proceeding. Perjury, regardless of the setting, is a serious offense that results in incalculable harm to the functioning and integrity of the legal system as well as private individuals.

[*United States v. Holland*, 22 F.3d 1040, 1047-48 (11th Circuit 1994), cert. denied, 513 U.S. 1109.]

- Read you a quote from a Supreme Court case on perjury. Tell me if you have any quarrel with its concept:

    False testimony in a formal proceeding is intolerable. We must neither reward nor condone such a flagrant affront to the truth-seeking function of adversary proceedings. . . . In any proceeding, whether judicial or administrative, deliberate falsehoods may affect the dearest concerns of the parties before a tribunal and may put the factfinder and parties to the disadvantage, hindrance, and delay of ultimately extracting the truth. . . . Perjury should be <u>severely</u> sanctioned in appropriate cases. [*ABF Freight System, INC. V. NLRB.* 510 U.S. 317. 323 (1994)]

- As the man who appoints all the federal judicial vacancies in America, would you have any toleration for federal judges or federal judicial nominees who commit acts of sexual harassment in the workplace?

    - Would it surprise you to know that the last three federal judges who were impeached by the House of Representatives, and removed from office by this body, were removed for some form of lying under oath - either in a judicial proceeding or on income tax returns.

    - Do you think impeachment and removal from office for high crimes and misdemeanors is an appropriate constitutional remedy for committing perjury in a sexual harassment lawsuit?

    - How about for pejury in general?

        - [Are you saying you think there are degrees of perjury?]

        - [How do you define degrees of perjury?]

        - Do you draw a distinction between lying to preserve national security, and lying to defeat a lone woman's claim of sexual harassment?

- As the man who appoints all the members of the cabinet, from the secretary of state to the attorney general, would you have any toleration for cabinet members who commit acts of sexual harassment in the workplace?

    - If one of your appointees was accused of committing sexual harassment, would you demand they cooperate completely in the investigation?

    - If they testified under oath and lied, or gave a

federal judge misleading and incomplete answers to
important factual questions, would you fire them?

- Why / why not?

- We've heard from a bevy of your defenders, both in the media
and at our Judiciary Committee hearings, that perjury is
almost never prosecuted. Do you believe that?

  - Would it surprise you to know that just during your
  administration, from 1993 to 1997, your Department of
  Justice has prosecuted, convicted and sentenced almost
  700 people for perjury related offenses?

  - Would it surprise you to know that, as we speak, there
  currently are over 100 people sitting in federal
  prisons alone (not counting the hundreds of state
  prisons) who are imprisoned for their crime of perjury.

  - Do you have any plans for any sort of blanket amnesty
  for federal perjury convicts?

    - What if there perjury consisted of lying about
    sex?

    - What if there perjury consisted of lying about sex
    in a civil, instead of criminal case?

    - What if there perjury consisted of lying about sex
    in a civil case that was later dismissed - - that
    is, dismissed after the perjury occurred?

- Do you have any quarrel with the notion that every citizen
is expected to tell the truth under oath, even if it might
cause them embarrassment?

- Do you have any quarrel with the notion that every citizen
is expected to tell the truth under oath, even if it might
cause them to pay money to the victim for wrongful conduct?

- Do you have any quarrel with the notion that every citizen
is expected to tell the truth under oath, even if it might
cause them to lose their job?

- Do you think that a president of the United States should be
allowed to commit perjury when he is a defendant in a sexual
harassment lawsuit, and then keep his job?

  - [How it differs from other jobs?]

- What legal precedent is set if we turn the courtroom into a
forum where the better liars are rewarded?

- Do you believe, as some of your defenders have claimed, that

any perjury you may have committed in the Jones case is
irrelevant because the case was eventually dismissed?

- Are you aware that, in that context, the legally
relevant question is whether the statement was perjury
when it was made, not whether the case was ultimately
dismissed?

= = = = = = = = = = = = = = = = = = = =

- At the Jones deposition, when you were asked about Monica
Lewinsky, you weren't caught off guard?

  - Knew since early December her name was on the witness
list.

  - Knew ahead of time she had been subpoenaed in the case?

  - You had VJ help her with a job search before your Jones
deposition testimony?

= =

Were you ever physically intimate with Monica Lewinski?
[read prepared statement: GJ, 9:13]

= = = = = = = = = = = = = = = = = = = =

The Prepared Statement: Grand Jury

Read prepared statement at grand jury when asked specific
questions about relationship with ML [gj, 9:25-11:1]

- "When I was alone with Ms. L on certain occasions from early
1996 to 1997.

  - How many?

- Said your contact with ML involved "inappropriate intimate
conduct," but it did not constitute sexual relations as you
understood the term?

- You understood PJ was entitled by law to know if your
contact with her was sexual within the scope of the
definition given you by Judge SWW

- You refused to answer specific questions about what your
contact with ML consisted of;

- You basically read a statement telling the attorneys your
contact did not fit the description, but you refused to
elaborate on what that contact was?

- Were you asking the attorneys just to take you at your word that your contact did not fit the definition?

- Did you have a motive to lie to them when you read your prepared statement?

  - Jones case still active then

  - Could have faced perjury charges from the Jones deposition

  - Could have paid money damages to PJ

  - In fact, after the case was dismissed, you paid her about $800,000 just to settle it and keep her from appealing the dismissal?

- "I regret that what began as a <u>friendship</u> came to include" this undefined conduct

  - ML: first spoke to you on 11/15/95, during govt shutdown

  - First day she spoke to you, you invited her back to the Oval Office area and allowed her to perform a sex act upon you

    - true?

    - how long was this friendship blossoming until physical contact began

    - before you allowed her to perform sex acts on you, how did you manifest your friendship for her.

    - Were you "ministering" to her?

      - [if yes] what does that mean?

      - did you tell the First Lady you were ministering to her?

      - you are aware the First Lady told one of your aides when the story broke 1/21/98 that the charges were untrue, and that you were just "ministering" to her?

Under your interpretation of the definition of sexual relations from the Jones deposition, you never had sexual relations with Monica Lewinski?

- She had them with you?

- You never touched her in an intimate way during this lengthy relationship?

  - talk on telephone the whole time?

  - stand there?

  - at some point did she complain to you about your total inability to touch her?

  - ever tell her you couldn't touch her because some day you might have to answer a technical definition of what constitutes sexual relations?

  - initially never expected to be deposed about all this, did you?

Lewinsky Case: Case Dismissed

- The law in the United States is that we look to <u>when</u> the statement was made, not what happened later to the case.

- If someone commits perjury in a case, and for some reason the case later is dismissed, it doesn't change the perjury.[1]

- What would be the results if the opposite were true.

    - Wouldn't the law then encourage perjury, because if a party was a good enough liar, and their lies could get their case dismissed, they would always be shielded from the consequence of their perjury, even if it later was discovered.

---

[1] See Joseph Gibson memo, pages 6-7, on perjury.

Lewinsky Case: Evidence Irrelevant?

- Lewinsky evidence was not excluded from the Jones case by the judge because it was irrelevant.

- It was excluded for other reasons, like the court finding that allowing exploration of the Lewinski matter might interfere with the grand jury's criminal investigation.

- In fact, the court said the Lewinsky evidence might well be relevant to the trial; the court simply wasn't ruling on that question.

· APPENDIX 3 ·

Original First Draft
Clinton Senate Impeachment
Trial Outline

Prepared by Congressman James E. Rogan

For House Judiciary Committee Chairman

Henry Hyde, January 2, 1999

```
                    Preliminary Order of Proof
                        Impeachment Trial of
                  President William Jefferson Clinton
                     Before the United States Senate

Prepared by Congressman James E. Rogan
First Draft
January 2, 1999
```

The Constitution

- Oath of office ("before he enters...")
  [Judicial notice: Article II Section 1]

- Obligation to take care the laws be faithfully executed
  [Judicial notice: Article II Section 2]

- WJC twice duly elected president and took the required oath
  at the legally designated times. He has served continuously
  in the capacity of president since January 20, 1993 without
  any interruption of service.
  [Judicial notice] [and/or] [Video of oaths]

The Paula Jones Incident

- Relevant dates WJC was governor of Arkansas
  [Stipulation]

- On **5/8** , 1991, then-Governor Clinton was present at the
  Excelsior Hotel in Little Rock, Arkansas, to [attend/speak]
  to _____ .
  [Stipulation]

- On that date, Paula Jones was an employee of the Arkansas
  Industrial Development Corporation
  [Paula Jones] or [Stipulation]

  - In that capacity, she was a state employee; her
    position was subordinate to that of the governor of
    Arkansas.

  - On that date, she was working at a meeting in the
    Excelsior Hotel in Little Rock, Arkansas.

  - As a result of an act she claims Governor Clinton
    committed in her presence that day in his hotel room,
    Mrs. Jones later filed a civil rights sexual harassment
    lawsuit against WJC.

- Question: how far into the Jones case do we want to go?

1

Just establish the bare predicate for the later
violations, or air the facts before the country?

- [If Jones called to testify for any lengthy purpose:
  reasons why she didn't come forward earlier against
  him; how her name got dragged into case; any "dirty
  laundry" issues relating to her possible financial gain
  from filing suit; later settlement, etc.]

The Paula Jones Suit

- Filed in May 1994 / WJC served and responded / Case still
  active until _on Sept 1, 1998_
  [Certified copies of court documents]

- On May 27, 1997, the United States Supreme Court unanimously
  ruled that Paula Jones could pursue her civil rights case
  against WJC [Judicial Notice]

- Language of Sexual Harassment Statute
  [Judicial Notice]

  - include penalty section that highlights relevance to
    "personal gain" allegation in articles of impeachment

Jones Litigation Discovery
[Judge Susan Webber Wright]

- For purposes of pretrial discovery, WJC was required to
  answer under oath routine questions relating to certain
  information about his alleged relationships with other
  subordinate female employees while governor and president.
  [Certified copy of Court's order of December 11, 1997][1]

---

[1]As to "materiality" issue, Judge Wright noted in her order
that

The Court finds, therefore, that the plaintiff is
entitled to information regarding any individuals with
whom the President had sexual relations or proposed or
sought to have sexual relations and who were during the
relevant time frame . . . State or federal employees.
Plaintiff is also entitled to information regarding
every person whom the President asked, during the
relevant time frame, to arrange a private meeting
between himself and any female.

Further, in a U.S. Court of Appeals decision (3-0) filed
under seal on May 26, 1998, the court rejected ml's argument that

procedural
- BC's ^attempts to avoid novembe error
- BC november discov 1997 regs
  a) December 1997 deposition
  b) Jan 17, 1998 deposition

- Reasons for discovery order / common in sexual harassment cases / questions not designed specifically for WJC or to embarrass him / Paula Jones also required to provide truthful answers to him under oath / etc.

WJC's Discovery Responses in Jones Lawsuit

- December ___, 1997 Interrogatories

  - When asked to identify all women who were state or federal employees and with whom he had "sexual relations" [not defined for purposes of this interrogatory] since 1986, he answered under oath "None."
    [WJC response to plaintiff's second set of interrogatories at 5; WJC supplemental responses to plaintiff's second set at 2]

- January 17, 1998 Deposition

Monica Lewinski Relationship: In General
[Monica Lewinski] *Summer 95 to Dec 95: intern*
Dec 95 - April 96: O fix leg. Affairs

- When/how she got started at White House, in what capacity, and her job description *April 96 - DOD - public affairs dept*
to 12/26/97

- Her age when she began at White House [21 years old]

- November 15, 1995: her first intimate contact with WJC

  - She never spoke to WJC until she had her first intimate contact with him *- alone @ least 21 X*
  Contra - Clinton testimony *- @ least 11 sexual*
  - The nature of her physical relationship with WJC *encounters (excluding phone sex) 3-1995; 5-1996; 3-1997*
  Contra -
  - Cover stories to disguise nature of the relationship *@ least 55 TTC; @ least 17 misdated phone sex*

  - She would carry papers when she went to see WJC to *BC gave her 24 presents*
  MC gave him 40 presents

---

she could not have committed perjury or obstruction of justice because her false affidavit did not contain facts material to the Jones case. The court examined whether her affidavit was predictably capable of affecting the official decision. The court concluded

There can be no doubt that Lewinski's statements in her affidavit were . . . predictably capable of affecting this decision. She executed and filed her affidavit for this very purpose. [Citation omitted].

3

pretend she was delivering them to him

- After she left White House employment, she would return to White House under guise of visiting Betty Currie, and not WJC (the real person she was coming to see).

- Monica Lewinski promised WJC she would always deny the sexual relationship and would always protect him; WJC would always speak words of approval and encouragement to this pledge.

Monica Lewinski: The Corruption

- The Initial Job Search

  - Monica Lewinski looking for a good-paying job in New York since July 1997 without much luck, despite WJC's promise of helping her

  - November 1997: Betty Currie arranged a 20-minute meeting with Vernon Jordan, who was supposed to help.

    - No action followed, no interviews, and no further contacts with Vernon Jordan.

  - [Vernon Jordan testimony: no recollection of the early November meeting; finding Monica Lewinski a job not a priority]

  - Nothing happened during November re a job search for Monica Lewinski. Vernon Jordan either was gone, or would not return Monica Lewinski's telephone calls.

- Friday, December 5, 1997

  - Monica Lewinski asked Betty Currie if WJC could meet her the next day; Betty Currie said WJC was meeting with his attorneys all day

  - Later that day, Monica Lewinski spoke briefly with WJC at White House Christmas party

  - After speaking to WJC, Monica Lewinski drafted letter that day WJC saying she was ending their relationship

  - That same evening, Jones attorneys fax list of potential witnesses to WJC's attorneys. Monica Lewinski is on the list

    - Monica Lewinski does not know she was a potential witness at this point; she would not find out

4

until 12 days later, on December 17th.

- Saturday, December 6, 1997

  - In morning, Monica Lewinski went to White House to deliver her letter and some gifts to WJC. She intended to deliver these items through Betty Currie.

  - At White House, Monica Lewinski spoke with several Secret Service officers.

    - One officer told her WJC was not meeting with his attorneys; he was meeting with Eleanor Mondale

  - Monica Lewinski left White House angry; she called Betty Currie from a pay phone and exchanged angry words. Monica Lewinski then went home.

  - After that telephone call, Betty Currie told the Secret Service watch commander that WJC was so upset about the disclosure that he wanted somebody fired.

  - 12:05 p.m.: Betty Currie paged Bruce Lindsay with message to "Call Betty Currie ASAP."

    - About that same time, Monica Lewinski was back at her apartment speaking with WJC on the telephone. WJC very angry; he said nobody had ever treated him as poorly as she had.

    - WJC invited Monica Lewinski back to White House that afternoon.

  - Monica Lewinski cleared into the White House at 12:52 p.m. to see WJC.

    - WJC's was now "sweet" and "very affectionate" with her. He told her he would talk to Vernon Jordan about finding her a job when she complained she was unable to get in touch with him, and that he had done nothing to help her.

      - [Vernon Jordan met with WJC the next day; the meeting had nothing to do with Monica Lewinski]

  - Betty Currie told some officers that if they kept quiet about the Monica Lewinski incident, there would be no disciplinary action.

    - Secret Service watch commander, Captain Jeffrey Purdue was told by WJC "I hope you use your

5

discretion," or "I hope I can count on your
discretion."

- After his conversation with WJC, Purdue told
  a number of other officers they should not
  discuss the Monica Lewinski incident.

- Deputy Chief Charles O'Malley, Captain Purdue's
  supervisor, said he knew of no other incident in
  his 14 years of service at the White House that a
  president raised a performance issue with a member
  of the Secret Service Uniformed Division.

- WJC testified before grand jury he learned Monica
  Lewinski was on the Paula Jones witness list this
  evening at a meeting in the White House.

  - At Jones Deposition, WJC testified he heard about
    the witness list before he saw it

  - In answers to House Judiciary Committee, he
    learned about it at a meeting in the White House
    about 5:00 p.m. [House Judiciary Committee Request
    #16]

- Thursday, December 11, 1997

  - Morning: Judge Susan Webber Wright ordered that Paula
    Jones was entitled to information regarding any state
    or federal employees with whom WJC had sexual relations
    or proposed or sought to have sexual relations

  - Vernon Jordan met with Monica Lewinski and gave her a
    list of contact names. They also discussed WJC.

    - Vernon Jordan remembered this meeting

    - Vernon Jordan immediately called two prospective
      employers.

    - Later that afternoon, Vernon Jordan called WJC to
      report on his job search efforts.

- Wednesday, December 17, 1997

  - Between 2-2:30 a.m., WJC called Monica Lewinski at
    home. WJC told her he wanted to tell her two things:
    first, Betty Currie's brother killed in auto accident.
    Second, he had some more "bad news": he had seen the
    Jones witness list, and her name was on it.

  - WJC told Monica Lewinski that if she were subpoenaed,

6

she should let Betty Currie know.

- When Monica Lewinski asked what she should do if she were subpoenaed, WJC said maybe she could sign an affidavit.

- WJC did not directly ask Monica Lewinski to lie; he said she could say she was always coming to see Betty Currie or that she was bringing him papers. Thus, WJC reminded her of their prior cover stories, and how she was now to respond.

  - Monica Lewinski testified that when WJC brought up their prior pattern of deception, she understood that to mean she should continue their preexisting pattern of deception

Friday, December 19, 1997

- Monica Lewinski was subpoenaed to testify in a deposition in the Paula Jones case on January 23, 1998

  - She immediately called Vernon Jordan, who invited her to immediately visit his office

  - Around the time Monica Lewinski arrived at Vernon Jordan's office (about 5:00 p.m.), Vernon Jordan called WJC and told him Monica Lewinski had been subpoenaed.

- During the 5:00 meeting, Monica Lewinski was very distraught

  - Vernon Jordan decided to call a lawyer to get someone to represent her

- Later that evening, Vernon Jordan met with WJC and relayed his conversation with Monica Lewinski earlier that day.

  - Vernon Jordan again told WJC that Monica Lewinski had been subpoenaed, that he was concerned about her infatuation with WJC, and that she had asked if he thought WJC might leave the First Lady when his term was over.

  - Vernon Jordan asked WJC if he was having sexual relations with her.

  - In his deposition testimony, WJC said he did not remember this meeting

7

- Sunday, December 28, 1997

  - Monica Lewinski met with WJC at the White House; she discussed her subpoena, and that it called for production of gifts.

  - She said the subpoena called for a hat pin; both WJC and Monica Lewinski said the specificity of this request bothered them.

  - Monica Lewinski suggested she take the gifts somewhere, or give them to someone like Betty Currie. WJC responded, "I don't know," or "Let me think about it."

  - WJC gave Monica Lewinski gifts on that date, including a bear, which he described as a symbol of strength.

    - Why would WJC give her additional gifts when he now knew gifts were being subpoenaed? Monica Lewinski testified that she never questioned "that we were ever going to do anything but keep this private," and take "whatever appropriate steps needed to be taken" to keep relationship a secret

  - Several hours after Monica Lewinski left the White House, Betty Currie called Monica Lewinski and said, "I understand you have something to give me," or "The President said you have something to give me."

    - Betty Currie said she thought Monica Lewinski called her; Monica Lewinski said she thought Betty Currie called her from a cell phone. [Betty Currie's cell phone record shows she called Monica Lewinski at home at 3:21 p.m.]

  - Betty Currie took the gifts and placed them under her bed

- Monday, January 5, 1998

  - Monica Lewinski met with her attorney Frank Carter to discuss the affidavit she was to sign

  - After meeting, Monica Lewinski called Betty Currie and said she wanted to speak with WJC before she signed anything

  - Monica Lewinski met with WJC; she discussed how she would answer under oath if she was asked about how she got her job at the Pentagon. WJC told her she could say the people in legislative affairs got it for her.

8

Appendix 3: Original First Draft Clinton Senate Impeachment Trial Outline

- Tuesday, January 6, 1998

  - Monica Lewinski picked up draft copy of affidavit from Frank Carter's office

  - Monica Lewinski delivered a copy of it to Vernon Jordan. She felt if Vernon Jordan approved of it, then WJC would also approve of the language.

  - [Monica Lewinski testimony] Monica Lewinski and Vernon Jordan discussed the contents of the affidavit, and agreed to delete a line that they felt might open questions regarding whether she had ever been alone with WJC.

    - [Contra: Vernon Jordan testimony] Vernon Jordan said he had nothing to do with the contents of the affidavit

    - Vernon Jordan admitted he spoke with WJC after conferring with Monica Lewinski about the changes that had been made in the affidavit.

- Wednesday, January 7, 1998

  - Monica Lewinski executed the false affidavit

    - Paragraph 8: "I have never had a sexual relationship with the President. He did not propose that we have a sexual relationship. He did not offer me employment or other benefits in exchange for a sexual relationship. He did not deny me employment or other benefits for rejecting a sexual relationship."

  - Monica Lewinski showed Vernon Jordan the signed affidavit the same day so he could report to WJC that it had been signed.

- Thursday, January 8, 1998

  - Monica Lewinski had an interview arranged by Vernon Jordan with MacAndrews and Forbes in New York

  - The interview went poorly; Monica Lewinski was upset. She called Vernon Jordan and told him.

  - Vernon Jordan called the CEO of MacAndrews and asked Mr. Perelman to make things happen if they could happen.

    - Vernon Jordan knew people with whom Monica

9

Lewinski worked at the White House did not like her, and that she was unhappy with her Pentagon job.

- Vernon Jordan said he never worried about her qualifications for employment because "that was not my judgment to make."

- Vernon Jordan said Monica Lewinski had hounded him for help finding a job, she had unrealistic job and salary expectations, and told him a disturbing story about WJC leaving the First Lady and how WJC wasn't spending enough time with her.

- despite this, Vernon Jordan told Mr. Perelman that Monica Lewinski was a bright young girl who was "terrific."

- Perelman testified Vernon Jordan had never called him before about a job recommendation.

- [Contra: Vernon Jordan said he had called in the past for job recommendations. Who? The former mayor of New York, a distinguished attorney from Akin Gump, a Harvard Business School graduate, and Monica Lewinski.]

- Vernon Jordan called Monica Lewinski back and told her not to worry.

- That evening, MacAndrews firm called Monica Lewinski and told she would be given more interviews the next morning.

- Friday, January 9, 1998

  - After a series of new interviews, Monica Lewinski was informally offered a job with MacAndrews.

  - Monica Lewinski called Vernon Jordan to tell him

  - Vernon Jordan called Betty Currie and told her to tell WJC: "Mission Accomplished."

  - [later-that day?] Vernon Jordan called WJC and told him personally of the job offer.

The Need To Make Sure Monica Lewinski's Affidavit Was Filed

With the Court in the Jones Case

10

- Wednesday, January 14, 1998

  - WJC's lawyer called Monica Lewinski's lawyer and left a message

- Thursday, January 15, 1998

  - WJC's lawyer called Monica Lewinski's lawyer twice; when he finally reached Monica Lewinski's attorney, he asked, "Are we still on time?"

  - Monica Lewinski's lawyer faxed a copy of the affidavit to WJC's lawyer.

  - Monica Lewinski's lawyer twice called the court in Little Rock to make sure they could file the affidavit on Saturday, January 17 (the date set for WJC's deposition).

  - Michael Isikoff's call to Betty Currie; Betty Currie and Monica Lewinski's ride to Vernon Jordan's office; Vernon Jordan's advice to speak with Bruce Lindsay; Betty Currie's immediately telling Bruce Lindsay about Isikoff's call [worth getting into?]

- Friday, January 16, 1998

  - Monica Lewinski's lawyer completed his motion to quash Monica Lewinski's deposition early in the morning; he mailed to to the <u>Jones</u> court, along with the false affidavit attached. It was set for Saturday delivery.

  - WJC's lawyers called Monica Lewinski's lawyer and left message: "You'll know what it's about." - - to see if she had filed her affidavit with the <u>Jones</u> court.

<u>The Jones Deposition: January 17, 1998</u>

- WJC's answers under oath

- [Judge Wright's order prohibiting discussions about the deposition testimony]

- WJC's realization that somebody had been talking, and that the only person who could know such things was Monica Lewinski.

- 7:00 p.m. (following his deposition), WJC called Betty Currie and asked her to come in the next day.

  - Betty Currie: no recollection of WJC ever calling her

11

that late at home on a Saturday night.

Post-Jones Deposition Activity

- Sunday, January 18, 1998

  - At some point this day, WJC learned of Drudge Report concerning Monica Lewinski.

  - 11:49 a.m. - 2:55 p.m.: three telephone calls between WJC and Vernon Jordan.

  - 5:00 p.m.: WJC met with Betty Currie and said he had just been deposed; said the lawyers asked several questions about Monica Lewinski (a direct violation of the judge's order not to discuss deposition testimony).

  - WJC made "5 points" to Betty Currie indicating what he wanted her testimony to be: he made declarative statements to her, and did not ask her what she remembered

  - Betty Currie said she felt he wanted her to agree with those points

    From 5:12 p.m. to 8:28 p.m.: four pages from Betty Currie to Monica Lewinski to call her, using code name "Kay."

  - 11:02 p.m.: WJC called Betty Currie at home to see if Betty Currie contacted Monica Lewinski

- Monday, January 19, 1998

  - Between 7:02 and 8:41 a.m., Betty Currie paged Monica Lewinski another five times

  - 8:43 a.m.: Betty Currie called WJC to say she had been unable to reach Monica Lewinski.

  - 8:44 a.m.: Betty Currie paged Monica Lewinski with claim of a "family emergency."

  - 8:50 a.m.: WJC called Betty Currie.

  - 8:51 a.m.: Betty Currie paged Monica Lewinski with message "Good news."

  - 8:56 a.m.: WJC called Vernon Jordan, apparently to engage him in the search for Monica Lewinski.

12

518

- From 10:29 a.m. to 10:53 a.m.: Vernon Jordan called White House three times, paged Monica Lewinski, and called her attorney Frank Carter.

- Between 10:53 a.m. and 4:54 p.m.: flurry of telephone calls between Vernon Jordan, Monica Lewinski's attorney and individuals at the White House.

- 4:54 p.m.: Vernon Jordan called Frank Carter, who said he no longer represented Monica Lewinski.

- 4:58 to 5:22 p.m. (a 22-minute period): Vernon Jordan made six calls to the White House once he learned Frank Carter no longer represented Monica Lewinski.

  - Vernon Jordan testified he tried to relay this information to the White House because "The president asked me to get Monica Lewinski a job," even though she already had a job.

- In between these calls, Vernon Jordan again called Frank Carter at 5:14 to "go over" what they had already discussed.

- 5:56 p.m.: Vernon Jordan spoke to WJC and relayed information about Frank Carter having been fired.

- Tuesday, January 20, 1998

  - Late in evening WJC learns of Drudge Report, containing report of taped conversations between Linda Tripp and Monica Lewinski

- Wednesday, January 21, 1998

  - 12:08 a.m.: WJC called attorney Robert Bennett

    - Later that morning, Bennett quoted in Washington Post breaking news story that WJC adamantly denies he ever had a relationship with Ms. Lewinski and she has confirmed the truth of that."

  - WJC next called Bruce Lindsay: spoke for half-hour

  - WJC called Betty Currie at 1:16 a.m. and spoke to her for 20 minutes

  - WJC then called Bruce Lindsay again

  - 6:30 a.m. WJC called Vernon Jordan

  - After that, WJC called Bruce Lindsay again

13

- 9:00 a.m.: WJC met in White House with Chief of Staff Erskine Bowles and his two deputies, John Podesta and Sylvia Matthews

    - Bowles testified that WJC told them as they entered the Oval Office "I want you to know I did not have sexual relations with this woman Monica Lewinski. I did not ask anybody to lie." Podesta confirmed same in his testimony.

- Later, WJC met with Sidney Blumenthal.

    - WJC told Blumenthal that Monica Lewinski "came at me and made a sexual demand on me."

    - After WJC claimed to rebuff her, he said she threatened him and said she would tell people they had an affair.

    - WJC said Monica Lewinski was known as a stalker among her peers and that she hated it, and if she could have an affair or say she had an affair, she would not be the stalker any more.[2]

    - WJC said he was in earshot or eyesight of someone when this happened with Monica Lewinski.

    - Blumenthal described WJC's demeanor as telling a "very heartfelt story. He was pouring out his heart, and I believed him."

- Meeting with Dick Morris, pollster

    - After WJC denied the allegations, they decided to take an overnight poll to determine if the American people would forgive a president for adultery, perjury and obstruction of justice. Results: would forgive adultery, but not the other things. WJC: "Well, we just have to win, then."

- Friday, January 23, 1998

    - WJC met with John Podesta: WJC denied having sex with Monica Lewinski in any way whatsoever, and that they had not had oral sex

WJC's Grand Jury Testimony: August 17, 1998

---

[2]See Schippers statement at 26 re White House sources describing ml as a "stalker" and other unflattering commentary.

14

- WJC finally testified after turning down six invitations
- Testified he engaged in wrongful conduct with Monica Lewinski beginning in 1996 [not include 1995, when she was a 21-year old intern]
- Testified he was alone with her on certain occasions: it was more than 21 times
- Testified he had occasional telephone conversations with Monica Lewinski that included sexual banter.
  - He had at least 55 telephone conversations, and in 17 of them the two engaged in phone sex

WJC's Answers to 81 Questions from the House

-

Depo

Shorthand reporter?

Judge Wright?

15

521

"The Lost Closing Argument"

Prepared (But Not Delivered) Remarks of

Congressman James E. Rogan,

Impeachment Trial of President William

Jefferson Clinton, February 8, 1999

MR. CHIEF JUSTICE; DISTINGUISHED COUNSEL
FOR THE PRESIDENT; MEMBERS OF THE UNITED
STATES SENATE:

On behalf of the House of Representatives, we now prepare to deliver into your hands an obligation anticipated and designed by our Founders over two centuries ago.

You are faced with overwhelming evidence that the president repeatedly perjured himself and obstructed justice.

His actions were without noble purpose. He did it to crush a lone woman's constitutional right to access our courts in a civil rights sexual harassment lawsuit. His defenders now plead for no constitutional accountability for the one American uniquely able to defend—or debase—our Constitution and the rule of law. In so doing, they call upon this body to view his perjury and obstruction not with opprobrium, but instead as legal finesse shielded under the cloak of private conduct. They seek to save him who cares only about saving himself. And they call for this remedy at the cost of weakening Jefferson's revolutionary pledge, made only a few paces from this spot almost two centuries ago, of "equal and exact justice to all."

The words of another leader moved the youth of my generation when he reminded us that the rule of law must apply to all or it would apply to none. Shortly before his tragic death, President John F. Kennedy echoed Jefferson's sentiment. He said, "For one man to defy a law or court order he does not like is to invite others to do the same. This leads to a breakdown of all justice. Some societies respect the rule of force; America respects the rule of law."

His words are important, because President Kennedy, like Jefferson before him, recognized no exception for those who happened to share his Party affiliation or political agenda.

Up until now, the idea that no person is above the law has been unquestioned. Yet this standard is not our inheritance automatically. Neither the ghosts nor memory of ten generations of American patriots can compel us to preserve their bequest. Each generation of Americans ultimately makes that choice for itself. Once again, it is a time for choosing. How will we respond?

By impeaching the president, the United States House of Representatives made its choice. It went on record as saying that our body will not tolerate the most powerful man in America trampling the constitutional rights of a lone woman no matter how obscure or humble she might be. We refused to ignore presidential misconduct despite its minimization by spin doctors, pundits, and yes, the polls. The personal popularity of any president pales when weighed against one fundamental concept that forever distinguishes us from every other nation: no person is above the law. The House of Representatives jettisoned the spin and propaganda. We sought, and have now presented, the unvarnished truth. Now it is your unhappy task to make the final determination: face the truth and polish the Constitution, or allow this presidency, in the words of Chairman

Hyde, to take yet one more chip out of the marble.

The Constitution solemnly required President Clinton, as a condition of his becoming president, to swear an oath to preserve, protect, and defend the Constitution, and to take care that our nation's laws be faithfully executed. That oath of obligation required the president to defend our laws that protect women in the workplace, just as it also required him to protect our legal system from perjury, obstruction of justice, and abuse of power. Fidelity to the presidential oath is not dependent on any president's personal threshold of comfort or embarrassment. Neither must it be a slave to the latest polling data.

How important was this oath of office to our Founders? Did they intend the oath to have primacy over the shifting winds of public opinion, or did they bequeath to us an ambiguous Constitution that was meant to roll with the punches of the latest polls and focus groups? The Constitution gives us that answer in Article II, Sec. 1: "Before he enters on the execution of his office, he shall take the following oath...."

The mere fact that a person is elected president does not give him the right to become president, no matter how overwhelming his vote margin. Votes alone do not make a person president of the United States. There is a requirement that precedes obtaining the power and authority of the presidency. It is the oath of office. It is swearing to preserve, protect, and defend the Constitution of the United States. It is in accepting the obligation that the laws be faithfully executed.

No oath, no presidency.

It is the oath of office, and not opinion polls, which gives life and legitimacy to a presidency. This is true no matter how popular an elected president might be or how broad his margin of victory. The Founders did not view the oath as a technicality or an afterthought. They viewed it as the absolute requirement before entrusting the highest office in the land to any person.

The evidence shows the president repeatedly violated his oath of office. Now the focus shifts to your oath of office. The president hopes that, in this chamber, the polls will govern. We entreat you to require that the Constitution reign supreme. Should this issue be decided by reviewing the latest polling data? Would your vote on the articles of impeachment be the same if the president stood at a 6 percent job approval rating instead of a 60 percent job approval rating? If polling data governs here—if polls matter more than the oath to uphold the law, then another chip out of the marble is struck.

The cry also is raised that to remove the president is to create a constitutional crisis by undoing an election. There is no constitutional crisis created when the process of the Constitution comes into play. Listen to the words of Dr. Larry Arnn of the Claremont Institute:

[E]lections have no higher standing under our Constitution than the impeachment process. Both stem from provisions of the Constitution. The people elect a president to do a constitutional job. They act under the Constitution when they do it. At the same time, they elect a Congress to do a different constitutional job. The president swears an oath to uphold the Constitution, both in elections and in the impeachment process.

If the president is guilty of acts justifying impeachment, then he, not the Congress, will have overturned the election. He will have acted in ways that betray the purpose of his election. He will have acted not as a constitutional representative, but as a monarch, subversive of, or above, the law.

If the great powers given the president are abused, then to impeach him defends not only the results of elections, but that higher thing which elections are in service, namely, the preeminence of the Constitution[.]

The evidence clearly shows that the president engaged in a repeated and lengthy pattern of felonious conduct—conduct for which ordinary citizens can and have been routinely prosecuted and jailed. This simply cannot be wished or censured away.

In the shadow of America's last impeachment debate a quarter-century ago, a Democrat member of the House Judiciary Committee, Robert Kastenmeier, said about his vote to impeach a Republican president:

> Impeachment is one way in which the American people can say to themselves that they care enough about their institutions, their own freedom, their own claim to self-government, and their own national honor, to purge from the presidency anyone who has dishonored that office. This power of impeachment is not intended to obstruct or weaken the office of the presidency. It is intended as a final remedy against executive excess: not to protect the Congress against the president, but to protect the people against the abuse of power by a chief executive. And it is the obligation of the Congress to defend a democratic society against a chief executive who might be corrupt.

With his conduct aggravated by a motivation of personal and monetary advantage in the Paula Jones lawsuit, the solemnity of our sacred oath of office obliges us to do what the president regrettably has failed to do: defend the rule of law.

On the day the House impeached President Clinton, I said that when they are old enough to appreciate the solemnity of that action, I wanted my young daughters to know that when the roll was called, their father served with colleagues who counted it a privilege to risk political fortunes in defense of the Constitution. Today, I am more resolute in that opinion.

From the time I was a little boy, it was my dream one day to serve in the Congress of the United States. My dream was fulfilled two years ago. I am a Republican in a district that is heavily Democrat. The pundits keep telling me that my stand on this issue puts my political fortunes in jeopardy. So be it. That revelation produces from me no flinching. There is a simple reason why. I know that in life dreams come and dreams go, but conscience is forever. I can live with the idea of leaving Congress. I cannot live with the idea of remaining in Congress at the expense of doing what I know to be right.

I was about 12 years old when a distinguished member of this body, the late Senator Ralph Yarborough of Texas, gave me this sage advice about elective office. He said, "Always put principle above politics; put honor above incumbency."

I now return the sentiment to the body from which it came.

Hold fast to it, senators, and in so doing, you will be faithful both to our Founders and to our heirs.

Clinton Impeachment Chronology

1993

January   Bill Clinton takes the oath of office as the 42nd president of the United States.

November   White House employee and Clinton supporter Kathleen Willey claimed that on the same day her husband committed suicide, Clinton groped and kissed her during an Oval Office visit. Willey called Clinton's advances unwelcomed. Others claimed Willey sought a physical relationship with Clinton previously.

1994

January   Facing continued media scrutiny about his pre-presidential Arkansas investments, President Clinton requested the appointment of an independent counsel to investigate his involvement in the Whitewater land development project in Arkansas.

Clinton's Attorney General, Janet Reno, appointed Robert Fiske, Jr. as the independent counsel to investigate Whitewater.

May   Paula Jones, a former Arkansas state employee, filed a lawsuit against Clinton claiming that in 1991 members of then-Governor Clinton's security detail escorted her to a private meeting with Clinton in a Little Rock hotel room. At the meeting, she said Clinton groped and propositioned her while exposing himself. When she refused his advances, Clinton reminded Jones that her boss was his good friend, and then he added, "You are smart. Let's keep this between ourselves." Clinton denied the allegations.

August   Congress reauthorized the independent counsel Act after it expired. The statute required that, upon investigation and a finding of credible evidence, the independent counsel "shall advise the House of Representatives" of any impeachable offenses. Clinton signed the bill into law.

Under the terms of the special prosecutor statute, a three-judge federal panel appointed former federal appeals court judge and former U.S. Solicitor General Kenneth Starr to replace Fiske in the Whitewater investigation. Later, Attorney General Reno and the judicial panel authorized Judge Starr to expand his inquiry into other areas of potential Clinton wrongdoing.

1995

June   President Clinton's chief of staff Leon Panetta approved Monica Lewinsky, age 21, to work as an unpaid White House intern.

November   President Bill Clinton began a sexual relationship with Lewinsky that continued until mid-1997.

December   Lewinsky became a paid White House employee in the Office of Legislative Affairs.

1996

April   White House Deputy Chief of Staff Evelyn Lieberman transferred Lewinsky to a Pentagon job. Lieberman later told the *New York Times* the move was due to Lewinsky's immature behavior and marginal work product. While working at the Pentagon, Lewinsky befriended Linda Tripp, a career government employee.

May   The first Whitewater trial ended, with Jim and Susan McDougal (Bill and Hillary Clinton's Whitewater investment partners) convicted of fraud. Later, Judge Starr and his staff obtained 14 additional convictions for more than 40 Whitewater-related crimes. Among those convicted was incumbent Arkansas Governor Jim Guy Tucker, who later was removed from office. (On his last day as president in January 2001, Clinton issued presidential pardons to many of these Whitewater convicts).

Summer   Lewinsky began sharing with Linda Tripp the intimate details of her sexual relationship with Clinton.

November   Clinton reelected. The Republican Party won its first reelected House majority since 1928; Republicans also retained control of the U.S. Senate. The author was among those elected to the freshman House Republican class.

1997

May   Clinton told Lewinsky their affair was over. The United States Supreme Court ruled that Paula Jones may continue her lawsuit against Clinton while he remained in office.

Fall Linda Tripp began taping her conversations with Lewinsky, who continued sharing with Tripp private details of her sexual relationship with Clinton.

October   Tripp disclosed information relating to Clinton's and Lewinsky's relationship with Newsweek investigative reporter Michael Isikoff.

December   Lewinsky left her job at the Pentagon. As Paula Jones' attorneys prepared for trial in her sexual harassment case against Clinton, they knew that without something more, it would be her word against the word of the president of the United States. When they learned about Lewinsky, they knew this additional evidence of Clinton seducing other subordinate female government employees would bolster Jones' credibility.

Jones' lawyers named Monica Lewinsky as a witness in their case, and they subpoenaed the gifts exchanged between Clinton and Lewinsky. Rather than complying with the court's lawfully issued subpoena, Clinton directed his personal secretary, Betty Currie, to pick up Clinton's gifts from Lewinsky. Currie brought them to her own home and hid them under her bed.

Betty Currie called Vernon Jordan (Clinton's close friend who served on many corporate boards) and asked him, on behalf of Clinton, to help find Lewinsky an out-of-town job. Jordan met with Lewinsky, and then he referred her to several New York job leads.

According to White House logs, Lewinsky made her final visit to Clinton in the Oval Office. According to Lewinsky, during this meeting Clinton urged her to be "evasive" in her upcoming deposition testimony in the Paula Jones lawsuit.

1998

January 5   Clinton spoke to Lewinsky on the telephone. Two days after Clinton coached her, she filed an affidavit in the Paula Jones lawsuit in which she declared under penalty of perjury that she never had a sexual relationship with Clinton.

January 12   Linda Tripp turned over to Judge Starr's investigators the secret tapes she made of her conversations with Lewinsky. The tapes disclosed Lewinsky giving detailed accounts of her affair with Clinton, as well as Lewinsky confessing that both Clinton and his friend Vernon Jordan had told her to lie under oath about the affair.

Tripp met with Lewinsky at the Ritz Carleton Hotel near the Pentagon. During this meeting, Tripp again recorded their discussion. Lewinsky handed Tripp a sheet of "talking points" designed to coach Tripp on what to say to Paula Jones' lawyers if approached by them. The talking points were designed to contradict Kathleen Willey, who earlier testified in the Paula Jones case that Clinton made an unwanted sexual advance on her.

January 13   With Vernon Jordan's help, Lewinsky accepted a job in New York at Revlon, a company upon whose board of directors Jordan served.

January 16   After learning of the contents of the Tripp-Lewinsky tapes, Clinton's own attorney general, Janet Reno, and a federal judicial oversight panel directed Judge Starr to expand his investigation to determine if Clinton used Monica Lewinsky to suborn perjury and obstruct justice in the Paula Jones lawsuit.

Tripp met Lewinsky again at the Ritz-Carlton Hotel; FBI agents and investigators interrupted the meeting, escorted Lewinsky to a nearby hotel room for questioning, and then offered her immunity for her cooperation.

January 17   The U.S. Supreme Court required President Clinton to testify in the Paula Jones case. In his deposition testimony, Clinton denied Jones' allegation that he used his position as governor to seek sexual favors from Jones, his then-subordinate state government employee. While under oath, Clinton denied having any sexual relationship with Lewinsky. For the first time, Clinton admitted to having an affair with cabaret singer Gennifer Flowers, a charge he denied vehemently since it first surfaced six years earlier.

Newsweek magazine refused to publish investigative reporter Michael Isikoff's story about the Clinton-Lewinsky relationship. Later that day, Matt Drudge revealed on his Internet-based news magazine that Newsweek spiked Isikoff's story. Drudge's revelation received almost no attention in the mainstream media.

January 18   Clinton called his personal secretary, Betty Curie, into the Oval Office and coached her memory of his many White House meetings with Lewinsky. According to Currie, Clinton asked her leading questions regarding those meetings such as, "We [he and Lewinsky] were never alone, right?"

January 21   The morning edition of the *Washington Post* reported the Lewinsky story.

January 26 In what became perhaps the most iconic news clip of his presidency, Clinton wagged his finger at a White House audience and repeated his denial of any affair with Lewinsky. "I want to say one thing to the American people," he intoned. "I want you to listen to me. I'm going to say this again. I did not have sexual relations with that woman, Miss Lewinsky. I never told anybody to lie, not a single time—never. These allegations are false. And I need to go back to work for the American people."

January 29 The Gallup Poll reported Clinton now enjoyed a whopping 67 percent favorable rating, which was his highest approval rating to date. A mere 13 percent of America believed Lewinsky told the truth about her relationship with Clinton.

March 15 In a nationally televised interview, former Clinton aide Kathleen Willey claimed Clinton groped her in the White House in 1993.

April 1 U.S. District Court Judge Susan Webber Wright dismissed Paula Jones' lawsuit against Clinton. Later, Clinton agreed to pay Jones $850,000 to drop her sexual harassment claim, with no apology or guilt admission.

August 6 After receiving a blanket grant of immunity from Judge Starr, Monica Lewinsky testified before the grand jury.

August 17 President Clinton testified before the grand jury. Later that evening, in a nationally televised speech, Clinton admitted for the first time to having a relationship with Lewinsky that was "not appropriate." He denied committing perjury or asking anyone to lie on his behalf.

September 9   Judge Starr delivered his referral to the United States House of Representatives. His investigation uncovered substantial evidence of Clinton committing multiple felonies, including perjury and obstruction of justice, all of which warranted impeachment consideration.

October 8   The United States House of Representatives passed a resolution authorizing the House Judiciary Committee to begin an impeachment inquiry. The vote was 258– 176, with 31 Democrats voting "yes."

November 3   Democrats gained five House seats on Election Day. Polls showed almost two-thirds of voters opposed Clinton's impeachment.

November 6 House Speaker Newt Gingrich announced his intent to step down as speaker and to resign from Congress.

November 19   Judge Starr testified before the House Judiciary Committee during its Clinton impeachment inquiry.

December 11   The House Judiciary Committee approved three articles of impeachment that accused Clinton of perjury and obstruction of justice.

December 12   The House Judiciary Committee approved a fourth Article of Impeachment accusing Clinton of perjury. The committee rejected a Democrat-offered substitute resolution to void the impeachment articles and instead "censure" Clinton for his misdeeds and "reprehensible conduct."

December 17   The House of Representatives delayed its debate and vote on articles of impeachment after Clinton authorized an unexpected military strike against Iraq.

December 19   The House of Representatives impeached President Clinton, passing two articles of impeachment alleging perjury, subornation of perjury, and obstruction of justice. House Speaker-designate Bob Livingston announced his intention to resign from Congress after a previous extramarital affair became public.

December 21   Clinton's Gallup Poll approval rating reached an all-time high: 73 percent of voters approve of him as president; 68 percent did not want the Senate to convict and remove him from office, and 70 percent did not want him to resign.

1999

January 7   The United States Senate began its impeachment "trial" of President Clinton; Chief Justice of the United States William H. Rehnquist presided.

February 12 The United States Senate found Clinton not guilty on all charges. The impeachment "trial" ended.

2001

January 19   On his last day in office, President Clinton signed a plea bargain with federal prosecutors in which he admitted that he lied under oath in the Paula Jones sexual harassment lawsuit. Clinton surrendered his law licenses to avoid disbarment by the United States Supreme Court and the Arkansas Supreme Court.

As a result of his dishonesty and perjury, the United States Supreme Court ordered that Bill Clinton's name "be stricken from the roll of attorneys admitted to the practice of law before this Court." He also agreed to pay a $25,000 fine to the Arkansas courts to avoid disbarment for his dishonesty.

· APPENDIX 6 ·

House Managers Epilogue

(As of January 2021)

CHAIRMAN HENRY J. HYDE (R-WI)

Henry retired from the House of Representatives in 2007. On November 5, 2007, President George W. Bush awarded him the Presidential Medal of Freedom. He died two weeks later at age 83 on of complications following heart surgery on November 29, 2007.

JAMES SENSENBRENNER (R-WI)

First elected to the House in 1979, Jim retired from Congress in January 2021 after serving 42 years there.

BILL MCCOLLUM (R-FL)

After serving 20 years in the House, Bill ran unsuccessfully for the United States Senate in 2000 and again in 2004. In 2006, he won election as Florida's attorney general; in 2010 he lost his bid for the governorship. He practices law in Florida.

GEORGE GEKAS (R-PA)

After serving 20 years in the House, George lost his battle for reelection in 2002 following an unfavorable Democrat redistricting in his Pennsylvania region. He practices law in Pennsylvania.

CHARLES CANADY (R-FL)

Charles kept his pledge not to serve more than four terms; he retired from the House of Representatives in 2001. Following a stint as Florida Governor Jeb Bush's general counsel, he served as a judge on the Second District Court of Appeal from 2002 to 2008. Today, Charles is the chief justice of the Florida Supreme Court.

STEVE BUYER (R-IN)

Steve served nine terms in the United States House of Representatives until his retirement in 2011. He practices law in both Indiana and Washington, D. C.

ED BRYANT (R-TN)

After four terms in the House, Ed ran unsuccessfully for the United States Senate in 2002 and 2006. In 2008, he became a United States Magistrate Judge for the Western District of Tennessee, where he serves currently.

STEVE CHABOT (R-OH)

Steve continues serving in the United States House of Representatives.

BOB BARR (R-GA)

After the 2002 Georgia redistricting, Bob lost the Republican primary to another GOP incumbent congressman. He left the Republican Party in 2006 and became a Libertarian. In 2008, Bob won the Libertarian Party's presidential nomination, winning over 500,000 votes in the presidential election. He is a columnist and contributor to major news networks.

ASA HUTCHINSON (R-AR)

After winning three terms in the House of Representatives, Asa resigned from Congress to become President George W. Bush's administrator of the Drug Enforcement Agency. Following the creation of the U.S. Department of Homeland Security, he became the agency's first under secretary. Following a stint in private law practice (for a short time we were partners in the same Washington, D.C. firm), he returned to Arkansas and ran unsuccessfully for governor in 2006. Eight years later, he ran again for the statehouse and won. In 2018, the voters reelected him in a landslide.

CHRIS CANNON (R-UT)

After serving six terms in the House, Chris lost the Republican primary in 2008. He returned to Utah to run his family business.

LINDSEY GRAHAM (R-SC)

Lindsey ran successfully for the United States Senate in 2002. Now in his fourth term, he serves currently as South Carolina's senior senator.

JAMES ROGAN (R-CA)

After my defeat in 2000, I served in the Bush Administration as U.S. Under Secretary of Commerce for Intellectual Property, and as Director of the U.S. Patent and Trademark Office. I went home to California and practiced law for a couple of years before returning to our state court bench in 2006, where I still serve as a judge of the Superior Court of California. And, despite the political consequences of impeachment—

I lived happily ever after.

ACKNOWLEDGMENTS

Most people have no idea how much stress congressional life can be on families. My wife Christine and I went to Washington with twin four-year olds in tow. I'm still fascinated by this woman who brought balance to our lives and kept the engine running smoothly amidst unending political battles. After 33 years, she remains my most consistent cheerleader and the great love of my life—even though I often overlook showing it. No matter how the Senate and my Los Angeles County constituents felt about me, Christine and our daughters, Dana and Claire, always treat me as a winner. I can never express to them my gratitude and love sufficiently.

I became an author only because back in 2001 Speaker Newt Gingrich thought I had a story to tell, and then he introduced me to his literary agent Jillian Manus who agreed with him. Thank you, Newt and Jilly, for all of your encouragement and for the push that got me started down the road.

I started this book in early 2008. As it progressed, many publishers expressed great interest in it. I completed a first draft a few days after Barack Obama won his historic election to the presidency. When I submitted it for consideration, I couldn't get a publisher to read the first page ("Clinton? Who cares—he's old news. Do you have an Obama book?"). I decided to shelve the manuscript. Almost two years later, I had lunch with my old pal Warren Duffy and mentioned casually to him that nobody was interested in the book. On his own initiative, Duffy called our mutual friend (and a publisher) Joseph Farah at WND Books. Joe and his wife Elizabeth read the manuscript and agreed to publish it. Deepest thanks to Duffy, Joseph, and Elizabeth for your many years of friendship and for making sure my story was told.

To my original 2011 WND Books production team, thank you for helping bring forth an important historical account: Creative director Mark Karis; copy editor John Perry; proofreader Lauren Christopher; editor Megan Byrd; and publicist Tim Bueler. Thanks also to Trinity Booker, Ike Crumpler and Albert Thompson for their help in this effort.

For this special 2021 second edition, I am reunited with two great professionals with whom I have worked on my previous books, Mark Karis and Geoff Stone. Whenever I hand over to you fellows one of my manuscripts, I feel as secure as if I were in my mother's arms.

During the two years that it took me to write this book, I imposed on family and friends to read passages, chapters and, in a couple of cases, the whole manuscript. My thanks to Dr. Larry Arnn, president of Hillsdale College; my former congressional receptionist Linda Bonar; my long-suffering district director, Denise Milinkovich; The Honorable Christopher J. Evans; The Honorable Jonathan Fish; Trudy Kruse; my old boss in the Los Angeles County District Attorney's Office, Walt Lewis; my former chief of staff Wayne Paugh (still just fair, but improving); Jason Roe (my longtime political director); Patty Roe; Jeff Solsby (whom I plucked off a bakery truck in 1996 and watched him grow into a great congressional press flak); and The Reverend John Taylor and his wife, Kathy O'Connor (dear friends who devoted their professional careers to a man that, had he lived a few years longer, might have had some meaningful perspective to share about the Clinton impeachment).

A special word goes to my former constituents—the people of California's (then) 27th Congressional District. Whether you ended up loving or hating me, it was a privilege to represent you.

I did my best to be an honorable public servant, and I have only profound gratitude for your twice sending me to be your voice in Washington. Thank you for giving me the gift of being able to say I served in Congress, but not keeping me there so long that it did me any permanent damage.

Although we crossed swords in battle, the lawyers for President Clinton are outstanding professionals. Many became friends; one even became a campaign donor. To each of them I offer my congratulations on the superb job that they did for their client. My thanks and affectionate regards to my good friend, former White House Counsel Lanny Davis, and to President Clinton's incredibly effective impeachment trial team: the late Charles Ruff, David Kendall, Gregory Craig, Nicole Seligman, Emmett Flood, Cheryl Mills, Lanny Breuer, Bruce Lindsey, and the late Dale Bumpers.

Although I lost my reelection campaign in 2000, it wasn't (borrowing Senator Phil Gramm's phrase) for a lack of bullets in my gun. Because of impeachment, an unprecedented 66,000 people from all 50 states donated to my House race. The average contribution was about $50. Because of them, I was able to battle the forces unleashed against me. I didn't win, but their support allowed me to fight. Thank you for standing with me. I remain deeply grateful.

This book stands as a tribute to my revered Judiciary Committee chairman, the late Henry Hyde, and to my 11 House Manager colleagues and the incredible staff with whom we worked. To my own District and Capitol office staff; to the House Managers and their staffs; to the legal and investigative teams of the House Judiciary Committee and the Office of the Independent Counsel—all led by my brothers Tom Mooney, the late Dave Schippers, and Judge Ken Starr: you are patriots. It was an honor to fight at your side.

Finally, to you—the reader. You might now be perusing a recently published book, or you might be reading it 100 years after the gravedigger has laid me away. Either way, I hope you enjoyed this behind the scenes journey through one of the most contentious brawls in American political history. If I still have a pulse when you've read it and if you wish to share your comments, feel free to write to me through my website at www.jamesrogan.org. I read every email and I try to respond to as many as time allows.

J. R.

ORANGE COUNTY, CALIFORNIA,

[PUB DATE 2021]

CPSIA information can be obtained
at www.ICGtesting.com
Printed in the USA
BVHW091812190521
607714BV00010B/994/J

9 781735 131771